ENCOUNTERS WITH
THE CONTEMPORARY
RADICAL RIGHT

NEW DIRECTIONS IN
COMPARATIVE POLITICS

Series Editor
Peter H. Merkl

ENCOUNTERS WITH THE CONTEMPORARY RADICAL RIGHT

EDITED BY
PETER H. MERKL
AND LEONARD WEINBERG

Westview Press

BOULDER • SAN FRANCISCO • OXFORD

New Directions in Comparative Politics

Copyright © 1993 by Westview Press, Inc.

Published in 1993 in the United States of America by Westview Press, Inc., 5500 Central Avenue, Boulder, Colorado 80301-2877, and in the United Kingdom by Westview Press, 36 Lonsdale Road, Summertown, Oxford OX2 7EW

Library of Congress Cataloging-in-Publication Data
Encounters with the contemporary radical right / edited by Peter H.
   Merkl and Leonard Weinberg.
      p.   cm.—(New directions in comparative politics)
   Includes bibliographical references and index.
   ISBN 0-8133-1445-3.—ISBN 0-8133-1446-1 (pbk.)
   1. Conservatism.   2. Right and Left (Political science).
3. Comparative government.   I. Merkl, Peter H.   II. Weinberg,
Leonard B.   III. Series
JA83.E63   1993
                                                                                    92-31974
                                                                                    CIP

Printed and bound in the United States of America

The paper used in this publication meets the requirements
of the American National Standard for Permanence of Paper
for Printed Library Materials Z39.48-1984.

10   9   8   7   6   5   4   3   2   1

CONTENTS

PART THREE: THE ANGLO-AMERICAN DEMOCRACIES

ACRONYMS

ADL	Anti-Defamation League
ANC	African National Congress
ANL	Anti-Nazi League
ANS	Action Front of National Socialists (Germany)
BDS	British Democratic party
BHE	Federation of the Homeless and Dispossessed (Germany)
BNP	British National party
BUF	British Union of Fascists
CDS	Centre des Démocrates Sociaux
CDU	Christian Democratic Union (Germany)
CISNAL	Confederazione Nazionale Italiana Sindicati Lavoratori (Italian National Confederation of Union Workers)
CNI(P)	Independents' (and Peasants') party (France)
CNPF	Employers' Association (France)
CSA	Covenant, Sword, and Arm of the Lord (U.S.)
CSU	Christian Social Union (Germany)
CTIM	Comitato Tricolore Italiano nel Mondo (Tricolor Committee of Italians in the World)
DC	Democrazia Cristiana (Christian Democrats)
DDD	Federation of German Democrats
DG	German Community
DKEG	German Cultural Foundation of European Civilization
DN	Destra Nazionale (National Right)
DNVP	German Nationalist People's party
DP	Democrazia Proletaria (Democratic Proletariat)
DReP	German Right party
DRP	German Reich party
DVU	German People's Union
FANE	Fédération d'Action Nationale et Européenne
FAP	Free Workers party (Germany)
FDG	Fronte della Gioventù (Youth Front)
FDJ	Free German Youth
FN	National Front (Front National)

FNCR	Federazione Nazionale Combattenti Republicani (National Federation of Republic Veterans)
FPO	Austrian Freedom party
FUAN	Fronte Universitario de Azione Nazionale (University Front)
GBM	Greater Britain Movement
GRECE	Groupe de Recherche et d'Etude sur la Civilisation Européenne
HIAG	Mutual Aid Society of Former Armed SS (Germany)
IMF	International Monetary Fund
JCAR	Joint Committee Against Racialism (U.S.)
JDL	Jewish Defense League
KKK	Ku Klux Klan
LEL	League of Empire Loyalists
LIM	Land of Israel Movement
MHRS	Movement to Halt Retreat in Sinai
MSI	Italian Social Movement
NATO	North Atlantic Treaty Organization
NDPC	National Democratic Policy Committee (U.S.)
NF	National Front (Britain)
NPD	National Democratic party of Germany
NRP	National Religious party (Israel)
NSM	National Socialist Movement (Britain)
OAS	Secret Army Organization (France)
PCF	Parti Communiste Français
PCI	Partito Comunista Italiano (Italian Communist party)
PCR	Romanian Communist party
PLI	Partito Liberale Italiano (Italian Liberal party)
PLO	Palestine Liberation Organization
PPF	Parti Populaire Français
PR	Partito Radicale (Radical party)
PRI	Partito Repubblicano Italiano (Italian Republican party)
PS	Parti Socialiste
PSDI	Partito Socialista Democratica Italiano (Italian Social Democratic party)
PSI	Partito Socialista Italiano (Italian Socialist party)
REP	Republikaner party (Germany)
RPR	Rassemblement pour la République
RPS	Racial Preservation Society (Britain)
SRP	Socialist Reich party (Germany)
TNT	Terror Neged Terror (Israel)
UDCA	Union of Shopkeepers and Artisans (France)
UDF	Union pour la Démocracie Française
WAR	White Aryan Resistance (U.S.)
ZOG	Zionist occupation government

INTRODUCTION

Leonard Weinberg

Does the collapse of Communist rule in Eastern Europe and elsewhere bring an end to serious ideological conflict? Have the principles of liberal democracy become so widely accepted, at least among the politically articulate, that history has come to an end and no further challenges to democracy are likely to occur? As we approach the year 2000, do we also reach a new political millennium, one in which liberal democracy has triumphed over all its critics, left and right, past and future?

Perhaps, but if we use the recent past as our guide, positive responses to these questions seem both excessively optimistic and premature. It was not all that many decades ago when much of the world was gripped by a catastrophic depression. In the 1930s it did not appear as if liberal democracy, as practiced in the United States, Great Britain, and France, for example, was destined to triumph. Far from it: For many intellectuals, the future belonged to the dynamic Fascist, Nazi, and Communist movements that had come to rule Italy, Germany, and the Soviet Union. Like the divine right of kings, constitutional democracy appeared to belong in another century and a different context when politicians wore powdered wigs not paramilitary uniforms. But the results of World War II changed the outlook considerably. Fascist and Nazi regimes collapsed after having brought massive physical destruction and international moral condemnation to the countries they had ruled. The democracies, the United States especially, did not prove to be anachronisms after all.

A REVIVAL OF RIGHT-WING EXTREMISM

However, the Soviet Union and the official ideology in whose name it was ruled emerged from World War II with enormous accretions of power and prestige. Less than fifty years later, Communism collapsed on a worldwide basis, and the democratic prospect could hardly seem brighter. The train of

1

historical inevitability is now pulling liberal democracy behind it. Marxism-Leninism now appears antiquated, an ideology persisting in China, North Korea and a few other "isolated" or "peculiar" places here and there. Still, we need to remind ourselves, as Karl Popper reminded us many years ago, that trends are not laws.[1] In fact, there are no universally applicable laws of social and political development.

In place of the spell of Communist movements, there is now a revival of right-wing extremism or right-wing radicalism. As Communist regimes are overturned and Communist ideology is losing its vitality in much of the world, is it conceivable that another species of authoritarianism will emerge to challenge the democratic consensus? There are some disturbing signs that the answer is yes. (See Table I.1.) In the haunts of the old Nazi movement, in Austria and Germany, there have been significant revivals, or imitations, of the national socialism of old. In Italy the successors of Benito Mussolini's Blackshirts are still going strong, even as a brace of new libertarian, radical right leagues have arisen in northern Italy, especially Lombardy (Lega Lombarda), and even in Italian Switzerland (Lega dei Ticinesi) that feed on xenophobia and violent antipathy to the existing parties and the welfare state. The Automobilists party in Switzerland, formed along similar lines, is considered a party of the radical right. In Belgium, where Neo-Fascist organizations were one of the hubs of a kind of Neo-Nazi international in the 1960s and then declined, the Flemish Bloc (Vlaams Blok) achieved a spectacular comeback in 1991. Even staid and democratic Scandinavia had its radical right upsurge with taxpayers' revolt parties in Denmark and Norway and a new party of this description in Sweden.

Recently a former Neo-Nazi and Ku Klux Klan leader, David Duke, became the Republican candidate for governor in the state of Louisiana. His subsequent electoral campaign caught the attention of millions of people throughout the United States.[2] In France the National Front of Jean-Marie Le Pen, a party whose raison d'être is the exploitation of anti-immigrant sentiment, has become a significant electoral force.[3] The newly reunified Federal Republic of Germany has hardly escaped the growing antiforeigner sentiment either. Cities in eastern German (Halle, for example) have been the sites of skinhead attacks on guest workers and their families. This East German right-wing violence supplies instructive evidence for detailed analysis from several angles, as shown in the Conclusion. As in the United States, so too in Western Europe the number of assaults and acts of vandalism targeted against foreigners or ethnic or racial minorities has increased significantly in recent years. The nature of the phenomenon clearly suggests the need to distinguish the aggressive actions of prejudiced individuals and small groups from the threat posed by organized parties of the radical right vying for power in the state (see Table C.2). So far, in the older democracies such parties have not been of much danger. Still further to the east, organi-

TABLE I.1   Selected Voting Results of Some Radical Right or Neo-Fascist Parties in Europe

Party	Country	Year	Results
Freedom party (Jorg Haider)	Austria	1986	9% and 18 seats in parliament
		1990	17% and 33 seats
		1991	22.6% in Viennese regional elections
Republikaner (F. Schönhuber)	Germany	1989	7.5% in Berlin elections
			7.1% in European elections (W. Germany only)
			14.6% in Bavaria
		1992	10.9% in Baden-Württemberg
German People's Union	Germany	1992	6.3% in Schleswig-Holstein
Italian Social Movement	Italy	1983	6.8% in parliamentary elections
		1987	5.9% in parliamentary elections
Lega Lombarda (Umberto Bossi)	Italy	1989	8.1% in Lombardia (European election)
		1990	18.9% in regular elections
		1991	24.4% in Brescia (largest party in the city)
Lega dei Ticinesi (G. Bignasca)	Switzerland	1991	23% in Ticino (30% in Lugano)
Automobilists party	Switzerland	1991	10 seats in parliament
National Front (J.-M. Le Pen)	France	1988	9.6% in parliamentary elections
			14.4% in presidential elections (first round)
Vlaams Blok	Belgium	1988	18.8% in Antwerp municipal elections
		1991	12 seats in parliamentary elections (20% in Antwerp)
Progress party (M. Glistrup)	Denmark	1977	14.6%
		1988	9% and 16 seats in parliament
	Norway	1989	13% and 22 seats in parliament
New Democracy	Sweden	1991	6.8% and 25 seats in parliamentary elections

zations such as Vatra Romanesca in Romania and Pamiat in Russia have appeared, in circumstances of extraordinary social and economic dislocation, in order to mobilize popular support on behalf of chauvinistic goals and objectives. And in Israel an increasingly influential collection of religious and nationalist groups and political parties have coalesced in opposition to the idea of territorial compromise with the Palestinians and in support, in some cases, of their expulsion from their homes on the West Bank.[4] We are in the midst of a wave of right-wing radicalism in the democracies and in some posttotalitarian systems where the passing of communism has brought out old and new nationalist and xenophobic proclivities.

DEFINING THE RADICAL RIGHT

Discussions of left-wing political parties and political regimes that define themselves as Marxist-Leninist need not spend much time on their ideological thrust. There is a well-known body of "sacred texts" to which reference may be made. This is much less the case with right-wing politics of a radical or extremist bent. There is no immediately apparent body of thought that defines the phenomenon in which we are interested. There is, then, a need to clarify our terms.

To begin, when we use the two terms *right-wing extremism* and *right-wing radicalism,* are we really talking about the same thing? The latter term came into widespread use in the United States during the 1950s and early 1960s at a time when a variety of political organizations were formed to exploit popular fears of the Communist threat to American life.[5] Right-wing extremism, in contrast, is a label European analysts usually apply to various contemporary political movements and parties whose roots can be traced back to the forces of interwar fascism.[6] The question of how much continuity really exists between the old fascism and the post-1945 Neo-Fascist or Radical Right is examined critically in most chapters of this book (see also Table C.1 in the concluding chapter). The terms *radical* and *extremist right* alike are used to distance political groups on either side of the Atlantic from conservative movements with respect both to their aims and to the means they employ in their pursuit. Furthermore, the terms now migrate from one side of the ocean to the other. Illustratively, the Anti-Defamation League (ADL), a Jewish American organization, published a handbook devoted to *Extremism on the Right,* and a prominent observer of the contemporary Italian Right edited a collection of essays on *La destra radicale* (The National Right).[7] There may be authentic differences to be found from one country to another, but we believe they are not captured by the two terms. So hereafter we will use them interchangeably.

A case might also be made for applying the label Fascist or Neo-Fascist to the collection of groups, movements, and political parties to which this book is devoted. Indeed, a few of the right-wing organizations examined here, the Italian Social Movement (MSI) most obviously, have their roots in the Fascist movements of interwar Europe (see Chapters 2 and 3). But the case for using or attempting to use Fascist or Neo-Fascist is outweighed by other considerations. First, despite an oceanic body of literature on the subject, there is still widespread disagreement among scholars over the nature of fascism.[8] Was it reactionary or progressive? A mass movement or a class movement? Second, some observers insist that fascism was unique to interwar Europe, whereas others perceive it as alive today but as having migrated to parts of the Third World. Finally, for many people the word Fascist is hardly value-neutral. It has become a curse, a term to be hurled at politicians, political parties, or governments that the user finds offensive, almost irrespective of the nature of the offense. In short, by attempting to ground our discussion of right-wing politics in the vocabulary of fascism and neofascism we make the task at hand much more complicated than it needs to be.

What places a political group on the extreme right? Or, what attributes should such a group display for it to be defined as radical right? The political meaning of the words *extreme* and *radical* seem easier to assign than the directional term. Therefore, it makes some sense to say what we mean by the former notions before attempting to tell right from left.

In the context of democratic politics, extreme or radical groups are ones that do not abide by the rules of the game. To achieve their goals, they are willing to free themselves of the inhibitions against the use of such things as "dirty tricks," subversion, and violence that usually restrain other contestants for political power in democratic systems.[9] From the followers of Lyndon LaRouche in the United States to the supporters of the late Meir Kahane in Israel, the tendency is to go beyond or below the norms of democratic politics. Indeed, the impulse reflects a desire to shut down the democratic enterprise. Another important characteristic of political extremism, left or right, is the presumption that there is only one correct answer. Political life is a conflict between truth and heresy, with no tolerance for ambiguity. In this context individual politicians or political parties that pursue compromise and strike bargains with rival forces are perceived as if they were in league with the devil. The politics of democracy is pluralist; its presumption is that open debate and discussion among competing points of view is healthy. By contrast, extremist politics is monistic, driven toward the imposition of authoritarian solutions.

What does it mean to be on the right? What constitutes a right-wing outlook on the world at the end of the twentieth century? Are there certain views about the world that cut across national boundaries that, taken together, represent a distinctively rightist perspective? A desire to turn the clock backward is often identified with the Right. This connection is not completely valid, however. For instance, in the former Soviet Union these days rightists are widely perceived as defenders of Communist orthodoxy who hope to turn the clock back to a time when the principles of Marxism-Leninism went unchallenged in their country. But so far as the apparent fate of Communist ideology in the Soviet Union is concerned, the American Right, among others, could not be more delighted. As American rightists see it, by moving forward, time is now going in the right direction in the Soviet Union in more ways than one. Further, back in the nineteenth century, many defenders of the European status quo viewed the United States as a source of dangerous ideas about natural right and individual liberty.[10] Today, ironically, many American rightists lament the decline in standards and values the country has experienced since that halcyon era in the country's national experience.

In terms of substance, there has been a tendency dating from the French Revolution to link the Right with anti-Semitism, or Judophobia. It seems undeniable that many political movements widely identified as rightist in character, now and in the past as well, have made hostility to Jews a cornerstone of their various programs. Yet some Jews participated in founding Italian fascism, widely regarded as quintessentially rightist, although a movement not noted for anti-Semitism until Mussolini's entanglement with the Nazis began. Today Israel has a Radical Right (see Chapter 8) whose leaders define themselves as champions of Jewish interests in that nation and elsewhere. Also, we ought not to forget that there have been any number of spokespeople for various "progressive" left-wing causes in different parts of the world who articulate somewhat less than flattering views of the role of Jews, redefined as Zionists, in economic and political life. And, too, there are now right-wing Christian fundamentalists who look upon Israel with considerable sympathy. If it is not necessarily an approving attitude toward the past or a negative one toward Jews that defines the Right, then what does? One answer may be found in the structure of society or in the structure of international relations. Often *left* is a label attached to groups, movements, political parties, and even regimes that are committed (or at least say they are committed) to advancing the interests of the poor. If *left* means support for poor people in society and poor nations in the international arena, then it should follow that *right*, its opposite, should be defined as a defense of rich people and rich nations. Whatever the latter need or want to retain, their wealth is right-wing. This argument certainly has quite a bit to recommend it, not least of which is its simplicity. But there are problems here as well. If one of our goals is clarity, one obvious trouble with this solution (rich = right) is that rich people and rich nations often want different, sometimes even contradictory things. In the United States, for example, wealthy and well-educated whites are more supportive of African-American rights than are poor and less-educated whites. As many of our authors point out, radical right movements in all the countries discussed here attract not only a substantial working-class following but usually campaign against the rich and the established elements of their societies.

For better or worse, the terms *left* and *right* have taken hold. Not only are they widely used by journalists and politicians, but many citizens in the industrialized democracies are able to anchor their political views by placing them along a scale ranging from extreme left to extreme right.[11] No entirely satisfactory answer to the question of what is on the right seems likely. Rather than referring to a single trend or movement, the term applies to a collection of different trends or movements. Instead of dealing with *the* Right, we are really dealing with *several* rights. Right-wing politics in the Western world and since the French Revolution, according to the British political scientist Roger Eatwell, has been a succession of reactions against threatening changes at work in society.[12] Thus during the last decade of the eighteenth and throughout the nineteenth century right-wing politics and rightist thought was essentially a defense of monarchy, aristocratic privilege, agrarian values, and an established church against those forces working to undermine them: republicanism, liberalism, industrial capitalism, and so on. Right-wing extremism, the kind of right with which this book is concerned, is a more recent development. Originally, the threat to which the Extreme Right has been a reaction was that posed by communism. But although simple anti-communism may be the beginning, it is hardly the end of it. Some recent evidence even suggests that it may have been the New Left of the late 1960s and the 1970s and the social emancipation it advocated, in particular of women, that sparked the current right-wing revival.

DIFFERENCES AND COMMON THEMES

Despite differences from one nation to another, there are a number of themes that contemporary movements of the extreme right share and that justify their consideration in a common framework. First, they are not only anti-Marxist or anti-Communist but intensely nationalistic or racist.[13] If Marxists see the world in terms of social class and class conflict, radical rightists characteristically emphasize the overriding importance of ethnic, national, or racial group membership. From this perspective, extremists of the right stress the superiority of whichever group they belong to over all others. Either as the result of cultural or racial attributes, the group is or should be the dominant force in a particular territory. However, in the radical rightist's worldview, this dominance is threatened by other inferior ethnic, national, or racial groups. These days and on both sides of the Atlantic, right-wing extremism is defined in terms of its manifestation of intense hostility to various out-groups: Turks in Germany, North Africans in France, South Asians in Britain, blacks and Hispanics in the United States, even Hungarians in post-Ceaucescu Romania have been, inter alia, the targets of violent attacks. And although this obviously does not apply in the case of Israel's collection of radical right groups (see Chapter 6 by Ehud Sprinzak), anti-Semitism is usually common to these extremist organizations. Again except for the Israeli groups, most contemporary radical rightists not only express hostility to Jews but adopt the doctrine of Holocaust revisionism as well.[14] According to the latter view, the idea that the Nazis murdered millions of Jews during World War II is a hoax, one concocted by Jewish and zionist organizations in order to win undeserved sympathy for Jews in general and Israel more particularly.

The latter observation calls our attention to another aspect of the radical right worldview: the conspiratorial origins of adverse developments. For the extreme Right, there is typically a secret and powerful conspiracy behind the events its adherents find so threatening. Depending on the country and circumstances, Communists, insiders, Illuminati, Masons, and Jews (Zionists especially) are depicted as the evil conspirators out to subvert the interests of certain ethnic, national, or racial groups. The Israeli Radical Right, by way of contrast, ferociously attacks anyone who resists or criticizes its policy of claiming Palestinian lands (see Chapter 6).

Finally, though publicists for various radical right organizations claim to speak in the name of "the people," that is, on behalf of whichever group's interests they seek to defend, they are not democrats in the conventional sense of that word, but populists. From the point of view of right-wing extremism, most conationals belonging to their group have been deceived by the mass media and political leaders to a point where they are incapable of expressing their real interests. It is therefore incumbent upon the enlightened rightists to act on behalf of all "their" people. Heroic leaders with small bands of thoroughly committed followers, they believe, are capable of achieving great deeds through direct action.

The above remarks may not capture all the qualities that denote right-wing extremism. We believe, however, that they reflect the central tendencies. It is not correct to view this extreme right phenomenon as a "thing" apart from ourselves—to reify it as "the same thing" cropping up everywhere. Rather, there are latent radical right tendencies in most of us, usually related to the respective nation, and they are brought to the fore by economic or social crises. As with all political doctrines and movements that cut across national boundaries, especially if they are left and center as well as right, there will be some variation based on unique national experiences.

WHAT TO LOOK FOR IN EACH CASE

To capture the national variations on common themes, the contributors to this book follow a common outline, or conceptual framework, supplied by one of the editors—only Chapter 5, on Pamiat, follows mostly the author's train of thought to round out, without empirical material, what little we know about this influential movement in a major country. Inclusion in such form is justified because this mysterious group is prominent among several Russian nationalist movements and sympathetic groups that have been strengthened considerably by the crisis of the Communist system, including the abortive military coup of August 1991 and its aftermath. By disestablishing the Soviet Communist party, KGB, and bureaucratic-military elites, the coup attempt assembled powerful networks and political forces behind what used to be more the realm of literary groups like Fatherland rather than a political threat to the waning authority of leaders such as President Boris Yeltsin in the midst of economic and political crisis.

The common outline for studying the contemporary Radical Right involves three major foci: its ideological or intellectual traditions in a given country, its grassroots basis as a social movement, and its role in party politics and elections. The first-mentioned focus asks questions about its continuity or change from pre-1945 positions and its ideology in particular, naming a defensive nationalism, xenophobia and prejudice, authoritarianism, heroic pose, and cultural pessimism or sense of decline as likely characteristics. There is also a reference to strong underlying emotional reactions, for example, resentment of empirical decline or decolonization, shame, defeat, or ethnic prejudice. As a social movement, the Radical Right is studied with respect to the personal links of members of Fascist family traditions, socialization within a right-wing subculture, and the presence of partisans of the old predecessor movements in the contemporary ones. The examination of socializing mechanisms—such as leadership cults and authoritarian structures in family and school; backlash against minorities, women, immigrants, or foreign workers; and a climate of violent clashes with police or antagonists—is part of this approach. Generational angles within existing right-wing subcultures or against a gerontocratic establishment also inform this perspective. The Radical Right as a political party can be studied in terms of its electoral potential and successes, its social composition, the views of members and voters on salient issues (immigration, asylum, abortion, terrorism, etc.), and the role of the party amidst the established parties, in coalition with or opposition to the moderate Right and Left.

THE FUTURE OF THE RADICAL RIGHT

Armed with the answers to these questions, we asked, What are the Radical Right's political prospects at the end of the twentieth century? Is it a marginal phenomenon or a plausible threat to the achievement or maintenance of stable democracy? Naturally, the answer varies from country to country among the nations included in our analysis. But for the moment it makes some sense to look at the general situation and examine conditions likely to promote or retard the reemergence of right-wing radicalism as a significant political force.

To the extent radical rightism in the Western world has been a reaction to the threat of communism, its prospects appear at first glance to be pretty bleak. As communism has collapsed, the raison d'être for right-wing extremism would seem to have disintegrated as well: No Communist threat, no Radical Right. But there is another side to this story. Unlike the moderate, conservative Right, which has indeed lost its focus along with the "evil empire," the Radical Right was never just an anti-Communist Right but drew sustenance from other substantive issues and, of course, from its own psychological and irrational proclivities. In the Soviet Union and parts of Eastern Europe, furthermore, Communist rule had always acted to suppress right-wing extremism. Because the open expression of support for nationalism, ethnic exclusivity, and anti-Semitism was prohibited (or channeled in directions approved by the regime), the end of communism serves to stimulate the formation of political groups animated by these values.[15] Further, the prospects for a meaningful upsurge in radical right political activity should be enhanced in these post-Communist settings as the hardships associated with their conversion to market economies do not show signs of abating. Conditions making for a revitalization of right-wing extremism in the established democracies are somewhat different. For one thing, within certain constitutional limits in Germany, Italy, and a few other nations, political groups expressing the radical right worldview have long been free to compete at elections and say what is on their minds.[16] But even in these nations and even in the absence of a Communist threat, domestic or international, there exist certain circumstances the adroit exploitation of which would yield vigorous radical right movements.

Regarding their composition, the established democracies of Western Europe and North America are experiencing a progressive de-Europeanization of their populations. Segments of the previously dominant population come to feel threatened as immigrant groups from Eastern Europe and South Asia, the Middle East and North Africa, Latin America, and so on become a more visible presence in the various national communities. In addition to this component of the situation, economic conditions may make their contribution as well. In Britain, Germany, and the United States, where do the skinheads come from? The answer is that in many cases they are young men drawn from working-class segments of the previously dominant population who have left school and whose job prospects seem especially bleak.[17] As changes in the domestic economy make traditional blue-collar jobs less abundant or as firms that make use of them move their operations to Third World sites, the availability of white working-class youth for a politics of resentment and ethnic backlash would appear to be enhanced.

It may be argued that the collapse of communism rather than removing a major cause of right-wing extremism has instead facilitated its growth. Two reasons come to mind in support of this possibility. First, if the Communist critique of liberal or bourgeois democracy is no longer meaningful, the proponents of right-wing extremism have an opportunity to provide one of the few radical alternatives to the prevailing order available to alienated and discontented segments of the population among the Western nations. They may come to enjoy a near monopoly over radical dissent from the status quo. Second, whatever else we may say about it, Marxism-Leninism was a universalist ideology. So that, with exceptions here and there, movements and parties committed to its principles sought to minimize ethnic group differences by subordinating them to the role of social class. Followers of the Communist cause, schooled in the role of class and class conflict in history, sought to break down ethnic, racial and religious differences among members of the working class. With the influence of the Marxist-Leninist cause waning, "class" may lose its ability to inhibit the expression of interethnic resentments among the least-privileged segments of the public. Consequently, a political space may be expanding for those forces prepared to exploit its potential.

None of this is to say that a resurgence of right-wing extremism is inevitable. The atmosphere of Europe in the 1920s and 1930s is unlikely to be repeated as we approach a new century. Nonetheless, necessary though not sufficient conditions are present in the democracies to make such a resurgence a troubling possibility.

A GLIMPSE OF THE CHAPTERS AHEAD

This book furnishes the reader not with a crystal ball with which to contemplate the Radical Right's future prospects. Instead, it offers an examination of its recent past and current circumstances. We believe the book to be distinctive because of its unusually wide scope and comparative thrust. Studies of the Radical Right normally focus on either Europe or the United States, not both. Those that provide commentary on the European scene rarely cover eastern developments. Israel's robust Radical Right is treated sui generis. This volume offers essays devoted to the rightist phenomenon in significantly different national contexts.

The contributors who focus on France, Germany, and Italy, nations with long experiences of right-wing extremism, pay particular attention to political parties. This, of course, is no accident because significant segments of the electorates in these three nations have been willing to support radical right parties in recent years. In Italy, as Piero Ignazi notes, we are dealing with the Italian Social Movement, whose roots grew directly out of Mussolini's defunct dictatorship. Having recently celebrated its forty-fifth anniversary and having achieved representation in every Italian parliament since 1948, the MSI is Europe's most venerable party of the radical right. The situations in France and Germany differ from that in Italy. In these cases, as William Safran and Ekkart Zimmermann and Thomas Saalfeld emphasize, parties of the radical right have gone through periods of surge and decline during the postwar decades. At different intervals parties that appeared to pose serious challenges to the prevailing order, the Poujadists in France during the 1950s and the National Democrats in West Germany in the 1960s, found their support at the polls to have evaporated almost as quickly as it had materialized. But in both countries, as one radical right party passed from the scene another arose to take its place. Accordingly, the contributors devote considerable attention to the National Front in France and the Republikaner party in Germany, the most recent, and arguably the most successful, manifestations of the Radical Right the nations involved have displayed since the end of World War II.

The Italian case differs from the others in another way as well. As Ignazi points out, the MSI's fundamental appeal over the decades has been built around the fear of communism. Its principal domestic target has been the Italian Communist party (PCI), an ideological not a racial or ethnic opponent. This is not true, however, in France and Germany. There is no doubt but that in both these cases the level of popular support for right-wing extremism is based upon hostility toward the millions of immigrants in the two nations. It is probably not a total coincidence, but Italy is also distinguished by the absence of a significant tradition of anti-Semitism. In the Italian context, Holocaust revisionism and references to a Zionist world conspiracy have little meaning. In France and Germany, in contrast, however respectable National Front and Republicaner spokespeople wish their parties to appear, these conceptions are not too far below the surface.

In Romania and the Russia, the two East European countries whose radical right groups are discussed in this volume, we are clearly dealing with situations in which there is great uncertainty about the future. In both countries Communist rule has been brought to an end, competitive elections held, and nominally democratic institutions put in place, although in the Romanian case the ruling National Salvation Front's democratic credentials are questionable. In obvious contrast to France, Germany, and Italy, democratic regimes in Russia and Romania have not had much chance to acquire the kind of legitimacy they enjoy in the West. Earlier experiments with liberal democracy did not last in either nation. The populations of both Romania and Russia are experiencing great hardships as these nations go through transitions to market economics. And in both instances there are long traditions of political and widespread anti-Semitism to contemplate.

The contributors who focus on the emergence of right-wing extremism in Romania and the former Soviet Union approach the subject from different perspectives. Trond Gilberg's piece on "Ethnochauvinism, Agrarian Populism, and Neofascism in Romania and the Balkans" is fundamentally historical. It reviews the interwar experience with fascism in Romania as well as other Balkan locales before going on to examine the current situation. In "Pamiat: Russian Right-Wing Radicalism," Vladislav Krasnov's concerns are almost exclusively contemporary. He makes little reference to earlier manifestations of right-wing extremism in Russian politics, such as the brand of fascism that caught on among certain anti-Communist Russian exile groups during the 1930s. Krasnov's tendency is to treat the Soviet experience as so overwhelming and so devastating as to make a Russian Radical Right almost sui generis.

Despite these differences, however, both writers emphasize the existence of linkages between the old Communist dictatorships and the new radical right organizations. In the Soviet or Russian case, Krasnov argues that the linkage was organic in the sense that Pamiat was promoted originally by the KGB. Gilberg makes no such claim with respect to Vatra Romanesca and the Securitate under the dictatorship of Ceaucescu. In each instance, though, the claim is that both former Communist regimes displayed certain tendencies that extreme right-wing groups find appealing. After all, anti-Zionism, the denunciation of "rootless cosmopolites," and such were not invented by Pamiat. Likewise in Romania, the stress on the leadership principle and suspicions about the Hungarian minority in Transylvania accompanied by threats of violence were as much a part of the old Communist regime as the new post-Ceaucescu Radical Right.

France, Italy and Germany are bound together in that some five decades ago they were ruled by dictatorships of the extreme right—Vichyite, Fascist, and Nazi—respectively. Romania, Russia (or the former Soviet Union), and East Germany have in common long experiences of Communist rule, weak or nonexistent pre-Communist democratic life, and now the severe challenges posed by their economic transformation. When these economic woes are coupled with the revival of ethnic strife in most of the latter and popular backlash against African, Asian and Middle Eastern immigrants in the former group of nations the prospects for vigorous movements of the extreme Right appear pretty bright.

The situations in the two Anglo-American democracies are significantly different, even though both Great Britain and the United States have extreme right-wing and authoritarian traditions on which contemporary groups might base historical claims to power (see Chapter 7). And, although obviously beset by economic and social problems, these pale in comparison to those confronting Romania and Russia.

At present, and in part as a consequence, radical right groups do not pose a serious challenge to the status quo in either Great Britain or the United

States. This is not to say, however, that they do not possess an ability to produce some turmoil, particularly at the local level.

As Stan Taylor observes in his essay on the British situation, it was not too long ago that the radical right National Front showed some promise of being able to translate white resentment of "colored" immigrants from the Commonwealth into some electoral success. But its prospects waned as the Conservatives' restrictive views on immigration won back white voters who might otherwise have been drawn to the National Front.

The situation in the United States seems both more complicated and more dangerous. Given the well-known permeability of the American party system, groups and individuals representing the Radical Right have been able to capture major party nominations for public office lately. Thus the followers of LaRouche were able to win Democratic party nominations for local and in one case statewide office. David Duke, a former Ku Klux Klan leader, was recently nominated for Governor of Louisiana on the Republican ticket despite the active opposition of that party's national leadership.[18] By contrast to its British counterpart however, the American Radical Right stands out as a result of the influence of racism, a rather exotic religious perspective—Christian Identity—and the repeated resort to various types of political violence.

Ehud Sprinzak's intriguing piece on the Israeli Radical Right raises vexing questions. In many cases Jews play a central role in the demonology of extreme right-wing movements. Jews or Zionists are said to secretly control this or that country or institution in order to wage a destructive campaign against whatever the relevant rightist group believes to be of value. In the Israeli case, the radical right story is upside down. The groups involved are composed of Jews, intensely religious ones for the most part. Their enemies are those who have entered into a dangerous conspiracy to grant portions of the God-given land of Israel to its sworn enemies. Worse, some Israeli politicians are prepared to betray their country and religious tradition in exchange for such worthless pieces of paper as the Camp David framework agreements. In comparative terms, the Extreme Right in Israel is relatively large; as in France and Italy, for example, it has been able to win enough support at the polls to win parliamentary representation.

Even if the Israeli Radical Right does not win power, it possesses a significant ability to blackmail those who do. Any Israeli government that pursues a policy of land for peace, as Sprinzak's account of the withdrawal from Sinai illustrates, will be confronted by potentially violent rightist protests in the streets and by the loss of important support in the Knesset. In regard to the blackmail potential, the Israeli Radical Right is hardly unique. In France, Germany, and Great Britain, governments and major political parties have reacted to the anti-immigrant campaigns of the radical right organizations by proposing or implementing milder versions of the restrictions the extremists have advocated. Margaret Thatcher, Helmut Kohl, François Mitterrand, Jacques Chirac and other European leaders have had to respond out of fear that these organizations will make major political gains among their electorates.

This *introduction* ends with a question, one readers might keep in the backs of their minds as they explore the accounts of the various radical right groups in the preceding chapters. By the middle of the 20th century movements of the extreme right had been defeated or discredited. Could it be that now at the very end of this century they are undergoing a revival? Are old skeletons to come out of the closet to do new mischief?

PART ONE

WESTERN EUROPE

THE NATIONAL FRONT IN FRANCE: FROM LUNATIC FRINGE TO LIMITED RESPECTABILITY

William Safran

The rapid rise of the National Front (Front National, or FN) from an obscure formation to the rank of an electoral force to be reckoned with is a key sign of the transformation of French politics. For three decades following the Liberation, the dominant ideology of the intellectual elite had been leftism; this fact was reflected in an electorally significant Communist party and (since about 1970) a revived and dynamic Socialist party. From 1958 and in the early 1970s, socialism (Marxist and non-Marxist) was partly eclipsed by Gaullism, which managed to combine nationalism, populism, and republicanism. In the 1980s both Marxism and Gaullism lost much of their appeal as France began to move in an "Anglo-American" direction. That move has been manifested by an acceptance by right-wing and left-wing mass parties of the same rules of the game and by a waning of old legitimacy crises; a growing area of agreement about the mix among *dirigisme*, market liberalism, industrial policy, and the welfare state; the growth of a technocratic ethos; and a general impatience with ideology.

Throughout most of this period, the Extreme Right posed no threat to the political order. Its leaders had been discredited during World War II; some of its themes—monarchism, Catholic "organic" nationalism, and militarism—had become outdated; others—opposition to Algerian independence—had become irrelevant; and still others—the celebration of the family, the nation, or the state—had been incorporated into the ideologies of the moderate prosystem parties. To be sure, Fascist, monarchist, xenophobic, and anti-Semitic movements continued to exist; but they were small in membership, fragmented, impecunious, and lacking a reliable electoral base, so that they were hardly in a position to compete with "mainstream" political parties for national office.

The one exception was the Poujadist party, the electoral expression of the Union of Shopkeepers and Artisans (UDCA), which projected a mixture of antiparliamentary, anti-industrial, anti-Parisian, and anti-Semitic attitudes.[1] Capitalizing on the disaffection of those farmers and members of the petite bourgeoisie who were victims of economic modernization, the Poujadists sent about fifty deputies to the Assembly in 1956; but in 1958 the Poujadist movement, like many other political formations, was caught up in the Gaullist wave as many of its erstwhile supporters climbed on the general's bandwagon.

The chief heir of Poujadism is the FN. Founded in 1972 by Jean-Marie Le Pen, it has functioned as collecting point of antirepublicans, authoritarians, Pétainists, archconservative Catholics, imperialists—including former members of the terrorist military conspiracy, the Secret Army Organization (OAS), and other unforgiving proponents of Algérie française), of keeping Algeria French at any price—opponents of the welfare state, antiunionists, and racists. Between its founding and its first significant electoral showings in the early 1980s, the FN competed with, attracted members from, and gradually superseded a variety of extreme right formations.[2]

In the presidential elections of 1974, Le Pen, the candidate of the FN, received only 0.74 percent of the popular vote; and the party's performance in the parliamentary elections of 1978 and 1981 was equally poor. But in the municipal elections of March 1983, Jean-Pierre Stirbois, Le Pen's second in command, received 16.7 percent of the popular vote in Dreux, a small town near Paris, when the local Rassemblement pour la République (RPR) and Union pour la Démocracie Française (UDF), the Gaullist and Giscardist parties, threw their support to him.[3] At the same time, a Le Pen supporter received over 3 percent of the votes in Aulnay, another small town. Le Pen himself got 11.2 percent of the vote in a Paris district. In the elections to the European Parliament in 1984, the FN obtained 11 percent. In 1985, opinion polls suggested that in the parliamentary elections scheduled for March 1986, as many as 19 percent of the electorate might vote for the FN and predicted that the party would receive at least 7 percent of the popular vote. Polls also predicted that the Socialists would lose control over the Assembly. These forecasts encouraged the Socialist government to reintroduce proportional representation, for there was reason to believe that under such a system the FN would draw sufficient votes away from the Gaullist-Giscardist camp to prevent the victory of the latter, or at least to reduce its winning margins. In the 1986 elections, the FN received 9.7 percent of the vote— nearly as much as the Communist party—and entered the Assembly with thirty-five seats (out of 577). Two years later, in the first round of the presidential elections in April 1988, the FN obtained 14.4 percent of the popular vote. Many observers viewed that last result as a "political earthquake" that would permanently alter the French political landscape. They saw it as proof that fascism had come out of hibernation and was becoming respectable again.

However, the explanation of the rise in popularity of the FN is complex: It may be attributed in part to the personal appeal of its leader, the alleged failures of the major "republican" parties of the right and left, and the ambiguity of its ideology and platform. The FN adopted a multiple strategy: It kept the door open to the supporters of other extreme right organizations (most of them now discredited) without clearly identifying with them.[4] At the same time, it attempted to draw off support from the RPR/UDF by presenting itself in a double guise: that of a party that is not so different from the RPR or UDF in its support of democratic institutions yet different enough in terms of its policy positions to deserve support (see Table 1.1).[5]

When it was first established, the FN labeled itself a "national, social, and popular Right" and signaled its intention to work for "a just and strong state."[6] A close reading of Le Pen's writings reveals parallels between his thinking and that of François de la Rocque, the leader of the Croix de Feu, an organization composed largely of frustrated petit bourgeois types (many of them war veterans) who in the mid-1930s wanted to replace the republic by a Fascist regime.[7] Unlike Fascist parties, however, the FN does not want to destroy the old order, with its social hierarchies; on the contrary, it wants to preserve them. Moreover, the majority of its supporters do not have an "integral statist" view of politics. Although clearly authoritarian and nationalist, antilabor and racist, the FN has adjusted its party line to fit the audience of the moment. The party's far right ideas tend to be conveyed in watered-down versions and by innuendo—and are often articulated not by Le Pen himself but by his associates and by supporters formally belonging to other organizations. Thus the FN stresses the importance of patriotism, family, and work—recalling Phillippe Pétain's "patrie, famille, travail"—but counterbalances this theme by an emphasis on private initiative and individual liberty. The FN rejects the idea of human equality as preached in the Bible *and* in the literature of the Enlightenment but does not oppose equality before the law (except insofar as it applies to foreigners).[8] It charges immigrants with being the major contributing cause of social disorder, crime, unemployment, and the depletion of social security funds; but it does not openly advocate extreme solutions, such as massive expulsion.

Unlike much of the traditional Right (as represented, for example, in the ideas of Charles Maurras), the FN is neither anticapitalist nor anti-republican and is not identified with special interest groups such as big business, the military, or the church.[9] The FN favors a brand of Reaganite or Thatcherite market economics that implies deregulation, denational-

TABLE 1.1 Political Attitudes of Opposition Sympathizers, 1983–1984 (in percentage of respondents)

| | Sympathizers of | | | |
	FN	RPR	UDF	All French
Judge that the liberalization of abortion constitutes progress	53	40	34	49
Believe in respect for the family, work, and religion	35	47	47	33
Judge the word Gaullism positive	54	69	61	39
Hope that the opposition deviates from legality in facing the Left	27	8	10	7
Think that the politicians forget their promises once elected	72	57	54	42
Hope for the restoration of the death penalty	88	71	61	57
Hope for the reduction of the number of immigrants by use of departure subsidy	75	81	79	70
Think that respect for state authority should be a priority	35	19	11	21
Think that "putting the house back in order" should be a priority	62	54	49	37
Are hostile to a common European defense	43	38	34	39
Think that fighting for the defense of an ally is justified	56	48	46	35

Note: This table is to be read thus: Of 100 FN sympathizers, 53 judge that liberalization of abortion . . . etc.

Source: Edwy Plenel and Alain Rollat, *L'Effet Le Pen* (Paris: Le Monde–Editions de la Découverte, 1984), p. 127.

ization, and free enterprise within the existing political system—a position that permits the FN to claim that it is not of the *Far* Right but rather the *Liberal* Right. At the same time, there are allusions to elitism, traditional authority structures, marital virtues, and the problems of a permissive society.

These themes have made it possible for the FN to appeal to the old Far Right as well as the Moderate Right, in particular those who had become disillusioned with the mainstream right-of-center parties. Some members of the FN had been Gaullists or Giscardists but had left the RPR or the UDF because these parties had moved from the right to the center. The appeal of the FN has stemmed at least in part from the fact that the major political formations, the "gang of four"—(the RPR, UDF, Parti Socialiste (PS), and PCF), has been hampered in its ability to articulate clearly three most important policy concerns of the ordinary French citizen: immigration, unemployment, and security (or "law and order") (see Table 1.2).[10] The RPR and UDF, because of their support of the State Security Court and their sponsorship of the "anti-smashers' law" of 1970 and the security and liberty law of 1980, came to be identified with repressive measures vis-à-vis French

TABLE 1.2   Why Vote for the National Front? (in percentage of respondents)

Reasons	Total of Those Surveyed	Proximity of Voter to FN	
		Sure to Vote for FN	Practically Sure to Vote for FN
Want a reduction in number of immigrants	46	96	68
Support more severe measures against insecurity and criminality	38	60	52
Want to restore order in France	21	48	41
Need more vigorously to oppose leftist rule	10	8	13
Hostility toward present political class (right and left)	9	28	7
Discontent with "classical" opposition (RPR/UDF)	5	4	4
No opinion	26	–	6

Note: Intentions to vote in favor of the FN include about 10% of those surveyed. They come essentially from the group of young people (aged 18–24)—15% of those surveyed; laborers (16%); white-collar employees (10%), and farmers (10%). Among those who declare that they are practically sure to vote for the FN, we also find 8% to be RPR sympathizers, 4% UDF sympathizers, 3% PCF, and 2% PS.

Source: Le Monde, October 17, 1985, p. 7.

citizens rather than merely foreigners, whereas the PS has been regarded as too lenient.[11] The Socialists' appeal to many conservatives and hard-liners declined after 1981 when, upon assuming governmental responsibility, they abolished the death penalty (which is favored by the FN and has come to be favored by the population as a whole), decriminalized homosexuality, and extended the substantive and procedural rights of immigrants. Neither the UDF/RPR governments under Valéry Giscard d'Estaing nor the Socialist governments under Mitterrand managed to solve the unemployment problem. Thus the FN filled a void.

A PROFILE OF THE
NATIONAL FRONT ELECTORATE

The sociological profile of the FN supporter does not diverge markedly from that of the entire opposition electorate nor from that of the electorate as a whole in terms of age, religion, profession, area of residence, and gender—except that males have been dominant (see Tables 1.3 and 1.4). Unlike the Poujade movement, which appealed to farmers, artisans, and shopkeepers, the FN has appealed to managers, free professionals, and ur-

TABLE 1.3   Sociological Profile of National Front Electorate, 1984 (percent of total)

	FN List (Le Pen)	Total Electorate
Sex		
Male	59	48.5
Female	41	51.5
	100	100
Age		
18–24	14	14
25–34	18	24
35–49	26	24
50–64	23	21
65 and older	19	17
	100	100
Profession of head of household		
Farmer, paid farm worker	7	6
Small-business person, artisan	5	7
Cadre supérieur (free profession)	15	11
Cadre moyen (worker)	21	22
Laborer (unskilled)	25	28
Inactive, retired	27	28
	100	100
Religion		
Regular practicing Catholic	20	15
Occasionally practicing Catholic	16	16
Nonpracticing Catholic	53	51
Other religion	2	3
No religion	9	15
	100	100
Interest in politics		
A lot	23	16
A little	49	45
Very little	22	25
Not at all	6	1
	100	100

Source: Edwy Plenel and Alain Rollat, L'Effet Le Pen (Paris: Le Monde–Editions de la Découverte, 1984), p. 129.

ban workers. FN support has been especially strong in areas such as the southeast, where many immigrants have settled, where they account for a sizable proportion of the population, and where the growth of unemployment and crime is (however unfairly) attributed to them. It is estimated that 19 percent of those who had been mugged or burglarized in the preceding five years voted for the FN in 1986 and that such victims accounted for one-third of Le Pen's electorate.[12] According to one source, a significant number of FN sympathizers of the mid-1980s—workers, white-collar employees, and

TABLE 1.4   The National Front Voters, 1984–1988 (in percentage of total electorate in each category)

	FN Electorate				
	Europ., 1984	Legis., 1986	Pres., 1988	Legis., 1988	Europ. Parl. 1989
Sex					
Male	13	12	17	13	12
Female	9	7	10	6	10
Age					
18–24	12	7	16	11	9
25–34	11	8	11	9	9
35–49	12	12	17	9	10
50–64	12	12	14	9	13
65 and older	9	9	12	9	13
Occupation					
Farmer	13	11	18	10	19
Small-businessperson, artisan	21	14	31	16	15
Cadre supérieur (free profession)	12	9	17	7	9
Middle-level white-collar employee	13	10	12	8	9
White-collar employee	12	7	14	10	9
Blue-collar worker	9	11	16	11	10
Service personnel	6	6	15	–	–
Inactive, retired	10	9	11	10	11
Employment status					
Unemployed	13	14	19	10	11
Employed in public sector	9	7	13	9	10
Employed in private sector	13	12	14	9	11
Independent, self-employed	17	13	24	11	11

Source: Le Monde, *L'Élection présidentielle de 1988* (Paris: Le Monde, 1988), p. 44. Cf. Nonna Mayer and Pascal Perrineau, eds., *Le Front national à découvert* (Paris: Presses de la Fondation Nationale des Sciences Politiques, 1989), p. 61, which gives slightly different figures; and Pascal Perrineau, "Le Front national, d'une élection à l'autre," *Regards sur l'Actualité*, May 1990, p. 24.

the unemployed living in medium-sized towns—had voted for the UDF, the RPR, or even the PCF in 1981.[13]

   The aggregate of FN supporters is diversified in ideological profile and electoral background. French citizens who had belonged to the nationalist and ultraconservative groups mentioned earlier—and were looking for a congenial and "useful" substitute political formation—chose the FN more often than other parties. Surveys show that, as compared to supporters of other right-wing parties, many more FN sympathizers classify themselves as belonging to the Extreme Right. Of those whose earlier preferences had been for the more "respectable" right-wing parties, furthermore, a large proportion had been Gaullists rather than Giscardists (see Tables 1.5 and 1.6).

TABLE 1.5   Political Origins of National Front Voters of 1984 (in percentage of total)

	Percentage
Voted in first round of presidential elections of 1981 for	
Marchais (PCF)	
Laguiller or Bouchardeau (other Left)	
Mitterrand (PS)	24
Crépeau (Left Radicals)	
Lalonde (Ecologists)	2
Giscard d'Estaing	23
Chirac	27
Debré or Garaud (other Gaullists)	4
Abstained, no response, or too young to vote	19
	100
Voted in second round for	
Mitterrand	29
Giscard d'Estaing	50
Abstained, no response, or too young to vote	21
	100
Self-classification on left-right axis	
Far left	2
Left	5
Center	19
Right	25
Far right	44
No response	5
	100
Party preference	
PCF	1
Far left	0
PS	9
MRG	1
Ecologists	2
UDF	12
RPR	33
National Front or PFN	24
No response	18
	100

Source: Edwy Plenel and Alain Rollat, *L'Effet Le Pen* (Paris: Le Monde–Editions de la Découverte, 1984), p. 130.

In the second round of the presidential election of 1981, more than twice as many sympathizers of the FN as sympathizers of the right-wing camp as a whole voted for Mitterrand. Later, the loyalty of FN supporters solidified in the sense that 90 percent of those who had voted for a candidate of that party in the legislative elections of 1986 voted for Le Pen in 1988. Nevertheless, only 61 percent of Le Pen's hard-core supporters and 28 percent of his "new" supporters voted for the FN in the legislative elections of 1988, so

TABLE 1.6   Sociological Profile of Electorate of Major Presidential Candidates, 1988[a] (in percentage of total first-ballot electorate)

	Mitterrand	Barre	Chirac	Le Pen
Sex				
Male	32	15	20	18
Female	36	18	20	11
Age				
18–24	35	17	14	16
25–34	38	15	11	17
35–49	29	16	20	17
50–64	35	19	24	11
65 and older	33	15	29	12
Occupation				
Farmer	23	19	35	14
Small-business person, artisan	18	15	35	23
Cadre, teacher, professor	24	23	23	17
Middle-level white-collar employee	36	19	13	11
Blue-collar worker	42	11	10	18
Inactive, retired	37	17	24	12
Education				
Primary school only	37	12	22	15
Higher education	29	24	17	12
"Political family" (self-classification)				
Extreme left	46	0	0	2
Left	71	3	1	5
Center	24	35	19	15
Right	3	33	50	13
Extreme right	1	14	32	53
"Marais"[b]	31	22	17	18

[a]PCF and other minor-party candidates are omitted; therefore each line adds up to less than 100%.

[b]The alienated and other habitual nonvoter.

Source: Adapted from SOFRES, *L'État de l'opinion 1989* (Paris: Seuil, 1989), pp. 76–77.

that the party (with 9.8 percent of the first-round votes) lost one-third of its electorate.[14] This disparity is not surprising, for only 2 percent of those who had voted for Le Pen classified themselves as "far right" (the same proportion as those who had voted for Gaullist candidate Chirac); 27 percent as "right"; 15 percent as "fairly right"; 29 percent as "neither right nor left"; and 8 percent as "left"![15]

These survey results suggest that frustration over concrete policies may be as important as ideology. But even on specific issues, the policy positions of the FN and the preferences of its sympathizers and potential electorate do not completely match. This applies to attitudes toward abortion (FN sympathizers seem to be somewhat more liberal than the electorate as a whole) and religion (which has no greater hold among FN sympathizers than among the citizenry in general).

Many of the supporters of the FN and Le Pen did not really want—or expect—the party to come to power; nonetheless, these supporters did not regard their votes as wasted, for they wanted the FN to articulate positions about which the major parties had been too hesitant. This applied not only to traditional right-wing voters but also to left-wing voters. According to estimates, about a quarter of the first-round votes Le Pen obtained during the 1988 presidential elections came from voters previously identified with the Communist party.

The politicians of the FN, including its Assembly candidates in 1986, have had backgrounds as diverse as that of the FN electorate. Some candidates (e.g., Stirbois and Bruno Gollnisch) had a history of belonging to extreme right formations; others had been members of one or another component of the UDF; still others (e.g., Olivier d'Ormesson and Paul Arrighi) had been Resistance fighters in their youth; others again (like Yvon Briand) had once belonged to the conservative Independents' (and Peasants') party (CNI[P]); and many more had been Gaullists but had abandoned the RPR or its predecessor parties either because of Charles de Gaulle's "sellout" of Algeria or, later, because the party, in its Chiraquist incarnation, was not considered "liberal" or, conversely, nationalist enough. Far from constituting a Nazi-like rabble, some politicians of the FN have been Polytechnicians, *Enarques,* and physicians. One FN candidate (Michel de Rostolan) in 1984 even set up a French committee for the reelection of Ronald Reagan![16]

The *embourgeoisement* of the FN was clearly in evidence during the party's congress in Nice in March 1990, in which a significant number of notaries, technocrats, and local politicians took part, as well as in the composition of its "scientific council," which included a number of writers and university professors (many of them from Aix-en-Provence, Montpellier, and Lyons and including Bernard Notin, a notorious historical revisionist).

The leap of the FN to respectability and electoral significance, which was reflected in the increasingly "bourgeois" character of the party's candidates for parliamentary and municipal elections, was a consequence of the growing public approval of selected positions taken by Le Pen, who remarked on several occasions that he said out loud what much of the public was saying sotto voce. Indeed, most of the polls conducted between 1983 and 1988— and the election results themselves—indicate a range of electoral support of Le Pen, the FN, or both from 7 percent to about 15 percent. These figures must be used with caution, for they include "hard" and "soft" supporters. Moreover, it is difficult to determine reliably what proportion has supported the FN because of Le Pen's leadership. As the results of the elections of 1988 indicate, Le Pen personally has received far greater electoral support than his party—as was the case also with respect to de Gaulle and the Gaullist party and Mitterrand and the Socialist party.[17]

In any case, the RPR and UDF have been ambivalent in drawing conclusions from such surveys. There is no doubt that Le Pen gained an increasing measure of respect from important Gaullist and Giscardist politicians. Thus in 1984, Raymond Barre, a prime minister under Giscard and the right-of-center leader who, according to the polls, appeared to have the best prospect among the politicians of the RPR/UDF coalition as a presidential candidate, asserted that "M. Le Pen is not a scarecrow" and that he, Barre, could identify with several of Le Pen's themes, such as immigration, anticommunism, and excessive public spending.[18] Four years later, however, Barre had changed his mind—or his strategy: In a joint television appearance with Chirac, his Gaullist rival in the presidential election of 1988, Barre implicitly distanced himself from Le Pen by calling for tolerance and for a fight against racism.

National leaders have had to be more circumspect in their public appraisal of Le Pen than have local ones; and Gaullist leaders have been more positive about him than have Giscardist ones, because Gaullist sympathizers have tended toward to the hard-line policy positions of the FN and have been more willing to consider it a legitimate component of the opposition.

LE PEN: THE PERSONAL FACTOR

The growth of the FN has caused many to look closely at its founder and leader. Le Pen came from a poor family and sought refuge from a humdrum life by engaging in military adventures. As a law student in Paris in 1947, he was active in right-wing university groups. Before finishing school, he enlisted in the army in Indochina as a parachutist; later he joined the Poujade movement and with the elections of 1956 became, at age twenty-seven, the youngest deputy in the Assembly. He helped to set up the Front National pour l'Algérie française, which was quickly dissolved by the government. In the same year he again embarked on a military adventure, leaving his post as deputy and joining a parachute unit in Algeria. By 1957 he broke with Pierre Poujade because the latter had not fought hard enough for a French Algeria and had not done enough to undermine the Fourth Republic. (Much later, in 1983, Poujade said that Le Pen had always been a "neo-Poujadist," and that rather than promoting a cause consistently, he was mainly interested in exploiting discontent.) Algeria was to haunt Le Pen: In 1984 many newspapers ran stories alleging that he used torture there between 1956 and 1958. That period also changed Le Pen politically. Like so many French citizens, he considered himself "at once Pétainist and Gaullist," but later he became as anti-Gaullist as he was anti-Communist.[19]

On the political stage once again, Le Pen in 1965 managed the presidential campaign of Jean-Louis Tixier-Vignancour, who ran under the label of an extreme right and ultranationalist party. Tixier had been chief defense attorney for General Raoul Salan, head of the OAS, during his treason trial in 1962. Between 1966 and 1972, the year he founded the FN, Le Pen experimented with several right-wing groups together with Tixier. In the parliamentary elections of 1973, the FN got less than 2 percent of the vote; and as a candidate in the presidential election of 1974, Le Pen received fewer than 200,000 votes, that is, less than 0.74 percent.

The appeal of Le Pen widened gradually, despite the negative publicity surrounding his inheritance of $2 million from industrialist Hubert Lambert in 1976, an event accompanied by allegations of deceptive dealings.[20] In 19, Le Pen was still not popular enough to secure the 500 signatures needed for nomination as a presidential candidate. Since then, however, the legitimation of Le Pen and his FN has progressed rapidly. In February 1984 he was invited as a guest on the television program "L'heure de vérité," an honor usually reserved for important national politicians. At the same time, Le Pen began to be included among the figures whose political popularity is gauged regularly by means of opinion polls. These media successes were both a consequence of and a spur to the electoral successes referred to above.

How is one to explain how a politician who has cultivated proto-Fascist friends, "whose path is strewn with scandals, attempted murders, imprisonments, lawsuits, and financial controversies, and who has represented ideologies that, since Liberation, have been marginal and discredited, would become a veritable television star, a king of the electoral stage?"[21] Is it possible to argue that Le Pen perceived popular frustrations better than more traditional politicians and, by dint of personal charisma and a loyal following, maximized and exploited them?

It is tempting to compare Le Pen to Hitler (whom, according to his first wife, Le Pen admires) and the FN to the Nazis because both embraced the themes of nationalism and natalism, both militated against Marxism and international finance capital, and both exploited socioeconomic insecurities. Both had ideological ambivalences: Hitler had (until 1935) a right-wing and left-wing side, and Le Pen has a republican-liberal and an authoritarian-etatist one. Like Hitler and the Nazis, Le Pen and the FN have appealed to racism by playing on the fears of French men and women about "alien" elements. One example is a remark by Le Pen that Maghrebi (i.e., North African Arab) immigrants had only one wish: "to sleep with your daughter or your son."[22] Another example is an issue of *Figaro* magazine (whose editor, Louis Pawels, has tried to make Le Pen's views respectable) that projected the Islamization of French society by the end of the century and that had on its cover a bust of Marianne, the symbol of France, covered with a *chadur*.[23]

Such propaganda recalls that of the Nazis about the Judaization of Germany and the *Stürmer* cartoons depicting hook-nosed Jewish men preying on Nordic women. In keeping with contemporary fashion, Le Pen has used code language more refined than that of the Nazis; thus he speaks not of blood and soil but of "cultures" and "mentalities," not of racial inequalities but of differences, not of eugenics or annihilations but of "national preferences," not of France's fight for survival in a conflict of nations but of "liberty, property, security, and identity."[24] Le Pen has distorted the facts and has repeated his distortions so often that they have come to be widely believed. Thus he has asserted that 108 billion francs' worth of social benefits has been given to immigrants, whereas the true figure was 8 billion! Similarly, he has spoken of 6 million immigrants, whereas official sources have cited between 3.7 million and 4.5 million.[25]

Earlier in his career, Le Pen rejected any pretension to an intellectual approach to political problems; he preferred the "muscular" approach and tried to live according to the maxim that "he who cannot fight [physically] is a girl."[26] He surrounded himself with "young men whose ideas were as short as their hair" and who had grown up in antirepublican organizations. He expressed his admiration of Charles Maurras "for his nationalism," of Nazi collaborator Robert Brasillach "for his anthology of Greek poetry," and of the Chilean dictator Augusto Pinochet for his anticommunism.[27] Like Hitler, Le Pen has disseminated an image of the Jew as both the arch-Bolshevik *and* the archcapitalist, as when he said that "Marx and Rothschild are in a way the two sides of the same coin," and when he distinguished between "the Jews and the French."[28]

In contrast to Hitler, Le Pen does not seem to be preoccupied with the belief that the world has ganged up on his country. Le Pen's writings, like those of Hitler, are full of paranoid slogans and the rhetoric of nationalist populism. They feature a Manichean approach to reality and his self-portrait of a man of the people.[29] Le Pen's political autobiography, *Les Français d'abord*, contains a (somewhat romanticized) tale of an impoverished childhood and of military experiences, an avowal of patriotism, a call for the spiritual renewal of the nation, and an attack on the "politicians." But it contains none of the venomous harangues of *Mein Kampf.* Most of the book is an endorsement of such well-worn slogans as the lowering of taxes, the encouragement of property and stock ownership by the masses, and the fight against Communist aggression. Whereas Hitler stressed the importance of the community and the primacy of the state, Le Pen envisages a minimalist role of the state, whose

mission ... is to serve the French people; it is neither to bring them to heel nor to make them work for a state that is increasingly avaricious, costly, and powerless to assume its basic functions of national and civil defense and protection.

... Our political program may be summarized in these words: to turn our backs
to socialism, communism, social democracy, advanced liberalism, or *travail-
lisme à la française* [patriotic, i.e., non-Marxist, trade unionism]—all of which
... make reference to the same outdated analysis of the modern economy.[30]

These ideas are spelled out more fully in the official economic program of
the FN, *Droite et démocratie économique,* which celebrates the free market, the
entrepreneurial spirit, and responsible trade union leadership, and calls for
a more or less Thatcherite monetarism.[31] The FN is officially committed to a
policy of progressive privatization of economic transactions and of the educational system. Le Pen and his friends advocate the retention and expansion of parochial schools and often refer to the virtues of old-fashioned
family ties and authority structures; but these references are probably designed less to please the mass of Le Pen's sympathizers—many of whom are
not devout Catholics—than to earn the support of reactionary Catholic
groups and periodicals.

It has been argued that the FN represents all those latent restoration elements that have never accepted the ideals of the revolution of 1789—the
royalists, Catholic fundamentalists, and Fascists.[32] It has been suggested,
too, that "Le Pen rallies not so much fascist France as soft-brained France,
which follows its gut rather than its head."[33] Le Pen himself asserts that his
movement has nothing to do with fascism, which he dismisses as an out-
moded Italian doctrine—an assertion that did not prevent the FN in the European Parliament from associating with the Neo-Fascist Italian Social
Movement or keep Le Pen from being on friendly terms with Giorgio
Almirante, its late leader. Recently, however, his relationship with the MSI
seems to have cooled and been replaced by a close rapport with the German
Franz Schönhuber and his Republikaner party, because the racism of the latter is more akin to that of Le Pen.

Officially, it is true, the FN does not fit into the archetypic Nouvelle Droite
(New Right), which is in favor of an organic state, a sociobiologically based
elitism, and (in some cases) a centrally directed economy, and which does
not believe in human reason.[34] According to Alain Rollat, Le Pen's credo includes an authoritarian presidentialism led by an aristocratic-nationalistic
elite that inculcates Christian moral values in the country's youth and in
which the army plays a prominent role.[35] Le Pen himself denies that he is an
extremist; he refers to his admiration of the United States, and especially of
right-wing Republicans, and some of his ideas could have been lifted
straight from the presidential campaign platforms of Barry Goldwater and
Reagan. In fact, one pro–Le Pen book shows the FN leader at a meeting with
Republican politicians in the United States, photographed together with
former Senator Paul Laxalt.[36] This has not, however, prevented Le Pen from
playing on anti-American sentiments, as he did during the Gulf crisis.

The major difference between Le Pen and mainstream right-wing politicians is in his racism and anti-Semitism—more precisely, in his incessant exploitation of such attitudes among the electorate. To be sure, many voters,
and not a few politicians, of the other parties are afflicted with at least racist
and anti-Semitic sentiments. In contrast, many observers suggest that anti-
Semitism is the major ideological ingredient in Le Pen's complex of
heterophobic attitudes. Le Pen denies that he is anti-Semitic, indicating that
as a producer of phonograph records he brought out an album of Jewish
songs, referring to an article in *Tribune Juive* (Jewish tribune) that stated that
in thirty years of public life he had not uttered a single anti-Semitic statement, and pointing to the existence of Jewish activists in the FN.[37] Le Pen asserts that he "consider[s Jews] citizens like any others" but not deserving of
special treatment. He argues that "if any group is entitled to better protection, it should be the French"—a remark that implies that the Jews are *not*
French.[38] Occasionally he even appeals to Jewish voters—by inciting Jewish
shopkeepers in the Belleville section of Paris against Arabs and by stressing
the FN's stand against international terrorism and its fight against Soviet imperialism. In 1987 he sent a congratulatory telegram to the newly elected
chief rabbi of France.

Yet Le Pen permits his political associates in the FN and editors of *Minute,*
Présent, and other journals that support him to mount more direct attacks
on Jews, confining himself to allusions to politicians and other public figures whom he believes to be mischievous or incompetent and who happen
to be Jews (or of Jewish origin). He extolls the moral monopoly of Christianity and stresses the intimate connection between Catholicism and *francité*
(Frenchness).[39] There is an anti-Semitic flavor in Le Pen's argument that
the legalization of abortion sponsored by Simone Veil when she was minister
of social affairs was aimed at legitimating the "genocide" of the French people. In this case, the FN is following the pattern established by right-wing revisionists as well as some new leftists of misappropriating the Holocaust.[40]

Although Le Pen is "at once racist and prudent," it appears from the fore-
going that his racism sometimes triumphs over his prudence.[41] Some FN
strategists have argued that Fascist backgrounds in general and hostility toward Jews in particular are found among those segments that oppose him,
including "respectable" republicans. Thus *National Hebdo,* the FN's weekly
organ, recalled that Maurice Duverger, the prominent political scientist and
critic of the FN, had once been associated with Jacques Doriot's Fascist Parti
Populaire Français (PPF) and had published an ostensibly affirmative commentary to the anti-Semitic legislation of the Vichy regime.[42]

Le Pen's public expressions of anti-Semitism are held in check by the limited electoral utility of Jew-baiting: Jews are not the only—nor the most
visible—"foreign" element. Most Jews are well assimilated into French life
and the theological basis of anti-Semitism has been undercut by growing sec-

ularism. The association of Jewishness with bolshevism is hardly credible in the face of the Soviet Union's past anti-Semitic behavior. The Jews of France have even benefited in their relative position as antagonists of the Arabs, who constitute the biggest and most vulnerable target of French racists. A recent public opinion poll revealed that no more than 5 percent of the respondents had a clear antipathy toward Jews (compared to 12 percent toward Muslims and 20 percent toward Arabs) and that only 13 percent would refuse to vote for a Jewish candidate for public office (compared to 21 percent for an Asian candidate and 31 percent for a candidate of Arab origin).[43] Even among FN supporters, anti-Semitism (though higher than among the electorate at large) does not seem to be as pronounced as negative feelings toward other minorities.[44] For these reasons, most of the political discussions and academic colloquia on the subject of *l'identité française* (the French identity)—and they are numerous—deal much less with Jews than with Arabs because the latter, for reasons of physiognomy, culture, and religion, seem particularly inassimilable. Such perceptions account in part for the fact that the "respectable" Right (including the Club de l'Horloge, discussed in the following section) speaks with growing frequency of France's "Judeo-Christian civilization."

A major divergence of Le Pen and his FN from Hitler and his Fascists is that the former are neither antirepublican nor excessively etatist, even though at the time of its founding the FN proclaimed that it intended to work for a strong state. Le Pen has attacked socialism—not because it is subversive but because it is the ideology of "the old age of the world. … (Its) theoreticians … have chosen as their models the bearded men of the 19th century: Marx, Engels, Bakunin."[45] Le Pen is neither an irredentist nor a constitutional revisionist, and he has never questioned the legitimacy of the Fifth Republic or even the loyalty of the leaders of its (Gaullist or Socialist) governments. On the contrary, he has advocated such classic republican policies as an independent supreme court. In contrast to Hitler, he has oriented his political campaigns around neither territorial nor clearly economic frustrations. Unlike Germany after World War I, France was not the victim of a dictated peace treaty, and its populace is not aware of a scarcity of Lebensraum. Le Pen does not demand that France regain Algeria, nor does he go beyond the Gaullists in arguing that France retrieve lost military glory and a dominant position in Europe.

Although xenophobia is a principal stock-in-trade of the FN, and its program is most detailed with regard to foreigners and immigrants, it does not wish to lock them up or expel them forcibly. However, it proposes to make life in France less comfortable for them by withdrawing their privileges and so encourage them to return to their countries of origin. The FN advocates that foreigners be deprived of family allotments and subsidized schooling; that the residence permit of ten years, which can be automatically renewed, be abolished; that henceforth all foreigners admitted into the country come without their families; that immigrants have separate social security funds; that they no longer be eligible to vote in union or professional elections or to hold office in them; and that they—and their descendants, even if born in France—no longer have the right to acquire citizenship.[46]

Comparisons of Le Pen with Pétain or Poujade are as problematic as those with Hitler. Poujade appealed to provincial shopkeepers and artisans; Le Pen, for reasons of electoral pragmatism, appeals to urban workers and white-collar employees. Poujade railed against economic modernization, whereas Le Pen, insofar as he considers himself a classic liberal, is in favor of it. His acceptance of the Fifth Republic may be a tactical pose rather than a matter of conviction; but even if he were committed to an antisystem ideology, he would not be able to mobilize a segment of the domestic elite large enough to subvert the republic. Whereas the administrative, military, and academic elites of the Weimar Republic (and an important segment of the elite of the Third Republic) were hostile to the republic, those of France today overwhelmingly support it. Furthermore, the vicissitudes of industrial modernization, which had impoverished a large number of small shopkeepers and attracted them to Poujadism during the Fourth Republic, are no longer quite so threatening: Most French citizens live well, the currency is stable, and the industrial workers (and most of the unemployed) are cushioned against homelessness and starvation by extensive welfare-state provisions, which no major party has threatened to dismantle.

Unlike much of the traditional "Orleanist Right, the FN has vowed to retain these provisions, *grosso modo;* unlike the Nazis, Pétainists, and Poujadists, it has stressed the importance of the market and of individual rights and responsibilities. Unlike the Vichy regime, which tried to create a coherent philosophy, Le Pen has a set of eclectic and contradictory slogans that he uses in a demagogic manner.[47] Some of Le Pen's demagogy is reminiscent of that of the late Senator Joseph McCarthy, with its innuendos and its attacks on the motives if not the patriotism of the people who disagree with him.[48] Unlike McCarthy, however, Le Pen has been in no position to conduct inquisitions or to deprive his opponents of their jobs. There have been sufficient differences between the FN and the extreme right movements of the past to endow the FN with a certain republican legitimacy and to make it less embarrassing for the RPR and UDF to think in terms of collaborating with it.

THE NATIONAL FRONT AND THE "GANG OF FOUR"

The emergence of the FN from "lunatic fringe" status to partial respectability is indicated not only by the increased media coverage of Le Pen's doings and sayings and his standing in the polls. It is also signaled by the fact that the FN is now regarded by politicians, journalists, and political scientists as a fifth major political formation (or a sixth, if one still counts the PCF). Until recently, discussions about electoral coalition deals between Gaullist and Giscardist politicians on the one hand and FN candidates on the other were so commonplace on local levels that there was a growing tendency, both within the RPR/UDF and elsewhere, to think of the FN as a third *current* of the prosystem Right.

From 1958 to the mid-1970s, the Gaullists and Giscardists were regarded as barriers against the Extreme Right, just as General Paul Von Hindenburg had been regarded as a barrier against Hitler. But after 1981, this barrier began to weaken. The changes in the structure of French society, the growth of unemployment, the dislocations and insecurities that accompanied the process of rapid urbanization, and the immigrant phenomenon contributed to an increasing disillusionment with the Socialists, who proved not to be miracle workers. At the same time, the RPR and UDF were unable to exploit that disillusionment to their own advantage because of rivalries between the two parties and the ambiguities within each. Although some progressive politicians within the republican Right—including especially those in the Centre des Démocrates Sociaux (CDS) and the Radicals—continued to issue warnings about Le Pen, others adopted a more complacent attitude.[49]

A variety of pronouncements reflected a continuum of positions. At one extreme were statements by left-leaning members of the UDF (such as Lionel Stoléru) that it was better to support Laurent Fabius, a Socialist, than Le Pen, and threats from moderate Giscardists (such as Veil) that they would leave their party if it made any compromises with Le Pen.[50] Others, however, argued that the FN was not a foe but a rival of the RPR and UDF; and still others (such as Bernard Stasi of the CDS), though wishing to have nothing to do with the FN, conceded that "it is not altogether wrong in its analyses and propositions."[51] Others again tried to compete with the FN in its appeal to racism. This tactic began in the municipal elections of 1983, when the RPR and UDF used the same arguments as the FN in several constituencies. In Tourcoing and Toulon, UDF candidates referred to the dangers the presence of foreigners posed for France, and in Gennevilliers the RPR candidate resorted to anti-Semitic innuendos.[52]

For its part, the FN, in order to draw votes from the "gang of four," has used the vocabulary of the republicans, and even of the Left, and inverted it. Thus it talked about "red fascism" and "the dictatorship of the Left." It accused its opponents of "anti-French racism," of being Nazis, and of using the demogogic methods of Joseph Goebbels in defaming the FN, and has argued that the welfare state ends in totalitarianism. It defended its opposition to a massive presence of Maghrebis on the grounds that fundamentalist Islam is opposed to democracy and pluralism.[53]

Early in 1985, most of the national leaders of the RPR and UDF were still highly critical of FN ideology and against any electoral alliance with it, though they were unwilling to condemn selective alliances on local levels. UDF president Jean Lecanuet, although unenthusiastic about deals with the FN, thought that the Gaullist-Giscardist camp might need to make them in order to avert the greater evil of a victory of the Left in the Assembly elections of 1986—a position that did not prevent Lecanuet from joining RPR leader Jacques Chirac in a declaration to the effect that a vote for any other than the (then existing) *parliamentary* opposition would only help the Socialists.[54]

An interesting evolution in thinking was that of Chirac, who was prepared to occupy sectors of electoral terrain that appeared fertile. In 1976 he quit as prime minister because Giscard had evolved too far in the direction of the free market and had been unwilling to permit the government to take "energetic steps" and provide a "vigorous and coordinated impetus for the economy."[55] Subsequently, Chirac moved toward market liberalism because of the evolution of economic thinking in the country as well as the need to capture part of the Giscardist and CNI electorate and secure the support of the Employers' Association (CNPF), whose newly appointed leader, Yvon Gattaz, was defining the priorities of economic policy as the three D's: *"déréglementer, défiscaliser, désétatiser"* (deregulate, reduce taxes, and degovernmentalize).[56] This did not prevent Chirac from agreeing, early in 1986, to a joint platform with Giscard that would "respect the social achievements of the Left."[57] By the mid-1980s, Chirac, sensing the mood of the electorate, began to reverse his previous stand regarding the legalization of abortion (which had become effective in 1975 while he was prime minister): He moved toward the position of the FN, which opposed legalization even though many of its supporters favored it. In anticipatory justification of a postelectoral alliance with the FN (should the need for it arise), he suggested that such an alliance would be no worse than the Socialist alliance with the Communists. One of the most overt moves toward accommodation with the FN was a letter addressed by Marie-France Garaud, a former (independent) Gaullist presidential candidate, to Giscard, Chirac, Barre, *and* Le Pen proposing "an agreement about the essential objectives for France in 1986" and expressing the wish that a "majority of hope" would arrive at a common position on selected issues.[58]

One of the organizations that has helped to legitimate the FN is the federation of Perspectives and Realities clubs, conservative closet supporters of FN. Its president, Jean-François Deniau, referring to Le Pen as a *bon marin* (good fellow), said that "I don't share [Le Pen's] ideas [but] one must admit that his image is better known than his ideas. ... If the French vote for him ... they must have good reasons. ... A government of Marxist inspiration ... incoherent and inadequate, suffices to explain a drift in the direction of the extreme Right."[59]

Among the "respectable" conservative formations, the CNI became the closest ally of the FN. The slogan "no enemies on the right" was used with particular frequency by the CNI, which took so seriously its task of building a bridge between the FN and the RPR/UDF that it was referred to as "Le Pen Club."[60] Yet even within this most conservative of right-wing parties, there were differences of opinion. Some leaders (like Alain Robert, who had come from the Extreme Right and had once been secretary general of the FN) were severe critics of Le Pen's irresponsible behavior, which, they believed, harmed the image of the entire Right and would rebound to the benefit of the Left. Others (such as Philippe Malaud, a one-time minister in Georges Pompidou's government) thought that Le Pen and his friends were democrats and good citizens: "There is no proof that Le Pen is a fascist. His problem is the impression he conveys. When he talks about immigration, everybody thinks that he wants to put the immigrants on rafts in the port of Marseilles and throw them out right away."

These CNI politicians admitted that there might be a few Fascist lunatics in the FN that Le Pen was unwilling or unable to throw out; still, "there would be no harm in having some of Le Pen's people in the government, although they would of course have to be controlled."[61] A practical reflection of that position was that during the cantonal elections of 1985, CNI-FN collaboration was fairly close in a number of constituencies, with CNI candidates withdrawing in favor of the FN on the second ballot.

Another connecting link between the republican Right and the FN is the Club de l'Horloge. Founded in 1974 as a think tank for the UDF/RPR and open to academicians, civil servants, free professionals, and business managers, the Club de l'Horloge has propounded several theses to which both the UDF/RPR and the FN could subscribe: a rejection of egalitarianism, a preference for a private school system, a concern with the social consequences of the immigrant phenomenon, and a hard-nosed approach to law and order.[62] Unfortunately, the immigrant problem was in part created by the business community (many of whose members now supported Le Pen), which thought that importing labor was cheaper than modernizing industry. Furthermore, a tough approach to criminals would require an enlarged police force and more jails, and that implies greater, not lesser, state involvement. In this respect, both the Club de l'Horloge and the FN resemble the Reagan-Bush Republicans, who want to spend less public money on everything except the military and the police.

Ambivalence, contradiction, and uncertainty about the implications of the relationship—or "connivance," as Socialist leader Lionel Jospin has called it—between the FN and the mainstream Right is found within the FN as well.[63] For a decade, Le Pen repeatedly suggested that all members of the "gang of four" were in collusion and that the RPR/UDF, in refusing to make deals with the FN, was playing the game of the Left (much in the same way that the PCF has accused the PS of playing the game of the Right); at the same time, however, the FN implied that a deal with the RPR and UDF was difficult because they constituted "the liberal and decadent parliamentary opposition."[64]

The FN's ambivalence stemmed from an uncertainty about the extent and intensity of its electoral support. There were half- supporters and putative supporters, and it was not easy to determine their mobilization potential or their motivations. Many were prepared to vote for the FN not in order to help Le Pen achieve power but in order to "punish" the Socialists and to get the RPR and UDF to do something about the (real or imagined) dangers posed by the immigrants. Others who were themselves not prepared to vote for the FN hoped nevertheless that it would achieve noticeable representation in the Assembly and stir up debate on a variety of issues.

Some voters have supported Le Pen because they are hostile to democracy and because his movement has the best electoral position within the antidemocratic Right. For them, any turn by Le Pen toward an acceptance of the republican system constitutes a betrayal. This position was exemplified by a minor politician (Michel Faci) who had come to the FN from the Parti des Forces Nouvelles but in the mid-1970s left the FN because it had become too "moderate," and joined the Fédération d'Action Nationale et Européenne (FANE), a Neo-Nazi movement that was eventually dissolved by the government.

The perception of a bifurcation of its electorate has prompted the FN to present a double face—of both extremism and liberalism. There is a kind of division of labor: Leaving the articulation of ultranationalist and racist themes to selected associates and periodicals, Le Pen has tried to take the high road, spouting phrases about productivity, democracy, and individual freedoms. One measure of the adaptation of the FN to the reality of technocratic liberalism is an increasing tempo of recruitment of graduates of *grandes écoles* (the elite universities, such as the Ecole Nationale d'Administration) and managers of business firms into its active ranks.[65]

Curiously, the support of these categories for the FN does not seem to have been hindered by Le Pen's periodic abandonment of the high road: his involvement in a number of trials (with judgments going against him), his demagogic attacks on journalists, his ex-wife's risqué exposure in *Playboy* and his own subjection to ridicule in *Canard enchaîné,* his statements about AIDS, or his allusions to Hitler's crematoria.[66] He did lose some support in the fall of 1987 after his remarks about the gas chambers, but that occurrence may perhaps be explained by the French people's resensitization to the Holocaust by the trial of Klaus Barbie, which had ended earlier that year.[67]

SCENARIOS FOR THE FUTURE

Writing in mid-1985, and prognosticating about the prospects of the FN in the Assembly elections that were several months away, Le Pen said:

> If, by some misfortune, the parliamentary opposition should obtain a majority by itself in March 1986, the FN would be eliminated from the game [écarté des affaires]. In the contrary case, the [UDF/RPR] would have to choose to govern either with the FN or with the Left. If they govern with the Left, the discontent would grow and the FN would find its prospects for the presidential elections strengthened. If they govern with the FN, the program that we would impose upon them would reinforce the image of Le Pen. In either case, we will be the gainers.[68]

None of these scenarios materialized. The RPR/UDF, the erstwhile parliamentary opposition, won control of the Assembly and the government. To be sure, it fell short of a majority, but its plurality was sufficient for it to govern without FN support. The FN was in no position to endanger the Gaullist-Giscardist control of the legislative agenda; nevertheless, with its thirty-five seats it achieved a presence in a national institution and enhanced its legitimacy.

However, legitimacy does not automatically bring respectability. A full acceptance of the FN as a respectable party would depend on the behavior of its deputies and, above all, of Le Pen himself. Some observers predicted that the FN deputies would behave so destructively that the party would look like a group of fanatics who could not be entrusted with a responsible place in the national decisionmaking arena, thereby forfeiting all chances of being considered by the RPR/UDF as a coalition partner and weakening the presidential prospects of Le Pen in 1988. Others argued that parliamentary experience—and the esprit de corps and ethos of compromise associated with it—might so domesticate the FN that it would come to resemble the RPR/UDF, lose its mystique, and alienate its extreme right supporters. When the RPR/UDF formed a government under Chirac's leadership, the three possible roles of the FN were equally problematic:

Joining the government coalition, the first scenario, was unrealistic from the perspective of both the Gaullists and the FN—for the former, because it would taint the UDF/RPR and introduce unnecessary conflict; for the latter, because it was hard to imagine Le Pen, a demagogue and street fighter, as a minister tied down to a specific administrative task. The second, functioning merely as a group apart, as an enfant terrible of the Right, would hamper the efforts of the FN to achieve respectability and policy payoffs. Finally, assuming an intermediate role between support and sectoral opposition would be somewhat akin to the role of the Communist party during periods of Socialist control of the government, but it would introduce policy instability *and* increase the impatience of the RPR/UDF and confuse the FN's own electorate.

The actual behavior of the FN was a compromise: the ambivalent stance of being partly pragmatic and partly extremist, a position that made Le Pen both respectable and exciting enough to be a candidate in the presidential election of 1988 and that tempted the mainstream parties to adopt some of his policy positions. The response of the RPR and UDF to Le Pen's candidacy was equally ambivalent. Before the first ballot, hard-line Gaullists adopted tough anti-immigrant rhetoric in order to keep Gaullist voters from deserting to Le Pen.

The position adopted by the FN paid off, for in the 1988 presidential elections Le Pen got 14.5 percent of the first-round vote. Yet it is doubtful whether the majority of his electoral supporters wanted him to come to power: A significant proportion of them shifted their support in the second round to Mitterrand, who had been publicly identified with positions on immigrants and law and order that were at odds with those of the FN.

Before the second ballot, Gaullists attempted to retrieve the votes of Le Pen supporters for Chirac by suggesting that the alternative, the reelection of Mitterrand, was much worse for them. Charles Pasqua, the Gaullist minister of the interior, appealed for FN support by saying: "Surely there are certain extremists in the FN, but basically it has the same concerns and the same values as the [Gaullist-Giscardist] majority. [It is] only that [the FN] expresses them in a more boisterous manner."[69] Conversely, Michel Durafour, a UDF politician, announced his support for Mitterrand as the person who could best keep the nation united in face of the threat posed by the FN.

How serious is that threat? Predicting the prospects of the FN is a hazardous enterprise. There is no doubt that it will maintain itself as a party in the immediate future and that it will continue to be an electoral factor in certain local constituencies, especially where immigrants are heavily concentrated, where socioeconomic conditions are unhealthy, and where the candidates of the mainstream parties are unappealing. However, the long-range prospects of the FN do not seem to be favorable. A number of recent developments have worked against it: (1) reversion to the single-member constituency system of elections, which since 1988, has left the FN with only one Assembly deputy;[70] (2) the official decision of the RPR in the fall of 1988 to distance itself from the FN and to refrain from collaborating with it on national and subnational levels in future elections;[71] (3) the accidental death of Jean-Pierre Stirbois, the party's secretary general, in November 1988; (4) the municipal elections of March 1989, which produced impressive gains not only for the Socialists but also for a number of Gaullist politicians who had taken a strong position against the FN, among them Michel Noir, who was elected mayor of Lyons (to be sure, the FN received 11.7 percent of the vote in the elections to the European Parliament in June 1989; but that score reflected expressive rather than instrumental attitudes, the rate of electoral participation being only 54 percent); (5) the increasing reluctance of municipal councils to permit the FN to hold large public meetings in their cities.[72]

One indicator of the evolving position of the FN on the French political scene was the growing indifference of the mass media, in particular the television networks, to Le Pen, a situation about which he complained bitterly in the late 1980s.[73] The media, by depriving Le Pen of a national audience, reduced his political prospects, and in view of the poor performance of the FN in the 1988 Assembly elections, it was no longer important to devote much attention to the FN. Le Pen's charisma had been so counterbalanced by irresponsible public statements that he was increasingly seen as an aging buffoon. Such a situation was uncomfortable, if not disastrous, for the FN. Within the party itself a certain disunity could be detected as one member of its executive committee criticized the party's "extremist" positions and another complained that Le Pen's self-destructive behavior was dragging the party into the gutter.[74] One recent consequence of such perceptions was the desertion of several prominent (and "respectable") politicians and eighteen regional councillors to the CNI, the RPR, and the UDF.[75]

Nevertheless, certain episodes periodically force the media to pay attention to Le Pen. One such episode was the affair of the religious headscarves (foulards) worn by three Muslim girls to public elementary school classes in Creil, a small town in northern France, in September 1989.[76] This affair contributed to a renewal of the debate on the Islamic impact of Maghrebi immigrants and to the victory of the FN candidate in the parliamentary by-election in Dreux, an industrial town southwest of Paris, two months later.

In 1990 the FN tried both to improve its image of respectability—to appear as democratic as the mainstream parties—and to regain the limelight by marking itself off from them. The first aim was promoted by the convocation of a party congress whose delegates were duly elected by local and regional FN echelons (unlike earlier party congresses, whose delegates had been chosen by the national party leaders). But it was clear that this did not greatly affect the hierarchical principle that dominated party organization: The national leadership still appoints all the departmental and district secretaries, who commit themselves "scrupulously to follow the directives of their superiors."[77]

The opportunity to promote the second aim was provided by two events during the same year. When in the wake of the desecration of a Jewish cemetery in Carpentras the leaders of virtually all the national parties participated in mass demonstrations in support of the Jewish community, the politicians of the FN were notably absent. During the outbreak of the crisis in the Persian Gulf, the overwhelming majority of Socialists, Gaullists, and

Giscardists joined President Mitterrand in condemning the Iraqi invasion of Kuwait, showing solidarity with the U.S. position. Le Pen (like PCF leader Georges Marchais) came to the support of Iraqi president Saddam Hussein, perhaps in order to differentiate himself from the mainstream parties, to show his independence vis-à-vis the United States, or to suggest that he was not anti-Arab. More probably, he wished to foster good relations with Arab countries in order to limit immigration, and to express hostility to Israel and the Jews.[78]

A similar desire for differentiation was signaled when, in August 1990, Le Pen called for the disappearance of the Oder-Neisse line and the return of Germany to its "historic" dimensions, at a time when many French citizens showed a certain apprehensiveness about the impact of a reunited and powerful Germany.[79] In short, such positions ignored public orientations shared across the ideological spectrum and put in question Le Pen's commitment to important national interests.

The tactical position of the FN has been weakened, too, as its ability to exploit the differences within the "gang of four" has been reduced. Le Pen was able to draw support both from Gaullist voters who were leaving the RPR because it had given up its populist etatism and nationalism for neoliberalism and from leftist parties because these were abandoning their commitment to equality.[80] But such votes are not reliable, for the former cannot regard the FN as sufficiently etatist, and the latter cannot view it as sufficiently egalitarian. Moreover, the FN can no longer credibly argue that it is necessary to fight the "socio-Communists," because the PCF has been marginalized and the PS has shed its Marxism (if not its socialism). There has been a gradual convergence between the PS and the RPR/UDF on constitutional, domestic, and foreign policy issues and a growing impatience with ideology. The FN no longer can maintain the appearance of being "moderately extremist."[81]

But Le Pen is faced with a dilemma: If he and his FN are convincingly moderate, that is, republican, they will not be regarded as much different from the "established" right-wing parties, and a vote for the FN would therefore be wasted. Such a view was expressed most recently by Bernard Antony, an extreme rightist who complained that a "process of conservative banalization" has afflicted the FN.[82] But the extreme right electorate that feels this way is too small; in order to remain electorally significant, Le Pen must proclaim himself to be a republican because, as a spokesman of the Club de l'Horloge admitted, "the large majority holds republican values."[83]

CONCLUSION

French scholar René Rémond once distinguished between the Bonapartist and the Orléanist Right—the former being more populist (and hence lay-ing claim to greater democratic legitimacy) than the latter.[84] Another scholar has complicated the categorization by including the typologies of: the counterrevolutionary Right, the antivoluntarist Right, the anticonstitutional Right, and the metapolitical Right, and by adding the distinction between the rationalist and the irrationalist Right—the former (e.g., Libertarians) being optimistic and the latter (supporters of Joseph de Maistre) pessimistic.[85]

The FN does not fit easily into any of these categories. It represents them all but has woven them together to reflect Le Pen's complex personality and to create a modern catchall party. It has adjusted its vocabulary, depending upon the particular electorate it addresses: It is Bonapartist in its populism, it is Orléanist in its exploitation of the penchant for self-enrichment, and it practices rational calculation in its attempt to garner votes by appealing to the irrational fears of citizens.

The FN *electorate* is even harder to categorize, both in terms of general ideology and political efficacy. Polls have revealed that many FN supporters have a greater degree of trust in institutions concerned with law and order—the army and the police—and a correspondingly lower esteem for those institutions that appear to encourage permissiveness—the courts, the trade unions, and the public schools (see Table 1.6). But a significant proportion of FN sympathizers also distrust the business community, the banks, and the church, and in that respect it is closer to the Socialist electorate than to the traditional Right. Such patterns of political efficacy do not bear out the belief of those who tend to see Fascists everywhere.[86]

One scholar has divided the FN electorate into three groups: voters of the traditional ("republican") Right who have become radicalized—about 49 percent; new voters (former abstentionists and those who had been too young to vote)—32 percent; and elements of the traditionally leftist electorate (including Communists)—18 percent.[87] Another observer has offered a different breakdown: old reactionaries, Neo-Fascists, and other adherents of the Extreme Right; those who agree with most of Le Pen's ideas; those who have a special concern about immigration, unemployment, insecurity, and violence; and those who are angry with Gaullist, Giscardist, or Socialist leaders.[88]

In several elections since 1983, Le Pen and the FN went beyond the "natural" ideological limits of the Extreme Right. However, as opinion polls indicate, there is no complete congruence between a vote for Le Pen and endorsement of his ideas. A poll conducted in 1984 showed that 14 percent of the electorate considered itself close to Le Pen, 28 percent approved of his position on immigrants (as did 21 percent of Socialist voters), and 26 percent approved of his stand on law and order (as did 14 percent of Socialist voters).[89] However, a poll conducted during the same period revealed that 76 percent of those identified with the Right and 70 percent of those

TABLE 1.7   Issue Concerns According to Presidential Candidate Preferences, 1988

	Le Pen (FN)	Chirac (RPR)	Barre (UDF)	Mitterrand (PS)	Lajoinie (PCF)	Total Electorate
Immigrants	59 (38)[a]	21	17	13	12	22 (8)
Law and order	55	44	31	21	18	31
Unemployment	41 (19)	41	41	47	59	45 (28)
Taxes	24	20	18	20	27	20
Social security	21	20	16	28	41	24
Competitiveness of French industry	21 (6)	35	35	16	12	23 (12)
Education/vocational training	20 (14)	26	33	31	33	29 (11)

Note: Because several responses were possible, numbers add up to more than 100 percent.

[a]Figures in parentheses are from an Institut Français d'Opinion Publique poll following the legislative elections of 1986.

Sources: Adapted from Nonna Mayer and Pascal Perrineau, eds., *Le Front National à découvert* (Paris: Presses de la Fondation Nationale des Sciences Politiques, 1989), p. 62; and Jean Chatain, *Les affaires de M. Le Pen* (Paris: Editions Messidor, 1987), p. 168.

who labeled themselves as extreme right (compared with 77 percent of the population as a whole) thought that openly racist behavior of a serious kind should be brought before the courts—an interesting instance of a concern with law and order moderating the concern over immigrants.[90] Only 60 percent who voted for Le Pen in the first round of the presidential elections of 1988 shared his ideas. Of the 19 percent of the first-ballot supporters of Le Pen who switched to Mitterrand on the second ballot, 27 percent did so in order to block the path of another candidate; only 45 percent planned to vote for the FN in the legislative elections; and 25 percent considered Le Pen a danger to democracy.

Exit polls during the first round of the presidential elections of 1988 indicate that observers of the FN are correct in asserting that immigration has played a major role in the appeal of the FN, along with unemployment and insecurity.[91] However, the relative saliences of these and other issues (such as AIDS), and the causal connections between them, have not been very clear; moreover, as Table 1.7 shows, these were not the only concerns: Unemployment figured as heavily among the Chirac and Barre supporters, and more heavily among the supporters of the candidates of the Left.

These polls do not suggest that typical FN supporters have authoritarian personalities nor that they are looking for the kind of national savior the Germans saw in Hitler. Unlike most Germans during the Weimar Republic, most French citizens care more about democracy than about specific (economic and other) policy matters. Few French citizens who have voted for Le Pen have voted for fascism. The prominence of young voters among the FN electorate implies that they were neither worried about fascism and its possible impact on France nor did they know enough about it to make comparisons or share the guilty conscience of their elders.[92]

It appears that the support Le Pen has gained from the immigrant issue has been partly offset by a loss of support from those who take democracy seriously. In recent years, the number of those who consider Le Pen a danger to democracy has steadily increased—from 38 percent in 1983 and 55 percent in 1987 to 65 percent in October 1987, declining only slightly (to 61 percent) in April 1988.[93] The proportion of people holding a positive opinion of Le Pen in the past few years varied from a low of 9 percent in January 1984 to a high of 17 percent in April 1986 and stabilized at about 15 percent in mid-1991. In April 1987, 24 percent were in agreement with his ideas; in October of that year, only 18 percent. At the same time, 12 percent thought that he would make a good president and 86 percent that he would not.[94] During the same period, the proportion of people holding a negative opinion of the FN varied from a low of 62 percent in January 1984 to a high of 81 percent in April 1988.[95] One sign of the reduced respectability of the FN may be that many protest votes that had previously gone to that party went to a more credibly "republican" alternative party, the Greens, who got increasing support (especially in the second round of the 1988 legislative elections) in selected areas (for example, 13 percent in Strasbourg and 15 percent in several towns in Brittany). Curiously, 31 percent of those who voted for Le Pen in the presidential elections of 1988 expressed satisfaction with the results of the ensuing legislative elections that almost wiped out the Assembly representation of the FN—an attitude that indicates a cognitive dissonance between the impact of Le Pen's personal magnetism (if not his promises) and a wide public commitment to democracy.[96]

That dissonance is sometimes exploited by leaders of the mainstream right-wing parties. Thus, in justifying his refusal to make concessions vis-à-vis the FN, Chirac said, "I have not seen in the Resistance many people who adhere to the extreme Right; rather, they were among the collaborators ... and [their] roots have always been the opposite of ours."[97] Such talk is less risky for RPR and UDF politicians than it had been only a decade earlier, because most of them are too young to have been collaborators during the Vichy regime. However, the RPR's fight against the FN has its limits: It is not intended to provide electoral advantage to the Socialists. During a parliamentary by-election in Villeurbanne (Lyons) in October 1990, when Alain Carignon, the Gaullist mayor of Grenoble, called for the support of the Socialist candidate in order to keep the FN candidate from winning, he was roundly criticized by Chirac and "furloughed" from membership in the RPR.

The agreement (Charte de l'Union) signed in June 1991 by the RPR and UDF to present common first-ballot candidates in future legislative elections was designed in part to strengthen these conventional right-wing parties vis-à-vis the FN. But in view of the growing public concern over riots in public housing projects and street violence in immigrant neighborhoods, it was doubtful whether this move would suffice to keep the FN in check. Chirac made a speech in Orléans in which he asserted that France suffered from an "overdose" of immigrants.[98] Chirac's subsequent remark that he was merely saying out loud what many were thinking was patently designed to retrieve traditional Gaullist voters who had gone over to the FN. Le Pen, however, was not worried: He rejoiced that Chirac had seemingly embraced the thesis of the FN, but he did not think this would help Chirac, for the French "always prefer the original to the copy."[99]

These Gaullist maneuvers suggest that the FN is not regarded as so threatening as to necessitate a "republican defense" in which the leaders of all mainstream parties put aside their partisan selfishness. Nevertheless, they suggest that the FN is now sufficiently "rooted" to be a recognized protagonist in "the war of the Rights" *(la guerre des droites)*.[100] But that war is of limited comfort to the PS, whose leaders began to notice a growing appeal of Le Pen to elements of the traditional Socialist electorate, an appeal that has accounted for Premier Michel Rocard's open reference in 1990 to a "threshold of tolerance" beyond which immigration must not go. Moreover, Edith Cresson, the newly appointed prime minister, though criticizing Chirac's appeal to racism, announced that her government would take tough steps to apprehend and expel illegal immigrants.

Despite these developments, there are several reasons to project an eventual decline of the appeal of the FN. Some of the issues that gained support for the FN have been handled with reasonable effectiveness by the parties in power, for example, the fight against terrorism. Much of the "neoliberal" program of the FN is already found within the RPR/UDF and is being selectively absorbed by the Socialist party as well. Other issues have become irrelevant, such as the fight against the menace of bolshevism, in view of the changes now in progress in the former Soviet Union and the collapse of Communist regimes in Eastern Europe. Still others will be solved with the passage of time; this would apply above all to the issue of immigrants. On that issue Le Pen reflects the preferences of a large proportion of the electorate: In 1988 approximately 45 percent of the citizens wanted the nationality code to be made more restrictive, and an equal proportion favored sending immigrants back to their countries of origin.[101]

The clear pronouncements of Mitterrand against racism and in favor of an open and tolerant society (in contrast to the behavior of German chancellor Kohl, who continued to insist that the Federal Republic was not a country of immigrants) seemed to bear fruit in the 1988 election and "shamed" the leaders of the republican Right into adopting similar public positions. Moreover, the French tradition of *ius soli* will continue to facilitate the relatively rapid naturalization of immigrants and lead to the eventual in-

tegration and assimilation of the Maghrebis. Already, the political mobilization of both "second-generation immigrants" and naturalized Maghrebis
has been proceeding rapidly enough for the Socialists and politicians of the
RPR/UDF to take increasing cognizance of their electoral potential.

There are no parallels in France to the situation that brought about the assumption of power by the Nazis. In Germany, nationalism (after the failures
of 1848) tended to be associated with antidemocratic positions; in France,
nationalism and patriotic behavior were more often associated in the minds
of the majority of its citizens (other than committed Vichyites) with liberation from Nazi occupation and from an authoritarian puppet regime. (It is
for that reason that Le Pen has found it useful to claim that his father, whose
fishing boat capsized in the Atlantic during World War II, fell for the homeland.)

Moreover, the combination of socioeconomic circumstances and class relationships that prevailed in Weimar Germany and that led to fascism (and
that accounted for the appeal of Poujadism during the Fourth Republic) is
not replicated in today's France. Fascism appealed to a middle class affected
by relative status decline, aggravated by a collusion between industry and
the farmer.[102] In France, in contrast, the nature of the marginalized element
has been changing: The provincials who once felt alienated from the national scene are now brought in closer contact with it through an expanded
welfare state and a modern system of communication; the peasantry is declining as a political force; and the relative status of the French lower-middle
and working classes has been raised by the presence of the immigrants, who
constitute the underclass. Because of the appeal of the FN to racism, however, that underclass, once politicized, is not likely to support the party.

In sum, although the electoral successes of Le Pen and his FN have given
them legitimacy, they have not gained enough respectability to pose a serious challenge to the established parties or a threat to the republican system.
Both election results and public opinion data suggest that between two-
thirds and three-quarters of the French electorate are repelled by Le Pen,
his outlook, and his behavior. It appears that the votes that he attracts from
the established parties—notably the RPR—are "soft" and temporary votes
and that there are limited prospects for the FN's drawing additional support
from elements of the Extreme Right that are currently outside its embrace.
Thus in the eyes of royalists and openly avowed Fascists, the FN has been
hopelessly co-opted by republicanism. Another extreme right organization,
the Groupe de Recherche et d'Étude sur la Civilisation Européenne
(GRECE), is interested in ideas and not in day-to-day political struggles; it is
also opposed to the Christianity that the FN and Le Pen have been preaching.[103] Conversely, in the eyes of fundamentalist Catholics, the FN is too populated by secular elements. Le Pen himself, despite his assertion that future

governments should be inspired by the Ten Commandments, is regarded as too hedonistic.[104]

It is possible that in order to maintain its electoral appeal, the FN will evoke the dangers posed to France by the "Europe of 1992" and seek to reunite those business, farming, and other sectors that might be overwhelmed by serious competition from outside. In a recent interview, a leader of the FN in fact hinted that the party was favorable to a degree of protectionism.[105] But that position is inconsistent with Le Pen's professed interest in productivity and competition. Moreover, with the increasing institutionalization of supranational patterns in the context of the European Community—such as the movement of workers, labor relations, social security coverage, and the right to vote in municipal elections—a purely "national" solution to the immigrant problem and for that matter, to the problem of security, is no longer possible, and, hence much of the nationalist rhetoric of Le Pen and the FN is no longer so credible as it may once have been. Although these developments do not augur well for the FN, however, the party is likely to maintain itself in the near future as an alternative political movement and, by appealing to discontented and diffuse elements of the electorate, to function as an arbiter in closely contested races.

THE THREE WAVES OF WEST GERMAN RIGHT-WING EXTREMISM

Ekkart Zimmermann and Thomas Saalfeld

It won't be a second Hitler who is going to challenge the Bonn state, no imitator who will captivate our attention. It will be a unique original, a personality appropriate in its time and responding to its needs. Similar cues will at best be evident to experts, but not to the mass electorate. The seduction approaches its victims imaginatively and with fantasy, it doesn't come about in a stereotypical and recognizable manner.[1]

—Harald Neubauer

Even though in early 1991 political and economic conditions were nowhere close to what is suggested in this quote from a former political leader of the (West) German Republikaner party, the public should be forewarned. More relevant than such prophesies by leaders of the Extreme Right, however, is a solid analysis of West German right-wing extremism. That right-wing extremism represents a fundamental challenge to liberal democracy is one of the lessons of the fall of the Weimar Republic. Understanding the conditions and correlates of its success thus may contribute to its containment.

We begin this chapter by characterizing the main features of right-wing extremism; we then attempt a longitudinal analysis of its three major waves in West Germany since World War II, thereby highlighting continuities and changes. Using the rich body of empirical data, we set up a simple theoretical model to account for the phenomenon in West Germany (and possibly in other Western countries).

DEFINING RIGHT-WING EXTREMISM

Right-wing extremism is defined here as efforts of political sects, movements, and parties to affect the development of society in such a way that the democratic rules of the political game will eventually be abolished and instead a political and social ideology introduced that is characterized by ultra-nationalism and ethnocentrism (expressed, for example, against foreign workers and asylum seekers), anti-Americanism, anticommunism, antiparliamentarianism, antipluralism, antiegalitarianism, militarism, law-and-order thinking, a demand for a strong and charismatic political leader or executive, cultural pessimism, and corporatist notions in politics and to some extent the economy. On the individual level, such an ideology is often coupled with rigid belief systems, stereotypes of friends versus foes, conspiratorial thinking, fanaticism and activism.

The driving force behind these goals is the effort to correct radically those societal and economic developments that are perceived as unfavorable both to individuals and for society at large. In addressing these goals, values and forms of organizations of a prior historical period are frequently invoked. We largely omit political sects and movements from our discussion in this chapter, but with a few adjustments, similar arguments would apply to them. A party is categorized as an extremist right-wing party on the basis of slogans and platforms, public speeches and interviews of party leaders and high officials, numerous in-depth survey materials of party sympathizers as well as a consensus in the expert literature. Any such classification necessarily contains arbitrary elements, but there is no way to avoid these. A formal content analysis of party platforms or a literal analysis of campaign speeches would be misleading because extremist right-wing parties often tune their rhetoric to democratic requirements. The results of placing a party on the extreme right, as done by both adherents and opponents of such parties, further justify our procedure.[2] The latter in a sense is the hardest attitudinal indicator, revealing more than the often pseudodemocratic rhetoric of right-wing extremist party leaders. Researchers in the past always had to follow such a strategy of mixing harder and softer definitional elements in classifying a party as extremely right-wing. Anything else would be underestimating the dangerous potential of such parties. That they partly adapt to other issues and more democratic styles of self-presentation should not detract from their fundamental opposition to democratic pluralism.

WEST GERMAN RIGHT-WING EXTREMISM
AFTER WORLD WAR II

Parties and Movements

It is impossible to cover the whole, diffuse spectrum of organized right-wing extremism in West Germany in this chapter.[3] Therefore, we focus upon (1) extremist right-wing parties that gained at least 5 percent of the vote in at least one election on the national or federal state level and (2) non–party or-

ganizations that were not confined to specific regions.[4] Five political parties
meet our 5 percent criterion: the Socialist Reich party (SRP), the German
Reich party (DRP), the German Community (DG), the National Democratic Party of Germany (NPD), and the Republikaner party (REP).[5] We
deal with these parties first and then turn to non–party organizations.

After the Allied licensing system for political parties had been abolished
in 1949, the Socialist Reich party was founded in October of that year. In
terms of ideology, policies, and leadership, the party was a successor to the
National Socialist German Workers party. SRP leaders considered the last
Nazi cabinet under Admiral Karl Dönitz as the only legitimate German gov-
ernment and saw the Bonn system and the administration of Konrad
Adenauer as an illegitimate imposition of the Allied powers. As Stephen
Fisher put it,

> The SRP put forth a typically Nazi doctrine of the Reich as a kind of mystical
> blood union of the German people. Party leaders declared that Germany
> should become a "leadership democracy" ruled by a "national chief," who
> would direct the nation as chief executive, assisted by a corporate parliament.
> The SRP openly expressed its admiration for Hitler and his regime, stating that
> it wanted to retain the good aspects of Nazism and desired to perfect the Nazi
> social revolution.[6]

The SRP's support was concentrated in the Protestant parts of northern
Germany. Almost two-thirds of its 10,000 or so members (1951) lived in
Lower Saxony. It was tightly and hierarchically organized in accordance with
the Nazi leadership principle. In 1951 the party had its biggest electoral success when it gained 11 percent of the vote in the state diet (Landtag) elections of Lower Saxony, and 7.7 percent in Bremen. In 1951 the Adenauer
government appealed to the Federal Constitutional Court to ban the SRP
on the grounds of its antidemocratic, overtly Nazi program, and in 1952 the
party was outlawed. Afterwards, most SRP leaders joined the German Reich
party. Its voters, by contrast, were largely integrated by the bourgeois
prosystem parties.[7] After 1952, none of those German parties having an
explicitly Nazi or Neo-Fascist program achieved any significant degree of organizational continuity or electoral success.

After the banning of the SRP, the German Reich party remained as the
strongest extremist right-wing party of the 1950s and early 1960s. It existed
from 1950 to 1965. Prior to 1952 the party had played a secondary role to
the SRP. Most of its leaders were former Nazi functionaries, and a large percentage of its membership had belonged to the National Socialist party. In
the early 1960s, the DRP had about 4,500 members, of whom approximately
50 percent were former Nazis and 20 percent ex-members of the SRP.[8] Its
support was largely restricted to those regions in which the SRP had its

strongholds. The party competed in three general elections on the federal level (1953, 1957, 1961) but never succeeded in gaining more than 1.1 percent of the total vote (1953). The best individual DRP results at the level of federal states (Länder) were reached between 1955 and 1959, when it polled 3.8 percent of the vote in the state diet elections of Lower Saxony (1955) and Bremen (1959), 3.6 percent in Lower Saxony (1959) and 5.1 percent in Rhineland-Palatinate (1959).[9] At the time of its foundation (1950), five members of the 1949–1953 Bundestag joined the party. It was also represented in the state diets of Lower Saxony (1951–1959) and Rhineland-Palatinate (1959–1963).[10]

In terms of programmatic statements, the DRP leaders were more careful to pay lip service to the Basic Law (the German constitution) than those of the SRP, but by and large their propaganda themes were similar. "Party programs cast aspersions on the honesty and patriotism of government leaders, expressed a belief in a German national community *(Volksgemeinschaft)*, demanded the release of all German war criminals, called for the creation of a 'new Reich' with a real German culture, emphasized what was 'worthwhile' in the Third Reich, demanded the restoration of the historic German frontiers, and insisted on the withdrawal of foreign troops."[11]

The SRP and DRP had its strongholds in some Protestant regions of northern Germany, whereas the German Community acquired significance only in the south, especially in Baden-Württemberg and Bavaria. "The DG originally sought to appeal to the dispossessed, particularly to those whose houses had been taken by the occupying forces, the victims of bombing, the returned prisoners-of-war, and those who had lost money through the currency reform."[12] Compared to its major rival on the radical right, the DRP, the German Community has more consistently pursued a nationalist-neutralist line in foreign policy, demanding an end to "the rule of the Communist and of the Capitalist internationals over German soil." Its economic policies were less conservative and put more emphasis on a petit bourgeois "socialism" that involved the destruction of the power of finance capitalism and the nationalization of key industries.[13] In this respect its policies recalled early Nazi party programs of the mid-1920s. The party enjoyed some initial electoral success in an alliance with the Federation of the Homeless and Dispossessed (BHE) in Bavaria and Baden-Württemberg. According to Fisher,

The alliance between these two movements was ended soon after the BHE decided in favor of participation in the government and the DG chose to pursue a course of radical opposition. ... As the DG began to denounce the parliamentary regime, the Western Allies, and the Bonn government, the BHE leaders came to view the DG as a handicap to the BHE's efforts to obtain government offices and benefits for refugees. Thus the alliance was dissolved, and, by 1952, almost the entire refugee electorate of the DG had crossed over to the BHE. From that time on, the DG never enjoyed any significant electoral success.[14]

In 1964 the DRP leaders initiated the foundation of the National Democratic party of Germany. After the formation of the NPD, the DRP dissolved. Its members, leaders, and organization became the backbone of the NPD.[15] In its initial phase, the party membership was heavily infiltrated by former Nazis.[16] Like most extremist right-wing parties, the NPD formally emphasizes its loyalty to the Basic Law. The fundamental issues of its propaganda in its most successful period, the late 1960s, were "the rehabilitation of nationalism and the Nazi past; a bitter hatred of all things non-German; a denunciation of the decline in traditional morality and values; the alleged sell-out by the enemy within; the call for a return to militaristic, authoritarian discipline."[17] These attitudes have largely persisted, supplemented by radical anti-Americanism, anticommunism, and ethnocentrism. The party is committed to the establishment of an ethnically defined "national community" based on corporatist rather than competitive decisionmaking rules and directed by a strong and nonpartisan executive. It also demands a significant reduction of immigrants and asylum seekers. Before the process of German unification commenced (1990), the party wanted to achieve national reunification—by then *the* central programmatic issue for all parties on the extreme right—by a neutralization of Germany. The NPD supports a "third way" between capitalism and communism. In its new program, stressing environmental protection and rejecting major nuclear power plants, the party attempts to modernize and to escape its former image of neonazism.[18]

Between 1966 and 1968 the NPD overcame the 5 percent threshold of West Germany's electoral law in seven out of the eight state diet elections of that period. It was represented by a total of sixty-one members in seven state parliaments and built up a solid organizational base in southern Germany (Bavaria and Baden-Württemberg), where its precursors, SRP and DRP, had lacked success. The electoral and organizational base of German right-wing extremism has since shifted from northern to southern Germany. However, with 4.3 percent of the total vote the NPD failed to gain parliamentary representation in the Bundestag elections of 1969. Afterwards, its electoral fortunes dwindled. Between 1972 and 1990, its best results in Bundestag elections were 0.6 percent (1972, 1987).[19]

The lack of electoral success encouraged bitter internal quarrels on the party's strategy. Although the leadership and a majority of its activists continued to favor the pursuit of parliamentary representation and eventually of a coalition with one of the established bourgeois parties, a militant minority demanded a more radical strategy. In frustration, most militants left the party in the early 1970s; many of them, especially younger members, joined nationalist-revolutionary or Neo-Fascist groups. The party's membership declined from a high point of 28,000 in 1967 and 1969 to 5,900 in 1982. By 1989, it had slightly recovered to 7,000 persons.[20]

In 1983 the Republikaner party was founded by two former Christian Social Union (CSU) Bundestag deputies, Franz Handlos and Ekkehard Voigt, and the prominent journalist Franz Schönhuber, who had for a long time been close to the then CSU leader and prime minister of the federal state of Bavaria, Franz-Josef Strauss. Handlos and Voigt had left the CSU because they felt alienated by what they considered as Strauss's too reconciliatory policies toward the German Democratic Republic.[21] After internal quarrels, the first REP leader, Handlos, stepped down in 1985 and Schönhuber became his successor. This change in the party's leadership brought a shift from largely conservative policies as represented by Handlos and Voigt to a more nationalist orientation. In consequence, the REP became more attractive to members of the traditional parties on the extreme right. The party's program bridges the gap between traditional conservatism as represented by the right wing of the Christian Democratic Union (CDU)/CSU and extremist right-wing attitudes as articulated by NPD and the German People's Union (DVU).[22] By 1991 the REP party was characterized by deep internal splits between a moderate wing led by Schönhuber, who favors a conservative strategy emphasizing nationalism and law-and-order issues, and those who wish a more intensive cooperation with traditional extremist right-wing parties such as NPD and DVU.

The REP can be conceived as a radical, populist right-wing protest party.[23] It tries to present itself as a prosystem party, stressing law and order and claiming to represent the interests of ordinary people. Its central programmatic objective (until 1990) was the reunification of Germany. The REP's apologetic views of German history during the era of National Socialist rule and its aggressive agitation against immigrants, asylum seekers and foreign workers, whom it deems a danger to Germany's national identity and public order alike, are classical statements of extremist right-wing parties.[24] In its platforms, the REP attempts to mobilize protest against certain grievances in state and society, against the "established" parties, especially against the CDU/CSU and the incumbent federal government. Its lack of a thorough organization, the limited opportunities for participation in politics, and the lack of intraparty democracy additionally contribute to the impression of a populist protest movement rather than a political party.[25]

In 1989, the year of its greatest electoral and organizational success, the REP's membership rose from 8,000 (January 1989) to roughly 25,000 (January 1990). Its organization is strongest in Bavaria, Baden-Württemberg, and West Berlin. To a large extent its leadership is recruited from three sources: former CDU/CSU activists, functionaries of expellees' pressure groups, and former NPD and DVU activists. Its first electoral success was in the 1986 state diet elections of Bavaria, where it polled 3 percent of the total vote. In the

1989 state diet elections of West Berlin, the party won 7.5 percent, and in the same year it repeated its success in its first contest on the national level, in the European Parliament elections (7.1 percent). This nationwide election confirmed, however, that its strongholds remained in the south of Germany: The REP gained 14.6 percent of the vote in Bavaria and 8.7 percent in Baden-Württemberg, whereas its results in northern Germany remained modest. In 1990, it declined as rapidly as it had risen. Even in its stronghold, Bavaria, the party failed to overcome the 5 percent threshold in the 1990 state diet elections, reaching just 4.9 percent. In the 1990 Bundestag elections it gained only 2.1 percent of the total vote.[26]

Organized right-wing extremism in West Germany has not only taken the form of various political parties; the latter are part of a broader social movement organizing its supporters either in nonpartisan activities or groups pursuing a militant strategy of direct (violent) action. Under the conditions of Allied occupation, it was impossible for former Nazi activists to restore the old National Socialist party. Some withdrew from politics, some turned to conservative nationalist parties which were licensed by the Allies, and many entered "parapolitical" organizations such as the Mutual Aid Society of Former Armed SS (HIAG) founded in 1949, the German Cultural Foundation of European Civilization (DKEG) founded in 1950, or journal circles such as the Euro-Fascist "Nation Europa" founded in 1951.

These organizations agitated against "denazification," glorified the German soldiers of World War II, and tried to build up contacts with conservative political movements. They offered help to the Nazi leaders sentenced in the Nuremberg war criminal trials and their families, and attempted to establish a network of contacts, personal relationships, ideas, and strategies. Outspoken National Socialist propaganda was avoided, but ethnocentrist and nationalist thinking circulated around the idea of the German Reich and attempts to rehabilitate the allegedly "positive" aspects of the Third Reich. Quickly an extremist right-wing network developed that was characterized by harsh opposition toward Bonn democracy and by a fortress mentality based on myths of conspiracy and deprivation.[27] Following the banning of the SRP in 1952 and owing to the declining attraction of extremist right-wing parties at the polling booths in the early 1950s, many SRP and DRP activists withdrew from party politics and increasingly attempted to work through organizations such as those mentioned above. The retreat into subcultural networks has generally worked as an important survival strategy of German right-wing extremism in times of electoral failure. Moreover, it was attempted to maintain the continuity of extremist right-wing beliefs among subsequent generations by establishing youth organizations such as the Viking Youth founded in 1952.[28]

In the 1970s, after the NPD's failure to establish itself as a permanent political factor in West German politics, the "Old Right," biographically still closely tied to national socialism, was largely absorbed by Gerhard Frey's German People's Union, founded in 1971.[29] Similar to the late 1950s, parapolitical networks functioned as "reserve positions" after the major extremist right-wing party had failed electorally. Since 1980 the DVU has had the highest membership of all organizations on the extreme right.[30] Until 1987, it has operated as parent organization of a number of "action groups" that articulate such demands as a general amnesty for sentenced Nazi war criminals, the repatriation of immigrants, a reunification of Germany in its 1937 borders, or the reduction of foreign influence in German radio and television programs. In the DVU's various action groups, its supporters attempted to continue the strategy of parapolitical organizations of the 1950s.

Only since 1987 did it begin to put forward its own lists at elections (DVU Liste D). Although previously the DVU harshly criticized the NPD, and even occasionally recommended that its supporters vote for the CDU/CSU in general elections, it has cooperated with the NPD in most general elections since 1987. The leaders of both parties, Frey (DVU) and Mussgnug (NPD), agreed that the two parties should support each other in certain elections rather than compete against each other.[31]

The DVU's publications exhibit massive historical revisionism, denial of German responsibility for the outbreak of World War II, and aggressive campaigns against the constitutional right to political asylum.[32] In its election campaigns of 1987, it accused leading politicians of the CDU/CSU of participating in foreign "instigation" against the German people, and inactivity in what the DVU conceives as the threat of immigration and ethnic "alienation." In the European elections of 1989, the party also attempted to mobilize nationalist, anti-European sentiments; again, immigration was a central issue.[33] With only 1.6 percent of the vote, however, the DVU Liste D was clearly overtaken by its major rival, the REP. Apart from its relatively large financial resources, the DVU's backbone is made up of the various extremist right-wing newspapers, magazines, and books published by Frey.[34] His weekly papers have a total circulation of more than 100,000 copies and are of crucial importance for the maintenance of ideological traditions and values of the Extreme Right.[35]

Younger right-wing radicals, who were disappointed by the NPD's and DVU's "bourgeois" strategy, were attracted by Neo-Nazi action groups such as the People's Socialists or the Action Front of National Socialists (ANS) or paramilitary associations such as the Military Sport Group Hoffmann (banned in 1983).[36] Most of these groups have pursued a militant strategy, using or provoking political violence especially against immigrants as well as Jewish citizens and institutions. They are largely recruited from working-class juveniles, soccer fan clubs, and skinhead groups. The Neo-Nazi action groups have infiltrated the marginal Neo-Fascist Free Workers party (FAP) and maintain close personal ties to members of the Young National Democrats, the NPD's youth organization.[37]

Besides parapolitical organizations and militant groups, there is a third strand, consisting mainly of intellectuals who have attempted to follow the French Nouvelle Droite and to develop a modern theoretical foundation of right-wing extremism, aware that the traditional ideologies on the right have failed to give answers to current political and social problems. This discourse takes place primarily in journals. The authors involved have consciously, and with a certain degree of success, sought to reach moderate conservative readers and bridge the intellectual gap between right-wing extremism and conservatism. The interpretative patterns developed here can be found in the current programs of the NPD and the REP: Neutralism between the two blocks, reunification as confederation, a "third way" between Soviet communism and American cultural imperialism, and national identity and patriotism as surrogates of the old imperial idea of the Reich.[38]

Voting, Membership, Violence

The organizational and electoral history of organized right-wing extremism in West Germany is characterized by three cyclical ups and downs. These cycles are reflected both in the cumulative share of votes gained by extremist right-wing parties at the national and regional levels, including in the European elections (Figure 2.1), and in the membership of extremist right-wing parties.

Each bar in Figure 2.1 represents, in chronological order, the cumulated share of votes gained by extremist right-wing parties in all Bundestag, federal, state diet, and European Parliament elections between 1949 and 1990.[39] Only in 4 out of 133 elections was the cumulated share of votes obtained by extremist right-wing parties higher than 10 percent of the total vote. In fourteen elections extremist right-wing parties surpassed the 5 percent threshold of the West German electoral system. Apart from the European elections of 1989, where the REP gained 7.1 percent of the vote, these instances were on the regional level (that of the *Länder* rather than the national level. In none of the twelve Bundestag elections did extremist right-wing parties individually or in combination gain 5 percent of the vote. Only the NPD came close to the 5 percent margin in the Bundestag elections of 1969 (4.3 percent). A second look at Figure 2.1 shows that the elections where extremist right-wing parties were relatively successful are not distributed randomly over time, but in clusters. Nor is it possible to explain the variance by recurrent successes in certain "strongholds" of the far Right. Rather, we can distinguish three phases in which extremist right-wing parties were particularly successful.

The first cluster represents the phase of postwar right-wing extremism that commenced in 1945 and gradually came to a close in the 1950s. The

Figure 2.1   Cumulative Share of Votes Obtained by Extremist Right-wing Parties in West Germany, 1949–1990

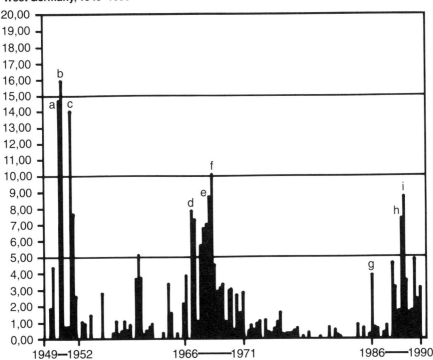

Legend: Federal state diet elections of (a) Baden-Württemberg, 1950; (b) Bavaria, 1950; (c) Lower Saxony, 1951; (d) Hesse, 1966; (e) Bremen, 1967; (f) Baden-Württemberg, 1968; (g) Bavaria, 1986; and (h) Bavaria, 1989. European Parliament elections are indicated by bar i.

Note: Each bar represents the cumulative share of votes obtained by extremist right-wing parties at Bundestag, Federal state diet, and European elections (in chronological order). For all elections of 1990, only the results in the former Federal Republic were entered.

Sources: For 1949–1989, Federal Office of Statistics (1989). For 1990, information obtained by the State Offices of Statistics of Bavaria, Lower Saxony, North Rhine–Westfalia, and Saarland, and German Bundestag (1990: 5–11).

most remarkable election results can be observed in 1950–1951. The DG received 14.7 percent of the vote and sixteen parliamentary seats at the 1950 state elections in Baden-Württemberg and—on a common ticket with the Federation of the Homeless and Dispossessed—12.3 percent of the vote and six parliamentary seats in the 1950 Bavarian state elections.[40] In 1951, extremist right-wing parties (including SRP and DRP) obtained 14.1 percent of the vote in Lower Saxony and 7.7 percent in Bremen.[41] In spite of a few remarkable DRP results, the period between 1952 and 1958 was a phase of decline. In the years of the "economic miracle," the "nationalist opposition" suffered electoral failure, fractionalization, organizational and personal rivalries, and social isolation. Its electoral clientele was diminished to a small core of antidemocratic outsiders.[42]

The early 1960s, the second phase, witnessed massive efforts of the Radical Right to join forces and set up a bigger party. The major result of these efforts was the formation of the NPD.[43] The NPD's support in the 1965 Bundestag election was modest (2 percent). However, the first major economic recession after 1949, the disintegration of the bourgeois postwar coalitions, the grand coalitions of CDU/CSU and SPD at the federal and state levels, as well as the activities of the left-wing extraparliamentary opposition contributed to the rise of the NPD between 1966 and 1968, when the party succeeded in overcoming the 5 percent threshold in seven state diet elections.[44] After the NPD had failed to win more than 4.3 percent of the vote in the 1969 Bundestag elections, its electoral fortunes declined. Between 1972 and 1986, it fell back to a position close to nil. The CDU/CSU reintegrated most of those voters who had shifted their allegiance to the NPD between 1966 and 1968. In the 1970s the NPD declined and was eventually outdone by the DVU, which, at least in terms of membership, became the strongest extremist right-wing organization in the Federal Republic in 1980. In 1989 the NPD succumbed to the REP.

The third surge of extremist right-wing voting was mainly due to REP success. In 1989 it overcame the 5 percent threshold in the state elections of West Berlin and in the European elections.[45] Although elections to the European Parliament are not usually considered as important as Bundestag elections, this was the first time an extremist right-wing party gained more than 5 percent of the vote in a nationwide election. However, the spectacular success story of the REP seems to end as quickly as it began. In the subsequent federal and state elections the party failed to repeat its gains of 1989.

A similar cyclical pattern emerges if we look at the membership in extremist right-wing organizations. Figure 2.2 exhibits a pattern largely analogous to the one observed in Figure 2.1 with regard to the electoral support of extremist right-wing parties. The dotted line marks the total membership of all such organizations from 1954 to 1989. The bars refer to the most important groups. The total number of members organized in extremist right-wing groups and parties declined rapidly from 1954 until the early 1960s. The rise between 1964 and 1967 was largely due to the growing attractiveness of the NPD, whereas the downward trend after 1967 also correlates with a continuous loss of membership of the NPD. Between 1978 and 1988 the number of organized right-wing extremists grew by about 60 percent. The most remarkable increases occurred in 1979–1980 and between 1986 and 1988. By and large, they seem to be a consequence of the growing organizational strength of the DVU (after 1987, DVU *and* DVU Liste D).

Despite the concentration process in favor of the DVU, the West German Extreme Right has retained one of its traditional characteristics: its high de-

Figure 2.2 Membership of Extremist Right-wing Parties in West Germany, 1954–1989

Thousands

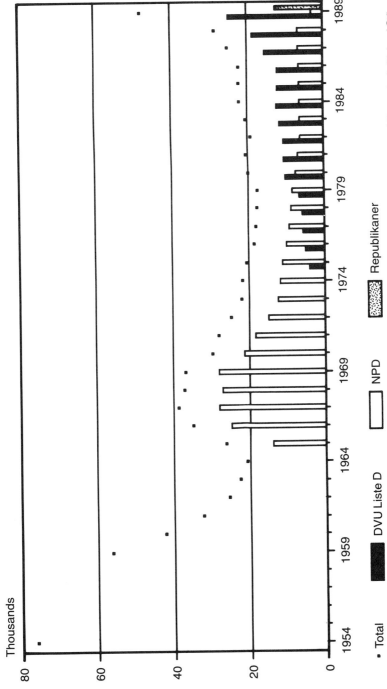

- Total
- DVU Liste D
- NPD
- Republikaner

Sources: For 1954–1989: Federal Ministry of the Interior, *Verfassungsschutzbericht* (Report of the Office of Constituional Protection); Richard Stöss, *Die Republikaner*, 2nd ed. (Cologne: Bund Verlag, 1990), p. 54.

gree of fractionalization. Between 1970 and 1989 the number of extremist right-wing organizations recorded by the Federal Ministry of the Interior oscillated between a minimum of sixty-two (1973) and a maximum of ninety-one (1975).[46] Nevertheless, in terms of organizational stability, NPD and DVU remain the dominant groups, despite the short-lived rise of the REP.[47]

Apart from the dominant traditional organizations, NPD and DVU, the small militant groups had considerable growth rates. Their membership increased fivefold between 1975 and 1989. In absolute numbers, however, they remained insignificant. In 1989 the Federal Ministry of the Interior counted twenty-three organizations with 1,500 supporters. Their highest growth rates were between 1975 and 1979. After a period of stagnation in the early 1980s, which was probably caused by the banning of many militant groups in 1983 and the prosecution of its leading members by the courts, these militant right-wing organizations experienced another growth period in 1987. Its militant core group, from which most of the extremist right-wing terrorists are recruited, is estimated to comprise about 200 persons.[48]

Sometimes the literature mentions a fourth phase of extremist right-wing activity that does not coincide with the electoral and organizational cycles sketched above. The phase of 1977–1985, a period of electoral failure for the whole extremist right-wing camp, was characterized by the growing militancy of Neo-Nazi groups. Figure 2.3 illustrates the number of legal offenses committed by right-wing extremists as recorded by the Federal Ministry of the Interior. The lower parts of the bars signify violent offenses and the upper parts threats of violence and nonviolent offenses such as racist or anti-Semitic insults or graffiti and the like.[49] Figure 2.3 demonstrates that the total annual amount of recorded offenses committed by right-wing extremists grew continuously between 1976 and 1982. After 1982 the number stagnated, albeit on a level considerably higher than in the 1960s and 1970s. Only a small portion of all legal offenses committed by right-wing extremists were of a violent nature. Nevertheless, the number of violent attacks also rose between 1977 and 1989. Some observers believe the confrontational relationship between government and opposition after 1969 and the extraparliamentary resistance against the socialist-liberal *Ostpolitik* on the nationalist right stimulated right-wing militancy, especially among younger members. Another factor might have been the frustration over the persistent electoral failure and lack of unity of traditional right-wing parties. From 1977–1978 onward, this increased militancy occasionally escalated to terrorism. The phase of stagnation of extremist right-wing offenses after 1982 is explained by the banning of militant Neo-Fascist groups and the authorities' successful prosecution of the leaders and activists.[50]

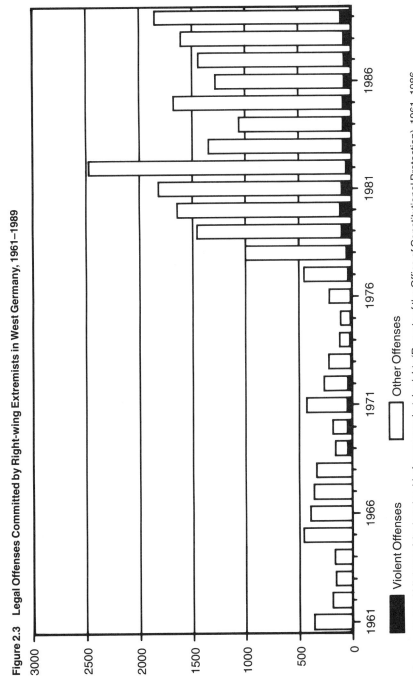

Figure 2.3 Legal Offenses Committed by Right-wing Extremists in West Germany, 1961–1989

Violent Offenses

Other Offenses

Sources: Federal Ministry of the Interior, *Verfassungsschutzberichte* (Reports of the Office of Constitutional Protection), 1961–1986.

Radical Right-Wing Voters

Extremist right-wing parties become politically relevant as soon as they influence the arithmetics of majorities and coalitions in the political
decisionmaking system. The collapse of the Weimar Republic illustrates this:
At that time extreme fragmentation among the constitutional moderate
parties made it harder and harder to form majority governments, and both
extreme wings, Nazis and Communists, benefited from mounting voter frustration. Surveys have repeatedly shown that there is a (mostly) latent
authoritarian-conservative potential among the West German electorate
that is considerably higher than the corresponding shares of votes obtained
by extremist right-wing parties at elections.[51] "In past elections, some of
these men and women abstained from voting altogether; others voted for a
variety of right-wing splinter groups; still others, for lack of a suitable alternative, supported the right-wing of the CDU or FDP."[52] Under certain conditions, however, extremist right-wing protest parties are able to mobilize
this potential.

One of the most influential explanations of right-wing extremism is
Seymour Lipset's hypothesis of middle-class radicalism. According to Lipset,
"each major social stratum has both democratic and extremist political expressions"; fascism and right-wing extremism are basically middle-class
movements.[53] Middle-class voters, especially self-employed small-business
people, farmers, and craftspeople, tend to be radicalized if they feel threatened by general processes of concentration and centralization—developments characteristic of modern industrial societies—and by specific economic crises.[54]

As an explanation of the Nazi party's rise in Germany, Lipset's thesis was
rejected from different perspectives.[55] The social roots of right-wing extremism in the FRG do not provide straightforward evidence in support of
Lipset's thesis either. Unfortunately, we do not have any survey data on the
electoral clientele of the extremist right-wing parties of the early 1950s. Aggregate data seem to support Lipset's hypothesis in this period, albeit with
the danger of ecological fallacy. The extremist right-wing parties of the
1950s were particularly successful in rural-agrarian constituencies and small
towns where the old middle classes were overrepresented.[56] Similarly, most
NPD strongholds were dominated by a rural-agrarian and middle-class population.[57] Survey data on the NPD voters confirm that the NPD was overrepresented among the self-employed (farmers, small-business people, and
professionals), but it has to be emphasized that it also gained a high share of
votes from unskilled blue-collar workers, especially in small firms.[58] Although empirical evidence so far is compatible with Lipset's thesis, it largely
fails to account for the causes of voting for the REP. In 1989 it was found that
members of the old middle classes were less prone than working-class peo-

ple to support extremist right-wing parties such as the REP. The most striking over-representation among the REP voters was among skilled and
unskilled workers.[59]

Although Lipset's *specific* thesis is only of limited value in order to explain
the broad electoral appeal exerted by the REP in 1989, its underlying *general*
assumption is plausible, namely, that the processes of economic and societal
modernization cause economic deprivation of individuals or certain groups
that are likely to be attracted by extremist right-wing parties. Proponents of
this hypothesis argue that a majority of extremist right-wing voters were losers of the societal modernization process.[60] In this context "deprivation," or
frustration of expectations, can either be conceived as an objective process
of economic marginalization or as subjective feelings of insecurity or fear of
expected loss of social status.[61] Moreover, it seems plausible that phenomena of relative deprivation should become more virulent in times of economic crisis.

On the basis of the aggregate data available for the 1950s, it seems likely
that relative deprivation was an important explanatory variable in the immediate postwar years. The German Right party (DReP), DRP, SRP, and DG
mobilized the protest of the unemployed, expellees, and former Nazis.[62]
Werner Kaltefleiter estimated on the basis of aggregate data that in 1949
half of the German Right party's voters in Lower Saxony were refugees and
expellees. Moreover, the DReP was also successful among the native population where unemployment was relatively high. A pessimistic perception of
the personal and general economic situation seems to have contributed to
the DRP successes in the 1959 state elections of Rhineland-Palatinate.[63] Although we do not have any precise data on the DG's voters in southern Germany, the German Community appears to have addressed its propaganda to
similar groups as did the DReP and the SRP.[64] The decline of voting for extremist right-wing parties in the second half of the 1950s can also be explained on these grounds: After 1951, improving economic prospects had
begun to reduce the protest of the Extreme Right against economic deprivation. The main beneficiary was the CDU/CSU.[65]

For the second half of the 1960s, the economic situation and resulting
phenomena of relative deprivation can be interpreted as a necessary but not
sufficient condition of the NPD's electoral rise at that time.[66] Sympathy for
the NPD was not confined to those who were most affected by the recession
of 1966–1967. On the contrary, voters with higher incomes were more
prone to sympathize with the NPD than were voters with lower incomes. The
crucial variable was not an individual's objective economic situation but his
or her economic expectations for the future. The NPD was particularly successful among those who were pessimistic about future economic development.[67] The decline of the NPD after 1969 could be explained by the economic recovery since 1968. However, the disastrous results of the NPD at the

polls during the two major recessions of the 1970s demonstrate that the shape of the economy and resulting symptoms of individual deprivation are only a contributing condition of increased voting for extremist right-wing parties.

The surge of REP votes in 1989 cannot easily be explained on the grounds of relative deprivation either. Although the 1980s witnessed split economic development—sustained economic growth coupled with long-term unemployment—that broadened the gulf between the majority of well-off and a minority of those hit by economic distress, surveys failed to detect a clear statistical relationship between income and voting for the REP. As regards household income and house ownership, the REP's supporters of 1989–1990 were largely representative of the total population.[68] Nevertheless, voting for the Republikaner party was in part motivated by a *perceived threat* to the individuals' social and economic status, by a feeling of being handicapped politically and economically.[69] There seems to be a negative correlation between satisfaction with personal economic situation and future expectations on the one hand and voting for extremist right-wing parties on the other. Feelings of dissatisfaction and fears of future developments are widespread among REP voters.[70] Thus, at least on the subjective level, there is some evidence supporting the thesis of relative deprivation.

In their analysis of the NPD's success of the 1960s, Erwin Scheuch and Hans Klingemann attempt to explain the existence of an extremist right-wing potential as a phenomenon that is present in all industrial societies; they consider right-wing extremism "a 'normal' pathological condition":

> In any industrial society undergoing rapid change, tensions are produced in various sectors and at various levels of the social system. These tensions often take the form of a conflict between primary-group-oriented values and the functional requirements of secondary institutions. The individual experiences this conflict in the contradictory (situational) demands of day-to-day life. ... One way of adjusting to these environmental conditions is rigidity or closed-mindedness. Hence, if the individual's affective and cognitive structure is induced by the social structure in this way, any industrial society must have a considerable number of persons with such belief systems.[71]

Jürgen Falter and Siegfried Schumann, elaborate on this theory. They claim that especially

> many older voters and a considerable proportion of the youngest age group do not possess the necessary analytical or cognitive tools to cope with the ever changing demands of modern society: the older age-groups because they may have acquired certain authoritarian habits and interpretive cues during their early years of intellectual and social formation and also because of a natural tendency to become less flexible and tolerant with age; the younger, because

they may belong to a "no-future generation" with high levels of unemployment and a general uncertainty about the prospects for the future.

Both groups "often display a tendency toward simplistic interpretations of a complex and bewildering world. In order to cope with the demands of modern society, they tend to develop—unconsciously, of course—certain psychological defence mechanisms, such as cognitive rigidity, an affinity towards stability and clear-cut but inadequate interpretations of the world. Such defence mechanisms tend in turn, in certain circumstances, to favor right-wing extremism."[72]

Similarly, Klingemann and Franz Pappi stress the importance of the combination age and education as explanatory variables: The higher the formal education, the more explicit and intensive is the intermediation of those values that are characteristic of the respective political system.[73] With this system-specific socialization hypothesis, Klingemann and Pappi try to explain why support for the NPD was comparatively high among older people with relatively high standards of formal education who had the bulk of their schooling in the period of the Nazi dictatorship; higher education in the post-1945 democratic system obviously favored the inculcation of democratic values and thus reduced the probability of voting for extremist right-wing parties. The social composition of NPD voters seems to support the theoretical assumptions quoted above. Representative survey data of 1970–1971 show that the general receptivity for right-wing extremism declined with a rising level of formal education. However, among those respondents with higher education, the age cohorts of forty-six and older exhibited an NPD potential far higher than among those under forty-six.[74]

The composition of potential REP voters according to age and education seems to contradict the Klingemann-Pappi thesis only at first glance. A total of 51 percent of the 1989 REP supporters absolved some kind of elementary school and an apprenticeship. The respective share of the total population was 38 percent. Only 8 percent of the party's electorate were in the highest educational group, with a high school education or a university degree. These findings on the aggregate level vary if the age variable is controlled for. REP voters under fifty tend to belong to strata characterized by lower levels of formal education. Among the REP voters older than sixty, the differences in formal education largely disappear.[75] This is at least compatible with Klingemann and Pappi's as well as Falter and Schumann's results.

An alternative structural explanation could be derived from William Kornhauser's theory of mass society. According to Kornhauser, differences in the receptivity to mass symbols and leaders "are due primarily to the strength of social ties, and not to the influence of class, or any other social status, by itself."[76] Modern industrial society has contributed to "social alienation" and has atomized traditional social groups. In a pluralist demo-

cratic system social groups mediate between elites and nonelites and thus reduce potential social alienation. To the extent that these groups have lost
their capability to fulfill their intermediary function, its members become
socially isolated; in consequence, a mass society develops where receptivity
for totalitarian leaders increases.

In the theory of mass society, it has been assumed that close ties to social
milieus as provided by the Catholic church or the trade-union movement
tend to work as barriers against the propaganda of extremist right-wing
movements. For the Nazi party of the early 1930s, the thesis is at least plausible regarding ties to the Catholic church; ties to the trade-union movement,
in contrast, do not necessarily seem to have been an effective barrier.[77] For
the voters of extremist right-wing parties in the early 1950s, it could be
shown that the DReP, DRP, and SRP were most successful in Protestant regions with a rural-agrarian structure and in Protestant small towns, that is, in
areas where neither the Catholic church nor the trade unions were able to
build up dominant milieus.[78] The NPD was also more successful in regions
with a high share of Protestants.[79] The closer the ties to the Catholic church,
the lower was the probability that a voter supported the NPD.

Trade-union membership was found to be a similar barrier against extremist right-wing voting. This is not to say that close ties to one of these intermediate organizations provided an absolute protection against NPD
voting, but they obviously contributed to stabilizing the SPD's and
CDU/CSU's electoral clientele in times of economic and political stress.[80]
Among the REP voters, there is no overrepresentation of Protestants as traditionally observed for the voters of extremist right-wing parties. This is easily explained in that the REP is a phenomenon predominantly in south
Germany and Bavaria, where the share of Catholic voters is disproportionately high. If one considers the *degree of identification* with the Catholic
church, the expected pattern reemerges, that is, the closer the ties a person
has to the Catholic church, the lesser the probability he or she votes for the
REP. By contrast, membership in trade unions is no longer a barrier against
extremist right-wing parties. Trade-union members even tend to be more
likely to vote for the REP than nonmembers.[81]

The theories mentioned largely fail to explain or even to address the two
most striking characteristics of extremist right-wing parties' electorates in
the late 1960s and the late 1980s: gender and region. Almost two-thirds of
the potential NPD voters of 1965–1966 and of the potential REP voters of
1989 were male. Both parties are traditionally drawing the bulk of their support from southern Germany, namely, Bavaria and Baden-Württemberg.[82]
The assumption that men were more interested in current political affairs
than women and that women generally tended to react more cautiously to
new political developments did not hold in a cross-national test.[83] The relative strength of the NPD and REP in southern Germany can be explained

with some plausibility by the relatively high levels of organization both parties achieved in Bavaria and Baden-Württemberg. Moreover, the REP's charismatic leader, Schönhuber, is Bavarian, and the party is making extensive use of specifically Bavarian symbols at campaigns and rallies.[84]

All theories sketched so far explain—to varying degrees—the existence of a radical right-wing *potential* in the German population. They have greatly contributed to understanding the social roots of right-wing extremism. However, they do little to explain under which circumstances the potential of right-wing extremism remains latent and under which conditions it becomes manifest.

Studies of the causes of NPD and REP support have demonstrated that political factors—besides those worked out in sociostructural voting analyses—must be taken into consideration if we want to understand the surge of voting for extremist right-wing parties in the second half of the 1960s and 1989. Compared to the total electorate, a disproportionly high share of NPD and REP voters expressed considerable dissatisfaction with the working of the political system, with its ability to cope with economic challenges, and with the established political parties.[85] This draws our attention to political variables on the supply side of the political process. Given a more or less constant demand for extremist right-wing interpretation patterns (8 percent to 15 percent of the electorate), political factors should help to explain the variation in the *manifestation* of right-wing extremism in political behavior.[86]

ANALYTIC SUMMARY

In an analytic synopsis we have listed six variables (variations in party system space, that is, complexion of government coalition, economic crisis, issue space, government repression, factionalism on the extreme right, and charismatic leadership) and classified the descriptive material. At the same time we have developed the rudimentary, yet parsimonious causal model shown in Figure 2.4.

Conservatives in the government coalition are perceived to be the most important, necessary, causal variable for the electoral success of an extremist right-wing party. In contrast, economic crisis only possesses the status of a necessary but not sufficient variable. Issue space, in particular an issue monopoly in the long run, however, also approaches the status of a necessary condition. The model is discussed elsewhere in theoretical and empirical detail.[87] A preliminary and indirect empirical test at the level of all state elections in West Germany leads to encouraging results.

In the case of the *first wave* of West German right-wing extremism, there was an opening in the party system space with the conservatives (the CDU/CSU and minor parties such as the conservative German party) in a

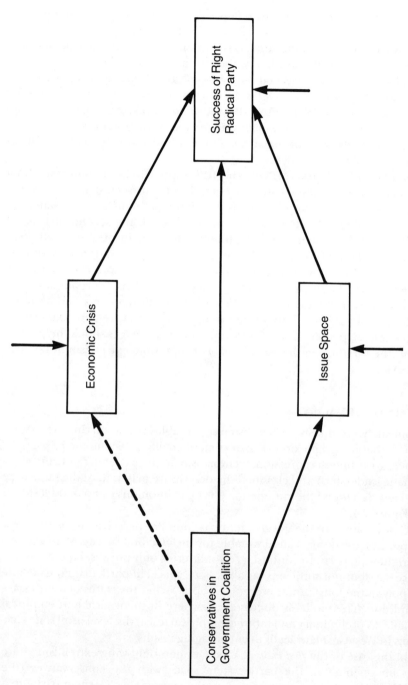

Figure 2.4   Three Key Variables Accounting for the Strength of Extremist Right-wing Parties

government coalition and economic problems such as postwar reconstruction and integration of German refugees persisting in portions of Lower Saxony, Upper Franconia, Hesse, and Western Palatinate. Yet four factors worked against the ability of any strong extremist right-wing party to persist: (1) From the beginning the Radical Right was fractionalized into numerous splinter parties (DReP, DRP, SRP, DG);[88] (2) from 1950 on, the BHE turned out to be a strong competitor on the radical right that opted for a pragmatic refugee interest policy; (3) government repression worked against the SRP in 1952, and the semiauthoritarian, charismatic leadership style of Adenauer kept under control some of the more authoritarian radical right-wing voters; (4) the economic boom proved so strong that till the end of the 1950s the Radical Right withered away, even with a conservative party in government.

In the *second wave* of extremist right-wing challenges, the NPD turned out to be the major new party. Its support was more evenly spread across the entire electorate. Radical right-wing voters no longer came from particular geographic areas, although milieu factors in regions such as Lower Saxony and Middle Franconia were still noticeable. The grand coalition in 1966 and the first major economic crisis in the history of the Federal Republic opened up the party system space on the right and gave the NPD a boost through economic protest voting. The party stylized itself as different from the "occupation-licensed parties in Bonn." Apart from the always looming national issue and the massive economic crisis, however, there was no specific issue for the NPD. The electoral 5 percent hurdle in the federal election of 1969 finally did in the NPD. Both conservatives (CDU/CSU) and the right-wing extremists lacked charismatic political leadership at that time. Thus, in spite of relatively low fractionalization on the radical right, at the moment of a massive economic crisis and a grand government coalition under conservative leadership, the NPD eventually failed, the main reasons being first political (in the form of the vigorous new opposition formed by the CDU/CSU in 1969) and then economic (when the trough of the recession passed in 1968).[89] Again the dominant factor appears to be a political one, namely, which party or party coalition is in government. Though fractionalization was lower on the radical right in its second phase, its eventual fate was similar.

Just as much as the second wave of right-wing extremism differed from the first (less fractionalization, much political leeway with the grand coalition in office), the *third* differs from the second. Our major variable, however, operates again, the only difference being that the government coalition is not composed of the two major parties, CDU/CSU and SPD. Yet as the many former SPD voters who voted for the REP or expressed sympathy for the party demonstrate, the SPD opposition is not perceived as an acceptable alternative. The SPD is not addressing the issues of immigration, law and order, and nationalism in the desired way. In contrast to 1966 through 1968, the general economic outlooks are good, in spite of the split economic development (e.g., agriculture versus high-tech industries). There is and most likely will remain, however, some structural unemployment affecting the less-educated and less-skilled as well as older persons. Thus subjective fears and negative expectations make for sympathies for the REP, not necessarily objective economic circumstances that are excellent for the vast majority. This makes it understandable why the questions of granting asylum, East European and Mediterranean foreigners in the country, and economic competition for housing and jobs could become the focus of attention. These issues serve as a scapegoat for imagined problems or expected problems, and only in this domain do REP voters and sympathizers agree and give their party higher marks of competence than with respect to running the economy or guaranteeing social security.[90]

This poor image of competence makes it understandable why there have been so many rivalries, why fractionalization on the radical right has remained so high, and why the pseudocharismatic "telegenic" appeal of Schönhuber has largely disappeared. The major difference over prior waves of right-wing extremism seems to be the focal point of foreigners in the country. (In contrast, anti-American sentiments were most salient in the late 1940s and early 1950s.) Yet the fractionalization of the Radical Right, the generally good shape of the economy, and the realization of German unification make it unlikely that an organization like the REP will be able to capitalize on this issue immediately or in the near future. In contrast to the Green party's environmental and peace issues, the issue of foreigners in the country would not alienate sympathizers or voters of the major parties if the Republikaner were to address it. What is more, this issue would not capture clearly defined social milieus needed to sustain a new protest party.[91]

Is there no right-wing extremism to be predicted, then, because conditional (and thus more guided) forecasts look fine for (western) German democracy? The persistence of milieus in Bavaria, Upper and Middle Franconia, Lower Saxony, and elsewhere calls for close attention, though the factor of milieu strength may be vanishing if compared to the continuity of results in the early 1950s and even 1960s.[92] Bertolt Brecht called it the womb that is still fecund: The 13 percent or so sharing extremist right-wing sentiments and ideology are those to worry about in the long run, especially *conservatives* that are more inclined to authoritarian rightist policies.[93] Perhaps this is the most dangerous group of all: former conservatives drifting toward right-wing radicalism, in particular if this implies institutional changes such as the breaking away of entire party wings. The crucial role played by the conservatives is corroborated by findings of comparative political research, namely, that "the conservative or Christian democratic parties, except for Italy, in all countries including those with extreme right parties, capture the relative majority of the extreme right's potential" (measured in terms of placement on the left-right scale).[94] Consequently, "the percentage of people placing themselves to the far right is significantly higher than the corresponding voting figures for parties of the extreme right."[95] If conservative parties or party wings were to turn to positions of right-wing extremism, it might conjure up memories of the final phase of Weimar. Yet again, because of the integrationist power of the CDU/CSU, there are hardly any such signs in Germany now or for the immediate future.

Given this marginal position of right-wing extremism, one might wonder whether the ghetto situation of that segment of 13 percent plus, hiding their attitudes and political sentiments under a democratically conditioned "spiral of silence" is the best democracy can do psychologically.[96] If their political attitudes (and prejudices) are not actively addressed and debated (as well as refuted) in a local environment, they may simply wait for the right moment and the right leader to disclose their "suppressed" sentiments. The outburst of xenophobia and increased activity of extremist right-wing parties in the former East German territory, where right-wing extremism had been suppressed more vigorously than in former West Germany, also point to this conclusion.[97] Merely legal responses to and public tabooing of rightist sentiments force those radicals to cultivate their ideas in secret and let a dangerous potential persist with their ideas uncontested in public debate.

CONCLUSION

Given German unification, the issue of nationalism is "deader" now than it ever was for the large majority of West Germans.[98] There will, of course, be fanatic rightists who claim the territory of 1937, but this is an even smaller minority than other German ultranationalists were before. The issues of xenophobic sentiments against East European and Mediterranean workers as well as asylum seekers and (perceived) competition for housing and jobs are, however, more likely to persist and to make for another focus of German right-wing extremism. Social upheaval caused by the processes of unification and economic adjustment in East Germany is also not to be ruled out. There is, too, the possibility of an enormous influx of refugees from Russia and Eastern Europe, if the reform processes there fail. Yet given the organizational chaos on the political right, the "excessive burden" issue of economic adjustment right now, and the good long-run economic forecast, it will take some time before another rise of a radical right-wing challenge will occur.

By then German democracy may have developed to such a degree that we need only worry about the warning signals. As important as issues are, the most important of all the variables in the causal model is the position of the major conservative coalition partners in the party system space. If they occupy potential issues that their competitors on the radical right might fasten upon and if they are in opposition, the chances of right-wing extremism are virtually nil. And even if the conservatives are in power, the complex set of factors worked out and the conditions on those variables right now make it unlikely for another Schönhuber to emerge as a phoenix from the ashes.[99]

3

THE CHANGING PROFILE OF THE ITALIAN SOCIAL MOVEMENT

Piero Ignazi

THE EXTREME RIGHT IN ITALY: DEFINITIONS AND BOUNDARIES

The Extreme Right in postwar Italy is made up of three elements: (1) the "official" Neo-Fascist party the Italian Social Movement (Movimento Sociale Italiano, MSI); (2) the Radical Right; and (3) the Nouvelle Droite.[1]

The MSI is a well-established political party founded in 1946 and represented in the Italian parliament since 1948. Its electoral strength has oscillated between a minimum of 4.5 percent (1968) and a maximum of 8.7 percent (1972) (see Table 3.1). In the past twenty years the MSI has been the fourth largest Italian party in electoral terms. Moreover, the party has a strong organization characterized by high membership (more than 100,000 members), a diffuse territorial presence (some 1,000 branches), and numerous flanking organizations (youth, women, veterans, ecologists, emigrants, and a massive trade union).[2]

By the Radical Right, I mean the movements that left the MSI in order to carry out revolutionary action against the democratic system. All these minor groups quit the MSI after denouncing its acceptance of (and subjection to) the system and calling for a tough opposition implying a resort to violence. Within this category we can count all the movements that emerged in the 1960s and early 1970s, from the older Ordine Nuovo (New Order) and Avanguardia Nazionale (National Vanguard) to such terrorist groups as Ordine Nero (Black Order), Squadre di Azione Mussolini (Mussolini Action Squads), Nuclei Armati Rivoluzionari (Nuclei of Armed Revolutionaries), and Movimento Politico Ordine Nuovo (Political Movement of the New Order). Finally, the latest generation of the Radical Right, Costruiamo l'Azione (Let's Do It) and Terza Posizione (Third Position), is quite extraneous to

TABLE 3.1   MSI Votes in the Parliamentary Elections, 1948–1987

	Percentage of Valid Votes
1948	2.0
1953	5.8
1958	4.8
1963	5.1
1968	4.5
1972	8.7
1976	6.1
1979	5.3
1983	6.8
1987	5.9

the MSI because of the latter's origin and its political strategy: The MSI is considered not just a "wet" member of the revolutionary right but a traitor and an enemy, more or less as are all the other parties.[3]

The third component of the Italian Extreme Right is the Nouvelle Droite, basically a cultural movement that has taken on the ambitious task of proposing new theoretical bases for the Right. Opposition to economicism and mercantilism, utilitarianism and individualism, liberalism and egalitarianism constitutes the cornerstone and the point of departure for this movement. The Nouvelle Droite emerged in France in the early 1970s with the philosopher Alain de Benoist at its head and found audiences in Italy, primarily among young MSI members. This dynamic and intellectually brilliant group seeks to recover some forgotten traditions of the rightist cultural patrimony—the German Conservative Revolution of the 1920s and French "Fascist romanticism" plus such unclassifiable philosophers as Ernst Jünger and Schmitt—and to introduce some contributions from the social sciences. At its beginning, the movement was made up of young MSI members (*missini*); however, after the MSI's expulsion of its very young leader, Marco Tarchi, it now attracts mainly former party members.[4]

These three components of the Italian extreme Right, though contiguous, differ on the basis of their organizational complexity, political strategy, and cultural references.[5] The organizational complexity is high for the MSI, which is structured along a mass-party model; limited in the radical right groups, who organize themselves as small underground sects; and negligible for the Nouvelle Droite, a loose network of cultural clubs.

The political strategy as concerns their relationship to the system and acceptance and practice of democratic rules appears to be contradictory for the MSI, which formally opposes the regime but in fact accepts its democratic rules; revolutionary for the Radical Right, violently pursuing the collapse of the system and opposed to its democratic principles; metapolitical for the Nouvelle Droite, which demonstrates both opposition and indifference to the political system and believes in overcoming democracy through a process of cultural renewal and hegemonization.

The cultural references take into account the respective importance assigned to Julius Evola, the leading extreme right intellectual, and to the Fascist tradition of Giovanni Gentile, Ugo Spirito, Alfredo Rocco, Carlo Costamagna, and others. On the basis of these two main poles, the MSI is Fascist (although the party has paid homage to Evola from time to time); Evolans dominate the Radical Right; and the Nouvelle Droite remains indifferent to both references.[6]

Because of its size and importance, the MSI, will serve as the focal point for this chapter; more specifically, I will discuss its historical evolution and recent dramatic changes in the outlook of the party's middle-level elites.[7]

HISTORICAL PROFILE OF THE MSI

The MSI story has been highlighted objectively only very recently and still only partially.[8] It seems useful, then, to offer a quick overview of the most important moments in the party's evolution. According to the crucial changes in terms of party strategy, distribution of internal power, and ideological debate, the MSI's history may be divided into six phases.[9]

1946–1950: Party Structure and Leftist Leaning

The Italian Social Movement was founded on December 26, 1946. Only one and a half years after the fall of fascism and the end of the civil war, a group of self-declared Fascist veterans set up a partisan organization and quite overtly entered the political arena.

However, this official declaration of birth was not a complete surprise: Immediately after the war, a plethora of newspapers and magazines flourished to express the voices of the "defeated" and the "survivors." The leading magazine of this era, *La Rivolta ideale* (The ideal revolt), had already tried to develop a network among its readers, collecting thousands of supporters. The MSI was established in the midst of this revival. Officially, the party was led by a group of young ex-Fascists with a very low profile: The general secretary was a young ex-journalist and Italian social republic official, Giorgio Almirante. But behind them, the Fascist old guard, which was still free and active, controlled and gently guided the party.

From the beginning, the MSI decided to fight in national and local elections. In particular, the party's electoral campaign for the Rome city council in October 1947 produced widespread publicity of its presence throughout the country. Moreover, the far from negligible result of that contest (24,575 votes: 4 percent of the valid votes) enabled the MSI to present itself as the focal point for all the tiny, extreme right-wing groups active in that period.

As for the relationship between the MSI and its extreme right competitors, the party had become the most authoritative structure of neofascism. On the other side, the variegated world of right extremism continued to operate via "exemplary behavior" and terrorist actions. But these initiatives began to conflict more and more with the MSI's increasingly legalistic attitude. A Neo-Fascist party could only survive in an "anti-Fascist" regime by exhibiting obedience to the democratic rules and distancing itself from the extralegal right-wing groups. Quite often, however, the same persons were active inside the party and in terrorist groups.

The MSI had a great deal of trouble organizing and campaigning in 1948 in the first parliamentary elections in the north of Italy. The still vivid memory of the civil war and terrorist actions of some right-wing extremist groups kept a militant anti-Fascist attitude alive. Although the party could operate without much difficulty south of Rome (where no resistance movement had arisen), it was compelled to lead a semiclandestine political life in the north, where the confrontation between the Fascists loyal to Mussolini's Repubblica di Salò (Salò Republic) and the anti-Fascists had been harsh and violent. The 1948 electoral results confirmed the relevance of the north-south cleavage for the MSI: The party elected six deputies, all from southern constituencies, and 69.6 percent of its votes were cast in the region south of Rome.

This skewed geographical distribution of votes had a direct impact on the relationship among the party's factions. The MSI was in fact internally divided according to the cleavages that shaped fascism's internal ideological debate. Fascist political culture was a vast sea in which different sources merged: from anarchosyndicalism to nationalism and revanche; from futurism to clericalism; from revolutionary tensions toward the future, the new order, the new man to petit bourgeois conservatism; from industrial modernism to ruralism; from worker's control over industries to industrialists' control; from authoritarian corporatism to laissez-faire.[10] The best way to reduce the complexity of this constellation of cultural and ideological references has been highlighted by one of the leading scholars in the field, Renzo De Felice, who distinguishes between the "movement of fascism"—a "left" fascism (revolutionary, antibourgeois, anticapitalist, nonconformist, utopian, etc.)—and the "regime of fascism" (conservative-authoritarian, clerical, corporatist, etc.).[11] These two main streams of the Fascist ideological tradition were at the core of the Neo-Fascist political-ideological debate from the beginning. Moreover, another dividing line was particularly salient in the early years: the cleavage between those who fought until the end with Mussolini in the north and those who had remained in the south after the Allies' landing and the fall of Rome. In reality, this "geographical" cleavage overlaps quite well with the ideological one, as the northern Fascists (the *salotini*) reflected the Fascist movement tendency, whereas the southerners represented the Fascist regime.

The first party leadership was inclined exclusively toward the movement position and fiercely opposed to opening the party to the "traitors" from the south. However, as has been emphasized, the vote distribution in the 1948 elections showed that the MSI had its electoral reservoir in the south. As a consequence, even if the young radical leadership kept control of the party at the First National Congress (held in Naples in 1948), the move toward a more traditional approach was under way.

1950–1956: Organizational and Electoral Development

In January 1950, General Secretary Almirante was obliged to resign. He was replaced by Alfredo De Marsanich, a former member of government of the Fascist regime and leader of the moderate faction. Whereas the leftist faction guided by Almirante expressed radical opposition to the democratic system, the moderate faction was more inclined to exploit whatever circumstances might emerge in order to intervene in the political scene. Instead of stressing the antisystem profile of the party, the new leaders attempted to fit it into the system. Therefore, party politics shifted from total opposition to support for the ruling Christian Democrats (DC). De Marsanich's regime emphasized the MSI's role as a *national* force against communism and for the defense of the Christian, Western world.

Such politics had three outcomes: the electoral alliance with the monarchist party; the declaration of acceptance of the North Atlantic Treaty Organization (NATO), which the MSI had opposed in parliament a few years earlier; and an alliance (aborted at the last moment) with the DC for the 1952 Rome municipal election. This pro-NATO, moderate, and proclerical stance was amply rewarded by the MSI's electorate, which voted massively (11.8 percent) for the Neo-Fascist monarchist alliance in the municipal elections throughout the south in 1952.

The sudden growth of the party provoked a twofold reaction from the DC: On the one hand, its minister of interior, Antonio Scelba, wanted to outlaw the MSI as a Fascist party; on the other hand, it offered cooperation and alliances at the local level, as in the case of a common anti-Communist list for the Rome municipal election. This ambivalent behavior vis-à-vis the MSI became a standard rule for the DC, which alternated carrot and stick.

The MSI's moderate politics did not go without protest inside the party. Despite the MSI's electoral successes, the radical faction remained very active and militant and tried at each national congress to overthrow the majority. The last and fiercest assault on the party leadership was undertaken in

Milan in 1956 at the Fifth National Congress, where the Almirante left faction lost by a handful of votes (307 to 314).

1956–1969: The Rise and Fall
of the *Inserimento* Strategy

After the 1956 showdown, the domination by the moderate faction became overwhelming. General Secretary Arturo Michelini's era began. This setting provoked the most dramatic split up to this point: the Ordine Nuovo group, led by Pino Rauti, left the party, advocating a radical, noncompromising opposition to the democratic system and a new order inspired by the aristocratic-esoteric principles of Evola. Michelini's leadership covered a long period that can be divided into two phases: an ascending one up to 1960 and a descending one from 1960 until his death in 1969.

In the first period the party achieved unprecedented political success, arriving at the threshold of government. At first, together with monarchists and liberals, it supported the Adore Zoli (1957) and Antonio Segni (1959) governments; then it was alone in backing the Giuseppe Tambroni (1960) government. The political impact of the last agreement was enormous: For the first time in the postwar democratic regime, a government received the vote of confidence thanks *exclusively* to Neo-Fascist support. The MSI was on the verge of final "acceptance" as a legitimate governing partner for the Christian Democrats.

Michelini's strategy of accommodation seemed totally successful. The Sixth National Congress planned for July 1960 in Genoa was intended to celebrate the accomplishment of his *inserimento* (literally, insertion) politics. However, a militant anti-Fascist reaction by leftist parties broke out in Genoa, then spread for a fortnight to other Italian cities. The protests culminated in clashes with the police and the death of some demonstrators, and the government prevented the congress from taking place. As a result, the MSI was again sent to the corner. The MSI was defeated in both the street confrontations and in Rome. The setback was particularly painful as hopes for a final entry into the system had become widespread among the party's faithful.

Michelini's strategic defeat had two main effects: On the one hand it gave new strength to his traditional internal opponents; on the other, it set the conditions for the development of autonomous extreme right organizations. This latter aspect is quite relevant and deserves particular attention. Until the beginning of the 1960s, the MSI had a monopoly on the representation of the Far Right. All the numerous attempts to create competing organizations did not last, with the notable exception of Ordine Nuovo (which, by the way, never challenged the party in the electoral arena). After Genoa the MSI gradually lost its capacity to control the extreme right environment. The recurring attempts at *inserimento* even after the establishment of the center-left coalition government (i.e., the entry of the Socialists into the government) demonstrated an amazing blindness toward the new circumstances.

As a consequence, new proposals and new organizations started to flourish on the extreme right. The starting point of all the initiatives concerned the MSI's unreliability: The party was no longer "revolutionary"; it sought to cooperate with the system and was prone to all the DC's whims and blackmail. Faced with "the subtle and undermining communist strategy of world domination," the Extreme Right looked for new actors beyond the MSI. More militant groups arose, and, for the first time, an organic alliance with the military was envisaged. Because of the 1943–1945 civil war, the MSI-military relationship had been almost nonexistent. No high official in the postwar army fought in the Fascist camp; on the contrary, many were active in the resistance. The extreme right movements, then, could become active in virgin territory and establish profitable alliances.

At the end of the 1960s, the MSI was almost at its end: It had lost its monopoly among the extreme right, its blackmail or coalitional potential, and its organizational and electoral strength.

1969–1976: The Destra Nazionale and Almirante's Triumph

As had the riots in Genoa in 1960, Michelini's death in 1969 represented a watershed. The moderate majority perceived it to be a critical moment for the party and decided to select as secretary Michelini's historical antagonist, the "radical" Giorgio Almirante, who made his presence felt in three ways: organizational, strategic, and ideological.

On the organizational level, the party was remobilized with a series of mass meetings and then reformed in its internal structures. The internal changes involved the establishment of a new youth organization, Fronte della Gioventù (Youth Front) instead of the three preexisting youth organizations: RGSL, Giovane Italia (Young Italy), and Volontari Nazionali (National Volunteers)—a renovation of the central apparatus, stronger control over (but at the same time a higher support for) local party cadres, and a strong centralization of the decisionmaking process.

The party strategy was at first glance the most novel feature of Almirante's leadership, but in reality it was just a lifting of the traditional *inserimento*. Almirante proposed to exit from the Neo-Fascist ghetto and to create a new party that could collect other political groups and independent opinion leaders. This meant that the party would end its Neo-Fascist nostalgia and become a modern, updated National Right (Destra Nazionale, or DN).[12] This transformation was successful, as the monarchist party merged with the MSI and some DC and Partito Liberale Italiano (Italian Liberal party, or PLI) politicians and many of the army's high-ranking officers entered the party. The updated version of *inserimento* also included an appeal for a tough confrontation in the streets with the "Reds." In this way Almirante tried to mobilize the party and, above all, to dominate the Extreme Right. In fact, the radical group Ordine Nuovo, led by Pino Rauti, controlled the MSI.[13] All these changes were intended to present the party as the true defender of the silent majority and, at the same time, as a respectable, "clean," and updated party that offered itself for a government coalition.

The third major change, closely related to the preceding one, regarded ideological renewal. Almirante officially declared his acceptance of the democratic system. He attempted to create a new image of a democratic right-wing conservative party. Following this line, the MSI promoted new journals, research centers, and cultural foundations. It also supported conferences and colloquia with an unprecedented variety of intellectuals.

In sum, Almirante's project pointed to the MSI's recapturing dominance over the Extreme Right and to the deemphasis of its Fascist heritage in order to acquire more legitimacy in the electoral and political arena. Up to 1973–1974, this strategy largely succeeded. The MSI reached its highest electoral score (8.7 percent in 1972) and its strongest organizational development. However, the inherent weaknesses of the Destra Nazionale strategy—a superficial and not very sincere ideological revision, and an inability to control the often violent radical right groups and even some fringes of the party's own youth organization—and the tactics used by the DC in order to stop the MSI's rise—denunciations of the connections between the radical right groups and some MSI party leaders and accusations of party responsibility in various violent actions, including assassinations—endangered the party's strategy. The superficiality of its ideological renewal plus the party's responsibility for the increasing spiral of violence produced a backlash. The brutal fall of the MSI's hopes was manifested in the 1976 parliamentary elections, in which it lost 2.6 percent of its vote, falling back to 6.1 percent.

This defeat opened the way to a reconsideration of Almirante's leadership and politics. The party split into two factions: one supportive of the leader and another, led by the MSI's speaker in the Chamber of Deputies, Ernesto De Marzio, which wanted to transform it into a right-wing conservative party and to develop a better relationship with the DC. On the eve of the Ninth National Congress, the moderate faction left the MSI and founded the ephemeral party National Democracy (Democrazia Nazionale, or DN), which disappeared three years later after its failure in the 1979 parliamentary elections (0.6 percent).[14]

1977–1983: Radicalization, Marginalization, and Ideological Renewal

The dramatic Ninth National Congress (January 1977) represented the collapse of the Destra Nazionale strategy. The exit of the prosystem faction led the party to engage in some ideological soul-searching. The faction led by Rauti, which had supported the Almirante leadership in its clash with the "moderates," constituted the laboratory in which this rethinking took place. Its starting point concerned the collapse of the liberal and Marxist ideologies: No current ideology had been capable of responding to popular needs, especially to those of youth. The capitalist influence on Western societies had dispossessed people of a real, authentic, communitarian life: Massification, consumerism, and alienation were the troubles to which Rauti's new stream wished to respond. This cultural wave, largely derived from the French Nouvelle Droite, had an impressive impact on younger generations. Evola was no longer the most admired guru because of his nonpolitical perspectives (the *mito incapacitante*). Other leading figures such as Jünger, Schmitt, Mircea Eliade, and Konrad Lorenz, entered the cultural constellations of the young *missini*.

In the late 1970s an unprecedented number of students and youth joined the MSI and stimulated a new style in part led by the Hobbit camps, youth summer camps where politics and fun were combined. This constituted the best expression of the new cultural mood; the gloomy and militaristic atmosphere of previous initiatives left the scene in favor of an open and ironic (and self-ironic) discussion on every topic without any taboos. Above all, these young activists expressed a clear desire to stop the bloody confrontation against the "Reds" and to get out from the Neo-Fascist ghetto: they expressed a need to take part in Italian society.

In the second half of the 1970s the MSI was highly isolated, even more than after 1960, mainly because of its (more or less conscious) complicity with terrorist groups. The party had failed to offer a clean and respectable image to the urban and northern bourgeoisie, the "silent majority" that voted for it in 1971–1972. Therefore, Almirante's leadership moved to initiate changes. New terms such as *rule of law (garantismo)*, *peaceful confrontation*, *civil rights*, and *minority rights* entered the MSI vocabulary for the first time; new electoral support was seen—young and southern protesters rather than the northern middle class; and a new political strategy was deployed—the appeal for an anti-Communist front was substituted by a call, addressed even to the left side of the political spectrum, for a common antisystem opposition. The MSI did not abandon anything of its traditional ideological patrimony but, inspired by the breakdown of ideologies, youth dissent against the regime, and the "historic compromise" (the Communists' willingness to form a ruling coalition with the Socialists and Christian Democrats), claimed to be a "protest party." Its main concern was no longer the Communist danger but the regime: All parties, Christian Democracy included, were responsible for Italy's agony. The strategic electoral reference was no longer the silent majority but the (young and southern) protesters. The shift in party strategy and analysis was momentous.

1983–1990: Legitimation and Crisis

The protest phase culminated in a positive outcome in the 1983 parliamentary elections, the party obtaining its second best result (6.8 percent: up 1.5 percent). At the beginning of the 1980s, the many changes inside the party and in the political system found the MSI unprepared. Two changes were crucial: a different outlook vis-à-vis fascism and a quick decline in the ideological temperature. In the early 1980s, the Fascist era ceased to be just dismissed as an all-negative period; on the basis of a new vogue of studies, fascism was neutrally interpreted as a period in Italian history. The attempt was to understand and analyze the interwar years. Historical studies, art exhibitions, and cultural debates produced a shift in the public attitude toward fascism. Neither indulgence nor nostalgia developed from this change; it merely produced the end of a black-and-white perception of the 1920s and 1930s.

The bloody season of violent confrontation and terrorism had come to an end; all radical groups perceived that they had gone too far and it was time to stop. The spiral of violence had involved so many young militants from both sides that everyone sought a way out. The new left militants and the young *missini* called a truce in their street confrontations and declared that all had the right to their own thoughts.[15] Tolerance and nonviolence suddenly broke out with unexpected consequences.

Thanks to this development, characterized by the historicization of fascism and the deradicalization of political debate, the MSI became less stigmatized than in the past. For the first time it could end its isolation. It is paradoxical that this favorable condition, from which the party had profited in the 1983 elections, produced serious problems for the MSI. In fact, the MSI had not been the *agent* of its integration and its legitimation; such processes had been initiated autonomously by external force. The MSI, moreover, had not elaborated any coherent strategy for this new political phase. Almirante kept the antisystem traits of the party intact but at the same time offered the MSI for an alliance against the DC-PCI duopoly, that is, for an alliance with the Socialists and the laic parties. However, the party had to decide whether to abandon part of its cultural and ideological identity and accept the democratic system or to maintain its advocacy of an alternative regime in favor of a corporatist system.

In the mid-1980s the MSI was deeply involved in this debate but incapable of reaching a conclusion: It continued to oscillate between radicalism and acceptance of the regime. Even Almirante's resignation after the 1987 electoral defeat and the new leadership of young Gianfranco Fini did not help to resolve the issue. On the contrary, the MSI was even more sharply divided, some factions pushing for change in favor of a more flexible attitude and ideological revision and others advocating continuity with Almirante's politics. In his first run, the new secretary, Fini (1987–1990), followed the line of continuity, but he was defeated at the Sixteenth National Congress (1990) by Rauti, who was more inclined to revise the ideological principles and to insert the party into the political and cultural scene.[16]

Rauti's election represented a turning point in MSI history. Rauti concentrated in himself many experiences of the Extreme Right: from voluntary participation in the civil war to terrorist activity in the early 1950s, from opposition inside the party to secession (1956) at the head of the Evolan group Ordine Nuovo, from intense and obscure relationships with the military and revolutionary proposals to reentering the party at the moment Almirante resumed the leadership (1969), from a low profile and acquiescence to Almirante until 1976 to an alternative candidacy to party leadership and, above all, to leadership of the ideological renewal.

Rauti certainly passed through all the extreme right components, but in particular he played a crucial role in the MSI's internal debate since the mid-1970s. His faction, to which most of the young members adhered, offered—through congressional documents (1977, 1979, and 1982), journals, and magazines (*Elementi* [Elements], *La Contea* [The earldom], etc.)—the key elements of a new identity.[17] It was to be found in (1) an abandonment of the reference to the Right: Fascism is (and was) not a rightist conservative movement but a leftist revolutionary one; therefore, the MSI should look to the left of the political spectrum in trying to attract that electorate; (2) a rejection of the so-called values of Western liberal civilization and of the Americanization of society—agnosticism, materialism, hedonism, egotism, and consumerism in favor of an authentic, spiritual life; (3) rejection of capitalism and of the "money power"; (4) anti-Western and anti-American attitudes and pro–Third World and pro-Palestinian ones; and (5) exaltation of "differences" against the "false egalitarianism" and the homogeneity of mass society.

In sum, according to Rauti, the MSI should appeal to the Left for a common struggle against capitalist and U.S. domination and for the affirmation of a national identity: Rauti was to replace the MSI's traditional authoritarian, conservative, petit bourgeois political culture with a leftist, anticapitalist, and anti-Western one. Such change in the ideological references is best understood if one thinks of the movement tradition of "fascism." Most of Rauti's positions come from that tendency—and in fact fascism is always exalted with mythical reverence—but at the same time many other themes derived from the Nouvelle Droite are included.

TABLE 3.2   Party Strategy

Action	% (N=173)
Develop relations with parties sympathetic to MSI proposals	26.6
Return to its origins	21.3
Relaunch strategy of National Right	14.5
Stay in opposition and refuse any opportunity to participate in ruling coalition	37.6
	100.0

THE CHANGING PROFILE
OF MSI POLITICAL CULTURE

The crucial question to be answered here is whether or not this recent cultural-ideological wave is consistent with the beliefs of the MSI's cadres, members, and voters. Unfortunately, no data are available for members and voters, but we can test the hypothesis of the diffusion of a changing or traditional political culture on a reliable sample of party cadres, or middle-level elites.[18] Data have been collected among the delegates participating in the Sixteenth National Congress held in Rimini in January 1990. As it has been argued elsewhere, participants at the party's national congress could be considered representative of the party's local leaders.[19]

To analyze the present cadres' ideological profile, two main topics were taken into consideration: the presence and degree of antisystem attitudes and the value system. The investigation of the antisystem attitudes utilized six items. The first three refer to the relationship with the political system in a specific way, that is, the likelihood of adopting a bargaining and coalitional attitude vis-à-vis other parties; more specifically, the three items concerned questions of future party strategy, hypothetical alliance with other parties, and sympathy for other parties.

As for the first item, Table 3.2 shows the existence of a cleavage among MSI middle-level elites: On the one hand there are the "politicians" (41.1 percent), those who are inclined to develop political relationships with other parties (items one and three); on the other are the "hard liners" (58.9 percent), who regret the MSI's lost purity and disdain any contamination by the system (items two and four). The majority supporting the latter attitude shows that the party is far from isolating itself in a radical opposition: On the contrary, it seems to be looking for a way of approaching other political partners.

The second indicator refers to the likelihood of accepting a hypothetical alliance with other parties in the future. In this context I disregarded the responses given to the various alternatives indicated in the questionnaire

TABLE 3.3   Sympathy for Other Parties (0 = maximum distance; 10 = maximum closeness)

Party	Mean Score	Score Zero
DP	0.7	77.0
PCI	1.0	64.6
PSDI	1.0	63.4
PRI	1.0	62.4
PLI	1.4	51.7
DC	1.5	55.6
PR	2.0	47.2
PSI	3.4	20.2
Greens	3.7	22.6

(from an MSI = DC coalition to an MSI = PSI coalition, as well as the intermediate formulas) and focus on the missing values because I want to know whether or not respondents accepted the idea of an alliance with another party. Almost one-third rejected all the possible coalition partners offered.[20]

The third indicator is provided by the sympathy scale (from zero, or minimum closeness, to ten, or maximum closeness) for the other parties. Again, it doesn't matter which party is the closest or the furthest, rather the degree of general antiparty feeling. Two measures were adopted: the mean value and the percentage of the lowest attributable score (zero). The sympathy mean (Table 3.3) is much below the hypothetical one (score five): It reaches score three in two cases and drops under two in all the other cases. Analogously, the same two parties, Greens and Socialists, collected a moderate percentage of the minimum score (zero); all the others focus on the lowest score around half of the responses. These data show a pervading feeling of distrust and alienation.

The second set of questions is related to a more general antisystem attitude. Two of these consist of direct questions: One asks whether "given the overall situation, to support boycotts is right"; the other states that "with violence one does not gain anything." The first statement, vague enough to collect a general mood instead of a precise proposal, causes a split of the MSI sample into three balanced groups: radical antisystem (35.4 percent), uncertain (32.3 percent), and conservative prosystem (32.3 percent). On the second statement the MSI delegates are more prudent: Half oppose violence as a useful tool for achieving one's goals, but a quarter are willing to adopt violent means.

This picture is clarified by a battery of questions derived from the study on protest and unconventional forms or participation by S. H. Barnes and M. Kaase.[21] Table 3.4 shows the items in the order in which they were listed on the questionnaire; respondents were asked to express their judgment on a standard Likert scale. Excluding the first two items, which received general support, we find two subgroups. The first is composed of the delegates who endorse such activities as factory occupation, sit-ins, and street blockage (al-

TABLE 3.4   Agreement/Disagreement on Unconventional Forms of Participation for the MSI

Form of Participation	Agree	Don't Know	Disagree	N
Petitions	92.5	6.1	1.3	363
Demonstrations	92.5	6.4	1.1	361
Reducing rent payments	49.7	19.8	30.5	359
Wildcat strikes	22.7	15.0	62.3	359
Sit-ins	44.9	13.9	41.2	356
Graffiti	25.7	12.6	61.8	357
Squatting	46.0	15.5	38.5	357
Confrontations	19.8	15.5	64.7	355

TABLE 3.5   Clericalism Scale

	Year	Agree	Don't Know	Disagree
Religion at school should be	1987	54.4	17.3	20.3
compulsory	1990	45.1	20.6	34.1
Religious education is	1987	38.1	24.4	37.5
indispensable	1990	33.9	24.0	42.1

most half of the sample). The second group, which includes around 20 percent of the delegates, supports such "innocent" acts as writing graffiti as well as such tough actions as wildcat strikes and clashes with police.

In sum, the MSI cadres at the beginning of the 1990s seem to be divided into two distinct groups: In the first there is a high degree of antisystem potential suggested by positive evaluations of protest (and even violent) acts, widespread distrust of the other parties, and a drive toward isolation. However, a consistent portion of MSI delegates moves in the other direction: They are willing to cooperate with other parties, oppose boycotts and violence, and want to work out a modus vivendi inside the system.

Both groups represent traditional alignments inside the MSI. The first embodies the militant antisystem tendency, the second the more bargaining-oriented one. In this case, the impact of the new elements of the MSI's political culture is not ascertainable. Yet Rauti and Almirante alike always overtly denied legitimacy to the system *and*—at the same time—tried to operate inside the system: in the political-parliamentary arena for Almirante, in society and the collective movements for Rauti.

A better test of the Nouvelle Droite's impact and that of Rauti's ideology can be made by taking into account a series of attitude questions that highlights the MSI cadres' values system. Moreover, it is possible to show a change over time in the delegates' beliefs, as the same questions were asked in a previous survey at the Fifteenth National Congress (1987). All the questions refer basically to five different scales: clericalism, militarism, anti-Westernism, racism, and authoritarianism.

The first scale, clericalism (Table 3.5) shows that although the MSI cadres declare themselves to be overwhelmingly Catholic (79.3 percent), they are

TABLE 3.6   Militarism Scale

	Year	Agree	Don't Know	Disagree
Increase military	1987	44.7	31.3	24.0
budget	1990	26.3	30.7	42.9
Keep mandatory military service	1987	25.1	31.5	43.4
as a learning experience	1990	23.7	30.7	42.9
Maintain Euromissiles	1987	57.3	10.7	32.0
	1990	49.9	22.1	28.1

TABLE 3.7   Anti-Western Scale

	Year	Agree	Don't Know	Disagree
United States is	1987	82.5	4.5	13.0
imperialistic	1990	86.5	6.6	6.9
Palestinian cause	1987	54.6	8.4	27.0
is just	1990	69.8	17.6	12.6
Europeans are	1987	74.9	10.9	14.2
disregarded in NATO	1990	67.3	17.6	15.1

not inclined to assign great importance to the role of religion in society: They are quite skeptical about the place of religion in the schools and even more so doubt the relevance of religion for a full education. Moreover, the tendency toward a lax attitude grew between 1987 and 1990.

The militarism scale (Table 3.6) touches a nerve of the extreme right tradition. These data destroy the standard militaristic image. The myth of military service as a fundamental step in a male's maturation is limited (as already in 1987) to a handful of nostalgics (23.7 percent). Moreover, the collapse of Communist regimes also affected MSI attitudes toward a strong defense. The demand for higher military expenditures collapsed in 1990 to just 26.3 percent, compared to 44.7 percent in 1987. Agreement on the need to increase the military budget and suspicions of Mikhail Gorbachev's peaceful intentions have decreased. In international politics, one notes (Table 3.7) that the attitudes toward the United States, NATO, and Israel reflect the anti-American and pro-Arab tradition of the extreme right. It is plain that the United States is considered "imperialist" (82.5 percent in 1987 and 86.5 percent in 1990), the Palestinians are strongly supported in their struggle for independence (from 54.6 percent to 69.8 percent), and the Europeans are perceived as constantly disregarded inside NATO (74.9 percent in 1987 and 67.3 percent in 1990). MSI cadres massively support Rauti's European-nationalist and anti-Western line.

Racism has recently returned as a major factor in determining the success of extreme right parties throughout Europe.[22] The MSI and above all the Rauti faction have quite a different approach to this crucial topic. Immi-

TABLE 3.8   Racism Scale

	Year	Agree	Don't Know	Disagree
Immigrant fertility is too high	1987	68.6	13.7	17.7
(threatens national identity)	1990	80.5	7.6	9.9
Illegal immigrants should be	1987	72.1	19.6	8.3
deported	1990	62.1	19.5	18.4
More aid should go to	1987	27.1	31.7	41.2
Third World	1990	54.9	23.4	21.7

grants are not stigmatized per se because they are the last link in the chain of exploitation. Rather, immigration is the result of capitalist domination over the Third World. In order to stop immigration, the North-South relationship should be modified. This line of reasoning is quite peculiar and reminiscent of certain Fascist justifications for the Italian colonial presence in Africa.[23] However, it remains abstract and far from the delegates' feelings: Two out of three respondents disagree (Table 3.8). Only on the item concerning more aid to less-developed countries was there majority support, which increased from 27.1 percent in 1987 to 54.9 percent in 1990. On the other two items, fear of the subordination of the white race is strikingly widespread and even increasing, and the support for the expulsion of illegal immigrants is very high, though declining.[24] In this case, Rauti's views on the North-South relationship find a hostile reception: Le Pen's xenophobia seems more appealing to the MSI cadres.

The last attitude measure uses items from the authoritarian personality scale. The items revolve primarily around civil rights. As one can see from Table 3.9, only four items received more than 50 percent of support from the delegates: the centrality of discipline in contemporary society, opposition to free circulation of pornography, the demand for total obedience from one's own children, and the development of nuclear energy. At any rate, though still majoritarian, all these items received less support than in 1987.

Responses to two other items are more balanced. The first concerns the outlawing of strikes in the public services and the second the acceptability of abortion. It is quite surprising that the level of antiabortion sentiment has increased so much that it now exceeds the proabortionist view. This is the only case of a marked increase of an authoritarian attitude that has inverted the balance between agreement and disagreement compared to 1987 data.

For the other six items, the number of "libertarians" is higher than authoritarians. The statement regarding the introduction of the death penalty divides the cadres into two camps of almost the same size. But the opponents of the death penalty win by a neck. In gender relationships, the MSI cadres (who are overwhelmingly male) show a libertarian approach: They support

TABLE 3.9 Authoritarianism Scale

	Year	Agree	Don't Know	Disagree
Discipline is the pillar	1987	82.1	9.2	8.7
of social order	1990	75.0	13.9	11.1
Forbid pornography	1987	63.4	15.5	21.2
	1990	71.3	16.5	12.2
Parents do not	1987	61.7	24.0	14.3
discipline children	1990	57.3	22.9	19.8
Nuclear energy is	1987	64.4	13.9	21.7
desirable	1990	52.5	16.2	31.3
Forbids public	1987	44.7	24.0	31.3
strikes	1990	45.7	18.6	35.7
Abortion is legal in	1987	39.1	23.0	37.2
special circumstances	1990	28.9	22.9	48.2
Introduce the death	1987	44.1	16.8	39.1
penalty	1990	39.9	19.1	41.1
Homosexuals should not be	1987	43.1	23.6	33.3
employed in bars,	1990	34.2	24.0	41.0
cafés, etc.				
There should be no	1987	26.0	14.1	54.9
control on police questioning	1990	28.8	16.2	55.8
Male is the authority	1987	26.0	16.2	57.8
in the family	1990	24.0	33.9	42.9
Men and women deserve	1987	70.8	15.2	14.0
equal rights	1990	71.3	14.6	14.1
Drug addicts should	1987	78.3	13.1	8.6
be helped	1990	87.4	7.1	5.5

full equal rights between men and women (71.3 percent) and disagree on male dominance inside the family (signaling a slight shift respecting the past). Their attitude toward homosexuality has changed spectacularly. In 1990 only one-third would prevent homosexuals from running bars, coffee shops, restaurants, and so on. Analogously, the MSI cadres agree massively on more initiatives to help drug addicts (87.4 percent). Finally, as the death penalty proposal is opposed, support for a police "without rule" in questioning criminal suspects is strongly rejected.

In sum, on a total of twelve items on the libertarian-authoritarian dimension, six show the prevalence of an authoritarian attitude but with a declining emphasis (except for the abortion issue), one is evenly balanced (the death penalty), and the other five receive more support for the libertarian side.

CONCLUSIONS

The MSI has gone through a process of change. The decline of political radicalism in Italian society during the 1980s affected the MSI and obliged it to leave its ghetto. Although all the MSI's leaders sought such an exit, in reality the party had to face a totally novel situation in which it could no longer just recall the Fascist mythology but was required to act inside the system. As has been emphasized, in this crucial transition Almirante tried to continue as usual in a radically changed political setting. Moreover, Almirante did not encourage the cultural changes that had been shaking the party from within. As a result, the MSI's external image of the late 1980s did not change much: The MSI was still perceived as a Neo-Fascist, violent, old-fashioned, extreme rightist party, just less dangerous because its strength was declining and social tensions and political conflicts cooled down.

However, the cultural initiatives carried on by the Nouvelle Droite young intellectuals, and the theorizing of Rauti's faction penetrated into the party rank and file. The survey data I have presented show that a dramatic change in the attitudes and beliefs of party cadres is occurring. Some of the old strongholds of extreme right thinking have been abandoned in favor of "libertarian" positions not so different from those of other parties. Some responses are quite astonishing for an extreme right-wing party: for example, on opposition to the death penalty, support for equal gender relationships, willingness to increase aid to the Third World, the relative empathy for such marginal groups as homosexuals and drug addicts (but not for immigrants), and a cautious attitude toward the police. These preferences do not fit the standard profile of an extreme right party.[25]

The shift in the MSI political culture is quite impressive. The exit from the ghetto and the receptivity to modern issues—and even postmaterialist ones—are pushing the MSI cadres far from the traditional Fascist (of whatever tendency, either regime or movement) ideology. This relative abandonment of its original identity and its current fascination with novel themes, alien to extreme right thinking, may prove fatal to the Italian Social Movement.

PART TWO

EASTERN EUROPE AND ISRAEL

4

ETHNOCHAUVINISM, AGRARIAN POPULISM, AND NEOFASCISM IN ROMANIA AND THE BALKANS

Trond Gilberg

Neo-fascism is often used to discuss a condition that allegedly exists in parts of contemporary Eastern Europe. The usage of this term is often loose— indeed rather indiscriminate: It refers both to attitudes and behavior and characterizes a number of phenomena without any real attempt to distinguish among them. It is certainly a pejorative term that signals phenomena we do not like. It is, therefore, essentially a label and a slogan. An attempt to examine the existence and effects of neofascism requires a more accurate definition that can then be used to test hypotheses and assumptions. When we employ the prefix *neo-*, we assume that something that existed before has appeared again. We therefore cannot define *neofascism* without detailed reference to *fascism.*

Fascism, according to James Gregor and others, is a political and socioeconomic phenomenon, with other important characteristics attached to these two main facets. The economic doctrine of fascism emphasizes a corporate organization of economic life that involves significant elements of public works, protectionism, and state control over economic activity. Fascism establishes the notion that participation and representation in politics are based upon economic units, not territorial entities or individuals, as is the traditional way of establishing representation in democratic political systems. Fascism also relies heavily on nationalism as a mainstay of the doctrine itself and as a vehicle for mass mobilization. It focuses on notions of organic government and the direct connection between rulers and ruled, without the segmentation usually found in pluralist societies. Fascism stresses total solutions and eschews compromise and bargaining. It tends to preach strong leadership, emphasizing "men on horseback," even though the corporate notion of leadership is also strong.

Fascism tends to be intolerant of others, those who are not part of the collective entity or enterprise or choose to set themselves outside of it. In the doctrines of fascism there is little room for the dropout, the derelict, the dissenter, and those who think differently. Fascism also tends to be anti-Semitic—which is not to say that fascism is inherently afflicted with this deficiency; rather, the doctrine and practice of fascism became prevalent in societies in which there was already a rather high level of anti-Semitism. Under these conditions, the intolerance of others that *does* characterize fascism became focused on the Jews. The most notorious example of this aberration is German national socialism, but similar (if less technically advanced) examples of anti-Semitism abounded in many other areas as well, notably in Eastern Europe.[1]

Because of its emphasis on the notion of the "organic" unity of the nation with its leaders, fascism often became an example of the most advanced (or egregious) form of nationalism. This included almost xenophobic hatred of certain other nations and their political structures. Coupled with this emphasis was the notion that the soil had a special place in the hearts and minds of the people. All of these factors produced a tendency toward agrarian populism, chauvinism, and an aggressive stance against those who did not fit the Fascist schemes of politics, economics, and social life. The same aggressiveness could be found in the foreign policy stance of Fascist leaders.[2]

The various aspects of fascism, as discussed above, constituted a package with considerable appeal for the masses and certain societal elites in much of central and Eastern Europe. The package touched upon a number of enduring facets of political and socioeconomic life in the region and thus had the ability to arouse enthusiasm and promote political behavior. Because the Fascist outlook was part and parcel of deep-seated values and attitudes, it was natural that it did not disappear with the demise of fascism as a system of rule but rather went into hibernation until circumstances would again favor its resurrection. According to some observers, this is why neofascism is surfacing in post-Communist Eastern Europe. Essentially, this revival shows that ideas will overcome even the most decisive material defeat, as was the case with fascism as a system of rule in World War II.

HISTORICAL FASCISM, POPULISM, AND NATIONALISM IN THE BALKANS

During the decades that preceded World War I, the newly independent states in the Balkans exhibited a number of characteristics that later combined to produce a special blend that we can call (with Peter Sugar) "native fascism." There were several ingredients in this mix, chief of which were ul-tranationalism, anti-intellectualism, populism, agrarianism, and a deep reli-giosity that underlined the organic links between God and country, ruler and ruled.[3] This was seen in the newly established states of Romania and Bulgaria, and similar tendencies were found in Serbia as well. In contrast, those parts of the Austro-Hungarian Empire that later became the republics of Slovenia and Croatia in Yugoslavia were part of the central European cul-tural sphere and exhibited different characteristics. Albania, predominantly Muslim, was quite different.

In the Balkans, the establishment of independent states toward the end of the nineteenth century thrust upon the world scene some political con-structs we may call structural democracies, which contained little within them that represented the values, attitudes, and behavioral proclivities of democracy as usually perceived in the West. Specifically, the new states had adopted constitutions, institutions, and procedures that looked similar to those of their French, British, or American precursors, but there was no un-derpinning for such institutions in the hearts and minds of the masses or even most of the elites. The history of the Balkan states between indepen-dence and communism is, in many ways, the struggle between values and in-stitutions that did not fit each other. In that contest, it was inevitable that the artificial constraints of democratic institutions would lose to the deep-seated feeling of masses and many elites alike. Thus political life in those states was characterized by attempts to maintain institutions and promote democratic attitudes, on the one hand, and efforts to assert existing values through sub-version and the destruction of those institutions, on the other hand. In this context, fascism, Balkan style, played a prominent part.[4]

As Romania, Bulgaria, and Serbia emerged during the demise of the Otto-man Empire, nationalism and religiosity became the key elements in the construction of the new order. Nationalism had galvanized the societies of the Balkans against Turkish rule, but the fervor of this political phenome-non came about largely because religion was a major part of this national-ism; in other words, the struggle was not merely against the Turkish nation but also against the Turkish infidels. The influence of secular and religious nationalism and the emergence of religious leaders as secular authorities pushed aside any tendencies of intellectual or class-based nationalism. This development had clear ramifications for societal and political history for de-cades to come. In particular, it enthroned the notions of "organic society" (religious leaders are seldom content to relate to *part* of the flock) and disre-garded the concept of group autonomy and the possibility of secular plural-ism. Thus, the developmental path of Balkan nationalism took it in the direction of "organic government"—a concept that was to become a main-stay of fascism as well.

Nationalism, defined as part of a secular *and* religious package of thought, by definition had little tolerance for those who were not members of the religious and national community. This meant that, internally, the politically dominant majority (Romanians in Romania, Bulgarians in Bulgaria, Serbs in Serbia) discriminated against the ethnic minorities, who were different ethnically *and* in religious affiliation. Throughout the entire region, some ethnic (and religious) groups were mistreated in various ways; this pertained primarily to Jews and Gypsies. The confusing settlement patterns and the existence of various irredentist problems resulted in a great deal of instability and tension inside each state and in interstate relations. Again, there were clear similarities between this ethnochauvinism and ultranationalism and fascism; indeed, it can be argued that fascism was merely one of the offshoots of the more pervasive phenomenon discussed above. This also explains why this offshoot became more important in some states than in others.[5]

The nationalism of the Balkans was essentially agrarian nationalism because the overwhelming majority of the population was made up of peasants. This meant that there were important elements of antiurbanism in the mainstream of political thought and action in most of Balkan political history until the arrival of communism, with *its* emphasis on industrialization and urbanization. The almost mystical elevation of the significance of the soil and the relationship between human and nature further alienated peasants from urban dwellers, many of whom were also ethnic minorities. Such conditions clearly added to the level of intolerance against others and their ideas. Again, fascism as an ideology drew upon many of the same ideas, thereby emerging as a mainstream phenomenon and not an aberration.[6]

The quest for an organic society was clearly mitigated by the obvious existence of corruption and a wide chasm between ruler and ruled. The notions of direct rule by a strongman, bypassing the officials and their sycophantic praetorian guard, therefore had an overwhelming appeal for the average man and woman. Elemental concepts of fairness and justice, of retribution and the settling of scores, so often crucially important in the village community, were frequently contained in the ideas of direct leadership, so forcefully expressed by ultranationalists and Fascists. The emphasis on frugality and commitment to a seemingly noble cause of national regeneration also had a considerable impact upon many in the peasant masses.[7]

There is, however, a clear contradiction in the various messages emanating from the ultranationalists and the Fascists, on the one hand, and traditional Balkan culture, on the other. The nationalists preached unity between leaders and followers, whereas the Balkan peasantry was used to foreign rulers from whom they isolated themselves as much as possible. Popular perceptions looked upon the very notion of central power as alien and dangerous, yet the new nationalists preached the need for unity in thought and action. Religious leaders, past defenders of the local community against alien central authorities, now became the chief supporters of the very concept of such power. How could the masses accept the influence of nationalism and religion, of central authority and organic government, under such circumstances?

There appear to be plausible explanations for the existence of such a seeming anomaly, but perhaps the most persuasive idea is that the population, steeped in localism, cynicism, and suspicion, yearned for organic causes and strong leaders. Ironically, in the postliberation era they thought they had found such causes and leaders among their own. Under such circumstances, nothing and no one was to be allowed to stand in the way.[8]

The naive assumptions of early Balkan nationalism gave way to cynicism as it became clear that the new, good, organic society would not materialize and that, instead, corruption, neglect, and self-serving policies remained the hallmark of the national leaders, as it had under the foreigners. Thus the early nationalists, some of whom at best contemplated the establishment of a pluralistic democracy and a civil society, lost much of their credibility, and they soon became targets of the Fascists, who described the early leaders as corrupt, effete, and isolated from the population. The sneers of the Fascists were loudest when they talked about the "bourgeois intellectuals," the snobs of Bucharest and Sofia society who had never got their hands dirty with hard work, and those who preached "foreign" ideas of individual human rights and group autonomy. These messages had considerable impact on the masses of the peasantry, the rural proletariat, and the lumpen proletariat of the cities, who hated intellectuals, shopkeepers, and landlords alike. Even the more established elements of the village resented the betrayal of the "organic ideal" by the increasing squabbling of corrupt legislators and cabinet ministers.[9]

It is only through the combination of a desire for something to believe in and the sense of betrayal by those who had been entrusted with the leadership of the nation that the passions and ferocity of native fascism in the Balkans can be understood. Many of those who supported the Fascists were decent individuals, pillars of society who had a sense of justice, indeed of community and perhaps even compassion for their fellows (provided they were of the right ethnic background and practiced the right religion). As the years of disillusionment wore on, the negative messages of ethnic hatred, disdain for democratic practices, and refusal to accept city dwellers, intellectuals, and Jews, so prominent in fascism, were mixed with the yearning for simple solutions to complex problems and the quest for a cause and a community—also prominent features of fascism. In the end, this contribution was important in all of the Balkan countries. In one of them it became a dominant feature. That country was Romania.

ROMANIAN FASCISM AND ITS LEGACY

Romania became the most clear-cut example of Fascist influence among the masses as well as the elites after World War I, especially in the late 1920s and throughout the 1930s. This influence was pervasive directly and indirectly, in the sense that the basic tenets of fascism were widely held, thereby influencing mass behavior and the members of the leading political parties and the royal household. The Fascists themselves established an organization, the Iron Guard, that gathered considerable support and ultimately became part of the ruling establishment. An earlier mass organization, the League of the Archangel Michael, was heavily infested with Fascist sympathizers. The individual who eventually reined in the Iron Guard, Marshall Antonescu, also had strong Fascist sympathies. The same can be said for the king, who took power by a royal coup d'état and ruled Romania throughout much of the 1930s. Thus fascism was an integral and important part of Romanian political life for more than a quarter century.[10]

The Fascist political and socioeconomic program in Romania was similar in content to the basic aspects discussed earlier. It highlighted organic government, direct rule, individualized leadership, and a corporate form of economic organization. Religious fundamentalism was an important element, and there was a great deal of ethnic hatred and disdain for other religions, coupled with rabid anti-Semitism. Intellectuals and spokespeople for the notions of pluralistic democracy were held in contempt. The Fascists advocated (and practiced) terror, assassination, and physical intimidation of their opponents.

The progenitor of Romanian fascism was Corneliu Zelinski Codreanu, who became the leader of the Fascist movement. Codreanu, a failed law student at the University of Iasi, spent a considerable amount of time in Germany in the 1920s and came into contact with individuals and groups who advocated the ideas of national socialism. He was allegedly received by Hitler, and he certainly adopted the methods of the various Fascist groups that terrorized German political life during the fateful decade of the 1920s.

In 1927 Codreanu became the leader of the newly formed Legion of the Archangel Michael. The program of the legion was "to rejuvenate the public spirit, the national economy, and all aspects of public life, creating a new Romania by producing vast reforms of a Fascist character."[11]

The practical manifestations of this program soon became clear; they constituted mass demonstrations and campaigns (both verbal and physical) against intellectuals, those members of the aristocracy who were thought to have "incorrect" political views, students, and "careerists." The legion sent its members to various areas of Romania to preach its socioeconomic doctrine and its program of hatred for all citizens mentioned above as well as ethnic minorities and Jews. Throughout the 1930s, the program of the legion and the Iron Guard became a major feature in Romanian politics. According to the Romanian scholars Mihai Fatu and Ion Spalatelu, four basic aspects of the program are discernible:

1. Irrationalism: The Iron Guard's basic program was based upon mysticism and emotions, with a corresponding rejection of rationality and respect for the thoughts of others.
2. Mystical religiosity: The irrationality of the guard's program was deepened by the emphasis on religion, mythology, and mystical symbols, parades, and rituals. The "organic" nature of the program was readily apparent.
3. Emphasis on action rather than analysis: The action-oriented philosophy of the guard derided rational discussion of problems and emphasized "life" over "effete rationality."
4. Emphasis on struggle to the death: It is clear that part of the cult of the guard and the legion emphasized struggle to the death and, in fact, contributed a cult of death. This represented a political philosophy of zero sum, in which the winner takes all in the political struggle and the loser loses all. In such a philosophy, there was no room for compromise or half measures. This focus on struggle also led to the glorification of war and the physical destruction of all opponents.[12]

The socioeconomic tenets of fascism were fully incorporated into the ideas of the legion and the guard. The foreign policy orientation of this movement was, naturally, toward Nazi Germany and resulted in Romania's participation on Hitler's side in World War II. All of this is well documented elsewhere and needs no elaboration here.[13] In this chapter the emphasis is on the philosophical underpinnings of Romanian fascism, because these elements were to become crucial in the political thought of Nicolae Ceausescu and his successors. But more about this later.

The Legion of the Archangel Michael and the Iron Guard became important forces in the political life of interwar Romania because they represented attitudes and values that were part of the mainstream of Romanian political culture. These organizations had the support of many of the most important political parties of the right, the landowning class, the forces of big business, and the hierarchy of the church. The dividing lines in Romanian political life in those troubled decades did not go between the Fascists and others; rather, it isolated the political Left and the more liberal elements of society, fascism and agrarian populism joining hands with traditional conservatives and reactionaries in the political mainstream. It is important to remember these facts as we turn to Romanian communism and, more importantly, Ceausescuism.

ROMANIAN COMMUNISM AND CEAUSESCUISM: HISTORY CONTINUES

On August 23, 1944, a palace coup brought down the Fascist regime of Antonescu. Various coalition governments followed suit until the Romanian

Communist party (Partidul Comunist Roman, or PCR) took full power in 1947, forcing the abdication and exile of the king and the royal family. The new leadership, first under Ana Pauker and then Gheorghe Gheorghiu-Dej, was ostensibly dedicated to the dismantling of the old Fascist order and the establishment of a new, Socialist system. The early programs of the PCR certainly did this with some consistency, as it confiscated the property of industrialists and landlords, destroyed the political organizations of the old order, and severely restricted the operations of the churches. The new regime also removed official anti-Semitism; in fact, many of the new Communist leaders were Jewish and quite a few more from ethnic minorities, thereby severely weakening the "nativist" tendencies of the Fascists and their supporters during previous decades. The working class, subjugated and controlled during the interwar period, now experienced a form of political ascendancy through its leaders in the PCR. Ostensibly, then, the Fascists were decisively beaten by this process of political transformation.[14]

Despite these seeming victories over fascism as a system of rule, it became clear that the emotional and theoretical underpinnings of the Fascist order had not been exorcised from Romanian political culture but remained a crucial element in it. The survival of the values and attitudes of fascism depended upon a classical problem in revolutionary and transformationist political systems: Would the new political leaders, allegedly dedicated to the creation of a "new, Socialist man and woman" succeed in their quest for value transformation, or would the new structures and their leaders succumb to the prevailing values of the existing political culture? The ascent of Ceausescu and the Ceausescu clan to power resolved this question in a most decisive manner.

Ceausescu, who succeeded Gheorghiu-Dej in 1965, was an unlikely candidate for the role of Balkan potentate and the local duce (*conducator* in Romanian), yet that is precisely the position he eventually established for himself. As the Ceausescu era unfolded, certain characteristics became predominant: a personality cult, a centralization of power, clan rule, mysticism, Romanian chauvinism, and deification of Ceausescu.

An Extreme Personality Cult

Increasingly, the gray apparatchik Nicolae Ceausescu became the object of a personality cult that surpassed the worst Stalinist excesses in the Soviet Union. In the beginning, the cult was promoted by fawning subordinates who assumed that such servility would gain favor for them in the halls of central power. But as time wore on, the leader himself clearly began to believe in the notions perpetuated by his sycophantic praetorian guard and his court poets; these included the idea that he was the greatest political leader; the most accomplished scientist; the most inspired model for poets, writers, and filmmakers; and essentially the leading light of humankind. The hoarse chorus of worshipers used the occasion of his birthday in January to pronounce him the "demiurge of the universe" and the individual who would take Romania to the promised land, blazing a trail for other nations to follow.[15]

Extreme Centralization of Power

Ceausescu eventually gathered in his hand all executive power in the Romanian system. He was also involved in the most minute matters of decisionmaking to a point where no authority was delegated, and all levels of the system below the top lived in constant fear of direct interference by the *conducator.* This central power became more and more capricious, frequently altering course in economic planning and in goal setting, thereby creating insecurity in all ranks. This rule was also arbitrary in that Ceausescu increasingly tended to blame others for the disastrous results of the policies that were adopted and, just as abruptly, changed. In the final analysis, Ceausescu ruled in the spirit of personalized dictatorship; "Romania under my leadership" was strongly reminiscent of Codreanu's "the league under my guidance."[16]

Rule by Clan and Sycophants

The Ceausescu regime functioned very differently from most of the other communist systems of Eastern Europe. Elsewhere, there was an attempt at functional representation, rational rule, and some delegation of power and authority. In Ceausescu's Romania, entrance to the leading circles was by personal invitation only; it depended upon the likes and dislikes of the ruler and his wife, Elena. Maintenance of a place in the inner circle also depended upon the ruling couple's whims. The result was that the members of the central elite had no particular skills other than those associated with currying favor and no loyalty to any principle other than the acquisition and maintenance of their personal position. They could only do so by kowtowing and shielding the ruling couple from the unpleasant realities in the country, thereby creating a totally distorted view of the world surrounding the isolated leadership.[17]

Symbolism, Mysticism, and the "Organic" Nature of Ceausescu's Rule

After 1970, the nature of Ceausescu's leadership began to show heightened emphasis on symbolism and mysticism. Furthermore, Ceausescu came to see himself as the rightful inheritor of the tradition of prominent Romanian leaders such as Stephen the Great and Michael the Brave. The symbols of the offices he occupied started to change; he was no longer the leader of a

Westernizing, revolutionary movement but rather the embodiment of the Romanian nation as a historical construct. Increasingly, the exercise of power was surrounded by pomp and circumstance, rituals with mystical overtones, and the near worship of the *conducator* by his close associates and, in a very contrived sense, the masses as well, as they went through their well-rehearsed "spontaneous" shows of support for the "demiurge of human-kind."

The symbolism and ritual masked the outcome of economic and social policies that had had such drastic effects upon the well-being of the population that only the ties of fear and repression remained. Rather than organic government, Romania experienced dislocated rule; government in conjunction with the people became rapacious rule over the people. That, finally, helped produce revolution.[18]

Anti-Intellectualism, Anti-Semitism, and Ethnic Chauvinism

Ceausescu was a product of a peasant society located in the Balkans, with all the ramifications thereof for attitudes, values, and behavior. One of the hallmarks of the Ceausescu era was strong anti-intellectualism and stress on "culture for the people." The PCR leader had little use for the analysis and vacillations of intellectuals, who were not in touch with the "real" people. He despised the alleged (or real) snobbery of urban intellectuals, thereby focusing on an important fact of cultural life in Romania for many decades. As a Romanian chauvinist, he also resented Jews, despite his repeated professions to the contrary. During the last decade of his rule, his many court poets and spokespeople increasingly sounded like anti-Semites of the interwar period. By the same token, Ceausescu also became an ethnochauvinist who castigated Hungarians, Germans, and other minorities for their "divisive" attitudes and behavior. In this contest, he appealed both to the notions of organic government and the strong nationalism of the Romanian masses. As the years wore on, this ethnic emphasis became virulent, establishing scapegoats for the obvious failures of the PCR's policies. This vicious cycle of ethnic hatred and policies that were designed to prove the correctness of statements of prejudice drove Romania to the brink of the revolutionary abyss and, indeed, beyond.[19]

The Deification of Personalized Leadership

The concentration of power in the hands of one individual and the sycophantic nature of the personality cult soon acquired religious overtones, as Ceausescu was billed as an individual whose capabilities, responsibilities, and wisdom exceeded those of mere mortals. There is little doubt that Ceausescu himself began to believe in these notions, thus further distancing himself from the emerging societal elites of engineers, economists, and planners whose educational background was rooted in modernity and the concepts of industrial society. At the same time, the deification of personalized rule was part and parcel of the yearnings of the peasant masses. This conflict between the cultural norms of modern elites on the one hand and the values and attitudes of the peasantry (and the first generation of industrial workers we can call "peasant workers") on the other represented a serious breaking point in Romanian society. It could only be bridged by the common loathing of both of these population strata for the excesses of the Ceausescu regime as it matured and then deteriorated.[20]

The hero worship of Ceausescu and his wife became hollow as the conditions of life worsened and the repressive nature of the system spread a blanket of fear over Romanian society. The masses of the population became cynical, withdrawn, and resentful of the Ceausescus. But a similar process also beset the dictator couple, as they increasingly blamed the population for the problems of political and socioeconomic life and the disastrous performance of the system in all respects. Toward the end, Nicolae and Elena Ceausescu held the people in great contempt; this was clearly demonstrated at the military trial of the couple on Christmas Day 1989, before their execution. Said the fallen dictator, "The people have failed me."[21]

THE POST-CEAUSESCU LEADERSHIP: WHITHER ROMANIA?

The dramatic revolution of December 1989 toppled the Ceausescu regime. The dictator and his wife ended up before a firing squad (even though there is some evidence that at least Nicolae Ceausescu had been executed before the bullets of the squad hit his body). Some of his close associates were jailed, and some even brought to trial. Nicu Ceausescu, the son of the ruling couple, had his own trial, amidst much publicity. All of these events point to a drastic break with the political past of Romania, especially the golden era of Ceausescu. Yet, there are a number of disturbing signs that the past continues to haunt postrevolutionary Romania. In short, a number of events and tendencies point out the similarities between the current regime and the one that preceded it and, even more strongly, the system that went before the advent of the Communists to power. The most important of these are the following (not necessarily in descending order).

Continuity in Leadership

A number of the current leaders of Romania were politically prominent under the Ceausescus (even though they did not occupy top positions in the ruling clan, and a number of them had experienced serious disagreements with the clan leadership). The most clear-cut examples of this continuity are

Ion Iliescu, head of the National Salvation Front and the current president of the republic, and Petre Roman, son of the prominent "old Bolshevik" Valter Roman. There are many other examples as well, including foremost leaders of the military establishment. Furthermore, much of the leadership and membership of the feared and despised Securitate continues intact. Regional and local leaders remain largely unchanged.[22]

Part of the reason for this continuity is that Ceausescuites completely permeated the entire administrative and political structure, so that their removal would lead to complete collapse in the provision of public goods and services. But in part the continuity also reflects the tendency of the new leaders to protect their colleagues from the old order because they are all part of the same elite structure. This is clearly demonstrated by the leniency and forgiveness so often expressed when the Salvation Front leadership discusses the reckoning with the past. Under these circumstances, it can be assumed that the continuity will also lead to the perseverance of old attitudes and values, as well as actual political behavior.

Expressed Elite Views

It is not necessary to *assume* the continuity of views, goals, and values by examining the continual presence of representatives of the old order; it suffices to document expressed views and policies of the new leadership. Such examples do abound. Ion Iliescu has repeatedly expressed his distrust of ethnic minorities, especially during the period of actual confrontation between Romanians and Hungarians in Tirgu Mures and elsewhere in March 1990. At that time, Iliescu charged the Hungarians with seditious activity, designs on the unity of the Romanian state, and attempts to separate Transylvania from the rest of the country. These charges were startlingly reminiscent of the ethnochauvinistic speeches of Ceausescu. The outpouring of articles, statements, and books on this subject revealed the extent to which much of the Romanian intelligentsia was still inbred with such chauvinistic views.[23]

Part of the campaign launched against the ethnic Hungarians also contained strong elements of anti-Semitism. There was a tendency to underscore "nativist" messages, stressing the importance of the *Romanian* nation and its unity, with direct or indirect threats against those who might be seen as endangering that unity. Furthermore, it was clear that important elements of the policymaking elite had resurrected the notions of *Romania Mare*, of Greater Romania, which would include most of Bessarabia. Perhaps more importantly, the notions of Greater Romania constitute an integrated concept of territorial, historical, political, and cultural unity that ipso facto excludes the ethnic minorities and explicitly threatens Romania's neighbors. There are strong similarities between these views and those expressed by prominent leaders of Romania in the 1930s; among those leaders were the *conducators* of the Iron Guard and the Legion of the Archangel Michael.[24]

Disdain and Hatred of Those Who Think and Act Differently

Ion Iliescu and his close associates have also displayed their angry disdain for those who think and act differently in relation to some established "norm." This has been demonstrated repeatedly, as various groups regularly demonstrate for the implementation of their programs in Bucharest or elsewhere. A classical example of this can be found in the many statements that the president has made about student demonstrations and their quest for democracy and greater political pluralism and tolerance. Iliescu charges the students with "disruption, threatening the goals of the revolution," "endangering public order," and "defiling the sacred values of the nation." During the election campaign in the spring of 1990, many charges were leveled against the opposition parties for their alleged effort to dismantle the unity of the nation. Iliescu is a strong promoter of organic government, and despises the notions of "unity in diversity," which are the hallmarks of real, pluralistic democracies.

Violence as a Means of Solving Political Disputes

The Salvation Front and the Iliescu presidency have not shied away from using physical violence against political opponents. During the election campaign, intimidation of opposition candidates and their organizations was a frequent occurrence. The most egregious example of such tactics was the brutal suppression of student demonstrations in the summer of 1990, when "outraged miners" acted "spontaneously" to "save the revolution" from the "hooligans" in the streets. This claim was preposterous on its face because the miners had arrived in Bucharest by bus and train after several hours' ride; they had been plied with alcohol en route and were well armed with tools and clubs. They were not suppressing hooligans but abusing students demonstrating for greater democracy. The revolution, which was supposedly about democracy, had already been "hijacked" by elements of the old order and those populist and well-nigh Neo-Fascist forces that had gained a strong foothold in the national leadership.

These and other events once again demonstrated the intolerance of others so prominent in the current political system in Romania. As such, it bore a strong resemblance to the archconservative and Fascist attitudes of the political elites of the 1930s as well as the Ceausescu era.[25]

The use of physical force was also rather symptomatic of the continued acceptance of violence as a means to settle political disputes. The notion of civility and respect for others and their rights of expression is alien to much of this class, indeed much of the general population. Thus it will take a great deal of time to develop a "civil society" in Romania, and the likelihood thereof is rather slim under present conditions.[26]

Mysticism and the Cult of the Personality

Although the new leadership in Romania has asserted that it eschews the personality cult that grew up around Ceausescu, there are many signs that Iliescu is not adverse to elements of the cult himself, albeit in muted form. Some of the commentary about his policies published in the various papers of the National Salvation Front is clearly dedicated to the presentation of Iliescu as the greatest leader that Romania could possibly have, a statesman who enjoys the respect of the rest of the world, and a father figure for all Romanians. None of this is really true, if the actual political discourse of present-day Romania is to be believed. But it is also clear that the cult of personality is an integral part of Romanian political culture, as witnessed by the almost mystical veneration of the leader, especially in rural areas, during the election campaign in the spring of 1990. Romania indeed has a long way to go before it can claim rational leadership in reality.[27]

Mass Attitudes Resembling Neofascism

The attitudes, values, and behavior patterns of significant elements of the ruling elite are matched by important population strata, especially the peasantry, the peasant workers of the industrial cities, and even much of the second- and third-generation proletariat. There is a great deal of ethnic hatred in contemporary Romania, fostered in part by the policies of the Ceausescu era but, more importantly, reflecting decades-old animosities and prejudices that have been more forcefully expressed as a relatively free press developed in the aftermath of the Communist order. This is especially true among the Romanians; there is a widespread perception in this ethnic group of cultural particularism and superiority, which translates into hatred of others, especially the Hungarians, but also to some extent the remaining Jews in the country. The most extreme form of this particularism is the organization Vatra Romanesca (Romanian Flame), which emphasizes the notions of Greater Romania, including the acquisition of "lost" territories. It was Vatra Romanesca that perpetrated the violent clashes with ethnic Hungarians and the other minority groups in Tirgu Mures in March 1990. But it should be pointed out that the attitudes of Vatra Romanesca are also shared by many others, albeit in a more restrained manner. For example, there is a flourishing literature in books, pamphlets, and articles that can only be characterized as ethnochauvinism. There are pieces produced for the theater and the cinema that carry much the same, ultra-nationalist message.[28]

There is little doubt that important segments of the population also have an authoritarian outlook. This has been evidenced on several occasions, most dramatically in the bloody repression of student demonstrators in Bucharest in spring 1991; there have been numerous other manifestations as well. It would be a mistake to assume that the miners' brutal repression was merely an orchestrated attack on an opposition group; in fact, this action represented the practical manifestation of a deep-seated mistrust, indeed hatred, of intellectuals so often found in the Romanian proletariat and among the peasant workers.

A disturbing characteristic of much of public opinion in post-Ceausescu Romania is a volatile mixture of fear, distrust, and jealousy that resembles the attitudes and values of fascism in the 1930s. Fear still exists as a result of the Ceausescu era, when the Securitate and its myriad informers kept the population in an iron grip. Distrust is an equally understandable attitude, because in the past no one could be believed, friends, colleagues, even family members turning into informers and betrayers. This widespread social pathology represents an asset to those who advocate simplistic solutions to complex problems. In other words, it is a major advantage to the ethnochauvinists and Neo-Fascists of the new order.

Jealousy is also a characteristic of the post-Ceausescu era, again for understandable reasons. For a considerable time, economic resources were so scarce that one person's gain was clearly another's loss. Thus there developed a widespread dog-eat-dog attitude with little margin for the acceptance of inequality based upon performance. A perverse egalitarianism resulted, in which any differentiation was ipso facto perceived as unjustly acquired. This attitude remains a dangerous legacy for post-Ceausescu Romania.[29] The culture of jealousy lends itself to the establishment and persecution of scapegoats, such as a member of a minority or the ubiquitous "bad guys," the Jews and the Gypsies. At the same time, there is a marked tendency to believe that there *can* be a togetherness of the "nation" under strong leadership. This contradiction bears many of the hallmarks of the corporatist, populist, and Neo-Fascist order of the 1990s.[30]

It should be pointed out that the attitudes and values discussed above, though prevalent in many segments of the population, are not the only ones to be reckoned with in contemporary Romania. There *are* elements who favor the establishment of a pluralistic system with due regard for the rights of others and the autonomy of groups. Many of the student leaders who were prominent in the revolution itself and in the political struggle that followed see as their ideals the democracies of Western Europe, especially the Scandinavian countries. The future of Romania will depend upon the struggle between these elements and those that favor authoritarianism and the various practical manifestations thereof, as discussed above.

Although forces for pluralistic democracy exist in Romania, they carry with them their own liabilities. The demands for democracy heard so consistently in the plazas and streets of Romanian cities are uttered in the context of an authoritarian political culture. The Romanian democrats are impatient; they call for instant pluralism and immediate civil society with the establishment of Western-style procedures and institutions overnight, thus representing a special threat to the orderly development of a more decent political system. Their demands must be tempered with the patience necessary for a successful conversion to democracy in this troubled region.

CONCLUSION

As shown throughout this chapter, the history of Romania is replete with elements of extreme nationalism, ethnochauvinism, agrarian populism, and native fascism. Some of the same traits were also present in the Ceausescu era, particularly in its pathological phase (essentially the decade of the 1980s). In the post-Ceausescu era, the active elements of these political tendencies are less prominent because a more open political system makes scrutiny of such behavior, attitudes, and values more likely. No one wants to admit that he or she is a Neo-Fascist or ethnic chauvinist. But the more open political communication patterns also offer opportunities for elements representing such views to express them publicly and to organize themselves with relative impunity. If these views match some of the attitudes and values of the ruling political elite, that correspondence can produce much greater chance for such elements to exercise political power and influence. This is what is now happening in Romania. Under present political circumstances, it is likely that the socioeconomic crisis, together with the traditions of Romanian political culture and the attitudes and values of the current leadership, will enhance the influence of such groups and individuals, putting the forces opting for real, pluralistic democracy at a disadvantage. The possibility of such a scenario bodes ill for this troubled Balkan state.

Elsewhere in post-Communist Eastern Europe, there are dangers of similar developments because all of the states of the region have *some* elements of ultranationalism, populism, and native fascism. This is particularly so in Hungary, and the Polish and Bulgarian political cultures also exhibit characteristics of authoritarianism. But nowhere are these tendencies as strong as in Romania, and nowhere do they represent as much of a threat to future developments. Analysts and policymakers dealing with this part of post-Communist Eastern Europe should keep this caveat in mind.

5

PAMIAT: RUSSIAN RIGHT-WING RADICALISM

Vladislav Krasnov

Since May 6, 1987, when the Russian nationalist group Pamiat sponsored the first mass demonstration in Moscow since the 1920s, it has been roundly condemned in the USSR and abroad for its self-declared anti-Zionism and alleged anti-Semitism. It has also been denounced for being allegedly chauvinist, racist, xenophobic, Stalinist, Fascist, and pro-Nazi. Strangely enough, although Western reaction to Pamiat has been long on condemnation, it remains short on documentation, analysis, and understanding of that curious and potentially dangerous movement.[1]

A major reason for this lack of an objective scholarly approach has to do with two ready-made, interchangeable, and virtually unchallenged stereotypical "explanations" of Pamiat. According to the first, Pamiat is a peculiar Russian phenomenon rooted in prerevolutionary Russian history, with its anti-Jewish pogroms, the forgery of the Protocols of the Elders of Zion, and anti-Semitic activities of the Black Hundreds (violent right-wing groups in prerevolutionary Russia). According to the second stereotype, Pamiat is a proto-Fascist movement similar to those that existed in Italy, Germany, and other European countries prior to World War II. Both explanations are largely misleading because they ignore the obvious fact that, whatever its affinity with the Russian Black Hundreds, Italian Blackshirts, and German Brownshirts might be, Pamiat is first and foremost a Soviet phenomenon. As such, it is rooted in conditions that are essentially different from those of prerevolutionary Russia or pre–World War II Europe.[2]

In this chapter I discuss some of the original Pamiat documents, as well as Soviet responses to its activities. I treat Pamiat primarily as a defensive reaction of Russian nationalists against the oppressive conditions of the totalitarian (Communist) Soviet state that has since collapsed. Although recognizing the existence of various "informal" groups that call themselves "Pamiat," I focus on the so-called original Pamiat, that is, Dmitrii Vasil'ev's group.[3]

DEVIL'S ADVOCATE

Even in the Dark Ages it was customary to give accused "heretics" a chance to defend themselves with the help of so-called devil's advocates. That right should not be denied to Pamiat. It certainly behooves scholars to ask a skeptic's question such as: Has Mikhail Gorbachev renounced Soviet anti-Zionist policy? Has he instructed his "new-thinking liberals" to withdraw the Soviet signature from the 1975 UN Resolution 3379 condemning Zionism as a form of racism? Has he pledged to reverse the present tilt in Soviet foreign policy toward the radical Arab states?

Despite the end of the cold war and a substantial improvement of Soviet relations with Israel, the answer to the above questions is no. So why, then, does the West condemn Pamiat's anti-Zionism more and more vehemently than it condemns official Soviet anti-Zionism? The usual explanation is that Pamiat's anti-Zionism is much more virulent and more equatable with anti-Semitism, or Judophobia, as I will call it in this chapter.[4] Pamiat's Judophobia, it is argued, is more dangerous because it allegedly stems from a deep-seated popular Russian tradition. Although there is some truth to this explanation, its suffers from two essential defects. First, it implies that Russian people are not only incorrigible but almost congenitally anti-Semitic, an assumption that is historically incorrect and morally indefensible. In fact, it mirrors the racist assumptions that Judophobes make about the Jews. Second, the "Russian" explanation diverts attention from Marxism-Leninism as an intrinsically antinational and antireligious ideology that has for decades guided Soviet policy to the detriment of all nationalities of the USSR, including the Russians and the Jews. In particular, it diverts attention from the link between long-standing official Soviet anti-Zionist policy and Pamiat's anti-Zionist rhetoric.

A SOVIET PHENOMENON

Not only is Pamiat a Soviet phenomenon, but it is so in its two worst aspects: its dependence on official Soviet anti-Zionist propaganda and its connection with the KGB. The two aspects are interconnected. In fact, having originated before the advent of glasnost, Eastern European ultranationalists or Neo-Fascists often enjoyed the covert backing of the remaining Communist establishment, especially at the local level, as the interwar Fascist movements frequently depended on a consultative or reactionary establishment.

Pamiat could not have developed its "Zionist-Masonic conspiracy" rhetoric without the connivance and even the help of the KGB.[5]

I do not mean to suggest that either Vasil'ev or any other Pamiat leader did actually conspire with the KGB but rather that it was plausible and even probable that from the very start Pamiat leaders were made to understand that as long as they refrained from blaming the party for the destruction of Russian national monuments and instead blamed anonymous "Zionists" and "Freemasons," they would be immune from prosecution and would be allowed to use government buildings for their lectures.[6] At a time when any criticism of the official Soviet policy was a punishable offense, the sobriquet "Zionist-Masonic" certainly provided Pamiat with a perfect alibi for its activities.

For a few years Pamiat had no trouble keeping such a concordat with the KGB. However, the situation changed with the advent of glasnost. Now the people wanted to hear the names of the culprits. And when Pamiat began to point to such close associates of Lenin and Stalin as Leon Trotsky, Nikolay Bukharin, Lazar' Kaganovich, and Emel'ian Iaroslavskii (Gubel'man) as well as Gorbachev's Politburo promotee, Aleksandr Iakovlev, it became clear that Pamiat actually decoded the sobriquet differently than did the KGB.

Although agreeing to the use of the sobriquet, the KGB apparently reckoned it would be employed in the sense of "agents of Israel and its Western allies." It did not quite expect that it could be used to implicate the party itself. Nor did it foresee that Pamiat's defense of Russian national monuments would escalate to a defense of Russian national and religious values and thus challenge the Marxist-Leninist ideological monopoly. It is precisely this *implicit* anti-Marxist-Leninist thrust rather than its *explicit* anti-Zionist and anti-Jewish rhetoric that worried Soviet ideologists most when Pamiat's activities broke out into the open in May 1987. Only then did Soviet ideological watchdogs realize the real threat Pamiat posed to Marxism-Leninism and the one-party system. They naturally responded by subjecting the "Russian nationalists" to an unprecedented propaganda barrage, the intensity and the scope of which overshadowed their condemnation of renascent national sentiments among minorities. The details of the party's denunciation, in view of past anti-Semitic campaigns under Stalin, are illuminating.

EARLY ATTACKS IN THE SOVIET PRESS

The barrage was started by the most dogmatic wing of the Soviet propaganda apparatus. Shortly after Boris Yeltsin, then the party boss of Moscow, received the Pamiat delegation in May 1987, Elena Losoto of the Communist Youth League's mass-circulation newspaper, *Komsomolskaia pravda,* accused Pamiat of failing to define patriotism "as Lenin did," that is, "socialism as fatherland." She particularly denounced Pamiat for defending Russian religious tradition. "If one regards the Orthodox [Christian tradition] part of our history [worthy of preservation]," declared Losoto, "this kind of history we have knocked out from under our people's feet and that serves them [Christians] right."[7] She also denounced Pamiat for its admiration for the prerevolutionary reformer Petr Stolypin who, according to Losoto, "gave the green light to the *kulaks* [wealthy farmers] and whose name is a symbol of reaction." Pamiat activities are contrary to Marxist-Leninist principles of "class struggle" and "proletarian internationalism," concluded Losoto.

Another attack was mounted by Andrei Cherkizov of *Sovetskaia kul'tura* (Soviet culture), a mouthpiece of the Soviet cultural establishment.[8] Like Losoto, Cherkizov attacked Pamiat from "the positions of Marxism-Leninism" because, he said, "only this great philosophic teaching is convincing and provable for me." Saying that the majority of Pamiat members are "thinking people," Cherkizov urged them to return to the Marxist-Leninist approach to Russia's national heritage. In the spirit of glasnost, Cherkizov sought to mollify his ideological dogmatism by conceding that it was fine to discuss "the past and the present" in terms of alternative variants, but only as long as such discussions aim at "strengthening socialism." Nonetheless, he denounced Pamiat's leaders for their failure to define patriotism in Marxist-Leninist terms. He contrasted Pamiat's "false" patriotism with the "genuine Soviet patriotism" of "internationalist soldiers," who, according to him, performed their "patriotic" duty in Afghanistan. Appealing to ideological vigilance, Cherkizov asked, "Why do our Communists and *Komsomol* members not give a rebuttal to these whiners?"

Neither Losoto nor Cherkizov saw any connection between Pamiat's anti-Zionist rhetoric and official Soviet anti-Zionism. On the contrary, both denounced Pamiat for giving ammunition to Israel and the West to charge the Soviet Union with "anti-Semitism" and thereby undermine Soviet foreign policy. "To get to the bottom of the truth," declared Losoto, "Pamiat makes the Zionists happy because it plays into their hands by giving them a reason to shout about anti-Semitism in the USSR."

It is true that Cherkizov accused four Soviet anti-Zionist "specialists"— Valerii Emel'ianov, Vladimir Begun, Evgenii Evseev, and A. Z. Romanenko— of being either Pamiat members or at least sympathizers and "favorite lecturers." But by singling out the four, Cherkizov clearly wanted to create the misleading impression that the rest of Soviet anti-Zionist "scholarship" was both Marxist-Leninist and "scientific." Neither Cherkizov nor Losoto responded to Vasil'ev's allegation that Lenin kept the Protocols of the Elders of Zion in his Kremlin library for reasons other than mere curiosity.

On December 19, 1987, Losoto published another article in which she surveyed readers' responses to her May article. She selectively quoted some of them to buttress her two main contentions: In spite of its anti-Zionist rhetoric, Pamiat actually serves the interests of world Zionism, and its chief danger lies in the creation of anti-Communist opposition to the Soviet regime.[9] "Anti-Semitism is a dream of the Zionists," wrote Losoto. By fanning the flames of anti-Semitism in the USSR, Pamiat actually serves the interests of world Zionism. "Our anti-Zionist fighters," as she sarcastically called Pamiat supporters, "have swallowed the Zionist hook even without bait on it."

Quoting from one of the pro-Pamiat letters in which Lenin was denounced for conspiring with the "Jewish Bolsheviks," Losoto argued that Pamiat is actually not against Zionism, but against the Communist revolution. According to Losoto, Pamiat and world Zionism are ideological twins because both are guided by "counterrevolutionary concepts." If the Zionists search for a promised land in Israel, Pamiat looks for it in pre-revolutionary Russia, with the "church bells" and "patriarchal" way of life Pamiat wants to restore.

Losoto accused both Pamiat supporters and emigration-bound Soviet Jews of sharing the same "counterrevolutionary" ambition: "To get farther away from socialism! That's the main thing [that unites the two groups]. But whether one goes 'farther' away through emigration [*za kordon*] or 'farther' away from 1917 [the year of Communist revolution] is secondary." Going further than in her first article, Losoto directly accused Pamiat not just of deviating from Lenin and Marx but of creating "an embryo of an oppositional party of the Neo-Fascist type." She insinuated that during the war Pamiat members would have joined Hitler. To support her charge that Pamiat is anti-Communist she alleged that Pamiat was working hand in hand with other "anti-Socialist informal groups." An excerpt from the letter written by a certain Iu. Fedin, a young Muscovite who was not afraid to supply his full address (as Losoto noted), sheds some light on the importance of the issue of preservation of Russian national relics that Pamiat has raised:

> Lenin hated Russia, but why should I share his views? We have slain the czar's family, annihilated the nobles, got rid of the bourgeois *kulaks*, and destroyed the churches. What do we have left? Just a few remaining monuments, only because we did not have enough bulldozers to destroy them. ... That's why the enemies of the Russian people cannot stand hearing the name of Stolypin! ... And our culture! Truly Russian artists have nowhere to go [as] only Maiakovskii, a vicious proponent of the destruction of Russian monuments [represents it].

The author may or may not harbor anti-Jewish feelings, but he clearly indicts the entire Communist revolution by citing two ethnic Russians, Lenin and Vladimir Maiakovskii, as the chief destroyers of Russian culture. He compares them to Stolypin, whose reforms were indeed aimed at averting the revolution and who was by no means hostile to the Jews.

During 1987 and later there appeared in the Soviet press dozens of similar articles. With minor variations, all were uniform in condemning Pamiat for its alleged prerevolutionary "Black Hundred mentality" and "anti-Semitic hysteria."[10] None suggested even the slightest possibility that a connection between Pamiat and official Soviet anti-Zionism might exist. None suggested any connection with the KGB. Few found any justification for Pamiat's existence. None offered its pages to Pamiat leaders nor tried to interview them nor quoted extensively their documents. From about 1988 on, the situation changed, however, and this change I discuss later.

Ironically, the predominant Western reaction to Pamiat has been to join the chorus of Soviet propagandists without noticing their more subtle themes. Western reporters uncritically repeated Losoto's and Cherkizov's denunciation of Pamiat for its alleged prerevolutionary Russian anti-Semitic mentality. At the same time, they have largely ignored Pamiat's raising a number of very important issues whose appeal extends far beyond the circle of people guilty of, or susceptible to, Judophobia. They also ignored official Soviet sources of Pamiat's "anti-Zionist" rhetoric and conduct.[11]

PAMIAT'S PROGRAM

Let us now examine a few original Pamiat documents that, in the absence of a formal program, might give us some idea as to how Pamiat wants to project itself and how it imagines the country's future. These are a 1986 appeal, a 1987 proclamation, and a November 3, 1988, "credo." Issued in the name of its governing body, these documents may serve as primary sources on Pamiat. The first two documents were, to my knowledge, never published either in the USSR or the West.[12]

As one could expect, both the 1986 appeal and the 1987 proclamation are full of hateful rhetoric. Both blame the misfortunes of the Russian people on the Zionists, the Freemasons, and their friends. "Global imperialism, nurtured by Zionism and its mercenary Masonic lackeys, is trying to drag the world into the spiral of a new planetwide catastrophe," reads the appeal.[13] "[The] enemy is the one who regards the problem of Zionism and Masonry as an idle invention," ominously warns the proclamation.[14] The two documents differ, however, not just in size but in tone. The 1986 appeal exudes an air of optimism and faith in perestroika. It calls the faithful to unite "around the Central Committee of the Communist Party ... headed by M. S. Gorbachev" and to reject "those party members ... who are trying to adapt themselves to perestroika while discrediting the new political course."[15]

The 1987 proclamation, in contrast, issued after the media campaign against Pamiat, assesses the situation in a much less sanguine way: "The reasonable and healthy forces of our society ... have again been trampled into mud. This perestroika bluff can no longer be continued."[16] The proclamation protests against the campaign of defamation and repression against Pamiat members. For lack of a formal Pamiat program, it might be worthwhile to take a closer look at the proclamation's programmatic statements.[17]

Economy

Pamiat urges the restoration of private landownership to those who till it and decries the "unnatural" life in communal apartments in huge impersonal buildings crowded in "giant cities," advocating instead the construction of private family homes.[18]

For Perestroika

Declaring itself a force for perestroika and glasnost, Pamiat calls on people to exercise control over the Soviet media, "which continue to lie."[19] Pamiat deplores the suppression of heterodoxy (inakomyslie) "in violation of the [Soviet] constitution and the law."[20] It also advocates the use of referenda to decide vital countrywide issues and urges people to create their own committees for perestroika.[21]

For Ecology and Freedom of Religion

Pamiat warns of the impending "ecological catastrophe" and accuses the authorities of squandering the country's natural resources through foreign trade. Pamiat declares itself to be against both "the ideological and alcoholic poison that destroys the nation."[22] It further demands "freedom of conscience" and the separation of "atheist propaganda from the state."[23] Finally, without openly advocating the abolition of the one-party system, Pamiat in effect challenges it by insisting on an equal partnership between the party "minority" and the "nonparty [bespartiinoe] majority."[24]

Patriots of the World, Unite!

Although primarily concerned with ethnic Russians, Pamiat leaders profess a desire to act in concert with other peoples of the USSR. They have adopted as their motto, "Patriots of the world, unite!"—a sarcastic paraphrase on Marx's famous appeal to the proletarians to unite. They urge "brothers and sisters of all nations" to create their own Pamiat-type groups for preservation of their national cultures in their republics, cities, and villages and to assert their right "to be masters of their own land."[25] They denounce the destruction of "an enormous number of monuments of universal significance that belong to the Russian and *other peoples*" (emphasis supplied).[26]

In Foreign Affairs

Pamiat seems to take a strictly isolationist and pacifist line. It deplores the nuclear arms race and denounces all wars, including the "criminal blood-shed in Afghanistan."[27] Although it does not condemn capitalism as such, Pamiat decries "international Zionist capital," "imperialist forces," and their agents inside the country. "They re-animate Trotskyism in order to dis-credit socialism, to sow chaos and to open the country's gates to Western capital and Western ideology," fulminates the proclamation.[28]

These two documents demonstrate that were it not for its wild and vicious "Zionist-Masonic conspiracy" rhetoric, Pamiat could have passed for one of the radical reformist groups in the country. It has correctly identified a number of fundamental Soviet problems. Moreover, the solutions it has pro-posed, such as the reintroduction of private property, the separation of athe-ist propaganda from the state, and the sharing of party power with the rest of the population, are not out of line with the demands of such avowedly democratic groups favoring fundamental systemic change as the Demo-cratic Union or Sergei Grigoriant's newsletter, *Glasnost*.[29] Yet Western critics of Pamiat, having focused almost exclusively on the allegedly "Russian" roots of Pamiat's Judophobia, have largely ignored that Pamiat's specific proposals challenge the totalitarian soviet.

The "Credo"

The third original document is a statement issued by Pamiat's central coun-cil on November 3, 1988. It was printed in Lithuania on March 14, 1989, by a small Russian-language weekly *Soglasie*, sponsored by the Lithuanian Move-ment for Perestroika.[30] Calling it a "credo" and "one of the main docu-ments" of Pamiat, the weekly explained its decision to publish it as a desire to reveal Pamiat's secret and thus demonstrate Pamiat's "fanaticism," "anti-Semitism," and "conspiratorial" tactics. It is unlikely, however, that Pamiat leaders regarded this document as secret. But they would probably have pre-ferred to see it published without a negative preface. In any case, unlike the appeal and the proclamation, the "credo" appears to be an intramural doc-ument, not intended for outsiders. Entitled "Avtoritet vozhdia" (A leader's authority), this "credo" (I use that name for convenience) sheds additional light on the main tenets and the evolution of this movement.

The main purpose of the "credo" was to inform Pamiat's membership of the "unanimous" decision of the council to make Vasil'ev a formal head (*glava*) of Pamiat. The rest of this rather long document was devoted to justi-fying the concept of *vozhdizm* ("leaderism") and to explaining why Vasil'ev was elected to the new post. The country needs a *vozhd'*, a leader, "a strong personality," whose "moral and spiritual" qualities will "heal the nation, uniting it for a higher purpose," reads the "credo," arguing that Vasil'ev is fully qualified for that role. Among Vasil'ev's merits the "credo" mentions that he was the first to launch a mass campaign against the "Zionist-Masonic conspiracy" by reading in public excerpts from the Protocol of the Elders of Zion, a document the "credo" claims illustrates Zionist plans for world domination.

Like the two previous documents, the "credo" liberally indulges in denunciation of "the primary root of evil: a world-wide Zionist-Masonic conspiracy." With the help of the Trotskyists, who are alleged to be mere tools of the Zionists, that "conspiracy" is blamed not only for the destruction of the czarist monarchy but also for the "splintering" of Pamiat into several "surrogate" groups. The leaders of these groups are denounced for prostituting the "idea" (of Pamiat) for "their personal ambitions or at the behest of the Mossad" (the Israeli intelligence agency).

The above paranoid diatribe aside, the adoption of the concept of *vozhdizm* may signal the evolution of Pamiat ideology in the direction of totalitarianism. But to which extreme: left or right? The belief in a strong leader saving a nation from the chaos of ineffective democracy and parliamentarism was fundamental for both types. Personal dictatorships emerged in virtually all Communist countries: those of Lenin and Stalin in the USSR, Mao Zedong in China, Fidel Castro in Cuba, and Ceausescu in Romania, to name a few. Yet the concept of *vozhdizm* was no less important for both Fascist Italy, where Mussolini was the duce, and Nazi Germany, where Hitler was the Führer.

In a rebuke of the "cult of personality," the "credo" seems to reject the *vozhdizm* of the Stalinist type—though it does not praise "Western leaders" (Hitler and Mussolini) either. Instead, the "credo" urges the restoration of a more or less traditional Russian monarchy and portrays Vasil'ev not only as a *vozhd'* but also as a potential Russian czar. "The benevolent Leader, the beloved Leader comes to the world not in his own name, but in the name of the Lord. Therefore Christ the God-son stands above the czar and the Leader," says the "credo" in an apparent effort to project Pamiat ideology as consistent with the traditional view of the Russian monarch as a defender of Christianity. Pamiat's evolution toward a variety of the right-wing totalitarian *vozhdizm* thus appears to be somewhat tempered by its emphasis on the need to restore traditional religion and a state form that can be called autocratic and authoritarian but hardly totalitarian. At any rate, the "credo" evinces Pamiat's evolution toward a stronger identification with Vasil'ev's personality. Let us now review the development that occurred after the initial Soviet reaction to Pamiat in 1987.

SOVIET MEDIA RESPONSES AFTER 1987

The Soviet Marxist-Leninist propaganda barrage against Pamiat during 1987 proved not only ineffective but counterproductive. The more the propagandists attacked Pamiat, the more people became interested in this rather small and obscure but recalcitrant group. The decades of systematic vilification of all dissident groups made many people immune to propaganda. Some may have assumed that because a group was attacked by the official propagandists, there must be some virtue in it. By fall 1987, with Soviet intellectuals increasingly splitting into various factions—from the conservative Russian nationalists to "left-liberal" Westernizers and the "conservative" Communists—the unanimity of Soviet condemnation of Pamiat began to falter. The Soviet mass media became divided. Although "reform Communists" managed to retain control over its huge trunk, the radical "liberals" (also known as "democrats") and the "conservative" Russian nationalists consolidated their hold over two of its largest branches. Unable to control the media directly, the party increasingly relied on the tactics of indirect control by manipulating, not without the help of the KGB, both the "liberal" and the nationalist branches.

In the October 1987 issue of *Nash sovremennik,* a major Russian nationalist monthly magazine, Vadim Kozhinov, a prominent literary critic, disputed Losoto's assertion that her approach to Pamiat was based on Lenin.[31] Reproaching Pamiat leaders for their "infantilism" and "ignorance," Kozhinov nevertheless urged that positive aspects of Pamiat's activities not be overlooked. In January 1988 the same magazine carried Valentin Rasputin's earlier speech, in which he denounced the indiscriminate "bombardment" of Pamiat. Rasputin scorned the predominant "left-wing" Soviet press not only for denying glasnost to Pamiat but also for labeling all Russian patriots as the "Black Hundredists."[32] A very popular "ruralist" writer and an unabashed Russian patriot, Rasputin was later inducted into Gorbachev's Presidential Council.

Gavriil Popov's Article

One of the most extensive and authoritative assessments of Pamiat appeared in the January 1988 issue of the "liberal" magazine *Znamia.*[33] It was done in a lengthy interview with Gavriil Popov, a prominent Moscow University professor who was later (in 1990) elected mayor of Moscow. Popov's assessment was more sober, more objective, and more balanced than any of the previous articles. Although there are reasons to feel apprehensive about Pamiat, said Popov, we should not forget that among its members there are "many honest, sincere patriots." Popov admitted that "there are profound, objective reasons for the emergence of Pamiat," such as "the demographic situation (unfavorable to ethnic Russians), the (miserable economic) state of

Nechernozem'e (Russia's historical cradle), the scale of alcoholism, and much, much more."

Not only was "Russian historical memory subjected to a brutal, vicious persecution *(utesnenie),*" Popov acknowledged, but among all peoples of the USSR, "the heaviest blows of the ('administrative') system fell on the Russians, whose past suffered most." But why were ethnic Russians singled out for this especially harsh treatment? Popov offered several reasons. First, "the Church was against the revolution," and therefore the revolution had to wipe out Russian "religious memory." The second reason had to do with the strength of the monarchist tradition among the Russian people. Naturally, it had to be eradicated. (Popov failed to notice, however, that the entire body of Russian prerevolutionary political tradition, both monarchist and nonmonarchist, liberal and social democrat was likewise wiped out.) The third reason was that Stalin, according to Popov, rejected Lenin's idea of an alliance with "the peasant majority." Consequently, the Russian "peasant memory" had to be wiped out as well. Finally, Popov offered a fourth reason: "It was necessary to debase Russian culture and Russia's past, in order to turn the Russians into brutes, to free them from their memory, so that they could carry out the role that the administrative system assigned to them."

Concluded Popov: "One can understand, if not justify the emotions of Pamiat."[34] Popov thus became the first prominent Communist (he quit the party in 1990, however) to publicly admit that Communist rulers deprived ethnic Russians of their national memory in order to make them accept slavery for themselves and to make them more "efficient" in carrying out the party's orders to keep other nations enslaved. It is clear that such an admission could not have been made in the pre-glasnost period. The "conservative" Communists, that is, those who want to "conserve" the Soviet system in its Marxist-Leninist totalitarian mold, came up with yet another opinion that somewhat diverged from the Losoto/Cherkizov line. It was expressed in Nina Andreeva's notorious letter published on March 13, 1988, in *Sovetskaia Rossiia* (Soviet Russia), a major newspaper controlled at the time by the "conservative" faction of Egor Ligachev.[35] According to Andreeva, the system is caught in the cross fire from two "alternative towers": the tower of pro-Western "left-liberals" and the tower of "the preservationists and traditionalists." Without naming Pamiat, Andreeva nonetheless made it clear that by the latter "tower" she meant exactly the tendency that Pamiat and other Russian nationalist groups represent. This "traditionalist" tower, argued Andreeva, threatens the survival of the regime because it wants to "overcome socialism" by moving backward to the "pre-socialist Russia." She also disliked the "left-liberal" tower because it was largely manned by "nationless cosmopolitans" (a Stalin-era code for the Jews), that is, the modern descendants of the Trotskyites who have now become the refuseniks. Invoking the authority of both Marx and Engels, Andreeva applied their concept of "counterrevolutionary" nations to the Jews and the Israelis. (In the use of the code names, Andreeva was about as subtle as Pamiat.)

There were other independent opinions on Pamiat that were a far cry from the initial unanimity of scorn and condemnation. Writing in the pages of the liberal magazine *Novyi mir,* Alla Latynina, a literary critic and a member of the editorial board of the "liberal" weekly *Literaturnaia gazeta,* criticized Soviet intellectuals for their lack of the "culture of polemic."[36] In a footnote she compared the smear campaign against Pamiat with the one against Boris Pasternak in the late 1950s. Many prominent Soviet intellectuals who now call themselves "liberals" then went on record as saying, "I did not read Pasternak's novel, but I condemn it." Now, according to Latynina, even without being threatened by government repression, they say the same about Pamiat and are quick to condemn those who are in no hurry to follow suit.

Lena Zelinskaia, one of the editors of the "informal" ecological magazine *Merkurii,* in an interview with the official "liberal" magazine *Vek XX i mir,* announced her decision to devote an entire magazine issue to Pamiat as "the first group (of Soviet citizens) to speak openly of the tragedy of the Russian people."[37] Speaking of anti-Pamiat zealotry among her "liberal" friends, she concluded: "It is not clear to me who is more aggressive, Pamiat or my good friends, decent and intelligent people, who ... fight against Pamiat." At the end of 1989, *Sovetskii zhurnalist* (Soviet journalist), a professional magazine of Soviet journalists, published an article, "How Myths Are Created," disputing Losoto's insinuation that the Sverdlovsk group Otechestvo (Fatherland) was "a younger brother" of Pamiat.[38]

Rumors of Pogroms and the Norinskii Case

In May and June 1988 there were rumors circulating in Moscow that Pamiat was about to start pogroms against the Jews. After two months elapsed, however, no attacks on Jews had been reported. In July 1988 dozens of Soviet officials received a letter containing the following statement: "The vengeance is coming. We'll get rid of you." It was signed by "Storm troopers of the patriotic front Pamiat." One of the addressees was Grigorii Baklanov, the editor of *Znamia,* in which Popov's assessment of Pamiat had been published. Unfortunately, this time Baklanov failed to exhibit good judgment. Without waiting for the investigation, he jumped the gun and in the pages of his magazine denounced Pamiat for making the threats. Pamiat leaders indignantly denied the charge. Meanwhile, Leningrad resident Arkadii Norinskii, not a Pamiat member, was arrested as a suspect. After he confessed to writing and mailing the letters, on November 18, 1988, a Leningrad court found him guilty and sentenced him to a year and a half of forced labor.

The most bizarre and unfortunate aspect of this incident was that both the author of the libelous forgery and the editor who published it were Jewish, a situation which Pamiat did not miss the chance to exploit. Baklanov certainly committed a serious gaffe. His mistake was hardly offset by the publication in the "liberal" illustrated weekly *Ogonek* of an interview with the imprisoned Norinskii. Though acknowledging that he had violated both "our ethics and our Constitution," Norinskii awkwardly tried to justify his action by the anti-Semitic atmosphere in the country.[39] The interviewer made things worse by admitting that before the interview he and his colleagues suspected that Norinskii was an *agent provocateur* acting on behalf of Pamiat. At least one Jewish reader challenged the wisdom of publishing the interview with this "moron and scoundrel" who put in "an awkward situation Baklanov, the editor of one of the most progressive journals."[40]

Other developments suggest the fallacy of relying on the information of the "liberal" Soviet press alone. In April 1989 a court forced *Sovetskaia kul'tura* to retract its report that A. Z. Romanenko, whom Cherkizov called a Pamiat sympathizer, had publicly accused "a certain Zionist organization" of the destruction of both Russian nature and culture.[41] In June 1989 Vladimir Begun, who also sued both *Sovetskaia kul'tura* and Cherkizov for linking him with Pamiat, died after the first court session. Calling Begun a communist "with the capital 'C,'" the nationalist (or, rather, nationalist-Bolshevik) monthly *Molodaia gvardiia* immediately charged that the death was caused by the stress of being "libeled all around the country."[42] The third member of Cherkizov's "four," Evgenii Evseev, was hit by a passing car in Moscow on February 10, 1990, and died a few days later. Although the results of the police investigation were inconclusive, the nationalist press alleged it was a terrorist act connected with Evseev's founding, shortly before his death, an informal committee of the Soviet public against the restoration of diplomatic relations with Israel.[43]

Finally, the fourth person whom Cherkizov accused of affiliation with Pamiat, Emel'ianov, was confirmed to be a leader of a "pagan" Pamiat, a splinter group Vasil'ev denounced. In an ironic twist, Emel'ianov charged that the "so-called anti-Zionist" Evseev was actually a "Jewish Nazi" in league with Evgenii Primakov, a member of Gorbachev's "team." Emel'ianov claimed that he became closely acquainted with both while studying Arabic at the prestigious Moscow Institute of Oriental Studies.[44] As such developments clearly demonstrate, it is difficult to obtain objective and reliable information about Pamiat.

CHANGE OF OFFICIAL TACTICS

The Gorbachev leadership gradually began to recognize that a new approach to Pamiat had to be used. It was decided to embark on more cautious divide-and-conquer tactics. Those tactics probably included the authorization of the APN news report that Vasil'ev's "anti-Semitic Pamiat" was but a splinter group of an allegedly larger, older and truly patriotic Pamiat of Egor Sychev.[45] It also included efforts to isolate the "bad" Pamiat by the expulsion of its sympathizers from the party. A certain amount of police action was also to be used, but only selectively, and Vasil'ev did in fact receive a KGB warning.[46] On August 13, 1988, a group of Leningrad intellectuals, upset over a series of Pamiat-sponsored meetings in the Rumiantsev Square, published a letter in *Izvestiia* demanding a legal action against this "unregistered" group, no legal action was taken, even though *Izvestiia* endorsed the letter. On September 25 a certain Dekhtiarev, a Leningrad party leader, declared that there were no plans to disband Pamiat. He did not rule out "administrative measures" against its members, however.[47]

Apparently, even the highest authorities now felt it necessary to make a number of concessions, not directly to Pamiat but to the sentiments that nourished it. Several such concessions were made to the Russian Orthodox church in conjunction with its millennium in 1988. Moreover, in its authoritative April 1988 rebuke to Nina Andreeva, *Pravda* took notice of "the growing interest of popular masses in our past." The editorial was carefully worded so as not to antagonize either of the two alternative "towers."[48] *Pravda* made it clear that the main threat to the unity of the country came not from the two towers but from the dogmatic leftists, such as Andreeva herself. *Pravda* implied that, unlike Pamiat, the leftists knew how to enlist the authority of Marx and Engels on their side in their attacks of the "counterrevolutionary nation."

Another concession may be seen in Aleksandr Iakovlev's removal from his watchdog ideologist post after the September 30, 1988, shake-up in the Kremlin. The removal certainly did seem like a conciliatory gesture because Pamiat had long demanded Iakovlev's resignation. At any rate, it was an acknowledgment of the sentiments Pamiat shares with many Russian nationalists, including Rasputin, whose appointment to the Presidential Council was probably likewise intended to placate the restive nationalists bent on raising the Russian question. It is nevertheless quite possible that concessions have not come from a single center. Both the party and the KGB seem to be so internally divided that they can hardly follow through on any centrally devised tactics.

A major breakthrough for Pamiat came in June 1989 when *Sobesednik,* the weekly supplement to *Komsomolskaia pravda,* published an article written on behalf of Pamiat by Aleksandr Shtil'mark, a high school teacher and a leader of a Pamiat affiliate in a town near Moscow. Titled "Pamiat: We Are for a Spiritual Rebirth of Our Fatherland," the article was an exposé of the very same Pamiat ideology that the newspaper, in the person of Losoto, had so high-handedly denounced two years earlier.[49] Whether ordered from above or authorized by the editors, the publication was yet another victory for Pamiat, and, one might argue, for glasnost. Devoting the first half of his article to the refutation of the charges of "chauvinism" and "anti-Semitism," Shtil'mark used the second half to describe Pamiat's "concrete activities" helping "the rebirth of national self-awareness."[50] He disputed the charge of "chauvinism" by saying that none of Pamiat's documents contains statements suggesting that the Russians are superior to or better than other people. Pamiat membership is ethnically diverse, including Tatars, Kalmyks, and Jews, claimed Shtil'mark, who is himself partly of Scandinavian origin.

As to the charge of "anti-Semitism," he flatly dismissed it as stemming from "Zionist tactics" of pasting that "label" on anyone who opposes Zionism. Arguing that there was no discrimination against Jews in the USSR, Shtil'mark praised Gorbachev for his "worthy rebuttal to the Zionist squallers" when Gorbachev said that though the Jews constitute only 0.69 percent of the Soviet population, they occupy up to 20 percent of all positions in "the sphere of administration and culture."[51] Shtil'mark maintained that Pamiat's documents contain no overt denunciations of Jews as a people.

His other assertions were wide of the mark, however. "Fortunately, the Jewish population of (our) country is gradually beginning to realize that Zionism is one of the chief enemies of this ancient people," asserted Shtil'mark, claiming that having "surrendered millions of (fellow Jews) to their destruction by the hand of the National Socialists, (Zionist) leaders now shed crocodile tears and accuse of anti-Semitism all and everyone." He went on to blame the Zionists for virtually all Soviet problems, from the destruction of Russian culture during the 1920s to the Chernobyl disaster. However, the only "Zionists" he named—Leon Trotsky, Lazar' Kaganovich, Emel'ian Iaroslavskii (Gubel'man), Iakov Sverdlov, Lev Kamenev (Rozenfel'd), Grigorii Zinov'ev (Apfelbaum)—were all Jewish Bolshevik leaders. Convinced Marxist-Leninists, they were avowed anti-Zionists, no less dedicated to the destruction of the Jewish culture than the Russian. Nor did they care whether the cultures they were destroying were based on Christianity, Judaism, or any other religion.

Shtil'mark's diatribe against "the enemy: Zionism and Masonry" was the most noxious, and weakest, part of his article. One has the impression that in the hope of solidifying Pamiat's breakthrough to the mainstream press, Shtil'mark deliberately downplayed Pamiat's anti-Communist thrust, which is more evident in the three documents (the 1986 appeal, 1987 proclamation, and 1988 "credo") reviewed above. Feeling legally secure in the familiar domain of anti-Zionist rhetoric, Shtil'mark chose to ignore the charge of anticommunism and antisocialism that was so clearly spelled out by critics like Losoto and Cherkizov.

Although they accepted Shtil'mark's article, the editors gave equal space to a rebuttal by Pavel Kudiukin, a young sociologist and ethnic Russian. Like

Popov before him, Kudiukin acknowledged that Pamiat and the patriotic movement in general were "a response to the real problems of the Russian people." But he strongly disagreed with Shtil'mark on just about everything else. He particularly took Shtil'mark to task for his failure to distinguish between the Zionists and the Bolsheviks. Without denying that Jewish Bolsheviks played a significant role in the formation of the Soviet state, Kudiukin accurately pointed out that "these people did not regard themselves as Jews." "Proletarian internationalism," said Kudiukin in reference to their creed, "is based on other principles than the ideology of Zionism." Kudiukin made it clear that Pamiat is "anti-Semitic" mainly because of its tendency to regard every Jew, irrespective of convictions, as a Zionist.

Kudiukin correctly criticized Pamiat for its intolerance of different views, as well as for its *vozhdizm*. Saying that a true antidote to the totalitarian system must be sought not in a leader but in a "people's parliament" and through political pluralism, Kudiukin cautioned that Pamiat might lead merely to the replacement of the current left totalitarian system with a right-wing one. Kudiukin was less convincing, however, when he argued that Pamiat is "chauvinistic" because it professes to counter the belief that Jews are the "chosen" people with its own brand of messianism, the belief that Russians are a "God-fearing people." Apparently not a religious person, Kudiukin seems to regard both beliefs as "chauvinistic."

On the whole, Kudiukin's rebuttal of Pamiat was considerably more competent and convincing than those of Cherkizov and Losoto. He not merely denounced Pamiat, but tried to challenge its main tenets. His problem, however, was that he saw no need for Russian national rebirth. Nor did he seem to believe in Russia's ability to solve its own problems, hoping instead for some sort of help from the West. Whereas Shtil'mark named Stolypin as a model of a reformer, Kudiukin named Olof Palme, the late Social Democratic prime minister of Sweden. Besides the fact that both were assassinated, there is little in common between the two. Still, Shtil'mark's choice seems more realistic.

It appears that the Gorbachev government learned to live with Pamiat. They may have figured out that as long as it remained unregistered and existed only in limbo, Pamiat could be contained—and could even be useful for the government. It could act as a sort of lightning rod to divert Western criticisms from such warts of the existing left totalitarian system as official Soviet anti-Zionism, to a largely mythical threat from "the Russian New Right." The Ostashvili affair may be seen as an example. When Konstantin Smirnov-Ostashvili, a poorly educated worker and the leader of a small splinter group of Pamiat, was sentenced in October 1990 to two years of hard labor for taking part in an "anti-Semitic brawl" at a meeting of liberal writers in January, the Soviet mass media, controlled by reform Communists and democrats, greeted the sentence with jubilation. The Western press likewise saw it as "a further sign of the Soviet Union's increasing recognition of its human-rights obligations" and, consequently, as yet another reason for supporting Gorbachev.[52]

But not everyone in the USSR was so convinced. Aleksandr Podrabinek, a courageous human-rights champion and the editor of the samizdat magazine *KhronikaPress*, argued that Ostashvili's conviction was no reason for jubilation, certainly not among people caring for human rights. According to Podrabinek, Ostashvili was a victim of both the Communist government and the oppositional democrats, most of whom are former Communists. After having been servile apologists for Leonid Brezhnev's policy of suppressing the human-rights movement, these democrats now like to parade themselves as heroic champions of reform, said Podrabinek. He argued that Ostashvili should have been tried not for his convictions but for taking part in the brawl, for which crime he deserved no more than fifteen days of administrative arrest. A Jew and not a Pamiat sympathizer, Podrabinek further argued that Ostashvili's silly ideas about "Jewish-Masonic conspiracy" should be combatted "by other ideas, not jails or camps." By turning an essentially criminal offense into a political trial, he argued, Soviet authorities may have helped Pamiat create a political martyr.[53] Podrabinek made it clear that if it was winning sympathy in the West for its crackdown against the "anti-Semite" Ostashvili, the Gorbachev government actually created a precedent for legal persecution of any nationalist (Russian, Estonian, or Jewish) whose ideas—expressed in a public speech, newspaper article, or private letter—it did not like.[54]

VASIL'EV AS THE LEADER

Insofar as there is a strong identification of Pamiat with Dmitrii Vasil'ev, a few words about him might be in order. Among several interviews he gave to Westerners, the one with John Dunlop on June 21, 1989, was perhaps the most revealing.[55] Because the interview (and Dunlop's comments about it) have been published, there is no need to review it in detail. But some points deserve to be emphasized. First, Vasil'ev "repeatedly stressed that he is an anti-Zionist, not an anti- Semite," claiming that there were Jewish members of Pamiat. Second, Vasil'ev virtually equated all early Bolsheviks, including the ethnic Russian Lenin and partly Jewish Bukharin, with the Zionists. "To blame the problems of Russia and the world exclusively on the Jews would," he said, "be wrong." He suggested that "the (Marxist-Leninist) system is to be blamed" for all problems that have accumulated since the February revolution. Third, he wanted to see a more or less traditional monarchy and the Orthodox church reestablished in a future Russia. Fourth, "Vasil'ev said that he detested Adolf Hitler for his hatred of Christianity and for his racial theories, but he expressed warm sympathy for the 'idea' of fascism." These four points probably reflect Pamiat's ideology more accurately than did Shtil'mark's article.

For comparison, let us now turn to Vasil'ev's interview with a reporter of *Komsomolets Kubani,* as it was reprinted in another provincial publication, *Volzhskie novosti,* in April 1990.[56] This is one of the few interviews with Vasil'ev published in the Soviet press.[57] To the first question, about various Pamiat groups, Vasil'ev replied that all of them were formed on the initiative of the Moscow party organization to discredit his own "genuine" Pamiat. Neither Sychev nor Emel'ianov nor Ostashvili had anything to do with "our Pamiat," said Vasil'ev. Calling Ostashvili a "crazy" fellow, Vasil'ev denied any responsibility for acts committed by such people. He also denied that his Pamiat was involved in spreading the rumors that pogroms were imminent, blaming instead anti-Pamiat zealots. Vasil'ev claimed that there have been attempts on his life, that his "tires are being frequently slashed," and that he has received threatening telephone calls and "thousands of (hate) letters." His efforts to stop these threats through the courts, said Vasil'ev, were "futile."

As to the rumors that Evseev was assassinated, Vasil'ev answered evasively. He said that his attitude toward Evseev as a person was "negative" and that he regarded some of his methods as "provocative." But "as far as the assassination version is concerned ... I have nothing to fear. I am candid. I do not call for violence." He denied any connection of his group with the KGB, except that "they persecute us." He said that for Russia's future he favored monarchy rather than a parliament because "the (Russian) people subconsciously dream about monarchy" and "are categorically against all sorts of [political] parties." No admirer of either the October or February revolutions, Vasil'ev opposed them to such indigenous Russian institutions as monarchy, the Assemblies of the Land, and the local self-government in the form of zemstvo. Emphasizing that in quest for a spiritual rebirth, Pamiat's main activity continues to be the restoration of historical monuments and churches, he denied any connection with the official church, suggesting that its hierarchy was being manipulated by the KGB. Asked who his "political mentor" was, Vasil'ev named Stolypin. However, he held little hope for perestroika's success as long as it tried to combine Stolypin's ideas "with the vestiges of Communist dogmatism."

According to Vasil'ev, there are "only a few" Jews among Pamiat members "because they are afraid. They are not afraid of us, but of their acquaintances among Jews." About Pamiat's black uniform and its comparisons with prerevolutionary Black Hundreds, Vasil'ev said that Pamiat had adopted the color to express its "mourning" for the fate of Russia. He did not mind the analogy with the "Black Hundreds" as long as medieval warrior monks, not pogromists, were understood. "Do you have something in common with Solzhenitsyn?" asked the reporter. "No. Our views do not coincide. He rejected the idea of monarchy," Vasil'ev answered, without elaboration.

The above two interviews complement each other. Vasil'ev seemed to be sincere in both; he did not appear to be playing it up for the public, Western or Soviet. Both interviews probably reflect Pamiat's ideology and program more accurately than Shtil'mark's article. Dunlop concluded:

> I came away from my discussion with Vasil'ev convinced that he is a political force to be reckoned with. He is articulate and speaks with conviction and passion. To be sure, his program repels anyone accustomed to intellectual rigor, since it is riddled with historical inaccuracies, untruths, and half-truths. But Vasil'ev is not interested in attracting intellectuals. A former chauffeur, actor and photographer, he is a man of the people who finds an easy rapport with the Russian masses.

CONCLUSION

We cannot fully understand the phenomenon of Pamiat unless we see that there is more to it than the "Zionist-Masonic conspiracy" rhetoric. First of all, the group's name itself, meaning "Memory," evokes a very real problem that neither the prerevolutionary Russian Black Hundreds nor the European Fascists and Nazis had to face. It is the problem of the destruction of Russia's past, a direct outcome of the long-standing, deliberate, and systematic Soviet policy aimed at rewriting the past to fit Marxist-Leninist utopian ideology. This policy dictated Soviet efforts to destroy, distort, falsify, or ignore any element of the past that was believed to contradict the "only correct and scientific" Communist worldview. As George Orwell observed, if a dictatorship wants to control a country's future, it must take possession of its past. Whatever element of the past did not fit their scheming had to go into a "memory hole," added Orwell. That is exactly what happened in the Soviet Union. The more obvious it became that socialism did not work, the more ruthlessly Soviet leaders tried to put down Russia's "exploitative," "capitalist," and "imperialist" past. In order to make the new Soviet citizens obedient tools of the Soviet state, leaders tried to cut them off from their vital national, religious, and cultural roots (be they Russian, Jewish, or Lithuanian). The leaders carried out this campaign by the same ruthless methods they employed to wall the people off from the outside world, and with the same disastrous results. Pamiat's efforts to raise the issue of Russian national memory as a means of a recovery of national life seems legitimate.

It is another matter that Pamiat completely misidentifies the sponsors of this enforced amnesia as the "Masons and Zionists." On this score, Pamiat's views are not only incorrect but morally reprehensible. The true sponsors are, of course, Marxist-Leninists, including but not limited to those Jewish

Bolsheviks whom Pamiat mislabels as "Zionists." But why does Pamiat mis-
identify the culprits? There are several reasons, and not all of them are
necessarily rooted in ill will toward the Jews. First, until the late 1980s it took
considerable civic courage to publicly criticize the party and its ideology. Notice, for instance, that even in 1988 Popov timidly substitutes the code expression "administrative command system" for communism. As I argued at
the outset of the chapter, by blaming all misfortunes of the Russians on "Zionists and Masons," Pamiat felt assured that it had a perfect alibi for its otherwise questionable (from the official viewpoint) activities.

Whether the idea of blaming everything on the "Zionist-Masonic conspiracy" was suggested by the KGB or not, Pamiat clearly seized on the opportunity to advance its own goals by exploiting the fact that the Soviet government itself was committed to anti-Zionist policy and that there were plenty
of Soviet books to justify anti-Zionism "scientifically"—that is, from a Marxist viewpoint. It would be a mistake, however, to attribute Pamiat's anti-
Zionism solely to Judophobia and opportunism. We should not overlook
that Pamiat is a victim of that same malady, the amnesia of Russian history,
that it purports to fight. I am not referring to the personal ignorance of
Vasil'ev or other Pamiat ideologues but to the numerous gaps (called "white
spots" in the USSR) in the study of Russian and Soviet history. These gaps
are a result of official taboo on the study of certain "un-Marxist" topics. Although glasnost has helped fill in some of the holes, others remain.

As a radical right-wing movement, Pamiat has a number of features in
common with similar movements in the free world: anticommunism, nativism, populism, Judophobia, a tendency toward religious fundamentalism,
and an emphasis on traditional values and the need to return to "the ba-
sics." Ironically, among all such movements, Pamiat resembles most the Israeli right-wing radicals, especially the Kach movement of the late Meir
Kahane. Both Kach and Pamiat believe in a preordained mission for their
respective nations. Both are distinguished by ultranationalism, stridency, intolerance, antialien sentiments (Kach wants Arabs to be transferred and
Pamiat wants Jews to emigrate), antisocialism, and even anti-Westernism.
They also share a conspiracy paranoia, except that where Pamiat sees the
hand of "Zionists and Masons," Kach suspects the hand of the international
Left. With some justification, each feels it is being vilified by the mass media
at home and abroad.

But Pamiat has much that is entirely its own and is deeply rooted in Soviet
experience. Its mentality was formed by living in a country where Marxist
"internationalism" triumphed—only to produce a Soviet holocaust that
swallowed roughly 50 million lives.[58]

Russian nationalists, including members of Pamiat, find themselves in a
difficult predicament, qualitatively different from that of the nationalists of
small nations. Theirs is a revolt against the double yoke to which they were

subjected under communism: the yoke of enslavement, like any other people in the USSR, and the yoke of hatred and abuse for their involuntary role in keeping others enslaved. It is this special predicament of the Russians that the West has largely ignored. Even when Aleksandr Solzhenitsyn pointed out a number of Western misconceptions about Russia and communism, and in particular called attention to the tragic plight of ethnic Russians in the USSR, his efforts met with little sympathy among American Sovietologists and policymakers.[59] What was worse, many of the same labels that are now being pasted on Pamiat (for example, that of ultranationalism) were pasted on him. The West has yet to understand that there is no better antidote to Pamiat's extremism than recognizing the legitimacy of the Russian national rebirth movement that Solzhenitsyn so eminently represents.[60]

Few American scholars understand contemporary Russian nationalism like John Dunlop of the Hoover Institution, who in his 1983 book called it a "folly" "for the West to continue to ignore the concerns of ethnic Russians and not-so-few Eastern Slavs who identify with them."[61] Dunlop discerned several "faces" of Russian nationalism, including some ugly ones akin to Pamiat. But he also made it clear that its mainstream, which he identified with Solzhenitsyn and other proponents of Russian "national and religious renaissance," is both wholesome and moderate.[62] Dunlop recommended that the West try "to send a favorable signal to the moderate nationalists," perhaps through the use of foreign broadcasting. The negative Western attitude toward *all* manifestations of Russian nationalism has inadvertently contributed to the growth of anti-Western sentiments among the Russians, driving some back to co-optation by the regime and pushing others to the right-wing extremism that Pamiat represents.

THE ISRAELI RADICAL RIGHT: HISTORY, CULTURE, AND POLITICS

Ehud Sprinzak

1984: THE SHOCK

Most Israelis were greatly shocked when they learned on the eve of April 27, 1984, that a plot to blow up five buses full of Arab passengers during a crowded rush hour was barely prevented. In the following week, twenty-seven men suspected of forming an anti-Arab terrorist network were arrested. It was soon disclosed that the suspects had been responsible for an attempt to assassinate the Arab mayors of three West Bank cities in 1980; a murderous attack on the Islamic college in Hebron in 1983, which took the lives of three students and wounded thirty-three; and a score of lesser acts of violence against Arabs. An elaborate plan to blow up the Muslim Dome of the Rock on Jerusalem's Temple Mount, the third most sacred place in Islam, was also on their drawing board.

What surprised observers and political analysts in April 1984 was not so much the existence of the terror group as the identity of its members. They belonged to Gush Emunim (the Block of the Faithful), a religious fundamentalist group committed to establishing Jewish settlements in the West Bank (biblical Judea and Samaria). Though an aggressive (and sometimes even illegal) settlement movement, Gush Emunim had never openly embraced an ideology of violence. Its orthodox leaders asserted a biblically based Jewish claim to Judea and Samaria but had never advocated deportation of the Arab population.[1] Instead, they professed the belief that a peaceful and productive coexistence with the Arabs, under a benevolent Israeli rule, was both possible and desirable. That any of these highly educated and responsible men, some of whom were ranking army officers and all but one of whom were heads of large families, would resort to terrorism was completely unexpected.

The exposition of "respectable" Jewish terrorism was followed, three months later, by another unexpected event: the election into the Knesset (Israel's parliament) of the late Rabbi Meir Kahane, an extreme religious fundamentalist (assassinated November 5, 1990). Nearly 26,000 (1.3 percent) Israelis voted for Kach (Thus), the political party that called for the expulsion of the Arabs from historical Palestine, and 2.5 percent of Israeli soldiers were among them. Almost everybody remembered that it was Kahane who since 1974 had advocated publicly Terror Neged Terror (TNT), which in his terminology stood for Jewish terrorism versus Arab terrorism.[2]

The astonished Israelis did not have to wait long in order to discover what the new party was about. A day after the elections, Kahane and his supporters held a victory parade to the Western Wall in old Jerusalem. Passing intentionally through the Arab section of the old city, Kahane's excited followers smashed through the market, overturning vegetable stalls, hitting bystanders, punching the air with clenched fists, and telling the frightened local residents that the end of their stay in the Holy Land was near. This kind of street brutality has been repeated many times since especially following anti-Jewish terror incidents. But instead of being shocked by what until that time could only have been seen in old newsreels of pre-1945 central Europe or in modern scenes from Teheran, some Israelis liked what they saw. Since the mid-1980s, the number of supporters of Kahane's political stance has increased by a great amount. Polls conducted as of summer 1984 have steadily given Kahane and his advocates between 2.5 to 2.7 percent of the total vote. Several attitude studies of high school students indicate an exceptional support for Kahane among the young. A general atmosphere of forgiveness and "understanding" of the acts of the Jewish underground has also surfaced.[3]

A careful examination of the evolution of religious fundamentalism, extreme nationalism, and aggressive anti-Arab sentiment since 1984 suggests a rise that is neither accidental nor isolated. This examination tells us the story of a large political process that until now has not been properly identified and named, the reemergence of the Israeli Radical Right. Before the establishment of the State of Israel, there existed in Jewish Palestine a small ultranationalist school that propagated the creation of a monolithic Jewish regime and was hostile to the dominant Zionist socialism of the time. This school was strongly opposed to the partition of Palestine between Jews and Arabs and exerted some influence over the young. The actual partition of Palestine in 1948 and the establishment of Israel under the domination of the social democratic Mapai (later the Labor movement) was responsible for the great decline of this Radical Right and for its eventual demise. The

nationalist scene was monopolized by Herut (Freedom party, later expanded to the Likud), which was a more moderate political party. It now appears that the Israeli nationalist Right, which had been revitalized since the
Six Days' War (1967), has undergone a significant political and ideological
transformation. In the last decade and especially since 1984, it has gone
from a unified political and ideological force headed unquestionably by
Menachem Begin, the leader of Likud, to a camp fragmented both politically and ideologically.

The concept of the Radical Right developed in the United States is useful
in the Israeli context because groups like Kach and Gush Emunim do not fit
the traditional features of the Israeli nationalist Right, yet they are neither
revolutionary nor Fascist. The parties to this camp earnestly believe that
they are the true Israelis and the genuine Zionists. The purpose of this chapter is to identify the sequence of events that produced the Israeli Radical
Right, portray it as a political culture, and examine its political dynamics.

THE ULTRANATIONALIST LEGACY

In the mandate period the school most identified with the idea of a Radical
Right was the maximalist wing of revisionist Zionism, the ultranationalist orientation linked to organizations such as Brith Habirionim (the Covenant of
Thugs) and Lehi (Israel's Freedom Fighters, also known as the Stern Gang).
The old Radical Right was moved by two fundamental beliefs: that the British were oppressive rulers who had to be expelled from Palestine by force
and that the emerging Extreme Right of the time, with perhaps the exception of the Nazis, represented a viable ideology and a relevant model of political action. The early ideologues of this camp, Uri Zvi Greenberg, Abba
Achimeir, and Yehoshua Heshel Yevin, represented an impatient Zionism
that concluded that the British betrayed the Jews and abrogated the terms of
the 1917 Balfour Declaration. Fascinated by other nationalist movements,
especially the Italian, the Polish, the Czech, and the Irish, all of which had
reached independence through military effort, they concluded that the
British had to be expelled from Eretz Yisrael (the Land of Israel) by force.
The fact that the Jews in Palestine were a small ethnic minority of mostly new
immigrants and that a much larger native community questioned their very
right to the land was not allowed to interfere in the great dream. Since its in-
ception, this ultranationalist circle was characterized by a conviction that
strong will and determination constitute the most important political re-
source and that they alone could change the world.[4]

This small group of ultranationalist ideologues, which started to write and
preach in the late 1920s, was not philosophically homogeneous, for each
member constructed an individual brand of ultranationalism from different
historical and philosophical sources. Profoundly influenced by the growing

European Radical Right, they all agreed on a principled rejection of democracy and a hostility toward socialism. Zionist socialism was perceived as a threat to nationalism. Only the Hebrew nation and its future instrument of power, the Jewish state, were sacred. Thus, in addition to their rejection of the policies of the yishuv (Jewish community in Palestine) vis-à-vis the British, the revisionist ultranationalists were driven by an ideological animosity toward the workers' parties. There was another important ingredient in their thinking: a romantic return to the biblical past of the nation and the aspiration to reconstruct the days of the early Hebrews who took Canaan by force and extended it by military means to the large Davidic kingdom.[5] Most appealing to these revolutionaries was not the image of the self-sufficient Jewish farmer-pioneer, idolized by Labor Zionism, but rather the model of the Jewish fighter, the Hebrew national who takes the land by force.

By calling itself Brith Habirionim, after a faction of the first-century Zealots, the small group of Greenberg, Achimeir, and Yevin clearly communicated radicalism, antiestablishment sentiment, and defiance. The rebellion was not only directed against the British, the Arabs, and the Labor establishment but also against the religious orthodoxy for whom the concept of *birionim* was anathema because their ennoblement of the Jewish past was not Halakic or historical. It was above all a mythological rediscovery of the glorious tales of the nation, a romantic glorification of the old days of blood, soil, heroism, and conquest. The intellectuals of Brith Habirionim mostly wrote and preached, and in the early 1930s they were involved in several symbolic demonstrations against the British, Nazi Germany, and the Arabs.[6] Nevertheless, their politico-cultural influence was considerable. Another contribution to Zionist right-wing radicalism was made by Vladimir Jabotinsky, the founder and leader of the revisionist movement that split off from organized Zionism.[7] Jabotinsky's admiration for Great Britain and for the virtues of democracy, liberalism, and the rule of law was responsible for his refusal to completely fight the British and relieve them from the moral duty of establishing a Jewish state as implied in the Balfour Declaration.[8] Nevertheless, there were certain radical elements in his thinking and political style that made it possible for the members of Brith Habirionim and other radical groups to admire him and include his thought in their extremist weltanschauung.[9] Jabotinsky's most important contribution to these younger followers was his integral nationalism, the fervent belief that the nation is the supreme foundation of legitimate political action.[10] His support for civil liberties, individual freedoms, and a free economy was somewhat at odds with his nationalist rhetoric and mode of action, which stressed monism, militarism, discipline, order, and bitter defiance of Zionism.[11] Jabotinsky's youth movement, Betar, which became the main politicization agent of revisionist activists, pioneers, and fighters, was a semimilitaristic entity that stressed hierarchy, discipline, obedience to superiors, rituals, and ceremonies.[12] Betar members wore brown shirts and stressed military virtues as a symbol of national sovereignty and an expression of collective national liberation. Jabotinsky cultivated romantic heroism and national fighters who gave their lives for freedom. Old and new battle sites like Massada, Betar, and Tel Hai were made sacred pilgrimage sites for thousands of Betar youngsters.[13] Other components of Jabotinsky's program included the unconditional demand that the future State of Israel be established on both sides of the Jordan River, a penchant for militarism, economic corporatism, and a fervent antiLabor stance. As Yonathan Shapira has shown, it was highly appealing to a whole age cohort of Betar activists who grew up in Poland between the 1920s and 1930s under the spell of Joseph Pilsudski and the Polish Extreme Right.[14]

Yet as Sholomo Avineri has pointed out, Jabotinsky was fully aware of the tremendous weakness of the Jews[15] and could neither support the politics of Brith Habirionim nor the underground operations of Etzel (the National Military Organization, a nationalist semimilitary organization close to Betar) in the closing years of the 1930s. Betar started to drift away,[16] and especially Etzel, which since 1937 had been engaged in active anti-Arab terrorism, could not accept Jabotinsky's hesitancy. They opted for a more radical direction expressed by an active military struggle against the British and a belief in military solutions for political problems. In 1940 Abraham Stern (Yair) split away from Etzel, and established Lehi. The Stern Gang went underground and hoped to lead the entire Jewish liberation movement toward the creation of the "Kingdom of Israel" free of the British and Arabs.[17]

THE MARGINALITY
OF THE OLD RADICAL RIGHT

Although the post-1967 Radical Right clearly has strong "classical" Zionist roots, there is hardly any question that before the Six Days' War it was a marginal phenomenon. The main force within the yishuv had been Labor Zionism. The political and cultural dominance of the Labor movement and Zionist socialism over the Zionist venture in Palestine and the emerging Zionist polity has been the subject of many studies and books.[18] The ideas and programs of the Radical Right appealed to relatively few Zionists, who were politically persecuted. The 1933 assassination of Labor leader Haim Arlozoroff and the 1935 crisis within the World Zionist Organization began a long period of marginalization of the Zionist Right and Radical Right. The "secession" of Jabotinsky from the Zionist movement and the later establishment of the "secessionist" underground, Etzel and Lehi, led to intense delegitimization of the Zionist Right.[19] To be a "secessionist" in the early 1940s amounted to membership in illegitimate subversive bodies that were considered Fascist by the official interpreters of Labor Zionism. Probably no more than 10 percent to 15 percent of the yishuv supported the Right, and most of these supporters were not very radical.[20]

The success of Labor Zionism in building the Zionist "state in the making" further diminished the historical role of the Right and the Radical Right. Etzel and Lehi played an instrumental role in driving the British out of Palestine in the 1940s—a role that was greater than was recognized by "legitimate Zionism"—but their support for the building of the Jewish polity in Palestine was minimal at best.[21] They made almost no contribution to the self-governing institutions of the state and to building the economic infrastructures of the yishuv,[22] and took almost no part in the great diplomatic effort to gain legitimacy and support for the emerging Jewish state in the United States and the post-Holocaust world. Furthermore, they were ill prepared to meet the real challenge of the newly created state: the war with the Arabs. By focusing all its efforts on the British, the Israeli nationalist Right became irrelevant the moment the British left Palestine.

World War II, the Nazi and Fascist experience, and the Holocaust also contributed to the historical irrelevance of the Radical Right. In the 1930s the historical Radical Right was a relevant ideological school, seen by many as a viable alternative to world communism on the one hand and "decadent" liberal democracy on the other. Not only the Polish Radical Right but also Italian fascism were highly attractive for the radical wing of the revisionist movement. The Fascist appeal was partly responsible for Abraham Stern's bizarre 1941 effort to form an anti-British alliance with the Axis powers.[23] The experience of the war and especially the Holocaust destroyed the fascination of fascism for the vast majority of the world. The loss of the war was also an ideological disaster for world fascism, driving it at once to the very margins of modern civilization. This was even more the case for Jews and Zionists. Very few ultranationalists remained loyal to their prewar political platforms, and many of them began to deny ever being close to the European Radical Right.

The 1947 United Nations Partition Resolution, the 1948 war of independence and the establishment of the State of Israel made the grand vision of the Radical Right rather unrealistic. It was therefore natural that despite some bloody incidents between Etzel and the new Israeli army, Etzel's political successor, Herut, became part of the Israeli parliamentary system.[24] Mapai's shrewd politicians constantly used Herut's past radicalism, extremist rhetoric, and commitment to the dream of "Shtei gadot laYarden zo shelanu zo gam ken" (There are two banks to the Jordan River, this one is ours and the other, too)—a principled rejection of the partition of Eretz Yisrael and the aspiration for a military conquest of the Kingdom of Jordan—to keep it out of the pale of complete legitimacy.[25] In September 1948, Lehi veterans committed their last defiant terrorist act, the assassination of Count Folke Bernadotte, the UN mediator in Palestine, and then gave up their underground life and in 1949 joined the new system. Organizing in the form of the Fighters party, they implied at least a partial recognition of the newly created Israeli state and its norms.[26]

The only organized component of the Radical Right that remained loyal to the old ideology and continued to function after 1949 was a small ideological group, Chug Sulam (Ladder Circle). Organized by Israel Eldad, a devotee of Greenberg and a former chief ideologist of Lehi, Chug Sulam vowed to preserve the dream of the greatest Kingdom of Israel. For that purpose, it published a highly ideological magazine, *Sulam,* and organized educational and ideological activities for youth. Completely detached from the historical reality of the newly created State of Israel, *Sulam* printed anti-British articles "exposing" the British intention to reoccupy Palestine via Jordan, antiregime articles attacking the decadent party system of the truncated Jewish state, and essays on the indivisibility of Eretz Yisrael and its promised borders. In an age of prestigious democracy, it called for the installation of a Jewish dictatorship and for a war of conquest against most of the new state's neighbors. The celebration of Israel's independence day was occasionally ended by the call "next year in Amman" (Jordan's capital).[27]

Chug Sulam's total isolation from the nation's public life and most Israeli citizens did not prevent the establishment, in the early 1950s, of two small underground groups that vowed to topple the regime: Brith Hakanaim (Covenant of Zealots) and Machteret Malchut Yisrael (Kingdom of Israel Underground). The first operated between 1949 and 1951 and was mostly interested in fighting the secular character of the new state; the second acted between 1951 and 1953 and was involved in "defending and uplifting" the national honor. Both groups were captured by the Shin Beth (Israel's secret service) before they caused major damage, but they left an impact nevertheless. Whereas Brith Hakanaim burned nonkosher butcher shops and set ablaze cars that were being driven on the Sabbath, the Kingdom of Israel Underground was involved in larger operations. Reacting to the 1952 doctors' trial in Moscow, it blew up the Soviet consulate in Tel Aviv and did the same to the Czech consulate following the Slansky purge trials in Prague. Following the intense public debate over the German reparations, the group conducted several symbolic attacks against artists performing German music.[28]

But the arrest of the members of this radical underground and the growing irrelevance of Chug Sulam to the problems faced by the State of Israel of the 1950s slowly brought about the final decline of the Israeli Radical Right. The army's aggressive retaliation operations against enemy targets in Jordan and Egypt in the first half of the 1950s, the 1956 Sinai campaign, and David Ben Gurion and Chief of Staff Moshe Dayan's hawkish posture became attractive to many people who had rightist tendencies and backgrounds. The illustrious operations of Commando Unit 191, and later the Israeli paratroopers under the command of Major Ariel Sharon, provided the old ultra-nationalists with new myths of Israeli heroism.[29] The publication of *Sulam* was discontinued in the beginning of the 1960s and Eldad became a full-time professor of biblical Jewish history at Technion College in Haifa. His devoted follower, Geula Cohen, started to write for Israel's daily *Maariv*, and the old Radical Right became passé. Neither its devoted ideologues nor its historical adversaries expected it to be resurrected.

THE RISE OF THE
POST-1967 RADICAL RIGHT

The Israeli Radical Right was reborn on September 17, 1978. On that day, when Menachem Begin signed the famous accords with Egypt, he gave a kiss of death to the unity of the Israeli nationalist Right. His agreement to return all of Sinai to the Egyptians, as well as his initiation of the Autonomy Plan (for the Palestinians of the West Bank), struck many of his political and ideological allies like bolts out of the blue. For many years these people had led themselves to believe that Begin, as the great champion of undivided Eretz Yisrael, was their safest assurance against territorial compromise with the Arabs. Most of them, not traditional supporters of Begin, were gradually swept into his political camp, which had gained national fame and legitimacy following 1967. In 1977 they were all thrilled when after thirty years of political opposition their man finally made it to the top. Immediately following his election, Begin pledged to have "many more Elon Morehs." Elon Moreh was the most controversial Gush Emunim illicit settlement in the West Bank. Located in the heartland of the Arab populated Samaria, it was never officially recognized by the previous Labor administration. The pledge signified Begin's total commitment to the settlement of all Eretz Yisrael.[30]

Most of the groups that were to form the new Radical Right had a distinct identity prior to 1978. The most influential among them was the Land of Israel Movement (LIM). This movement, a direct offspring of the Six Days' War, did not draw its ideas from the traditional ideology of Vladimir Jabotinsky—the fountainhead of Begin's convictions. Rather, it was a newly born ultranationalist creature that brought together strange bedfellows: religious fundamentalists, military hard-liners, and labor-settlement fanatics. As diverse as the LIM people were, they shared two politico-ideological characteristics that set them apart from other political schools: an immense confidence in Israel's might and a total suspicion of the Arabs. "Peace for peace" was their political slogan. It amounted to the proposition that under no conditions should Israel respond to an Arab proposal for peace by territorial concessions.[31]

The Land of Israel Movement was not the only component of the would-be Radical Right. Two other organized entities joined its elderly true believ-

ers in the 1970s: Gush Emunim and Kach. Gush Emunim was established as
an independent movement in 1974. Its members were never fully detached
from the LIM, and some of their spiritual authorities belonged to the found-
ers of this movement. But there existed a major sociological difference between the two. The leading figures of the Land of Israel Movement were elderly secular notables, well known and established in Israel's public life,
whereas the Gush people were young, inexperienced, and fresh. Totally religious, messianic, and fundamentalist in their beliefs, they introduced a new
component to the life of the nationalist Right, operational messianism.[32] In
the settlement of Judea and Samaria they saw not only a political act but a religious and metaphysical commandment. According to their theology, pioneering settlement meant a direct contribution to the imminent process of
redemption. It was consequently carried out with utmost enthusiasm and
total devotion. No wonder that the new spirit soon lighted the hearts of
many Israelis, right-wing and non-right-wing alike. Many Labor veterans, especially from kibbutzim and moshavim (collective and cooperative villages),
were deeply moved. For years these people had been longing for the lost old
spirit of Zionist pioneering. Charmed by the new mystique of Gush
Emunim, they did not care a great deal about the full politico-religious message of the new movement.

Although the official establishment of Gush Emunim did not take place
until 1974, Rabbi Meir Kahane appeared on the scene in 1971. Kahane, the
former head of the vigilante Jewish Defense League (JDL) in the United
States, established the Israeli branch of the JDL, which was later to become
Kach. Less than a year after his arrival, he discovered the Arab issue and
never let it go. By 1973 the well-known pattern of provocative visits to Arab
villages was established. Kahane, surrounded by several followers, would go
to an Arab town, demand to talk to its *muchtar* (village head), and deliver the
message that there was no room for Arabs in the Holy Land.

Although the Land of Israel Movement, Gush Emunim, and Kach maintained their organizational and ideological independence, they had one
common thread: a great admiration for Menachem Begin. This ardent nationalist had become their chief flag captain. In the elections of 1973, the
LIM, including former Labor members of the movement, endorsed Begin.
This was a watershed. One of the oldest legacies in Zionist history, the hatred between Labor and revisionism, was overcome. Gush Emunim had also
become close to this old commander of Etzel. The movement, initially a faction within the National Religious party (NRP), severed these ties a short
time after its establishment. Unhappy with the NRP's partnership in a Labor
government that did not pursue a total "Israelization" of Judea and Samaria, the youngsters of Gush Emunim decided to abandon politics and
concentrate on settlement.[33] No such frictions, on this issue or others, existed with Begin, the leader of the opposition. He was a frequent visitor of

their illicit settlements. In time he would describe them as his "dear children."

Of all the would-be Radical Right, Kahane alone did not endorse the Likud in the elections of 1973 and 1977 but was a devotee of Begin, whom he saw as the true successor of Jabotinsky and the spirit of Betar.[34] Kahane was an old Betar man. In 1947 in Brooklyn, he picketed Ernest Bevin, the hated British foreign minister who was responsible for pro-Arab politics in Palestine. This demonstration led to Kahane's first arrest under the banner of Betar.[35] His races for the Knesset in 1973 and 1977 were not directed against Begin but were meant to strengthen Begin's hand in the Knesset. He argued that he, as an orthodox rabbi, was capable of introducing a genuine nationalist religious party, one that could stand by Begin without selling out to Labor.[36] Kahane's reaction to Begin's 1977 election was total jubilation:

> For the first time since its establishment, the State of Israel has as its prime minister potential a man who thinks like a Jew, acts like a Jew, faces television with a yarmulke on his head, and actually speaks the "one little word" that we have waited to hear from the lips of Ben Gurion, Sharett, Eshkol, Golda, Rabin, and Peres. Menachem Begin, the potential prime minister of Israel, faces the nation and the world and thanks God, the one little word that the polysyllabic Eban finds impossible to pronounce. And he reads from Psalms and thanks the Almighty. Miracle? Miracle of miracles.[37]

The Camp David accords turned out to be a historic moment of truth. For the vast majority of the nationalist Right, Begin became a superhero. In less than a year the man had done the impossible. He first defeated the Left in the elections and later stole the whole "peace show" from their hands. For the minority, he instantly became a traitor, an imposter who either could not stand the pressures of the Gentiles or was never truly loyal to the nationalist legacy. They could never trust him or most of his Likud again.

The rise of the Radical Right from the ashes of Camp David was slow and tortuous. It was not easy to confront in public the immense elation of the majority of Israelis or to challenge the victorious prime minister. Several leaders of Gush Emunim were stunned. Camp David signified for them a religious affront of the first degree. It meant an inexplicable delay of national redemption, something they could not believe to be possible. Some of them renounced their Gush Emunim activity for a while and went back to their yeshivoth for several months of reflection and soul-searching.[38] But despite this first shock, the potential radicals survived. They apparently had sufficient stamina to endure and to start on a course based on strong political and ideological foundations.

The structure of the present-day Radical Right was shaped by three overlapping beginnings that took place at the end of 1978. The creation of Banai (the covenant of Eretz Yisrael's loyalists) and the establishment of the Tehiya (Renaissance) party, the ideological break of Kahane with Begin, and the crisis within Gush Emunim that produced (among other developments) the Jewish underground. At the time only the emergence of Banai was noticeable, but the other developments were to play a significant role.

Established on November 1, 1978, as a direct response to the "betrayal" of Menachem Begin, Banai-Brith Ne'emanai Eretz Yisrael (Covenant of Eretz Yisrael Loyalists) was a large coalition composed of prominent members of the Land of Israel Movement, Ein Vered circle (kibbutzim and moshavim supporters of the maximalist cause), Gush Emunim, and the Loyalists of Herut's Principles. Representatives of the settlers in northern Sinai and a small student organization named False Peace also joined.[39] At first, the movement did not consider itself a political association with electoral aspirations. It only tried to alert the public to the grave error Begin had committed. Its very establishment, however, indicated a significant political break. It was the first internal ideological revolt against the founding father of the party. Some of the rebels, the Loyalists of Herut's Principles, were old revisionists. They challenged Begin in the sacred name of Jabotinsky. Their leader, Gershon Solomon, was a distinguished representative of Herut (Begin's own party) in the municipal council of Jerusalem. Upon the prime minister's return from Camp David to Jerusalem, Solomon met him at the city gate carrying a large black umbrella, thus symbolically associating Begin's act with the shameful peace British prime minister Neville Chamberlain signed with Hitler in 1939.[40] The new movement operated on two levels. It organized public demonstrations in the streets of Israel's main cities and, in a desperate attempt to bring the nationalist Right back to its senses, lobbied within the Likud and NRP. But on March 29, 1979, any illusion of retreating from the Camp David accords disappeared. Menachem Begin, Anwar Sadat, and Jimmy Carter signed the official peace treaty in Washington. The only hope left for the opponents of the treaty was to take the issue to the Israeli voter. Yuval Neeman, a noted scientist, took the lead. Following Neeman's call, more than 1,000 people signed on to take political action. Gershon Shafat and Hanan Porat of Gush Emunim were highly supportive, and there was a growing interest in other circles. When the new religious-secular effort of professor Ne'eman got the blessing of Rabbi Zvi Yehuda Kook, the revered mentor of Gush Emunim, the other hesitant elements opposed to Camp David joined in. They established the Tehiya, a party totally devoted to the delegitimization of Camp David.[41]

The Camp David accords also had a profound impact on the stature of Meir Kahane. In the 1970s the vigilante rabbi was a very marginal figure. Only a small cabal of young, former American JDL members and Russian immigrants followed him. His efforts to establish in Jerusalem an influential ideological center under the title Jewish Idea were largely frustrated by lack of funds and supporters. The creation of Gush Emunim in 1974 and the highly acclaimed pioneering activities of its members left little room for Kach's self-styled radicalism before the accords with Egypt. But after Camp David, the previously admired prime minister of Israel became a traitor. By succumbing to the pressure of the Gentiles, "substituting fear of the finite gentile for Jewish faith in the God of creation and history," he had committed *hillul hashem,* "the humiliation and desecration of the name of God" to be fearful of the Gentiles.[42] Kahane was finally relieved of his former ideological allegiance to the successor of Jabotinsky. He was now free from an additional bond: the remainder of his loyalty to Israel's democracy. Kahane, it is true, had never been a great champion of democracy. But as long as he believed that a legally elected government under Begin was capable of solving the pressing problems of Eretz Yisrael, he maintained some allegiance to the system. Now it was all gone. Begin had proven himself part of a rotten system and the whole secular framework was corrupt. The post-1978 Kahane became a different political animal. Racial overtones entered his terminology as well as the operations of his followers. The first ideological target became Israel's declaration of independence. The 1948 document, which promised equal rights to all the inhabitants of the Jewish state, race, religion, and nationality notwithstanding, was now presented by Kahane as a contradictory document. Israel could not be Jewish and democratic at the same time because that meant political equality for too many hostile Arabs. So it had to be just Jewish.[43] Kahane's people in Kiryat Arba, the Jewish city adjacent to Hebron, acted accordingly. They accentuated their positions vis-à-vis the Arabs and became prime catalysts in the growing Jewish, anti-Arab violence in the area.[44]

The most extreme reaction to the Camp David accords was the crisis within Gush Emunim that resulted in the secretive establishment, in 1978, of what became known in 1984 as the Jewish underground. Until 1980, the only issue on the agenda of the group was the blowing up of the "abomination," the Muslim Dome of the Rock. The idea was brought up by two exceptional individuals, Yeshua Ben-Shoshan and Yehuda Etzion. Although both were closely affiliated with Gush Emunim and its settlement drive, neither was a typical member. More than most of their colleagues, they were intensely preoccupied with the mysteries of the process of regeneration that was about to bring the Jewish people, perhaps in their own lifetime, to its redemption. The two convinced themselves that the historic setback of Camp David must have had a deeper cause than Begin's simple weakness. It may have been a direct signal from heaven that a major national offense had been committed, a mistake that was responsible for the political disaster. Only one prominent act of desecration could match the magnitude of the setback: the presence, sanctioned by the government of Israel, of the "infidels" and their shrine on the Temple Mount, the holiest Jewish site, the sacred place of the first, second, and third (future) temple.[45]

Students of messianic movements have long noted that millenarian types are driven to extreme and antinomian acts when the imminent process of redemption is suddenly stalled. They become convinced that an exceptional operation is needed in order to calm the Lord's anger. Only such an action can restore the messianic process and ensure its consummation.[46] This psychological mechanism was probably involved in the Temple Mount plan. But the plan had an additional goal: Its perpetrators believed that it would ruin the peace treaty between Israel and Egypt and stop the evacuation of Sinai.[47] Following several tête-à-têtes between Etzion and Ben-Shoshan in which they cautiously studied the possibility of an operation on the Temple Mount, the two decided to extend the circle. They brought in several trusted friends. Three years were devoted to preparing the operation, and in 1982, just prior to the final Israeli retreat from Sinai, everything was ready. The plan, however, was shelved, because none of the rabbis with whom they consulted approved of the idea.

But though the Temple Mount operation was postponed indefinitely, other acts did take place. When six yeshiva students were brutally murdered by Arab terrorists in Hebron in May 1980 and a general outcry for revenge emerged in the community, it was only natural that Terror Neged Terror would strike, its members already having conspired to commit a major act of terror. Seeing it as a way to restore law and order at once, they attempted to assassinate the mayors of several Arab cities. With the same conviction—the belief that they, as the most dedicated, idealistic and pure had to fulfill the act[48]—some of these people attacked the Muslim college of Hebron in 1983 and prepared in the same year to blow up five Arab buses.

An event that greatly shaped the identity and style of the emerging Radical Right was the struggle of the Movement to Halt the Retreat in Sinai (MHRS). Mostly a Gush Emunim entity, the MHRS was organized at the end of 1981. It came into being following Begin's success in the elections of that year and the failure of the Tehiya to stop the peace process at the polls. The messianic members of Gush Emunim stepped in when all hopes for a secular solution faded. Armed with their illicit settlement experience of the previous decade, they convinced themselves that immense dedication and self-sacrifice could entice God to stop the evacuation of Sinai and prevent the self-imposed destruction of Jewish settlements. In line with Gush Emunim's tradition, the settlements of the Rafiah Salient in Sinai were flooded with colleagues from the West Bank. They came with their families, rabbis, yeshivoth, and logistics. All the veteran settlers, the heroes of the extralegal settlement of the early 1970s, were there. They prayed, conducted Torah courses, and were determined to reconstruct normal life in the area as if no evacuation were to take place in less than six months. It was an unparalleled show of faith and conviction.[49] All three Knesset members of Tehiya joined the struggle and settled in Yamit.

But Begin was determined to keep his word and was backed by his minister of defense, Ariel Sharon, a former ally of Gush Emunim. A full 20,000 experienced soldiers were mobilized for the evacuation, which only miraculously ended with no fatalities. Nevertheless, fierce struggles between soldiers and desperate settlers resulted. Distinguished rabbis were beaten up. Laws, rules, and formal regulations were systematically disregarded. The Israeli public witnessed the longest and most intense period of civil disobedience and organized extralegalism in the history of the state. Several members of the MHRS seriously considered armed resistance, and others suggested mass suicide. Twelve followers of Kahane locked themselves in an underground shelter full of gas tanks and explosives and threatened to blow themselves up. Begin had their rabbi rushed in from the United States and flown to Yamit by a special military helicopter in order to convince his devotees to give in.

When Yamit was finally evacuated on April 28, 1982, the exact date set by the peace treaty, it was clear that Begin's grand move was successful. However, it was also the coming of age of a new political camp and culture, a conglomerate of activists and movements whose loyalty to Israel's traditional foundations was significantly limited. The leaders and followers of the MHRS, who were taken from the scene bitter and frustrated, left no doubt that the struggle in Yamit had been a lesson. It was a warning of what would be done if the government of Israel ever conceived of territorial concessions in Judea and Samaria. The increased electoral strength of the Tehiya in the elections of 1984 (five Knesset members), the election of Kahane, and the growing support for "Kahanism" in the streets brought the large extremist movement into full swing.

CULTURE

Each of the responses to the Camp David accords was to evolve on its own course. But with time and against the background of a stagnating peace with Egypt, a sick Begin, a failing economy, and the fiasco in Lebanon, these responses also led to the formation of an unprecedented radical rhetoric and unrestrained street behavior. Extreme attitudes regarding the land and the Arabs, special expressions implying war and a never-ending struggle against the terrorism of the Palestine Liberation Organization (PLO), enthusiastic utterances about redemption, and a constant siege mentality have in recent years expanded upon the nationalist rhetoric of Herut's "New Zionism."[50] For a sizable public, these attitudes have produced more than a bitter mood; they have created a unique political and cultural life-style.

Within the nationalist camp, the Israeli Radical Right is presently a great deal more than the movements that are directly associated with it. It is a general climate of opinion and constitutes a syndrome of political behavior. It crosses party lines, economic divisions, and educational strata. The Israeli Radical Right is today again an integral part of the thriving general nationalist camp. But five salient themes, which bring together theory, practice, and special symbols, set it apart from the larger right-wing camp that wants Eretz Yisrael to remain undivided.

First, there is the nostalgia for the prestate Zionist community. In contrast to the popular image promoted by its rivals, the Israeli Radical Right is not Fascist. The political and social model that appeals to most of its leaders is neither drawn from foreign ideologies nor caters to antibourgeois, antiparliamentary, or antidemocratic ideas. It is instead a model of a limited democracy taken from the past, from the era that preceded the 1948 formation of Israel. Most of the leaders and followers of the Israeli Radical Right cherish the memories of the Zionist founding fathers, their values, and their behavior. Just like those members of the American Radical Right who constantly go back to the founding fathers, the Constitution, the rugged individualism of the time before Franklin D. Roosevelt, and the "American way of life," the Israeli radicals are nostalgic about the old days of the yishuv, the days when each Zionist settlement counted and Hagana (Defense Force) was a real thing; the times when Jews worried about Jews, not about Arabs. As Rabbi Moshe Levinger, Gush Emunim's settler number one, describes it, "In the old days Labor people have worked for settlement, immigration, security and peace with our neighbors. Today the political program of Labor has only one item, an agreement with the neighbors."[51]

The spokespersons of the Israeli Radical Right, very much like right-wing radicals in other countries, do not really understand what has become of their people, what corrupted them and turned them so soft, so liberal, and so pluralistic. They see themselves as perfect Zionists, the true inheritors of the old, prestate yishuv. Many of them also consider themselves good democrats or, more precisely, good Jewish democrats.[52] The Zionist yishuv, they argue, was established in a democratic way and was operated as a democracy. But everybody functioned in the framework of a limited democracy and did not think in terms of universal pluralism. The Zionist founding fathers were, therefore, not antidemocratic, but they were no fools either. Instead of reciting John Stuart Mill or John Dewey all day long, they set out to build a viable polity for their own people. The conclusion of this line of thinking is thus very clear. When the legal and duly elected government of Israel stands in violation of the primary tenets of Zionism, it has to be resisted just as the legal British government was resisted in the 1930s and 1940s by the Zionist founding fathers. Its "anti-Zionist" acts have to be overruled just as similar acts of the official organizations of the yishuv itself were overruled by zealous pioneers. "How is it possible to act against the government and the law?" asks an anonymous writer in an early Gush Emunim information leaflet, and answers:

> All through the history of yishuv, settlements were established as a result of a grassroots pressure, and official approval was only granted later. Ein Harod was established with no official license in 1921. ... Following the Six Days' war, settlements in the Golan Heights, Gush Etzion, and Kiryat Arba were formed in this way. ... The same procedure has been reactivated in the settlement of Keshnet near Kuneitra. ... Blocking Jewish settlement in Eretz Yisrael, by force, is graver when it is committed by a Jewish government than by foreign rule.[53]

The attachment to the yishuv era and to its political style, however, is not concrete but selective and normative. The leaders and the ideologues of this camp do not really want to go back to the old presovereign days. What attracts them is that aspect of the value system of the early days that prescribed and helped operate a framework of Zionist norms free of legalistic barriers and excessive democratic obsessions.

The second theme that distinguishes the Israeli Radical Right from the right wing in general is a religious fundamentalism or a secular neofundamentalism. The Israeli Right, like several similar movements in other countries, contains a prestigious fundamentalist element. The embodiment of this component is Gush Emunim and its ideology. This orientation is also evident in Kahane's writings. The special attraction of Emunim's belief in the fundamental truths of the Bible is that it is a partial system. It concentrates almost exclusively on the territorial sacredness of the "Kingdom of Israel in the making," which is the status of the present State of Israel. Unlike the ultraorthodox anti-Zionist fundamentalists, who live by every single rule of medieval Halakah as if the state did not exist and the world had not changed, the fundamentalists of Gush Emunim are modern, nationalist, and pragmatic.[54] They are full of admiration for the state and the instruments of its sovereignty—the government and the military. Their fundamentalism commands them to sanctify every single grain of soil that God promised to Abraham. It tells them that they are living in an age of redemption in which it is mandatory to follow the course of the great biblical conquerors, Joshua and King David. It requires them to become pioneers and personally to settle all the territories of Eretz Yisrael that were recovered by the Joshuas of our time. Benny Katzover, a leading figure in Gush Emunim, illuminated the group's special territorial fundamentalism: "In every age and time, there is one point, a special point, through which all that is good sheds light. ... In the beginning of the messianic age, the critical point is Eretz Israel and everything else derives from it. Without its settlement no holiness operates in the world."[55]

This new fundamentalism fits perfectly the psychology of many secular maximalists and the people who are nostalgic about the old Zionist community. The majority of these people, who were very active in pioneering settlement and defense in the prestate era, are charmed by the vigor and vitality of the youngsters of Gush Emunim's theology from a nonorthodox angle. The main proposition of the neofundamentalist school is that Zionism, though secular, was never devoid of deeply seated religious beliefs. It had been preceded by centuries of aspirations of returning to Eretz Yisrael. The theologians of Gush Emunim, the late rabbis Kook (father and son), had discovered the correct formula for future political Zionism according to neofundamentalist thinking. Arguing that the secular Zionists are as legitimate partners in the process of redemption as orthodox Jews, they made it possible for orthodox and nonorthodox Jews to ally and strive together for national grandeur.[56]

Third is the legitimation of radical right direct action and illegal practices. Students of the history of Israel's right-wing radicals are familiar with the methods of political protest, illicit settlement, and civil disobedience the radicals have introduced since 1973.[57] But they also remember that in the beginning and the mid-1970s, this camp was inexperienced and uncertain. Gush Emunim, whose theology had always expressed a great respect for the government, was highly apologetic. Its leaders conducted many soul-searching sessions in which a genuine attempt was made to limit excesses to the very minimum. Menachem Begin, for example, at that time the leader of the opposition, was especially equivocal. On the one hand he truly loved the youngsters of the Gush and visited some of their illicit settlements, but on the other he maintained a great respect for the rule of law and avoided many other settlements.[58] For most of the members of the Gush, the Camp David accords terminated the period of uncertainty. It was now clear to the growing Radical Right that efforts to maintain its grip on the totality of Eretz Yisrael had to involve a great amount of extralegalism. The parliamentary nationalist Right could no longer be trusted, and the land had to be defended by all available methods. In 1982 all the Tehiya Knesset members went down to resettle Yamit. By their very action they introduced a new doctrine that implied that illegal extraparliamentarianism, just as legal parliamentary action, was a legitimate avenue of action. The new doctrine has, since the retreat from Sinai, been widely applied. It became the guideline of Kahane's actions in the streets and has led many other Israelis to disregard law and order.

The extralegal doctrine of the Radical Right, which matured between 1979 and 1984, had a by-product that also emerged at that time: the settlers' conception of self-defense and vigilantism. Despite the successful attempts of the Likud government to intensify the Jewish settlement in Judea and Samaria, the settlers underwent in those years a crisis of confidence with the

cabinet and especially with Minister of Defense Ezer Weizman. Arab violence and terrorism in the West Bank had intensified a great deal, and the
settlers argued that because the state was not defending them, they were entitled to do it on their own. They developed a vigilante philosophy that prescribed that every Arab act they considered illegal called for retaliation. An
investigative report written by the state deputy attorney, Judith Karp, in 1982
revealed a comprehensive system of Jewish reprisals and retaliations.[59] The
whole phenomenon was verified by an academic study published in 1984. Of
a random sample of settlers, 68 percent answered positively to the question,
"Is it necessary for the settlers to respond independently and swiftly to Arab
attacks on settlers and settlements?" The 13 percent that disagreed represented a minority opinion that was occasionally heard but was increasingly
isolated.[60] Settlers' raids of Arab towns and villages, in reaction to previous
acts of terrorism, have become a common West Bank practice.

The extralegal attitude of the radicals reached its peak in the fall of 1985.
When Moetzet Yesha (the council of the settlements in Judea, Samaria, and
Gaza) learned about the prime minister's new initiative for peace (which involved the possibility of further territorial concessions), it issued the unprecedented warning that any Israeli government that would give up Jewish territories would lose its legal basis.[61] Elyakim Haetzni, a prominent attorney
who stood behind the pronouncement, did not hesitate to tell Prime Minister Shimon Peres that a territorial concession would put him in the position
of French general Pétain, who collaborated with the Nazis in World War II
and was later tried for treason.[62]

Finally, there were the themes of militarism and a belief in the use of
force. A leading segment within the Israeli Radical Right was convinced that
Israel's immense military might could be translated at any given moment
into political power and national achievements. A quick examination reveals that the source of this conviction goes back twenty years, to the Six
Days' War. The 1967 campaign, in which three Arab armies were defeated in
six days, proved that Israel was a major power and that a well-coordinated
military operation could change the balance of power in the area. For the
fundamentalist elements of the Radical Right, Israel's might does not require a rational explanation. In the age of redemption, in which the nation
is expected to reclaim the land, God is definitely standing behind the army.
This is, for example, the reason Kahane believed that it was *hillul hashem* (the
desecration of the name of God) to be fearful of the Gentiles.[63]

The secular neofundamentalists, in contrast, do not need the religious argument. Zahal (Israel Defense Force) is for them a highly qualified and well-
trained army that can beat any combination of its enemies at any given time.
The military setbacks that took place in the Yom Kippur War were caused by
a nonrepeatable combination of surprise attack and erroneous operation of
the army. Against all these odds, the war was won militarily. The same thing

happened in Lebanon in 1982. Had the army been led by a determined government, the war would have been terminated by a great victory and with the possible annexation of biblical Jewish territories.

Thus for the militaristic school of the Radical Right, there is only one explanation why the great potential of the nation is not realized. Israel's political life is dominated by a handful of leftists, Zionists without vision, and weak and hesitant individuals. The ranks of the people who do not stand up to the greatness of the nation are not only manned by Labor and left politicians but also by Likud members who are scared of their own shadows. Israel, according to this school, has never been so strong. Had military force been used correctly, the Jewish state would not now be in trouble. Judea and Samaria would have long since been annexed and PLO bases all around the Mediterranean destroyed. The Temple Mount's Muslim shrines would either have been demolished or kept under tight Israeli control and the "shameful escape" from Lebanon would have been prevented.[64]

The Israeli Radical Right, despite its consistent growth in power and popularity, is living a paranoid life. Its leaders and spokespersons are convinced that a conspiracy to betray the people of Israel and the destiny of Zionism is under way. Many political agents play leading roles in the grand conspiracy: the Jewish Ashafists (PLO members) who collaborate willingly with the enemy; the leftists who care about the sentiments of the international Left more than they do about their homeland; President Sadat (when he was alive), who "fooled" Israel into a phony peace; and the evil-mongers of the U.S. State Department. The result of all these evildoings is a Palestinization of the Jewish mind:

> Filastin [Palestine in Arabic] infiltrates Eretz Yisrael slowly through the radio and T.V. and not in the least through the military broadcasting system. Filastin is served by many of Israel's experts on the Middle East. Filastin has almost completely monopolized Israel's literature and poetry, theater and movies. Filastin does increasingly penetrate the schools and the youth movements and the army's chief educational officer invites Israelis, who are supportive of the Palestinian claim for rights in Eretz Israel (including Jerusalem), to "educate" the military. Former presidents of the World Jewish Congress are working hard to get money for Filastin and a helpful prime minister meets King Hussein's cousin, with whom Israel is in a state of war. ... A bridge for Filastin is constructed by thousands of Jewish demonstrators in "solidarity" protest in the midst of Ramaalla and Hebron and at the gates of Um-Al-Fahm and Ixal.[65]

It may of course be argued that because overt plans for territorial compromise with a Jordanian-Palestinian entity are constantly raised and discussed, fears such as those expressed above can be seen to be genuine. However, the writings and remarks of the spokespeople of the Radical Right disclose the difference. Most of the fundamentalists and neofundamentalists of this camp are unable to make the distinction between legitimate opposing schemes and conspiracy. Their political epistemology is not pluralistic but monistic. Their ideational world is simply divided between the children of light and the children of darkness. In such a world no room is left for legitimate opposition. Every political rival is a conspirator.

An outstanding example of the conspiracy mentality is the Radical Right view of the Israeli media. The spokespersons of the Radical Right are convinced that Israel's public television, the only channel in the country, is full of anti-Zionist leftists. These traitors project in their stories a negative image of the Right and instead of boosting public morale impair it greatly. The media are seen to be constantly presenting the case of the PLO and avoiding "constructive" national projections. They are responsible for Israel's lost war in Lebanon and for much of the present gloomy spirit of the nation. Elyakim Haetzni, a leading Tehiya activist and a Knesset member since 1990, reacted to a television interview with Shimon Peres: "The interviewers begged most of the political questions. But why the surprise? It was already pointed out by our Elders that a self-imprisoned person can never free himself from jail. Few television interviewers are people who are not imprisoned with Peres in the same spiritual and ideological jail of leftist, 'Peace Now-nics,' Jordano-Palestinian concepts."[66]

POLITICS

Although the Israeli Radical Right is gradually becoming a salient political culture, shared and espoused by many unrelated groups and individuals, it has at its core a very determined political infrastructure. The leaders of the movements that shaped the new culture know that as favorable as the Israeli political conditions have been to them in the last decade, nothing would have happened without their incessant struggle. They recognize just as well that none of their ultimate political goals have been secured and that the creeping annexation of the occupied territories has not yet reached the stage of irreversibility. This is the reason they continue to work hard and are today by far the most energetic ideological and cultural force in Israel. The radicals may not yet represent the majority of the nationalist Right, but their intensity and devotion make up for large numbers. These efforts help them create many "accomplished facts." Four movements or political schools—attracting only 5 percent of Israel's voters—shape the present and the future of the Radical Right: Gush Emunim, the Tehiya and its satellites, Kach, and those who might be called concealed radicals. Each of the groups and most of the individuals involved were active in the late 1970s when the Radical Right reemerged, but each has changed, grown up, and developed new perspectives. Thus despite some unavoidable internal conflicts and controver-

sies, the Radical Right is a functional system in which each of the components fulfills a different role and appeals to a different public.

Gush Emunim

Gush Emunim is by far the most dynamic component of the new radicalism.
Between 12,000 and 15,000 settlers in Judea, Samaria, and Gaza consider
themselves active members of this movement. Despite several recent internal conflicts that have damaged the political unity of the movement, Gush
remains a homogeneous revitalization movement held together by a cohe-
sive ideology, mutual sociocultural origins, common existential interests,
and shared aspirations.[67] Most of the members are well educated, idealistic,
and hardworking. They relate nearly every aspect of their daily lives to national goals and understand their existence in the context of a divine order.
The leadership of the movement is made up of talented and devoted individuals who bring together exemplary spiritual authority and first-class political performance.

As important as the spiritual devotion of the young members of Gush is,
the movement does not exist by enthusiasm alone. Its present power and influence are based on dozens of settlements and on a sophisticated organizational infrastructure. Ever since they assumed the mission of settling Judea
and Samaria, Emunim's leaders wanted to obtain legal status and institutional legitimacy. They were anxious to shed the youthful and adventurous
image that made them look like a belated youth movement during the
1970s. This goal was achieved during Begin's first administration. In 1978
Gush Emunim was allowed to establish Amanas (Covenant), an official and
state-supported settlement movement. By this very act it obtained the same
legal status as the prestigious kibbutzim and moshavim movements of Israel.
A civic legalization of Emunim's settlements as ordinary rural and regional
Israeli localities followed suit. The movement's most talented leaders, who
previously excelled as lawbreakers, became municipal and district officials
overnight, they and their councils entitled to state budgets and to alloca-
tions from the funds of the World Zionist Organization.[68]

Gush Emunim today is a great deal more than the political movement of
penniless true believers it was in the 1970s. From an organizational perspective it is a highly effective machine. Its members are spread out in many West
Bank settlements and control Moetzet Yesha, the actual government of the
West Bank. Through Moetzet Yesha and its regional councils, they are now
establishing economic corporations that could help them regain future independence from external constraints.[69] Moetzet Yesha, via its security committee, also has a say in military matters. Its experts, some of whom are ranking army officers in the reserves, maintain close contact with the military
government of the occupied territories. The settlers' opinion is heard and

attended to not because of its professional quality but because it reflects the attitude of those who are involved in the routine security of the area. Ever since 1979 this sensitive job has been handed out to the Regional Defense Unit, a local militia composed of armed settlers in the reserves. During the recent Arab uprising in the occupied territories, the settlers were kept constantly informed by the highest military authorities. The officials of Moetzet Yesha and the heads of Emunim's other organs are welcomed in the offices of the Knesset, the government, the administration, and the military. Several of their leaders, such as Hanan Porat and Gershon Shafat, have been Knesset members for years. This representation, and their very effective lobbying in the parliament and cabinet, make the Gush leaders partners to some of the most delicate political and military deliberations that take place.[70] No wonder that private interviews with these people reveal competence and self-confidence. Despite the historic setback of Camp David and the recent Palestinian uprising, most of Emunim's activists believe that they are, politically, in good shape and that their course is successful. At present unable to attract large numbers of new pioneering settlers or to get significant governmental support for newly planned settlements, they constantly strengthen their organizational infrastructure and are further developing existing settlements. Many of Emunim's members are scornful of Israel's established politicians and are certain about their ability to manipulate the system no matter which political party is in charge.[71]

Tehiya and Its Satellites

If Gush Emunim provides the radical right with pioneering quality and material resources, three political parties—the Tehiya (Renaissance), Tzomet (Crossroad), and Moledet (Homeland), together representing 5% of the nation in the Knesset—are its political spearhead. Tzomet and Moledet were formed in 1986 and 1987, respectively, as a result of disagreements within the Tehiya but have otherwise advocated the same ultranationalist views. They have also endorsed all the activities and positions of Gush Emunim. But there are, nevertheless, significant cultural and social differences between the Gush and its parliamentary supporters. Gush Emunim is a religious movement, solidified by a unique theology of national redemption, whereas the Tehiya and its satellites are basically heterogeneous secular parties. Their leaders are not religious, and all the political operations they conduct are explained in the context of secular symbols.[72] Two elements make this alliance possible: agreement on long-range goals and the neofundamentalism of many of the secular leaders. Many observers associate the radicalism of the parliamentary Radical Right with either the theology of Gush Emunim or the ultranationalist tradition of Lehi, whose main representative is outspoken Knesset member Geula Cohen. What they fail to recognize is that the dominant individuals in these parties identify with the prestigious tradition of Israel's Labor movement. The spokespersons of this school believe that they are the true successors of the "vigorous" David Ben Gurion (of the 1940s and 1950s).[73] They are convinced that the security of the State of Israel requires every single square inch of Eretz Yisrael, as well as a very tough stand vis-à-vis the Arabs. Raphael Eitan, the head of Tzomet and Israel's former chief of staff, is a typical representative of this school. He is an old Mapai man, a rugged moshavnik, who is ready to do whatever is necessary for security. If removal of an Arab village is needed in order to further advance the Jewish hold on the land, then it should be done, according to Eitan, "swiftly and without excessive noise."

A most controversial concept has been added to the slogans of the Israeli parliamentary Radical Right in 1987, the concept of transfer, a shorthand for the removal of the Palestinians of the occupied territories and their re-settlement in the neighboring Arab countries. The concept was first intro-duced by a retired general, Rehavam Zeevi, the leader of Moledet. Zeevi ar-gues that because the West Bank and Gaza are essential for the security of Israel and their 1.5 million hostile Palestinians are a mortal liability, the local residents have to be transferred out.[74] The introduction of the transfer to the nation's public agenda can be seen as a strong indication of the intense radicalization of the Extreme Right and its supporters. In 1984 there was only one party whose program called for the removal of the Arabs from the occupied territories; Kach of Rabbi Kahane. At that time everyone, includ-ing most of the spokespersons of the Radical Right, saw Kahane as a racist and believed that his opinions were beyond the pale of legitimacy. But dur-ing the middle of the 1980s, the public climate changed dramatically. The increasing friction between Jews and Arabs in the West Bank, the Palestinian uprising, as well as the intense Palestinization of the Israeli Arabs produced an atmosphere in which every radical solution became legitimate.

Kach

Whereas Gush Emunim and the parliamentary groups project the positive and creative face of the Radical Right in Israel, Kahane's movement, barred in 1988 from running for the Knesset, casts a hostile and negative image. Kach is a classical angry movement of protest, a right-wing backlash that is politically organized. The vast majority of the people who support Kahane have never read his books. They hardly know the man or his long-range goals. The movement has mostly been a one-man show that responds to events spontaneously and has a weak organization. Meir Kahane *was* the movement. He was the sole theoretician, its only public speaker, top orga-nizer, fund-raiser, and treasurer. There were many indications that his de-parture would mark the end of the movement.[75]

The recent decline of Kach, which is a direct result of the disqualification of the movement by Israel's supreme court, stands in some contradiction to the lingering popularity of Kahane's ideas and to the continuous functioning of his movement. A more general explanation for the Kahane phenomenon is therefore needed. Students of right-wing radicalism know the conditions likely to give rise to right-wing protest drives, which are neither anchored in a solid social class nor in significant economic resources. They know that what is mostly needed for the consummation of such drives are a prolonged sense of social alienation, a continuous period of economic insecurity, and the uneasy and threatening presence of an alien community.[76] It appears that the existence of a respectable right-wing radicalism, external threats, and military dangers also produce the conditions for the rise of a movement of this type. In the 1980s Israeli society experienced plenty of these conditions. The traditional social alienation of Jews from North Africa and the Far East and the security pressures of Arab terrorism have been joined by the grave agonies of economic insecurity and the political growth of a respectable Radical Right.[77] Kahane, who once lived in Israel's political wilderness, was able in the 1980s to emerge from his isolation not because of an ideological compromise on his behalf but as a result of the movement of the entire political culture in his direction. Extremist messages of racism and violence that were unheard of in the 1970s became acceptable in the 1980s. Kahane gradually became a legitimate vehicle for the enraged, the alienated, and the deserted. These people—the representatives of the weakest and most vulnerable stratum of Israeli society—could never be attracted by the cultural elitism of the Tehiya and Gush Emunim. For a long time they supported Likud. But following the retirement of Begin, the fiasco in Lebanon, and the economic blunders of their party, they discovered the eloquent rabbi.

The portrayal of the disqualified Kach as the protest component of the Radical Right does not exhaust the phenomenon. Right- wing protest movements vary a great deal. Kach, it appears, belongs to the quasi-Fascist breed that includes political groups that do not profess full ideological fascism but display typical Fascist behavior and politics. Kahane was never attracted by secular fascism. His belief system was always very religious and very Jewish. The special ideology that he carved out of his Betar training, rabbinical studies, and Brooklyn experience was always a mixed bag of fundamentalist readings of the holy scriptures, immense antiGentile sentiment, and an admiration of physical force. Today what makes Kach a quasi-Fascist phenomenon is not Kahane's ideology but Kahane's practice. The man was a combination of a very violent character with unrestrained ambitions. He was especially unable to separate strategy from tactics: The Arabs should be expelled *now;* Palestinian terrorism must be destroyed (by Israeli counterterrorism) *today;* the government, which does not do its job, ought to be brought down *tomorrow*. The sociopolitical result of this impatience cannot produce anything but Fascist behavior and politics. The syndrome is well known. It includes the preaching of vulgar Social Darwinism and antialien racism, a public legitimation of violence and terrorism, and a rapid shift from ideology to propaganda and from propaganda to smear campaign. It ends in street hooliganism and in the personality cult of the leader.[78] The quasi-Fascist nature of Kach has been most apparent since its 1988 disqualification. Followers of Kahane first formed an organization called the Independent State of Judea and later a secret assassin group named Sicarii. Although advocating typical Kahane ideas, both organizations gained notoriety for the application of unrestrained anti-Arab violence in the West Bank and for threatening moderate Israelis and issuing phony death sentences to Jews advocating direct talks with the PLO. Many of their activists have been detained and arrested.

The Concealed Radicals

Unlike the institutionalized movements of the Radical Right—Gush Emunim, the Tehiya and its satellites, and Kach—the fourth component of this camp, which I suggest naming the concealed radicals, has no formal existence. Its general ideological orientation lies somewhere between Kahane and Gush Emunim, but it is not yet clear whether its members will assume an independent existence or remain politically dispersed. Concealed radicals are people who, though they believe that Jewish moralists stand above conventional moralists and that the Arab question should be solved by deportation, do not propagate these views in public. They disapprove of the personality of the violent rabbi and were disgusted with his unpredictable drives, his rude style, and his vulgar propaganda. They think Kahane spoke too much and was therefore counterproductive. Things that may be done in ten, twenty, or thirty years (i.e., a possible expulsion of Arabs and a takeover of all the Temple Mount) should not be spelled out today.[79]

The concealed radicals come from the extremist circles of the settler community in Judea, Samaria, and Gaza and from former Kahane associates. Their radical approach is an ideological extension of the collective mood that was created by the crisis of Camp David, the struggle in Yamit, and the failure of the government to stop PLO terrorism in the West Bank. Many of the individuals who may be said to belong to this group did not study in Yeshivat Merkaz ha-Rav, the spiritual center of Gush Emunim, and were not students of Rav Zvi Yehuda Kook, the mentor of the movement. Thus they have little patience with what they perceive as Emunim's excessive homage to the Israeli government and its agencies. They are militant fundamentalists who trust the sword as much as they trust the book. Among them it is possible to identify some well-known rabbis such as Israel Ariel, the former cohead of Yamit's yeshiva, and Dov Lior, the cohead of Kiryat Arba's yeshiva. Several members of the Gush Emunim underground, like Yehuda Etzion and Menachem Livni, and some former Kahane supporters, such as Yoel Lerner and Yosef Dayan, also qualify as concealed radicals. A small Jerusalem youth movement, Hashmonaim, whose political activity rises and declines occasionally, may also be counted within this group.

The unorganized yet concrete existence of the concealed radicals is epitomized by the Jewish underground. It is clear today that the underground was not a hit squad of Gush Emunim, selected and operated by its heads in order to strike hard at the PLO centers in Judea and Samaria. Rather, it was a self-selected splinter group whose leaders had come to the conclusion that neither the government of Israel nor the settler community responded correctly to the post-1978 conditions. It is not clear how many of the concealed radicals were aware of the existence of the underground and of the theories of its leaders, but those who were not involved had entertained similar ideas in isolation. When the underground was exposed, the concealed radicals were thrilled. Although most members of Gush Emunim were greatly shocked and critical, the concealed radicals responded vigorously and in the summer of 1984 established a supporting association named Tzfia (Looking Ahead). They also started a new magazine under the same title and took upon themselves the job of challenging the moderate position of *Nekuda* (Point), the Gush Emunim–oriented journal of the settlers of Judea, Samaria, and Gaza. Yehuda Etzion, the leading spiritual force of the underground, has become an influential voice in *Tzfia*. In an exemplary act of moral support, Ephraim Caspi, the magazine's publisher, printed Etzion's account of his Temple Mount ideology.[80] In addition to supporting Etzion's "liberation theology," the magazine published extremist essays on the Arabs, on the need for a further territorial expansion, and on the misconduct of the Israeli government.

A typical concealed radical is Rabbi Ariel. In a private interview, he did not hide his opinion that it was high time for the nation to wage a war of conquest of all the biblical promised land (from the Euphrates to the Nile). Asked about current political constraints and diplomatic limitations, the rabbi replied that "Joshua had far worse political constraints and limitations but he did not question God's command to conquer the Land." When further pressed about potential casualties and national losses, the fundamentalist rabbi referred to a Halakic ruling that in a holy war no question about casualties is legitimate until one-sixth of the nation is extinct.[81]

At present the concealed radicals are not organized politically and cannot be seen as an active agent of political action. Some of them operate in the framework of the Temple Mount Loyalists, a small movement dedicated to the full Jewish return to the Temple Mount. Others collaborate with Kahane's people in several West Bank communities like Kiryat Arba, and still others teach and preach in their own yeshivoth or internal circles. Their impact and influence within the Radical Right should not, however, be underestimated. Theirs is a qualitatively distinct voice. In my opinion they form the potential nucleus that can play a critical role in times of national crisis. If the Radical Right is ever pushed to a final showdown, most probably in a situation of territorial compromise in the West Bank, they are likely to become the focus of armed resistance. The concealed radicals will draw the support of both Kahane's hard-liners, who would not trust the emotional and unstable rabbi, and Gush Emunim extremists. The concealed radicals of today may very well lead the real Sicarii of tomorrow.

The Impact of the Radical Right

Few observers, Israeli or non-Israeli, are prepared to recognize the magnitude of the new Israeli Radical Right and its influence on national politics. When faced with the attitudes of this camp and the operations of its members, they argue that it is made up of the lunatic fringe. As disturbing as these activities might be, so runs the argument, the Radical Right has no say in the government and its impact on critical national decisions is dismal at best. A formal examination of the case tends to support this proposition. The hard-core movements and parties of the Radical Right are small, young, and have relatively few economic assets. Their representation in the Knesset does not exceed 5 percent. They are no match for Israel's older and larger political parties such as Labor, Likud, the National Religious party, and even the smaller ultraorthodox parties of Agudat Israel and Shas. They cannot compete with the powerful Histadrut (General Federation of Labor) or challenge the old and prestigious kibbutz and moshav settlement movements.

But the proponents of this argument are missing three elements that make the Radical Right a most effective agent in present-day Israeli politics and culture: its sophisticated penetration of the larger parties, the exceptional determination of its members, and the strategic location of its constituency. One of the great successes of the Radical Right has been its ability to penetrate the Likud and National Religious party. Thus about 25 percent of the leaders of the Likud, and their followers, look at the world today through the ideological and symbolic prism of the Radical Right. The most outstanding representative of this Likud radical "rightism" is former cabinet member Ariel Sharon, a person with great charisma and a large following who thinks and talks like the ideologues of the Extreme Right and exerts a significant influence in the party's councils. The NRP, an old power broker in Israeli politics, has also been a target of the Radical Right, especially of the young and talented activists of Gush Emunim. Indeed, between 1986 and

1988 the NRP underwent a quiet ideological reshuffle that drove it to the bosom of the Radical Right. Two of the first three Knesset members of the NRP are devoted radicals, and its political platform reads almost like a Gush Emunim pamphlet. The radical leaders of the Likud and the NRP are not isolated in the Knesset. Their opinions are shared by several Knesset members of the ultraorthodox Agudat Israel and Shas, and they enjoy the support of hundreds of thousands of Israelis. In my estimation Radical Right ideas pertain to 20 to 25 percent of the Jewish citizens of Israel and are felt everywhere: in schools, military camps, the markets, and synagogues.[82] A proper measure of the real parliamentary power of the Radical Right is the recently established Eretz Yisrael Front in the Knesset, a political lobby of about thirty Knesset members (one-fourth of Israel's parliament), who have constituted themselves in order to express concern about the undue moderation of the 1989 Unity government and to block any compromise on the occupied territories.

Another fact about the Israeli Radical Right that many observers ignore is the high intensity of its operations and the great effectiveness of its activists. Israelis in general have never been silent, but some have been more vocal than others and much more effective. The hard core of the Israeli Radical Right is made up of true believers who are also pragmatic and politically skillful. These activists are totally committed to the defense of Greater Israel and will advance this cause in many sophisticated ways. Their leaders are good communicators, excellent political lobbyists, and, when necessary, skillful demonstrators and extraparliamentary activists. Several leaders of the Israeli Radical Right are former illustrious generals, scientists, and mainstream Zionist public figures who have been converted to the cause of Greater Eretz Yisrael by the traumatic experience of the Six Days' War. They speak in the name of traditional Zionism, of which they believe they are the only remaining representatives, and manipulate national symbols such as pioneering, settlement, and defense. Their leadership and dedication are respected well beyond their immediate constituency.

But perhaps the most important asset of the Israeli Radical Right is the strategic location of its hard core, the settlements of the West Bank. The Radical Right was crystallized around the demand to annex the occupied territories to Israel and has emerged in response to political developments that led Israeli leaders in the opposite direction. It is therefore no surprise that the settlers of Judea, Samaria, and Gaza, for whom the dilemma of annexation versus evacuation is an essential issue, have always been the most determined part of this camp. The Jewish underground of Gush Emunim was made up of devoted settlers; several supporters of Rabbi Kahane who are presently active in a few conspiratorial groups organized to prevent a similar retreat in the West Bank, also come from settler circles. The settler community may not be very large, about 110,000 strong in 1992, but it represents for many Israelis the true pioneering of the 1990s, the only meaningful Zionism of our time. The ethos of the Zionist pioneers who expanded the boundaries of the small Jewish community in Palestine and built this land from scratch is still very strong in Israel. Gush Emunim in particular represents for the entire Israeli Right (about 50 percent of the nation) the idealism and self-sacrifice of the good old days. In many respects the group fulfills for the Right the role the tiny kibbutz movement once fulfilled for the Labor movement. The settlers of Judea, Samaria, and Gaza are also the ones who maintain the daily contact with over 1.5 million unhappy Palestinians. In that capacity they have an impact on national politics that far exceeds their sheer numbers. In spite of the heavy presence of the army in the West Bank, the settlers, who are armed and well organized, could turn the occupied territories into hell if they wanted to. Therefore even hostile cabinets cannot afford to ignore the attitudes and demands of the Radical Right. Rabbi Kahane's thugs may still be beyond the pale, but not Gush Emunim, Tzomet, and Moledet. These movements and their leaders are part and parcel of the Israeli body politic and are considered legitimate partners to the political process. This is the reason why the presence of the Radical Right in Israeli collective existence casts a large shadow over the future of the Jewish state and is deeply involved in questions of peace and war. What the Radical Right does or does not do is a major question that no Israeli, Arab, or anyone interested in the Middle East can afford to ignore.

No fact dramatizes the centrality of the Radical Right to the life of Israel more than the Palestinian uprising in the occupied territories. It is true that the *intifada,* which broke out in December 1987, was not directed against the Israeli Radical Right and the settlers but was instead a Palestinian cry for self-determination, directed at Israel's occupation in general. But the outbreak of the *intifada* cannot be explained without the growing Arab-Israeli friction in Judea, Samaria, and Gaza, and the Palestinian fear that the Jews are about to take over the entire area through massive settlement. The settler community in the occupied territories and the spokespersons of the Radical Right have played a crucial role in instilling this fear in the collective consciousness of the Palestinians and, more importantly, in realizing it through the establishment of over 100 settlements in the occupied territories. Even moderate critics of the settlers maintain that they have created for Israel a huge time bomb whose safe detonation is becoming harder each day the occupation continues. There is, furthermore, no doubt that the settler community and the Radical Right are among the most concrete stumbling blocks against Israeli compromises with the Palestinians and the Arab world, a significant force to be reckoned with whenever a peace plan is worked out or speculated about.

CONCLUSION

The Radical Right can be viewed as a growing success story. Polls conducted since the 1987 beginning of the uprising in the West Bank and Gaza showed a growing radicalization within the Israeli Right and a movement of some of Herut's supporters to the small parliamentary ultranationalist parties. The Radical Right appears, in this perspective, as a thriving public culture and a sophisticated political system. Even strong adversaries agree that a long time will pass before the present rise of this camp is reversed or brought to a halt. By that time the Jewish polity is likely to be greatly different from the Israel of David Ben Gurion, Golda Meir, and even Menachem Begin.

PART THREE

THE ANGLO-AMERICAN
DEMOCRACIES

THE RADICAL RIGHT IN BRITAIN

Stan Taylor

We may, following S. M. Lipset and E. Raab, define radical right movements in terms of the structure and content of their ideologies.[1] With regard to their structure, such ideologies are (1) monist—based on the notion that there are fundamental truths about humanity and the environment that do not admit to question; (2) simplistic—ascribe complex phenomena to single causes and advance single remedies; (3) fundamentalist—involve a view of the world as divided into "good" and "bad" and; (4) conspiratorial—accept the existence of a worldwide conspiracy by a small group that seeks to manipulate the masses against their real interests in pursuit of the attainment or maintenance of dominance. With regard to content, radical right ideologies are characterized by the desire to create a mythical past when (5) economic, social and political relations were harmonious; (6) the nation was united, great, and in some cases dominant over others; and (7) the race, ethnic group, or both (sometimes regarded as coextensive with the nation) were "pure," great, and dominant.

Thus, in all, seven characteristics may be used to define radical right-wing ideologies and, hence, political movements. It may be noted that this is a general definition of the Radical Right, not one of fascism. There is a tendency to use the word *Fascist* to define all groups on the radical right, which renders the term virtually meaningless. For present purposes, Fascist movements are defined as a subset of radical right movements, that is, they share the seven attributes already mentioned but also have additional ideological characteristics. These, according to A. Gregor, include advocacy of (1) an authoritarian and antiliberal state, (2) control of labor and consumption in the interests of a state-managed and productionist economy, (3) differential access to resources and power by a managerial bureaucracy under the control of a single party, (4) totalitarian control over political aggregation, communication, and socialization, (5) creation of a self-sufficient society, and (6) belief in a charismatic leader who will energize the masses.[2]

Since 1970 the term *Radical Right* as defined above has been largely synonymous in Britain with one political movement, the National Front (NF). Formed in the mid-1960s as a coalition of "fringe" organizations, the NF emerged in the 1970s as a mass political movement that was modest on an international scale but in electoral support was unmatched by any previous radical right movement in Britain. Then, following a major reverse at the end of the 1970s, in the early 1980s the NF returned once more to the peripheries of the political system, where it has remained. My aims in this chapter are to (1) briefly consider the historical strands of radical right thought underpinning the ideology of the NF, (2) outline the movement's ideology, (3) discuss the NF as a social movement, (4) examine its role as a political party mobilizing electoral support in the 1970s, (5) look at reactions to its emergence as a political force, (6) consider its demise and subsequent developments in the 1980s, and (7) assess its prospects for the 1990s.

THE IDEOLOGICAL ANTECEDENTS OF THE NF

The ideology of the NF was influenced, as R. Thurlow has suggested, by five strands of radical right thinking in Britain, namely, die-hard conservatism, conservative fascism, radical fascism, anti-Semitism and racial nationalism, and racial populism.[3]

The roots of die-hard conservatism lay in the reaction of sections of the aristocracy to what was perceived as the decline of Britain and of British power in the late nineteenth and early twentieth centuries. Decline, as manifested in economic eclipse by the United States and Germany, military challenge in Europe by the latter, and colonial weaknesses exposed by the Boer War, was blamed upon the rise of liberalism. This was seen, in economic terms, as allowing a free-for-all in which resources were allocated by the market rather than by the needs of the nation-state; the result had been the diversification of resources into domestic consumption rather than defense or imperial expansion, and the opening up of the British economy to unfair competition from other countries.

A similar critique was applied in the field of foreign policy, with the substitution of internationalism for nationalism as the factor undermining British power in general and the maintenance of the empire in particular. Finally, in terms of a moral dimension, die-hards saw liberalism as destroying the sturdiness and independence of the British nation/race and hence its fitness to play a dominant role in world politics. For all of these reasons, then, the die-hards blamed liberalism for Britain's decline. In its place they sought to institute economic and foreign policies based upon Britain's interests as a great nation and a dominant player in world politics; domestic policies were to be devoted to improving the fitness of the race and thereby enabling it to fulfill its imperial destiny. Although the die-hards made little political impact in the era before World War I, their philosophy lived on to become, as will be seen, a potent strand of radical right thinking in the postwar era.

A second strand that was of little importance at the time but had implications later was that of so-called conservative fascism, which developed in the early 1920s. This was primarily a response to what was seen as the menace of communism and socialism as represented in the international sphere by the Russian Revolution and in the domestic one by the rise of the Labour party. Essentially it consisted of an extrapolation of die-hard ideas to cover the rise of socialism rather than liberalism as the major threat to British prestige and power. The solution was to deal firmly with the Socialists, as Mussolini had in Italy, but then to restore a traditional conservative society. This strand was associated with a number of groups in the 1920s, most notably the British Fascists, but these shared small size, a style of politics based as much upon personalities as issues, and almost total isolation from the political system.

The third input to postwar radical right thinking was the radical economic and political program linked with Britain's largest Fascist movement of the 1930s, the British Union of Fascists (BUF), and its leader, Sir Oswald Mosley. He had been first a Conservative and then a Labour MP in the 1920s and in the latter capacity became a junior minister in the Labour government that took office in 1929. But despairing of Labour's willingness to adopt the radical measures he saw as necessary to tackle Britain's pressing economic problems, especially continuing decline and high unemployment, Mosley resigned in 1930 and created first the New party and then, in October 1932, the BUF. As Mosley outlined it, the BUF's program was "distinctively English": For its historical inspiration it drew essentially on the Tudor period, romantically seen as an era that had permitted the full cultural, economic, and social flowering of the English spirit; since then, except for a brief era in the eighteenth century when the empire had been won, there had been darkness.[4]

But the aim of the BUF was not to restore Tudor England per se but to recreate conditions that would once more allow such a flowering of the national spirit, the key to which was seen as economic rejuvenation, which in turn demanded a strong state. For Mosley, then, the abandonment of liberal democracy was dictated by economic necessity, a means to the end of creating the centrally planned and corporatively organized autarkic economy that alone could restore Britain to its former glories.

In addition to this contributing factor of postwar radical right ideology, the BUF also became associated with another strand, that of anti-Semitism and conspiracy theory. This had been present in earlier radical right thought but mainly in muted form, as was initially the case with the BUF in the early 1930s.[5] But after failing to mobilize support on the basis of its economic program or via mass demonstrations and low-level political violence, the BUF in late 1934 turned to anti-Semitism and accusations of conspiracy primarily in an attempt to tap a new vein of support. Anti-Semitism took the form of attacking Jews because they held loyalties other than to Britain and were, particularly in the financial and media fields, pursuing objectives inimical to British interests. But the BUF was reluctant to present this publicly in terms of an all-embracing conspiracy that offered any kind of total explanation of the country's plight. However, there were certainly those within the BUF and outside who claimed that the (forged) Protocols of the Elders of Zion offered proof of such a conspiracy and detected its hand in every development, past and present, deemed inimical not just to British interests but to those of the Aryan or Nordic races. Among the most notorious of these racial nationalists were Mosley's lieutenant, A. K. Chesterton, and Arnold Leese of the tiny Imperial Fascist League, both of whom were to play a role in postwar radical right politics.

All of the strands identified above began prior to World War II, but the fifth and final strand, that of racial populism, was primarily a postwar development. After the end of the war, Britain, in common with other Western European countries, suffered from a shortage of labor. This was relieved in part by immigration from past or existing colonies. The new workers, mainly from the West Indies or the Indian subcontinent, had rights of citizenship and began to settle in Britain in increasing numbers from the late 1940s onwards.[6] Their reception by the indigenous population was, not surprisingly after centuries of colonialism, markedly hostile, that is, the appearance of "colored people" on the streets of a number of British cities triggered a racist response.[7] This offered, on the one hand, a new scapegoat for radical right ideology in the sense that "colored" immigrants could be blamed for Britain's ills and, on the other, a possible basis for mobilizing support, hence the term *racial populism.*

At least four of these five strands of radical right thought were represented in the organizations that came together to form the NF in late 1966 and early 1967. The first two, die-hard conservatism and conservative fascism, were transmitted via the League of Empire Loyalists (LEL), formed in 1954 by A. K. Chesterton. He had broken with Mosley in 1938 over the organization and tactics of the BUF, and, almost uniquely among BUF, leaders, he had not been interned as a potential traitor in 1940 and had served in the army during the war. After the war he had modified at least the more strident of his anti-Semitic and racial nationalist views and founded the LEL as a pressure group to influence the governing Conservative party against decolonization (the die-hard element) and welfare statism (the conservative Fascist one). The LEL had attracted a mixed bag of "Colonel Blimps" (elderly ex-officers convinced that Britain should continue to fulfill its imperial mission), right-wing Conservatives (including some MPs), and a younger generation of radical right activists.[8]

This younger generation soon tired of the tameness of both the LEL's political stance and its pressure-group tactics. In search of stronger meat, they sought out the trenchant anti-Semitism and racial nationalism of Arnold Leese. As noted above, Leese had been a virulent anti-Semite in the 1930s and was heavily influenced by national socialism during and after the war. Following his release from prison after a sentence for helping former SS officers to escape justice, Leese had started the Britons Society and the Britons publishing house as a means of keeping the flame of racial nationalism and national socialism alive. It was to Leese, then, that the discontented ex-LEL members turned for inspiration, and they established a number of specifically Nazi movements in the early 1960s, most notably the National Socialist Movement (NSM) and its offshoot, the Greater Britain Movement (GBM).

The fourth strand of radical right thinking, that of racial populism, was represented by two further organizations, the British National party (BNP) and the Racial Preservation Society (RPS). The BND, too, was the creation of former LEL members, but this time of those who rejected Chesterton's emphasis upon influencing the Conservative party and in favor of appealing directly for white support on the basis of the immigration issue. As such, the BNP had attempted to build an electoral base in areas that had been subject to extensive immigration, most notably Southall in London, where the party had some success in winning votes in the early 1960s. The other organization, the RPS, was not a movement in any formal sense but a grouping of local associations that had, as the name suggests, sprung up to preserve the British "race" in the face of colored immigration.

If these organizations stemmed from different traditions on the radical right, by the mid-1960s they had one thing in common, namely, a bleak political future.[9] The LEL had for a time been tolerated by the Conservative party, but in the wake of a series of political stunts at Conservative gatherings that had caused serious embarrassment to the leadership, it had effectively been outlawed and was under threat from a new right-wing pressure group, the Monday Club. The GBM for its part, had remained as no more than a tiny gang clustered around a self-appointed Führer, John Tyndall, and militant anti-Semitism proved inadequate to sustain the movement while it waited for the crisis that would sweep it into power. For the BNP, the problem was resources, without which it could not hope to expand beyond it heartlands and mount a serious challenge. Finally, at least for individual leaders of the RPS, the problem lay in ineffectiveness and a lack of any wider influence. Thus by the mid-1960s, these movements had an incentive to form a coalition, and this was arranged via a formal merger of the LEL and the BNP, with participation from members of the RPS; the new movement was called the National Front. Initially, the GBM was excluded because of its Nazi associations, but in 1967 it was disbanded and the NF accepted most of its members, several of whom rapidly rose to positions of importance in the new party. The only major movement missing from the coalition was the Union Movement, which Mosley had started after the war to project his ideas in a European context, but individual members who had rejected "Eurofascism" in favor of a specifically British version did become associated with the NF and hence represented the final stand of extreme right thought, radical fascism, in the new movement.

THE IDEOLOGY OF THE NF

The ideological synthesis that emerged from this amalgamation may, as I have argued elsewhere, be considered in terms of two components, the analysis of the past and existing state of the world and the prescription of an appropriate world order.[10] The former component was clearly derived from the anti-Semitic and racial nationalist tradition and was based on five propositions, namely, that (1) variations in physical attributes and social behavior and abilities among people reflected different genetic inheritances, (2) there were significant discontinuities between groups of people in physical and social characteristics that delineated humankind into "races" and "nations," (3) that these could be ordered hierarchically according to various abilities, and (4) that the highest races were locked in a deadly struggle to secure world dominance as manifested in (5) a "grand conspiracy" by Zionists to destroy other "higher races" by, among other things, miscegenation, internationalism, and internal division.

The first proposition, of course, represented the doctrine of biological determinism, that is, that human nature was predominantly if not exclusively determined by genetic inheritance. According to this notion, genetics accounted for physical features, skin color, size, weight, the structure of the brain, the nervous system, and the endocrine glands; and the protein structure of blood serum. But the influence of genes did not stop at this point: Patterns of "instinctual" behavior were also held to be genetically—rather than socially or environmentally—determined, as was a large proportion of non-instinctual behavior, including intellect, faculty for comprehension, cognitive intelligence, and ability to learn from experience.

The second proposition represented the core of racialist nationalism. The argument ran that though all differed somewhat in genetic inheritance and hence instinct and intellect, people could be meaningfully classified into "races" on the basis that these groups had more in common with each other than with other groups. In some instances a complex division of races was made, using, for example, the terms *Nordics, Caucasoids, Semites,* and *Turco-Armenoids,* but in most cases there was a simple blanket division between "white" and "black" races. The differences in "color" were held to be associated with other differences on the basis of discrete gene pools, and it was claimed that the "white" race was genetically superior to others as the creator of modern civilization. But the credit for this was not simply laid at the door of the "white" race as a whole, because different contributions had been made by different subsets of it, or nation-races. The latter were defined initially as an ethnic rather than a racial entity, which in the course of inbreeding over a long period of time took on a distinctive racial character, that is, became a race within a race or a nation-race.

The third contention was that there was hierarchy of such nation-races, which had made differential contributions to civilization. In line with the BUF in the 1930s, the NF considered that the major contribution had been made by the British nation-race, which by the sixteenth century at least had been forced into one entity from an initial ethnic mix of Angles, Saxons, Jutes, Normans, Norse, and Celts. Thus Tudor times had witnessed both major cultural advancement and the first growth of an empire designed to provide for the expansion and enrichment of the nation-race. The achievements of the empire, both then and later, were seen as nothing less than the bringing of civilization to the "black" race throughout the world, giving it a culture and enabling it to develop its natural resources, climb out of poverty, and achieve a reasonable standard of living.

The fourth proposition was that the British and other races were engaged in a Darwinian struggle for dominance, with each trying to put down the other by all means possible. These included denying "living room," that is, space for the race to expand and fulfill its destiny; diminishing the purity of the racial stock by encouraging miscegenation; inculcating values inimical to the selection of the best "natural" leaders; and ensuring the physical destruction of a race by involvement in war.

The final proposition was that the central enemies facing the British race were the Zionists, who were seen as undermining the British race in four main ways. The first was through their control over the international economy. The development of capitalism on an international scale was seen as giving enormous power to those who could control the means of financing it, with the Jews identified as the unseen hand behind international finance capitalism. Second, combining conspiracy theory and die-hard conservatism, the NF considered the Jews responsible for spreading the pernicious doctrine of liberalism. In liberal societies people were, the NF argued, given the illusion of power but were in fact manipulated by the conspiracy and its hold over finance and, most critically, the media. The promotion of liberalism by the conspiracy was blamed for the decline of Britain since the early nineteenth century, in particular in the postwar period, when the weak and pliable leaders elected had given away the empire and denied the nation the right to living space, at the same time encouraging immigration and the consequent dilution of the British race. Third, blending conspiracy theory and conservative fascism, the NF held the Jews responsible for spreading communism in the world in general and Britain in particular. In the international sphere, communism was seen as a device for presenting a serious external threat to the Western nations that, taken to ultimate levels, would destroy them. On the domestic level British institutions, including the Labour party, the trade unions, the media, the educational system, the churches, and even the Conservative party, were supposedly riddled by Communists dedicated to destroying the national spirit. Finally, the conspiracy was seen as lying behind the promotion of internationalist ideas and institutions as varied as the Council for Foreign Relations, the Trilateral Commission, the Bilderburg group, the International Monetary Fund (IMF), the World Bank, and the European Common Market. Such institutions were seen as designed to subvert and ultimately do away with nationalism.

The combined effects of Zionist-inspired liberalism, communism, and internationalism had, then, been to weaken and destroy the "white" race in general and the British nation-race in particular. The NF, like the BUF, saw its task as the reversal of this decline by means of the re-creation of the conditions of late and mid-sixteenth century England. The NF believed that it would be possible to recapture the greatness and harmony of this age by instituting several big changes. First, all those who threatened the purity of the British nation race would be removed, including Jews and the "colored" people who were a "fifth column" for the conspiracy. Once a homogeneous racial stock had been re-established, it would be maintained by encouraging the growth of eugenic consciousness among the people. Second, the NF would act to transform the political structures of society. The movement's contempt for liberal democracy has already been noted; this would be replaced by an organic state that would be a manifestation of a higher level of thought and action than that achievable by individuals alone. In the new order, individuals would be valued not mechanistically but in accordance with their contributions as agents in the destiny of the nation and the race. Third, changes in the political sphere would be complemented by changes in the economic sphere toward a true producer's economy entailing a centrally planned self-sufficient economy along the lines suggested by Mosley and the BUF in the 1930s. Fourth, in the social sphere, the NF stressed the need to reorganize the educational system and to control the media. With regard to the former, the educational system was to be purged of Communists, selectivity in access to schools was to be restored, and the curriculum changed toward the teaching of Britain's past and present glories, the inculcation of patriotism and nationalism, and stress on the need for perfect physical fitness. Finally, in external relations, Britain would cease to be a member of supranational and international bodies, including the European Community, the IMF, the World Bank, and the Commonwealth. In place of these, the NF would involve Britain in a "White Commonwealth" partnership in which would be included Canada, Australia, New Zealand, and South Africa. This would be Britain's only alliance; it would not cooperate with the United States, regarded as dominated by international finance, and would oppose Communist regimes and Israel might and main. Perhaps most controversially in the external sphere, the NF raised the prospect of the recolonization of Africa, on the ground that the resources of that vast continent were too important to be left in the hands of either the Africans or the Communists.

This, then, was the "core" ideology of the NF, one that clearly met the seven conditions (identified at the start of this chapter) as defining a "radical right" movement. In addition, it met four of the six conditions named as characteristic of a Fascist movement, the exceptions being with regard to control by a single party and belief in a charismatic leader. However, it may be noted that the NF did not claim to be opposed to a single-party state or to dictatorship on grounds of principle; their argument was that this was not good for Britain in their view, which implied that the NF was open to change depending on circumstances.[11] Thus the NF's denial that it was a Fascist party has to be interpreted in this light. An overt espousal of such doctrines would obviously have affected its support as a social and political movement.

THE NF AS A SOCIAL MOVEMENT

In a number of countries, postwar radical right movements have been able to mobilize support on the basis of their "core" ideologies, reflecting the existence of a Neo-Fascist subculture stemming from the interwar period or unpurged institutional leftovers from the latter or a cult of old leaders. In Britain, however, the NF was unable to follow suit. Apart from a small area within the East End of London, interwar fascism had relatively little political or institutional impact and old leaders had been discredited by internment as potential traitors during the war and had little following thereafter. Hence the NF could only rely upon its core ideology to recruit the relatively tiny number of people already active on the radical right, and the mass appeal of the movement had to be cast in different terms.

In fact, four central themes were apparent in party literature intended for recruitment and publicity purposes, principally the *National Front News*. The first theme was the fueling of racist sentiment. Issues of the *NF News* were replete with horrendous stories about immigrants, with headlines such as "Blacks Wage War Against Police," "Asians Import Bizarre Sex-Murder Rites," "Inter-racial Sex—A Mother Warns," "Black Savages Terrorize Old Folk," "Blood Flows as Frenzied Asian Gangs Battle," and "Jobs for the (Black) Boys." These were clearly intended to reinforce negative stereotypes of black people arising from colonialism and to blame them for Britain's problems. Second, other parties were castigated for allowing "colored" immigration or letting it continue. Sample headlines along these lines included "Labour and Tory Agree: Black Immigration Must Continue" or "What Future for British Children: One in Three to be Black: Official Plan." A third theme was to attack the activities of those working in the field of race relations, stressing that they were forcing unwanted integration upon the public and trying to destroy venerated British institutions. Thus, for example, the chairman of the Commission for Racial Equality was described as the "chief race traitor," NF members prosecuted for racial incitement were portrayed as "the patriots who won't be bullied," and the charge was advanced that the heir to the throne would be forced to marry a black: "Latest Gimmick from Race- mix Madhouse: Prince Charles is Pressured to Take a Black Bride." Finally, an attempt was made to portray the NF as representing the interests of whites ("We'll Put White People First—NF Elections Pledge") and as a growing force in British politics ("Establishment Panic Measures Confirm: Economic Decline + Racial Chaos = NF Road to Power"). Thus, in its public appeal, the NF attempted to tap popular racism and present itself in this context as the only party prepared to defend democracy, liberty, and traditional British institutions.

This appeal to popular racism within an apparently democratic context was successful in attracting support particularly on occasions, discussed in the next section, when the established parties were viewed as flouting popular opinion over immigration. As a result, large numbers of new members were drawn to the movement. Thus in addition to a hard core of 2,000 to 3,000 members with a long history of involvement on the radical right, the party won approximately 11,000 new members in 1972–1973 and 5,000 in 1976. Most of these were seemingly ex-Conservatives and from the lower middle and working classes.[12] However, relatively few stayed for any length of time, and it has been estimated that at least 12,000 people joined and left the party in the 1970s.[13]

This revolving-door aspect of NF membership would seem to have reflected two main factors: When large numbers of people were joining the movement essentially in a moment of anger and frustration, it was vital that they should be integrated within the organization as soon as possible to maintain enthusiasm within a supportive milieu. However, the NF's leadership was new to the role of guiding a mass party, and national and local structures were often inadequate in recruiting and maintaining membership.[14] Second, even among those who did stay the course initially, there was a high turnover as, sooner or later, they came into contact with the movement's "core" ideology. Re-socialization appears to have been undertaken informally at branch level with the circulation of the movement's journals or videos such as "Survival Ethics," advertised as propounding "sound principles for an ideology of racial survival."[15] A number of people were disturbed that, as one ex-member of the movement put it, "the NF should get people to join on the immigration issue and then slowly brainwash them into the real thing that the NF is about."[16] Yet it is clear that not all potential members were put off either by the initial difficulties in joining the movement or by the discovery of its inner ideology, and some indeed found that this ideology met their basic personality needs and so remained within the movement. In addition, at a much less exalted level, the association between the NF's inner ideology and racism and fascism proved attractive to an element among skinheads looking for an attachment that would shock their elders and contemporaries as well as the opportunities for "aggravation" afforded by life in the NF.

Such opportunities were legion in a movement that intended, in the words of one of its leaders, to "kick its way into the headlines." The standard tactic of the NF was to march, carrying the British flag, often in areas with large black populations, in the expectation that this would provoke a reaction from the Left and generate favorable publicity. The success of this tactic on at least one occasion, a demonstration in Red Lion Square in London, has been described by R. Clutterbuck in that:

> Of the groups which organized the Red Lion Square demonstration, the only one which advanced its cause was the NF, however little they deserved to do so. They set out to give a display of order and dignity to contrast with the disorder and violence of the left. They meticulously observed police instructions and maintained strict discipline. Television films showed the NF marchers standing stock still with closed ranks on one side of (the square) while "dirty, hairy lefties" swarmed about in a chaotic battle with the police on the other. The implied menace of the "defence sections" [of the NF] and of the metal spikes on top of the forest of Union Jack flagpoles made less impact on the public than pictures of students hitting out at policemen and charging them with banner poles. The result was precisely what the NF would have wished—publicity for the purposes of their demonstration, discrediting of the detractors.[17]

In this way, and frequently as well by the initiation of street brawling, the NF attempted to bring itself to the attention of the British public and so aid its campaign for votes.

THE NF AS A POLITICAL PARTY

What distinguished the NF from most of its radical right predecessors was its willingness to participate in the electoral process. This did not, as was noted above, represent any sort of commitment to liberal democracy as such but was seen as a means of building a mass movement by tapping popular racism. Although the BNP had attempted to win votes on this basis in the early 1960s, the real potential for such a strategy became apparent only in the wake of public response to a speech in 1968 by a "maverick" Conservative politician, Enoch Powell, which shattered the elite consensus on race relations and immigration.

The established parties had been slow to respond to public concern over immigration, and it was not until 1962 that action was taken by the Conservative government to restrict the flow of migrants from the New Commonwealth. Labour had bitterly opposed the introduction of restrictions, but after some of the party's candidates had been defeated on the immigration issue in the 1964 election, the Labour government had espoused even tougher controls—coupling them, however, with race relations legislation offering a measure of protection to Britain's own black population. This and a similar package of controls plus an extension of antidiscrimination measures in 1968 would, it was hoped, kill the race issue stone dead by, on the one hand, appeasing popular racism and, on the other, preventing the parties presenting a united front from capitalizing on the issue.

But these hopes were shattered when Powell made his speech on April 20, 1968. In what many considered to be a particularly lurid way, Powell gave vent to popular prejudices concerning "colored" people. He called for their repatriation, and prophesied racial war on Britain's streets, protesting the while that he was simply articulating "what thousands and hundreds of thousands were saying and thinking—not throughout Great Britain perhaps but in the areas which are already undergoing the total transformation to which there is not parallel in a thousand years of English history."[18] It is worth quoting D. Schoen's summary of the impact of the speech:

> One of the country's leading political figures, a man of cabinet rank and experience with powerful aura of cerebral severity, had made all his own the cause of the pubs and clubs, the bingo halls and the football terraces. The bitter anecdotes of a thousand Coronation Streets had poured forth from an apparent stalwart of the Establishment and were set amidst the classical allusions so long the hall-mark of the authoritative in British political rhetoric. Powell had moreover trodden an ambiguous line in his talk of the holocaust to come. While he had averred merely that racial conflict of some kind was sadly predictable, given the strength of native English resentment against the incoming immigrants, he had voiced the resentments sympathetically and not condemned them. The implication was strong both to his supporters and opponents that he was siding with a righteous assertion of yeoman English wrath against the threatening alien tide.[19]

For his pains, Powell was immediately removed from his position as a front-bench opposition spokesman, which occasioned extraordinary demonstrations in his favor and the establishment of a "Powell for premier" movement. The polls revealed that up to three-quarters of the electorate agreed with what he had said and that two-thirds considered that he had been wrongfully sacked.

The unintended effect of Powell's intervention was to boost the NF, which began to attract right-wing Conservatives, and to open up a potential role for the party in mobilizing racist opinion, which was not represented by either of the established parties. Thus in the late 1960s the NF began to fight local elections and achieved moderately encouraging results in seats in a number of cities.[20] This, however, failed to translate into support in the general election held in 1970, when the nine NF candidates averaged a mere 3.7 percent of the total vote, probably reflecting a drift back toward the Conservatives. Although Conservative leaders had disapproved of Powell's intervention, they could scarcely ignore the widespread support for his views, and the party adopted a tougher stance on immigration in 1970 that Powell endorsed; by doing so, he may well have won his party the election.[21]

As promised, in 1971 the Conservative government introduced tougher controls on immigration, but any political benefit was rapidly dissipated by its decision in late 1972 to admit, as political refugees, some of the Asians expelled from Uganda in the wake of Idi Amin's drive to "Africanize" the economy and society. This decision led to an immediate outcry in the popular press, which wildly overestimated the numbers involved, and to a campaign, orchestrated by Powell, to prevent their entry. Conflict within the Conservative party rose to a crescendo at the party's conference in October 1972, at which Powell and the party leader and prime minister, Edward Heath, clashed in a gladiatorial style unusual in the normally deferential atmosphere of Conservative gatherings.

This scenario—the Conservatives apparently reneging on their promises, a sudden and (according to the press) mass immigration, and Powell condemning his own party—could not have been better for the NF. The party's leaders milked it for all it was worth with marches and protest demonstrations against the incoming refugees, and they were rewarded by a rapid increase in membership and in their share of the vote in local elections in April 1973.[22] This encouraged the NF to mount a major campaign in a parliamentary by-election in May, when its candidate won 16.4 percent of the total vote—the highest ever won by a radical right candidate for a parliamentary seat. This was followed by further successes in local elections in June 1973.

The emergence of electoral support encouraged the party to mount a major effort in, as it turned out, the two general elections held in 1974, one in February, the other in October. In the former, the NF put up fifty-four candidates and in the latter ninety, but these did badly, with average shares of the vote at 3.2 percent and 3.4 percent, respectively, well below the level at which the party had been performing in the previous year. The most likely explanation of its failure would seem to be that once the initial fuss over the

Ugandan Asians affair had died down, voters had lost interest in the NF and, if they wished to register a protest vote against the major parties, had plumped for the established third party, the Liberals.[23]

In the wake of this defeat, the NF entered into a period of internecine strife, from which it was rescued in 1976 by a combination of the same factors that had helped it to emerge from the fringes in 1972–1973, namely, racialism in an African country and sensationalism in the British media. In this case, the catalyst was the decision of President Hastings Banda of Malawi to embark upon Africanization, which led, in the early spring of 1976, to a small number of Malawi Asians' taking up their right to British citizenship and to settlement. Immigrants began arriving at Gatwick Airport, and the local council housed some of them temporarily in an expensive hotel. This story was picked up by the British press in early May and spread under such headlines as "Scandal of £600 a Week for Asians" and "New Flood of Asians into Britain."

From the NF's viewpoint, neither the content nor the timing of this scare could have been better: The image of a sudden mass immigration was calculated to raise hackles, that they were staying in a luxury hotel at the taxpayers' expense added insult to injury, and the publication of these stories in the days immediately preceding the local elections ensured that the maximum advantage would accrue to the party. As a result, in May 1976 the NF enjoyed its finest hour, winning average shares of the vote of 15 percent or more in a number of major English cities, and a short-lived offshoot from the movement, the National party, actually won two local council seats in the Blackburn area, the first (and so far the only) political representation to be achieved by the Radical Right in Britain since the 1920s.

However, as in 1972–1973, this surge of support proved short-termed, as the Malawi Asians issue quickly died away, and in local elections held the following year, NF support fell sharply in the provinces. But this was more than compensated for by what was widely seen as a major growth of support in London. Elections had not been held in the city in 1976, but in 1977 the NF put up ninety-one candidates for the ninety-two seats. These won 120,000 votes, more than twice the total won in the whole of England in 1974, and though the average share of the poll was only 5.3 percent, this concealed shares in a number of individual seats of 10 percent or more. These results were regarded as significant for four main reasons. First, the NF's share of the poll in a number of constituencies, particularly in the East End of London, was much higher than it had been in the general election of 1974. Second, in many seats NF candidates had polled better than Liberals, which seemed to indicate that the former was replacing the latter as the third party in parts of London. The third reason was that these results had been achieved when there was no immediate scare over immigration, suggesting that the NF was, for the first time, tapping support upon a wider basis.

Fourth, given the sociogeographical distribution of NF support, this backing appeared to come from alienated working-class voters protesting inner city decay and decline, a basis that could offer the party a durable presence in the political system.[24]

Even though this interpretation of the NF's performance in London has been strongly disputed, the party itself clearly regarded the results as a major step along the road to power, and it announced its intention of putting up 300 candidates at the next general election.[25] This declaration, as well as a heightened program of NF marches and demonstrations designed to keep the party to the forefront in the run-up to the election, aroused considerable apprehension and anger among a wide range of groups in British politics and society, which led to the growth of two major opposition movements, the Anti-Nazi League (ANL) and the Joint Committee Against Racialism (JCAR). A loose coalition of groups on the left of the political spectrum, including left-wing Labourites and members of the Trotskyite Socialist Workers' party, the ANL was dedicated, as its name suggests, to exposing what it regarded as the fundamentally Nazi nature of the NF. The ANL managed to secure the endorsement of a large number of people prominent in public life, including left-wing politicians, union leaders, academics, show business and sporting figures, and church leaders, and embarked upon a dual campaign of using these spokespeople as opinion leaders to increase public awareness of the NF's core ideology and of countering, by force if necessary, the NF's public displays. The second organization, the JCAR, was also coalition, but intended to be publicity-oriented and to appeal to a more moderate spectrum of opinion. Support was attracted from the Labour and Liberal parties, the Board of Deputies of British Jews, the British Council of Churches, the Supreme Council of the Sikhs, the Federation of Bangladeshi Organizations, the Indian Workers' Association, the West Indian Standing Conference, the National Union of Students, and the executive council of the National Union of the Conservative party. Thus by the end of 1977, an unprecedented range of groups from almost every section of British society and from all parts of the political spectrum had declared an intention to oppose the NF and the racism upon which it fed.

It is, however, at least arguable that the efforts all of these groups were probably less important in the final analysis than the intervention in early 1978 of Margaret Thatcher, then leader of the Conservative opposition. In a television interview in early 1978, Thatcher had been asked about her views on immigration and had replied that new initiatives were necessary in light of the widespread feeling among whites that they were being "swamped" by "colored" immigrants.[26] She also, without prompting, mentioned the NF:

> I shall not make [immigration] an election issue but I think there is a feeling
> that the big political parties have not been talking about this, and sometimes,

you, we are falsely accused of racial prejudice. I say falsely accused and that means we do not talk about it perhaps as much as we should. In my view that is one thing that is driving some people to the National Front. They do not agree with objectives of the National Front, but they say that at least they are talking about some of the problems. Now we are a big political party. If we do not want people to go to extremes, and I do not, we must ourselves talk about this problem and we must show that we are prepared to deal with it.

When asked whether she would hope to bring back Conservatives who had defected to the NF, Thatcher replied, "Oh, very much back, certainly, but I think that the National Front has, in fact, attracted more people from Labour than from us, but never be afraid to tackle something which people are worried about. We are not in politics to ignore peoples' worries; we are in politics to deal with them." The Conservative leader did not elaborate on the policy changes that needed to be made, only that there would have to be a "clear end in sight" to immigration. These remarks created a political storm insofar as she was alleged to be pandering to the NF in the interest of winning votes, but she rode this out and pushed through policy proposals involving a significant tightening of immigration controls as part of the platform upon which to fight the forthcoming general election.

As promised, the NF fielded over 300 candidates in the election held in May 1979, the largest total by far ever put up by a radical party in Britain. These, however, averaged a mere 1.3 percent of the total vote, the lowest average at any election since 1970. Although this outcome in part reflected the fact that the NF was contesting many seats it had never fought before, even in those the party had previously contested, its share of the vote was down substantially, with the main beneficiary being the victorious Conservatives.[27] Thus the NF was effectively dished in 1979 by Thatcher's adoption of tougher policies on immigration; after this disaster, the NF fought few seats in elections, putting up only fifty-eight candidates in the general election of 1983 (they averaged a mere 1.1 percent of the total vote) and contesting no seats at all in the general election of 1987 or the European elections of 1984 and 1989.

It should be clear from the above that, in overall terms, the NF's electoral support was primarily a backlash against what was seen as the major parties' willfully ignoring public opinion on immigration, in particular in 1972–1973 and 1976, during the issue of the Ugandan and Malawi Asians, respectively. In this sense, then, it was a "flash" vote that flared up and then died away quickly after the crisis passed before remaining support was drained away in 1978–1979, when the Conservatives adopted new policies. But within this general context, there were some variations in NF support across social strata and geographical areas. With regard to the former, there is some evidence from national surveys that the NF appealed more to young, male, and working-class voters than to other groups.[28] In the case of the young, this probably reflected both high levels of racism and a greater openness than their elders to political mobilization by a new party identification.[29] In the case of males as opposed to females, no satisfactory explanation has been produced, but possibilities include the generally greater political interest of the former or the differential attraction between the sexes of the NF's violent style of politics. Finally, with regard to class, it may be that manual workers were more inclined to overt racism than their middle-class counterparts or at least more willing to reveal this to researchers, although analysis has suggested that such workers were simply more likely to live in areas where local circumstances were likely to promote NF support.[30]

Such circumstances included, first, the size of the "colored" population in a particular area that might have been expected to have resulted in backlash from the indigenous population and NF support. Aggregate data studies show that there was a fairly weak correlation between these variables.[31] Second, it has been suggested that the critical factor was not the large-scale presence of immigrants within an area but the extent to which people living in areas with small "colored" populations felt threatened by the prospect of a large-scale incursion; some, albeit inconclusive, evidence has been found to support this hypothesis.[32] Third, bearing in mind the substantial variation in NF support among urban areas, C. Husbands in 1983 suggested that differing localized economic conditions and political traditions may have been the key explanatory factors. His survey findings, however, offered only limited support to such explanations, with the outstanding exception of part of the East End of London. This was probably the only area of the country where the NF could rely upon raising support via its "insider" ideology, reflecting a local racist political culture probably originating in unique social and economic circumstances in the late nineteenth century and manifested in a long tradition of support for radical right movements stretching back to at least before World War I and encompassing the BUF in the late 1930s, the Union Movement after the war, and then the NF.[33] But in 1979 even this apparent bastion of the Radical Right largely deserted the NF, which proved unable to re-capture it during the 1980s, let alone to recapture the wider support it had enjoyed in the previous decade.

THE NF IN THE 1980s

For a movement that had deluded itself that power was just around the corner, the 1979 election results came as a traumatic shock to the NF, and in 1979 and 1980 various leaders left to form their own political movements, including the National Front Constitutional Movement, the British Democratic party (BDP), and the New National Front, which in 1982 became the British National party. Thus the Radical Right fragmented in the early 1980s, the ideological ground cut away from beneath its feet by the new Conservative government's adoption of tough legislation on immigration and by Thatcher's reassertion of nationalism in the context of both the war to recapture the Falklands and her opposition to European integration. Faced with this challenge, the NF and its offshoots all but abandoned the electoral road and descended into murkier activities. The latter, as revealed in the anti-Fascist monthly *Searchlight,* included gunrunning by some members of the BDP (formerly the Leicester branch of the NF); inciting racial hatred, for which the editor of the NF's youth paper, *Bulldog,* was jailed; furthering links with other movements, including Protestant paramilitary groups in Ulster and both legal and underground radical groups in the United States and Europe; and recruiting the violent skinhead fraternity at a number of soccer grounds, particularly in London. It was the skinhead element that provided the most public face of the Radical Right in the early 1980s, and the NF became identified in the public mind with the chanting of racial obscenities and mindless violence at soccer matches both at home and abroad.[34] This was hardly an image calculated to restore the party's fortunes or enable it to take advantage of the economic and social problems occasioned by the deep economic recession of the early 1980s, particularly mass unemployment.

The need to improve the party's image, to counter Thatcher's highly successful mobilization of nationalism and conservatism, and to appeal to new strata led in the mid-1980s to the growth of a new faction within the NF that differed from the movement's previous leadership in four main ways: in age, education, program, and strategy. A fresh generation of activists came to the fore. In the late 1960s the NF had been led by Chesterton, who was born in the nineteenth century and had been a leader of the BUF, and in the 1970s by activists such as John Tyndall and Martin Webster, born in the 1930s or early 1940s and socialized into radical politics via the LEL and other organizations, particularly the NSM and GBM. But the new faction was composed mainly of younger people, born in the 1950s, whose adult political socialization had been conducted within the NF itself—that is, a third radical right generation. Whereas earlier generations were not, in general, highly educated and had held fairly lowly jobs, the new generation had, in a number of cases, been to universities and achieved higher-status occupations. Accepting the bulk of the NF's core ideology as outlined above, they nevertheless regarded the party's attempt to appeal for support on the basis of economic and social prescriptions drawn largely from the BUF in the interwar period as wholly inappropriate in the 1980s. Instead, in order to contrast with the Conservatives and appeal to groups such as the unemployed, they attempted to provide an alternative in the form of a Socialist "back to the land" economic and social program variously inspired by writings of the Strasser brothers in Germany and Julius Evola in Italy.[35] Finally, with regard to strategy and tactics, the new generation favored a seemingly aboveboard legitimate political movement shorn of its hooligan associations, but this was to be secretly complemented by a disciplined underground army of so-called political soldiers.

This set the scene in the mid-1980s for a struggle within the NF between the old guard and the new, which precipitated a further series of damaging splits in the movement, a number of the old leaving to found organizations such as Our Nation and the Front Support Group. This left the so-called Strasserites in control of the movement, and their socialistic bias was evident in the mid-1980s in NF attempts to exploit left-wing issues, for example, by attacking unemployment or supporting strikes, including that of Britain's miners during their long struggle to prevent pit closures in 1984–1985. However, these and other attempts to mobilize support on the basis of left-wing nationalism were, except perhaps among younger people in a few areas, firmly rebuffed.[36] By the late 1980s the movement was not only without public support but suffering from continuing defections of members (membership was down to less than 2,000) and in serious financial trouble. This led to a desperate search for funding that took NF leaders as far away as Libya to seek help from Muhammar Qaddafi, but even he apparently refused to assist what was clearly a lost cause. Thus in 1992 the NF is in disarray and despair, and its very continuation as a political movement is in question.

CONCLUSION

The Radical Right in Britain has a pedigree, as was noted in the first section, stretching back to before World War I, and including a number of different ideological strands. Early in the postwar period these were represented by a range of "fringe" political movements, but they were brought together in the mid-1960s by the creation of the NF. The "inner" or "core" ideology of the new movement amalgamated existing radical right thought into a synthesis that was certainly Neo-Fascist, but the NF's mass appeal was cast in terms of popular racism. As such, on three occasions in the late 1960s and 1970s—in the aftermath of the Powell speech and during the crises over admission into Britain of Ugandan and Malawi Asians—the NF was able to take advantage of what was seen as the intransigence of the established parties and win members and votes. However, increases in both the party's membership and its vote proved transient, and eventually the party's appeal on the race issue was undermined by the Conservatives' adoption of tougher immigration policies. The NF then fragmented and in the 1980s became locked in a declining spiral of support from which the takeover of the movement by a new generation of activists failed to rescue it, leaving it almost moribund.

The future for the NF and the various organizations it spawned in the 1980s looks bleak, unless, as happened in 1972 and 1976, more of Britain's colonial past comes home to roost in the form of a wave of immigrants from the former colonies and once more triggers a "flash" racist vote. Although this is clearly not completely out of the question—for example, it is conceivable that there could be pressures for Britain to accept large-scale immigration from Hong Kong when the latter is handed back to China in the mid-1990s—the prospect seems unlikely. It is more probable that the Radical Right will remain where it has been for most of the present century, confined to the fringes of the British political system.

THE AMERICAN RADICAL RIGHT: EXIT, VOICE, AND VIOLENCE

Leonard Weinberg

Anyone wishing to provide an analysis of radical rightism in the United States these days faces a dilemma. It approximates one art historians must confront when they decide to assess the paintings of a heretofore obscure artist of the early Renaissance. If the scholars reach the conclusion that the work is trivial or derivative and the artist's obscurity deserved, it is hard to understand why they have lavished so much attention and written so many words only to reconfirm the judgment of centuries. Thus the art historian has a strong incentive to find importance in the paintings that others have missed. Likewise, most political observers will concede that groups promoting anti-Semitism, white supremacy, and nativism do not pose a serious challenge to American democracy at the present time. Even the Anti-Defamation League, hardly an organization inclined to minimize the threat, reported in 1988 that membership in the various Ku Klux Klan and Neo-Nazi groups active around the country had reached a low ebb.[1] If right-wing extremism is not a major force in American political life, why waste words on it?

There are several ways out of the dilemma that may furnish a justification for the analysis to follow. The most obvious and least desirable is to exaggerate the importance of the phenomenon. This may be accomplished by expanding the meaning of radical rightism to include such movements as the New Right and the New Christian Right, that is, a constellation of organizations with some mass support, considerable financial resources, and a good deal of influence in setting the agenda for recent conservative administrations in Washington.[2] To do this, however, is to distort the picture and practice a kind of academic McCarthyism. To be sure, there may be some blurring of difference at the fringes (e.g., the John Birch Society, former Arizona governor Evan Meecham), but New Right and New Christian Right groups publicly disavow racism and, if anything, represent themselves as more philo- than anti-Semitic. Their enemies are secular humanists, liberals, and Communists not blacks, Jews, and foreigners.

A more promising path out of the dilemma is to suggest the possibility that the current picture of right-wing extremism in the United States is a *pentimento* because under its visible surface design lies another far more substantial picture to be revealed. In the past American politics has produced powerful mass movements animated by ethnic, racial, and religious hatreds.[3] It follows that attention should be paid because, given the appropriate conditions, the old picture might emerge once again. But a more compelling justification for an analysis of the Radical Right may be derived not from a review of the past or speculations about future prospects, but through a brief glimpse at the present situation. In April 1985, 200 FBI agents invaded the compound of the Covenant, Sword, and Arm of the Lord (CSA), a group located on the Missouri-Arkansas border. Among other discoveries, the authorities found a rifle range known as Silhouette City. In polishing their shooting skills, CSA followers had practiced by firing their guns at man-shaped targets with Stars of David sketched over the chest areas.[4] In a disturbing number of recent incidents, individuals and small bands, either inspired by or affiliated with groups prophesying the values of right-wing extremism, have carried out politically motivated attacks on their racial and religious enemies. The shootings have not been restricted to Silhouette City. A few cases may serve as illustrations.

On Christmas Eve 1985, David Rice, a twenty-seven-year-old unemployed vagrant, walked into the home of Charles Goldmark, a Seattle attorney. Believing Goldmark to be Jewish as well as the head of the Communist party in the Pacific Northwest (neither of these suspicions conformed to reality), he proceeded to kill the attorney along with his wife and their two children. The killer had acquired his political beliefs through attendance at meetings of the Duck Club, a right-wing organization whose leaders were not only anti-Semitic but believed that Communist forces were massing on the Mexican border in preparation for an invasion of the United States.[5]

During the evening of June 18, 1984, Alan Berg, a talk-radio personality in Denver, was shot and killed by gunmen as he was about to enter his home. His killers were members of the Order, a group that believed the United States was controlled by a Zionist occupation government (ZOG). The Order's campaign of violence, of which Berg's murder was simply one episode, was intended to overthrow ZOG and restore the country to its rightful Anglo-Saxon owners.[6]

In January 1987, a federal grand jury in Raleigh, North Carolina, indicted five members of the White Patriot party for attempting to steal weapons from a U.S. military installation. The men had planned to use the weapons in order to rob banks and assassinate Morris Dees, a civil rights lawyer who had brought suit against the North Carolina KKK because of its establishment of paramilitary training camps in the state. The *Washington Post* reported that the indictments brought to twenty-eight the number of White Patriots and Klansmen who had been charged with violent crimes in North Carolina in the previous eighteen months.[7]

Late in the evening of November 13, 1988, in Portland, Oregon, a young Ethiopian immigrant, Mulugetta Seraw, was attacked and beaten to death in front of his home by members of a group of skinheads, a growing and now nationwide youth movement committed to the principles of white supremacy and anti-Semitism.[8] The racially motivated slaying of Seraw was preceded and followed by other skinhead killings and attacks carried out in various parts of the country.

The accounts of these violent events are intended to persuade the reader that radical right activity, though it may not pose a mortal threat to the republic, does represent an exceedingly serious political phenomenon to which attention should be paid. Let us, therefore, begin our analysis of it by seeking to specify the dimensions of the problem with which we are confronted.

DIMENSIONS

The 1988 edition of the ADL's compendium *Hate Groups in America* lists a total of sixty-four organizations, presently active, that espouse racist and anti-Semitic views.[9] To put this figure into some historical perspective, in his *Abandonment of the Jews,* David Wyman reports the existence of more than 100 such groups that were active in the United States during the decade preceding Pearl Harbor, and Arnold Forster, a former ADL official, compiled a total of fifty-seven like-minded groups in operation during the half decade following the end of World War II.[10] A more recent study, published by the ADL in 1983, reports the existence of twenty-two radical right hate groups active during the early 1980s.[11]

We can, of course, quibble about the numbers and the definitions used in their calculation, nevertheless, it seems fair to make at least one judgment based on these figures. Specifically, extreme right organizational activity and public opinion seem largely unrelated to one another. Various analyses suggest a long-term decline in the level of anti-Semitic and racist attitudes expressed by the American public.[12] But this trend appears to bear little relationship to the number of hate groups on the scene. The proportion of Americans willing to express racist and anti-Semitic views in the late 1980s is substantially smaller than in the post–World War II era, yet the number of groups active in the two periods is approximately the same.

TABLE 8.1   Radical Right Groups by Type, Frequency, and Region, 1988

Type	Frequency	Region
Ku Klux Klan	17	East = 4 South = 9 Midwest = 2 West = 2 17
Neo-Nazi	19	East = 0 South = 3 Midwest = 9 West = 7 19
Christian Identity	27	East = 0 South = 4 Midwest = 5 West = 18 27

Note: One group, the Liberty Lobby, headquartered in Washington, D.C., is not easily classifiable by this scheme.

Source: Anti-Defamation League, *Hate Groups in America* (New York: ADL, 1988), pp. 89–90.

The sixty-four groups identified by the ADL in 1988 may be classified in several ways. For one, they appear to belong to three separable species: Ku Klux Klan, Neo-Nazi, and Christian Identity groups. The KKK organizations, of course, have deep roots in American life, ones dating back to the Reconstruction era. Neo-Nazi organizations and the various groups linked to the Identity religious movement are of far more recent vintage, having emerged in the 1950s and 1970s, respectively.

Table 8.1 records the frequency of each type of group by the region of the country in which it is located. Several observations may be made based on these figures.

First, the most numerous kind of radical right group currently active in the United States is linked to a particular theology, Christian Identity. Second, with a handful of exceptions, there seems to be little organized radical right activity in the Northeast and Mid-Atlantic states. Although the South, not surprisingly, is the center for the various KKK-related groups, it is not the region where the preponderance of radical right organizations are to be found: That honor goes to the West. To the extent that neonazism manifests itself organizationally, it appears to be concentrated in the Midwest (Chicago, Detroit, and Milwaukee in particular) and the West.

The figures displayed in Table 8.1 do not provide a complete picture, however. Some groups do not fit easily into the three categories. There is an extensive network of organizations around the country composed of the cult followers of Lyndon LaRouche, who, until his recent criminal conviction, directed its operation through his National Caucus of Labor Committees from a heavily guarded estate near Leesburg, Virginia.[13] Originally a leftist of Trotskyite persuasion, and a pacifist, LaRouche turned to right-wing politics during the 1970s. By the end of that decade, he and his supporters had developed a complex and exotic conspiratorial view of the world in which anti-Semitism played a central role.

The Liberty Lobby, organized in 1957 by Willis A. Carto and headquartered in Washington, D.C., defines itself as a "pressure group for patriotism." In practice the latter word is identified with the promotion and dissemination of racist and anti-Semitic views. Its activities have taken a variety of forms. One is the Institute for Historical Review, an organization devoted to promoting the doctrine of Holocaust revisionism, a perspective that claims the Holocaust never occurred, that it is a hoax whose perpetrators are interested in stimulating unreasonable sympathy for Jews and Zionism.[14] Liberty Lobby also publishes a number of books and periodicals, most prominent of which is the *Spotlight* (whose current circulation is estimated to be 200,000), a weekly offering that exposes the destructive role Jews play in American life. Still another initiative is represented by the Populist party. The latter is a vehicle by which the Liberty Lobby has hoped to exploit the discontents of midwestern farmers by linking them to the designs of international bankers and the Jewish-controlled Federal Reserve system.[15]

Formed more recently and certainly far more colorful than the Liberty Lobby groups are the skinheads. They are gangs of white youth with shaved heads who often wear combat boots and display an affinity for Nazi swastikas and related paraphernalia. The American skinhead gangs are modeled after similar groups organized in Britain in the 1960s: "The skinhead nation was born in London in the mid-1960s, a direct descendant of the 'hard mod' subculture of the working class East End. ... The hard mods strove for a tough, clean style, in reaction to the androgynous finery of hippies and the sloppiness of the long-haired bikers known as rockers."[16] In keeping with their origins, the American skinheads are fond of a particular kind of rock music (there was a skinhead music festival on a farm north of San Francisco in the spring of 1989) started in Britain and known as Oi, whose lyrics stress the virtues of white supremacy and violence. Their favorite songs have such titles as "White Power" and "Nigger, Nigger."

Since 1986, skinhead gangs have emerged in many U.S. cities. Not all of the groups have become politicized on any consistent basis. For many young people, it is apparently the music, attire, and style that provide the attraction. But some gangs have become both political and violent: the Reich Skins in southern California, Romantic Violence in Chicago, and White American Skinheads in Cincinnati, among others. Furthermore, established Neo-Nazi and Identity groups, starved for youthful adherents, have conducted recruitment campaigns designed to bring skinhead gangs under their racist and anti-Semitic umbrellas.[17]

How many individuals are caught up in organized radical right activity at present? The available estimates are not precise, but they do provide us with at least a rough approximation. In 1988 the ADL believed that there were somewhere between 4,500 and 5,500 KKK members and that the various Neo-Nazi groups had a combined total of from 400 to 450 adherents.[18] But these estimates do not take into consideration either the skinheads or the followers of Christian Identity, the two fastest-growing components of the movement. (The Center for Democratic Renewal reports a figure of 3,500 for the racist, anti-Semitic segment of the skinheads.)[19] Nor do the accounts take into consideration the approximately 1,000 members of Lyndon LaRouche's organizations.[20] Affiliation with radical right groups is rarely as formalized as, say, membership in the American Medical Association. Observers refer to considerable overlap and turnover. Thus we are probably dealing with a pool of some 10,000 individuals with an unknown but likely much larger number of sympathizers.

There is some evidence concerning the backgrounds of those individuals who lead and publicize the various radical right groups and causes. Based upon biographical accounts the ADL assembled recently for fifty-five prominent radical rightists, the following portrait emerges.[21] We are dealing, first, with a group of males; not one of the individuals identified by the ADL was a woman. Not only are they men, but they are distinctly middle-aged as well; their average age in 1988 was slightly under fifty-two. Most were born in the United States, but a surprisingly high percentage of them (15 percent) were born in Europe. Almost two-thirds of these prominent radical rightists live in small towns. Few of the latter are to be found in the northeastern part of the country; the South is the most common place of residence, followed by the Midwest and West. Most of the leaders seem to hold middle-class jobs as insurance salesmen, real estate agents, high school principals, attorneys, ministers, state legislators, and so on; but a few, such as John R. Harrell, founder of the Christian Patriots Defense League, are independently wealthy. Some, such as Louis Ray Beam, the former grand dragon of the Texas KKK, are serving prison terms for violent crimes they committed in the course of their political careers. Most radical right leaders identified by the ADL are Protestants, though there are several Catholics. And one individual, Harold Von Braunhut, a businessman active in the Aryan Nations movement, was described in a recent *Washington Post* article as someone of Jewish origin.[22]

If the above commentary provides us with at least some sense of the Radical Right's leaders, what of its followers? Who are they? Where do they come from? Unfortunately, there is no easily accessible data on the followers of the various radical right organizations. They likely make up a relatively heterogeneous cast of characters. It is possible, nevertheless, to provide sketches of some of the participants' backgrounds.

On December 30, 1988, three teenagers belonging to a skinhead gang were arrested in Reno, Nevada, and accused of having shot a young black man to death; there was no motive other than their hatred of his race. Although their court-appointed attorneys did not wish me to interview their clients, some biographical information was obtained as the result of a conversation with a police detective involved in the case. The two boys (aged eighteen and seventeen) and one girl (aged seventeen) charged with the murder were described as having similar backgrounds. All three had dropped out of high school, left home, and moved from one community to another before coming to Reno. There they had a succession of menial jobs, most of them in fast-food restaurants. All three described themselves as "white working-class youth," but only the oldest boy was able to articulate coherent political views. Evidently acquired as a result of his involvement with the White Aryan Resistance (WAR), a Neo-Nazi group active in the Los Angeles area, these views emphasized a sense of loss and displacement. The United States been stolen from its rightful owners by Jews, blacks, and immigrants—groups that had no right to be in the country, much less seize control of it. Accused of murdering a perfect stranger, the three youths nevertheless felt themselves to be aggrieved and defenseless victims of injustice rather than perpetrators of violence.[23]

The University of Michigan psychologist Raphael Ezekiel recently conducted a series of extended interviews with members of a Detroit-area Neo-Nazi group.[24] These encounters occurred in the run-down, white, working-class neighborhood in which most of his subjects had grown up. The overwhelmingly male group of Neo-Nazis were young (half under twenty) and had been raised in fatherless households by mothers who held such full-time jobs as waitresses and beauticians. Most of his subjects had left school by the tenth grade; few were able to find work or express much optimism about their future prospects. They came to the group with deep feelings of racial hatred toward blacks and romanticized conceptions of nazism, the latter acquired from old films they had seen on television. The impact of group membership was to rationalize and refine these feelings as well as provide a means by which the members could express them.

Not all radical right activists are as youthful as the ones described above. Several years ago in Phoenix the FBI arrested eight members of the Arizona Patriots, a white supremacist band, and accused them of planning to rob an armored car and use the proceeds to finance the establishment of a paramilitary training camp. The suspects' average age was nearly forty.[25]

Middle-age was also a characteristic of the members of the Order/Silent Brotherhood, several of whom were convicted for Alan Berg's murder. The average age of those eventually arrested and charged with violations of the

RICO Act (passed to combat organized crime) for their participation in the group's violent escapades was thirty-six.[26] Members of the Order/Silent Brotherhood shared another characteristic with the Arizona Patriots and the more youthful skinheads and Detroit-area Neo-Nazis: They were predominantly males. Only two of the two dozen individuals linked to the Order were women.

Most members of the Order came to right-wing violence after having had earlier belonged to a number of radical right hate groups, usually to the Aryan Nations Church of Hayden Lake, Idaho.[27] Though there were a few exceptions, most were raised in small towns or medium-sized cities in California, the Pacific Northwest, and the intermountain West. In terms of their educational background, members of the Order were unlike the Detroit-area Neo-Nazis and the various skinhead bands. A few members were college graduates (mostly from institutions in the Pacific Northwest), and a few even showed signs of academic distinction.[28]

Radical right activism also has some allure for prison inmates and professional (nonpolitical) criminals. A 1985 Justice Department account reported the existence of 114 gangs in federal and state penitentiaries. They are typically organized along racial lines: black, Hispanic, and white. The white gangs, which emerged in the context of interracial tensions within the prisons, are often white supremacist and have such names as Aryan Brotherhood and Aryan Warriors.[29] As with the skinheads, leaders of radical right organizations have viewed the white prison gangs as a pool of potential recruits from which to draw members when the inmates are released from the penitentiaries. Accordingly, they have launched recruitment campaigns by providing the white prison gangs with supportive religious pamphlets and related literature.

In his important study of Christian Constitutionalists and Identity Church adherents in Idaho, James Aho emphasizes their normality. Aside from the fact that their occupations (e.g., independent contractor, itinerant preacher) tended toward the isolative, these radical rightists were virtually indistinguishable from other Idaho males.[30] For Aho, then, the family circumstances, educational attainments, income levels, and other characteristics of his sample of "Christian patriots" looked similar to a cross-section of other Idaho residents.[31]

The information concerning the social composition of the Radical Right, both leaders and followers, furnished in the accounts above is hardly comprehensive. Despite the fragmentary nature of the information, a few things seem clear. However the individuals differ from one another in terms of age, wealth, occupational status, educational attainment, and the like, the overwhelming majority are still white Protestant males. Do they constitute what Daniel Bell referred to many years ago as the "dispossessed"? Although "dispossession" does characterize a certain percentage, by and large they are not society's failures and losers as these terms are conventionally defined. Rather, it seems that they *feel* "dispossessed." Indeed, to the extent that there is a single overarching theme to their outlook, it is the sense that America has new owners: What was once theirs now belongs to someone else. If their social backgrounds do not tell all, they tell some things. They are whites in an era when major American cities have growing and highly visible black, Hispanic, and Asian populations. They are men at a time when women's issues have gained substantial public attention. They are largely Protestant during a period when Catholics and Jews have risen to positions of prominence in almost all walks of life. They live on the periphery (e.g., Idaho) when the center makes basic decisions (e.g., taxes) that affect their lives. The sense of loss, of dispossession, is palpable.

EXIT

One of the ways by which radical right groups have reacted to modern American life is by withdrawing from it. Sometimes their departure is purely psychological and takes the form of a utopian fantasy involving the creation of an imaginary, separate white Christian "Nordland," a nation to be established in the Pacific Northwest. On at least one occasion the exit has taken a more literal meaning, as when members of one group devised a plan to seize control of Dominica, a small island in the Caribbean, and establish an independent, white, Christian republic on it. Another collection of radical right bands, the Posse Comitatus, located in the West and Midwest, has sought to cope with the present situation by proclaiming all forms of governmental authority above the county level to be illegal. In this view neither allegiance nor taxes are owed to state and federal institutions.[32]

But the most prevalent kind of radical right exit combines religious ideas with isolative behavior. One observer refers to the groups displaying this type of response as the "compound dwellers."[33] As was the case with the number of radical right activists, there is no precise count of such compounds. The ones that have attracted the most public attention include the Aryan Nations (Hayden Lake, Idaho); Covenant, Sword and Arm of the Lord (Three Brothers, Arkansas); Church of the Living Word (Pineville, Missouri); Elohim City (Stillwell, Oklahoma); and the Citizens Emergency Defense System (Licking, Missouri).

The individuals who dwell in these and other encampments lead communal lives, engage in survivalist and paramilitary training, and adhere to Christian Identity theology. This doctrine provides a religious justification for their profoundly alienated view of American society. Begun in England during the nineteenth century and originally known as "British-Israelism," Identity theology was adapted to American circumstances in the twentieth century by the late John Wesley Swift, William Potter Gale, and the Reverend

Richard Girnt Butler. Identity offers a radical reinterpretation of common
Judeo-Christian beliefs.[34] It begins from the premise that the Anglo-Saxon,
or Aryan, race is the direct descendant of the ten lost tribes of Israel. Accordingly, the members of this race are God's chosen people. Jews, by contrast,
are the children of the devil, the literal biological offspring of Satan. Furthermore, long before God created Adam and Eve, the progenitors of the
white race, there were other human-like inhabitants of the earth, sometimes
referred to as "mud people." Because of their racial inferiority however,
Asians and blacks were unable to develop civilizations: hence God's creation
of Adam and Eve, whose racially superior offspring possessed this creative
ability. According to the theology, America was the land chosen by God to be
inhabited by the Anglo-Saxons. Yet because of a Satanic conspiracy un-
leashed by Jews, Aryan domination of this land has been usurped by the inferior races:

> In short, "white supremacist" racial theory is based upon belief in a kind of
> cosmic swindle, in which the birthright of the "Aryan" race has been taken
> from it, so that where it should exercise total domination over its racial inferi-
> ors, it must acquiesce in their parity or even dominance. Little wonder, then,
> that "white supremacists" have an obsessive concern to explain the deception
> and wreak vengeance on the putative deceivers, who in their cosmology, are in-
> variably Jews.[35]

The perpetrators of this "cosmic swindle" have formed ZOG to maintain
the subordination of the Anglo-Saxons to their racial inferiors in their own
land.

Identity doctrine holds out the possibility of redemption, however. Aside
from expressions of admiration for the Nazis, the theology contains a strong
element of millenialism. There is a belief in an imminent end to history in
which the wicked will be punished and the Aryan race restored to its rightful
dominance. The last days for America may be at hand. The compound
dwellers and other Anglo-Saxons able to absorb the doctrine believe they
will live through a seven-year period of tribulation, during which the existing social order will dissolve into chaos. This interlude will be followed by
the Second Coming of a white Aryan Christ. The Satanic Jews and inferior
races will be overthrown and the Anglo-Saxons restored to their preeminent
status. The purpose of the white supremacists' encampments is to prepare
for this eventuality.

In the past, right-wing extremism in the United States has been linked to
"super-patriotism." Superpatriots have been viewed as defenders of the U.S.
Constitution, traditional Protestant religious values, and "Americanism."
Their hatred was aroused when the status of these venerated symbols was
threatened by putatively subversive elements: Catholics, Jews, Communists,

TABLE 8.2   Origins of Hate-Group Periodicals by Region and Size of Community

	Number of Periodicals
Region	
East	4
South	14
Midwest	13
West	19
	50
Size of Community	
Rural, small town	34
Medium-sized city	9
Large city	7
	50

Source: Anti-Defamation League, *Hate Groups in America* (New York: ADL, 1988).

and others.[36] But it would be hard to define the compound dwellers and other adherents of Identity theology as patriots, super or otherwise. Their allegiance is to race and their longing is for the destruction of the United States and its constitutional government.

VOICE

In addition to exit, contemporary radical right activity in the United States also encompasses a repertoire of means the various organizations and publicists use to influence the general public and the political arena. First, let us consider activity intended to communicate their message. The ADL has compiled a list of fifty periodicals it considers to be published by right-wing hate groups.[37] The geographic origins of these undertakings are displayed in Table 8.2.

The center of newspaper and magazine publishing in the United States of course is the major cities: New York, Chicago, Los Angeles, Washington. But this is just as obviously not the case with hate-group publications. They typically emanate from small-town America and communities located outside the Northeast and Mid-Atlantic states. They are most prevalent in the West. Not surprisingly, this pattern corresponds, roughly, to the geographic origins of the radical right organizations themselves.

One unusual feature of the radical right publications, though, is that not all of them are printed in English. The largest distributor of Neo-Nazi publications circulated in Germany is an American, Gary Rex Lauck. He and his organization, the National Socialist Workers' Party—Overseas Division, are located in Chicago (although they use a Lincoln, Nebraska, post office box) and mail their German-language efforts to the Federal Republic.[38]

Some of the radical right organizations have taken advantage of modern computer technology in order to enable their members to communicate with one another. Anyone with a home computer, modem, and the appropriate log-in number can gain access to the Aryan Nations Liberty Net and receive a variety of appeals and sermons on screen. But for the already initiated Aryan Patriots who possess the correct access codes, there is detailed information available concerning upcoming meetings and the names and addresses of like-minded individuals in the vicinity.[39]

For the most part, the publications and computer-based network provide messages to those already sympathetic to the Radical Right's voice. Television and radio, in contrast, offer much greater potential for reaching the uninitiated. The ability of radical right spokesmen to gain access to or sympathetic treatment from network television is limited, though. One reason for this limitation may be that the reporters, directors, and staffs of the network news departments are overwhelmingly hostile to the messages these spokesmen are prepared to deliver. In terms of their social backgrounds and political beliefs, the employees of network news departments are almost polar opposites to radical right activists. The former tend to be from the Northeast and from relatively well-to-do families, have university degrees, and possess political views more liberal than the general public's, much less the radical rightists'.[40] Nonetheless, representatives of the various groups do appear from time to time on television talk shows, ones whose hosts seem to specialize in confronting their audiences with guests who exhibit exotic lifestyles and eccentric outlooks on the world. Also, Lyndon LaRouche has been able to purchase time on network television in connection with his 1980 and 1984 presidential election campaigns.

Right-wing extremists have had marginally better opportunities to make use of cable television. This medium has provided audiences in the millions for the televangelists associated with the New Christian Right movement. The political careers of such figures as Pat Robertson and Jerry Falwell have been made largely as a result of their public appearances on Christian Broadcasting outlets.[41] The Radical Right cannot come close to matching these achievements. Nevertheless, Tom Metzger, a defeated congressional candidate and leader of WAR, now produces a show titled "Race and Reason" that is shown on public-access channels in fifteen cable markets, including such major metropolitan areas as Los Angeles, San Francisco, Kansas City, Atlanta, Memphis, and Phoenix.[42]

Radio may be a more significant outlet for the expression of racist and anti-Semitic views. Small, locally owned AM stations that have adopted the news-talk format occasionally provide opportunities for radical right spokesmen to have their say. For instance, a Salt Lake City station recently began broadcasting a Saturday morning show called "The Aryan Nations Hour." In the mid-1980s a Posse Comitatus group gained control of a small station in Dodge City, Kansas, from which it broadcast messages attacking Jews, Catholics, blacks, the banks, and the Internal Revenue Service.[43]

Unlike television news, radio programming furnishes occasions for the audience to interact on the air with the broadcasters. Since in the late 1970s, there has been a proliferation of phone-in shows on AM stations whose format permits members of the audience to call the station and anonymously express their social and political views.[44] If the college-educated reporters on network television news shows routinely deplore expressions of racism and anti-Semitism, those who call talk radio programs often advocate racial and religious bigotry. One analyst recently referred to these shows as venues for the expression of proletarian despair.[45]

There is some information, admittedly fragmentary, concerning the social characteristics of both the talk radio audience and those individuals who call in to have their views broadcast. One study, done in the early 1980s, reported that the forty-seven stations in the United States that used the news-talk format had a combined weekly audience of 24 million people. By contrast to radio shows that play music, the news-talk programs deliberately target an older audience, individuals between the ages of twenty-five and fifty-four. Despite this intention, a substantial proportion of the listeners are in fact over fifty-five. Even though women dominate this older age cohort, a majority of listeners are men.[46] The phone-in shows often vary according to their hosts' political outlook: right-wing conservative, devil's advocate, and argumentative liberal are common bases of differentiation. Callers differ depending on the hosts' political inclinations. One analysis of those who call shows with right-wing conservative hosts reports the callers to be disproportionately composed of retirees, housewives, and those with high school educations.[47]

The evidence, again fragmentary, suggests these shows provide opportunities for older, less-educated people to voice bitter resentments against blacks, Hispanics, Jews, and those in positions of power who have extended unwarranted privileges to members of these minority groups. In addition, analyses of the contents of phone-in shows in Boston and Chicago, done at different times during the 1980s, indicate many callers denounce welfare recipients, permissiveness, affirmative action policies, and the general decay of American life. Conspiratorial explanations are not uncommon.[48] There is no evidence to suggest that the callers are connected to radical right hate groups. Instead, they seem to represent a not insignificant segment of the population susceptible to the appeals of such groups, if the latter were able to find effective means for making them.

Indeed there have been occasions recently when individuals affiliated with radical right groups have sought to exploit this sentiment by running for public office. For instance, in 1989 former Ku Klux Klan leader David Duke was elected to the Louisiana legislature as a Republican despite the public intervention of President Bush and other national GOP leaders. More recently Duke received enormous publicity during his unsuccessful gubernatorial campaign. In this contest his background in radical right politics became a central issue. Other examples could be brought to bear. An organized and systematic effort to tap the discontent was mounted in 1984 by the Populist party, a creature of the Liberty Lobby. Emphasizing the plight of the farmer and the U.S. government's refusal to alleviate it—all the while providing financial support to Israel, the Populists waged a presidential campaign on behalf of the Reverend Bob Richards. Richards, a former Olympic athlete, managed to win 10,882 votes (out of more than 11 million cast) in six farm-belt states.[49]

But by all odds the most elaborate and sophisticated effort of this kind was undertaken by the LaRouche organization. In addition to his 1980 and 1984 presidential campaigns, ones aided by federal matching funds as well as a complex credit card fraud, LaRouche formed the National Democratic Policy Committee (NDPC) as a vehicle to field candidates in Democratic primaries all over the country. Between 1982 and 1988, LaRouche-backed candidates contested close to 4,000 Democratic primaries and general elections in over thirty states. During these years his NDPC candidates received over 4 million votes. The most publicity accrued by LaRouche candidates was in Illinois, where two of them won Democratic primary nominations for state treasurer and lieutenant governor.[50] For the most part, though, the candidates achieved their successes when they ran unopposed in districts that were normally Republican and where serious Democratic challengers were, consequently, hard to recruit. No NDPC candidate was ultimately elected to any office higher than that of school board member.

Still, 4 million votes are not to be made light of. Evidence from the Illinois results suggests the LaRouche candidates did best among blue-collar workers living in communities where crime and unemployment were widespread and in areas where farming was an important activity.[51]

It was rare for either LaRouche or his candidates to unveil full-blown versions of the cult's ideology (which involves a theory according to which a global Anglo-Jewish conspiracy exists to weaken Western society, in the face of Soviet subversion, and makes possible its control by international bankers, drug merchants, and Zionists). Instead, they offered relatively specific proposals to deal with concrete problems, for example, repealing environmental protection laws as a way to save jobs in manufacturing.

The voice of the LaRouche organization was not limited to campaign activity on behalf of its candidates. In addition, it mounted publicity campaigns to promote the Strategic Defense Initiative, nuclear energy, as well as an end to U.S. support for Israel. It also sought to stimulate public support for ex-Nazi rocket scientists facing deportation. Using the last word in "dirty tricks," it tried to discredit 1988 presidential candidate Michael Dukakis and former secretary of state Henry Kissinger by disseminating rumors they were, respectively, mentally ill and homosexual. Perhaps the LaRouche organization's most significant achievement to date was getting 700,000 signatures on a petition in California (in 1986) on behalf of a ballot proposition to have victims of AIDS placed in quarantine.[52]

American radical right political activity is not confined to Americans or limited to the United States. There are international linkages to be considered. Aryan Nations holds an annual world congress at its Idaho compound at which individuals from like- minded groups in Canada and Great Britain have been in attendance. Some years ago when the World Anti-Communist League held a conference in Washington, it brought together delegates representing the Liberty Lobby with representatives of the Crown Commonwealth League of Rights and the Neo-Fascist Italian Social Movement.[53] But as is true for the domestic situation, so too in this case, the LaRouche organization seems to have developed the most extensive international network. There are LaRouche-affiliated groups in Latin America; in particular, there are LaRouche labor parties in Mexico, Peru, and Venezuela, and a rather misnamed LaRouche Club of Life in Colombia. There is also a European Labor party headquartered in Wiesbaden, Germany, that achieved some notoriety as the result of its ties to retired, high-ranking Bundeswehr officers.[54] It remains to be seen, however, whether or not these various international initiatives represent anything more than handfuls of multinational crackpots from isolated fringe groups talking to each other from time to time.

VIOLENCE

Data are available concerning the frequency of racist and anti-Semitic violence in the United States. For instance, the National Council of Churches issued a statement recently in which it reported that between 1980 and 1986 there were 121 murders, 302 assaults, and over 300 cross burnings carried out for racial motives. The statement went on to say that these figures reflected a dramatic resurgence of antiblack violence during the 1980s.[55] Likewise, the ADL's annual audit of anti-Semitic incidents for 1990 showed an 18 percent rise in their occurrence over the previous year (see Table 8.3). The ADL interpreted these figures to mean that an almost decade-long trend of decline in anti-Semitic violence had been reversed.

Various explanations have been offered to account for these developments. The ones probably mentioned most frequently in the press belong in the realm of atmospherics. The Reagan administration's hostility toward affirmative action and welfare state programs, the Bitburg incident, the Pollard spy case, and Israeli behavior in the Middle East have all been blamed for stimulating or facilitating a racist and anti-Semitic backlash.

No matter the immediate cause(s), it is hard to say how much of this violence is the direct result of radical right groups and of individuals inspired

TABLE 8.3   Frequency of Anti-Semitic Incidents in the United States

	Vandalism	Harassments, Threats, Assaults
1980	377	112
1981	974	350
1982	829	593
1983	670	350
1984	715	363
1985	638	306
1986	594	312
1987	694	324
1988	823	458
1989	845	587
1990	927	758

Source: Anti-Defamation League, Audit of Anti-Semitic Incidents, 1990 (New York: ADL, 1991), p. 22.

by their exhibitions of voice. The racially motivated killing of a black youth in the Howard's Beach section of New York City aroused widespread concern a few years ago. But the event was not caused by organized right-wing extremists. New York has consistently been the site of the highest incidence of anti-Semitic attacks over the years, but there is little radical right activity in the state. Acts of anti-Semitic vandalism, cemetery desecrations, for example, are often the product of teenage pranksters rather than organizationally inspired religious bigotry.

Illustratively, the ADL reports that 86 percent of those arrested in connection with such incidents in 1986 were twenty years of age or younger.[56] Yet sometimes violent events stimulated by radical right groups are not reflected in these figures. For instance, on May 16, 1986, a middle-aged couple, David and Doris Young, invaded an elementary school in Cokeville, Wyoming, and held its students and teachers hostage. The Youngs demanded a $300 million ransom and a talk with President Reagan. In the course of this episode, Mrs. Young was killed when a homemade bomb she was holding detonated accidently, and her husband then committed suicide by shooting himself in the head. From a diary Mr. Young left behind, the police learned that the couple had hoped to use the ransom to promote the restoration of Aryan supremacy. Mr. Young was a longtime member of the Posse Comitatus and a believer in Christian Identity.[57]

If many of the racist and anti-Semitic attacks were carried out by individuals unrelated to organized radical right groups, some evidence shows a particular type of violence committed by these bands. According to the Rand Corporation, which accumulates data on terrorist events within the United States on an annual basis, there was a general decline in the frequency of these planned and politically motivated acts carried out by small groups during the 1983–1986 period.[58] Another study, using FBI statistics, reported the same result.[59] Yet within this general pattern, the frequency of terrorist attacks committed by radical right organizations showed an increase. The numbers involved are small (there were only thirty-nine terrorist events recorded in 1986) and the period over which they were accumulated is short, but the evidence points to the growing domination of terrorist violence in the United States by radical right organizations.

The groups responsible for perpetrating acts of terrorist violence—the Order, Silent Brotherhood Strike Force II, Posse Comitatus, Arizona Patriots, White Patriot party—had in common their members' commitments to Christian Identity theology. It seems many participants in these groups hoped that by unleashing a terrorist campaign they would provoke a white racial revolution along the lines described in the novel *The Turner Diaries* by William Pierce, a longtime radical right leader. By robbing banks and armored cars, bombing synagogues and Internal Revenue Service offices, and murdering or planning to murder selected representatives of ZOG, they also believed they would restore Anglo-Saxon dominance, destroy the Jews, and thereby hasten the coming of the millennium. According to Thomas Martinez, a member of the Order who became an FBI informant, many of those involved in the terrorist campaign had grown tired of all the Identity sermons and talks to which they had been exposed and decided to translate the rhetoric into action.[60]

To date, what these groups have managed to achieve are extensive FBI manhunts and a series of federal and state criminal prosecutions. In Seattle, Denver, and Boise, convictions have been obtained against radical right terrorists for having committed a long list of violent crimes.[61] But the most far-reaching prosecution, one brought against the national leaders of the major Identity-related groups for sedition (i.e., organizing a violent nationwide scheme to overthrow the U.S. government), in a federal district court in Fort Smith, Arkansas resulted in an acquittal (1987).

Some federal authorities believe radical right terrorism has been dealt a fatal blow by the arrest and prosecution of many of those responsible for the recent violence. This may not be the case, however. After the destruction of the Order in 1985, some members of the Aryan Nations formed a successor group, the Silent Brotherhood Strike Force II, in order to continue its work. Will strike forces III, IV, and V emerge in the future? There are the already violent skinheads to contemplate, and the Identity movement continues to attract followers in various parts of the American West.

CONCLUSION

There are at least three ways by which contemporary American radical rightism may be explained. First, it may be understood historically as a continuation of what Seymour Martin Lipset and Earle Raab have called the politics of unreason.[62] Right-wing extremism, after all, is not a new phenomenon in American political life. Its organized manifestations have been present almost since the founding of the republic. At various times in American history, political groups expressing radical right views have been far more powerful than the current collection. The latter may simply represent a remnant, the modern-day bearers of the tradition.

But the groups and organizations with which I have been concerned in this chapter are not museums or historical societies whose curators are interested in displaying artifacts from the past to modern audiences. Their vitality seems to reflect that, at least for some people, they offer meaningful responses to current developments.

Accordingly, a second way of understanding the contemporary Radical Right is by reference to certain structural strains in American society. In a recent assessment, Robert Reich notes that "the American economy ... is creating a wider range of earnings than at any other time in the postwar era."[63] Reich cites figures from 1978 through 1987 that indicate the real income of persons employed in the securities industry (e.g., brokers, investment bankers) rose by 21 percent, while the number of Americans who were employed but whose incomes fell below the poverty line rose by 23 percent. The general beneficiaries of recent economic trends are those Reich defines as providing "symbolicanalytic services," jobs that require higher education and involve the manipulation of information. The principal losers are those workers engaged in "routine production services," that is, individuals whose occupations involve farming and manufacturing, and those who provide "routine personal services," such as truck drivers, custodians, restaurant employees, barbers, and beauticians. Individuals who earn their living by performing routine production or service jobs and who lack postsecondary educations have been hard hit by the changing nature of the American economy and the competition it faces from abroad. It would not appear to be an accident that the radical right groups apparently have drawn many of their members and sympathizers from whites employed in these increasingly distressed economic sectors.

Third, given the historical and structural explanations, what accounts for the particular attraction of the Christian Identity movement and its evident propensity to spin off groups committed to the restoration of white supremacy through violence? Protestant religious excitation, hatred of blacks and Jews, fear of foreigners are hardly new phenomena in American life. The answer seems to rest in the messianic element in the doctrine. According to David Rapoport, the rise to popularity of messianic movements is often associated with the presence of "signs" that the last days may be imminent.[64] At present, signs that the end of the world may be near abound: the threat (until recently) of nuclear war and warnings of ecological disaster coupled with the restoration of the State of Israel make such prophesies seem plausible.

At least for some individuals whose temporal experiences or personal lives reflect the economic strains just mentioned, messianic beliefs may become quite compelling. For those who have come to view the world in these apocalyptic terms, the desire to "force the end" and issue in the millennium by violent means has become exceedingly powerful.

CONCLUSION:
A NEW LEASE ON LIFE
FOR THE RADICAL RIGHT?

Peter H. Merkl

As Emperor Hirohito lay dying in late 1988, the mayor of Nagasaki, Hitoshi Motoshima (age sixty-seven), said in response to a question in city council: "I have been in the military and I think the Emperor bore some responsibility for the [Second World] war." His statement was hardly news, but he nearly paid with his life for breaking a long-standing taboo, as a gunman shot him from behind about a year later. The would-be assassin belonged to Seikijuku, a radical right organization that supports the old imperial system and, in particular, the once deified royal family and Japanese conduct in the war. This was not the first time that deadly violence had been threatened by the Japanese contemporary Radical Right, which otherwise has a reputation of involvement in local rackets and organized crime rather than political activity.

There is no need to repeat here the definitions of the Radical Right or of the more generic "right-wing extremism" (which includes avowedly Neo-Fascist movements) supplied by most of the contributors to this book. In fact, it is very important to resist the popular and journalistic tendency to reify the Radical Right, turn it into a "thing," a Platonic "essence" surfacing in many places. It would be more correct to say that there is a touch of Le Pen in most French people, a bit of Gush Emunim in most Israelis, or a little nativism in most of us, but that at the fringes of each modern society these little touches will *on occasion* become an obsessive concern, especially for certain personality types who may form dangerous, extremist, and often violently aggressive movements. This is also the reason why it is often difficult to draw the line between, say, a former Klansman and an America First candidate for president. It also does not help our understanding of the

204

phenomenon to exaggerate the "certain personality types and ignore the essential normality of most right-wing extremists, including those who act out their prejudices in a violent fashion. To be sure, these strong prejudices against Jews, people of color, women, foreigners, or religious minorities are dysfunctional to society and a menace to the designated victims, but so are nonpolitical crime, alcoholism, drug abuse, and many other activities that more or less rational people engage in. That radical right movements tend to crest "on occasion" constitutes their challenge to the system and should focus our attention on the kind of occasions that can make a real threat: In the cases of Great Britain, France, Germany, and the rest of Western Europe, for example, the concentrated irritant of seemingly uncontrolled immigration appears to provoke the equivalent of the "touch of Le Pen" in most of the population, leading to demands for *action* and, possibly, propelling irresponsible demagogues into positions of power.

The multifaceted crisis of post-Soviet Russia—national identity, the loss of power, and the intractable economic morass (plenty of parallels to the terminal crisis of the Weimar Republic)—raised the menacing hosts of Pamiat and, most recently, a would-be little Hitler in the person of Vladimir Volfovich Zhirinovsky of the misnamed Liberal Democratic party who won 7.8 percent of the votes in the Russian presidential elections. Fortunately for Russia, the entrenched Communist power structures are no easy match for this ambitious demagogue who advocates suppressing the remnants of Communist rule with a Communist-like dictatorship of the Right. His prescription resembles more the Fascist states of Hitler and Mussolini than the libertarian Radical Right of, say, the Italian Lega Lombarda, the Scandinavian tax revolt movements (the anti-immigrant Swedish New Democrats and Denmark's Glistrup party), the Swiss Automobilists party, or some of Reagan's radical right supporters in the 1980s. Of the authors in this volume, at any rate, only one attributes a crucial hold on national policy to the radical right movement he describes, owing to "its sophisticated penetration of the larger parties, the exceptional determination of its members, and the strategic location of its constituency," in the West Bank. Ehud Sprinzak could have added also its cohesion and skillful leadership, the lingering crisis of Israeli identity, and, most of all, the international situation of Israel after the decline of the East-West conflict in the Middle East, which places the government under extraordinary pressure to withdraw from the areas occupied since the war of 1967. This outside pressure on the recalcitrant settlers may well bring out the "little bit" of the Radical Right in many Israelis who have not been on its side before. The external pressure on Israel today, of course, is the equivalent of internalized controls in some other modern nations: Massive civil rights demonstrations (by SOS Racisme and others) and deliberate antiprejudice education in the schools, strong liberal traditions as in the United States and France, or massive guilt feelings as in Germany are needed to rein in the "little bit" of radical right feelings in many people before they can turn a time of crisis into one of shameful excesses.

There is violent radical right activity all over the world, as one can read in the newspapers almost every day, and not just in the countries included in this collection. There have been nationalist murder and mayhem from several sides in India, where Sikhs, Tamils, and fanatic Hindu groups have assassinated political leaders and engaged in sectarian killings on a frightful scale. In South Africa the lifting of the ban on the African National Congress (ANC), the South African Communist party, and other black liberation groups by President F. W. De Klerk on February 2, 1990, kicked off a furious mobilization on the radical right; by mid-August, no fewer than sixty-nine such organizations were known to be active. They engaged in vigilantism, bombings, and drive-by shootings directed at black youths, the ANC, and De Klerk's Nationalist party, and threatened the worst if an actual transfer of power should occur. Led by Eugene Terre Blanche of the Afrikaner Weerstandsbeweging, and others, they could probably muster a well-armed force of 40,000. Most young whites have been trained for at least two years in the armed forces and have access to more than 2 million registered guns. Their goal of resistance is articulated also by Andries Treurnicht's Conservative party, which received about one-fourth of the popular vote in the 1989 elections.

In Europe, too, there has been much more radical activity than this book could hold. In Austria, the place of birth of Adolf Hitler and some 700,000 members of the old Nazi party, there continue to be radical right incidents and attitudes that have kept alive the awareness of the past. There are a small but hard-core anti-Semitic percentage and active Neo-Nazi groups, such as the one associated with the South Tyrol activist Norbert Burger. Knowledgeable observers hesitate to relate the popular majority for President Kurt Waldheim, or the recent wave of the nationalist vote for demagogue Jörg Haider, to the Radical Right.[1] The patterns of Austrian xenophobic prejudice are clearly stronger in areas of the country's ethnic frontier, such as Carinthia and Styria, than, for example, in Vienna. Haider, until recently the *Landeshauptmann* (governor) of Carinthia and the head of the right-leaning Austrian Freedom party (FPO), lost his governorship in June 1991 over public remarks praising the employment policies of the Third Reich. It was not the first time that the flamboyant right-winger had offended even Waldheim's conservative People's party with statements reminiscent of the Nazi past. In the Viennese local elections of November 1991, his party beat the People's party with a tally of 22.5 percent. In Belgium a Radical Right connected to Flemish nationalism was extremely active until more than a decade ago. It maintained, in particular, close relations to Neo-Fascist groups in Germany and Italy and was known as the hub of a kind of Neo-Fascist international. Now it has reappeared as the anti-immigrant Vlaams Blok and raised its representation in the Belgian house of representatives from two to twelve seats.

In Spain and Portugal, too, radical right-wing forces have appeared in the wake of collapsing right-wing dictatorships. In Spain, for example, Francisco Franco's army was far less affected by the rupture with *franquismo* than most of Spanish civil society, and the fear of the "three black beasts" of separatism, terrorism, and communism characterized a Falangist hard core with a putschist mentality. This led to the coup attempt of Lieutenant Colonel Antonio Tejero Molina in 1981, allegedly in order to wipe out Basque terrorism by setting up a temporary military government under King Juan Carlos—who had not been consulted and resolutely squelched the putsch. On a paramilitary level, the small Fuerza Nueva (New Force) of Blas Piñar Lopez, a goon squad already in the service of Franco, became the last hope of the Falange after Franco's death: "If the government will not enforce General Franco's law, we men of Fuerza Nueva will take to the streets and do it ourselves." Piñar's list of enemies is long: "inorganic democracy," parliamentarianism and party government, liberalism, Jews, Marxists, the Bourbon monarchy, attacks on church and army, pornography, the breakdown of the family, urban crime, and drug abuse. He served as a Spanish senator from Toledo until 1982, when he announced the dissolution of Fuerza Nueva.[2] During its short post-*franquist* life, the organization had held a dominant place among smaller groups of the New Right and been linked more than once with Italian right-wing terrorism— for instance, in the case of the Bologna railroad station bombing of 1980. In 1986, moreover, half a century after the start of the civil war, it resurfaced as Frente Nacional (National Front), and the late Giorgio Almirante of the Italian Social Movement and Jean-Marc Brissaud of the French Front National were present at its official foundation meeting. There were bronze busts of Franco, Fuerza Nueva badges, the familiar blue shirts, and talk of the need to build "the Europe of Christianity." The Frente Nacional participated in the 1987 election to the European Parliament in Strasbourg but failed to obtain a single seat, in spite of winning 123,000 votes. Its members did no better in 1989, garnering only half as many votes, whereas their French comrades of the Front National held on to their ten seats and the German Republicans gained six seats in Strasbourg.[3] It was careful not to contest any domestic elections, although from 1988, right-wing radical violence in the form of the *bases autonomas* (independent local groups) was once more on the rise in the universities, at the secondary school level, and among the hooligans of soccer stadiums.[4]

A NEW SPECIES OF NEONAZISM?

If the question of continuity or renaissance of the Radical Right seems playful or even far-fetched in cases like Portugal, this is hardly the case with German Neo-Nazi groups. Too vivid is the memory of the Third Reich and its horrendous crimes against peace and against humanity. In Chapter 2 Ekkart Zimmermann and Thomas Saalfeld make clear how at least the first two waves of West German right-wing extremism, in the early 1950s and the mid-1960s, were characterized by a predominance of ex-Nazis and members of earlier postwar right radical right groups.[5] Even their programs resembled the old Nazi doctrines, except for planks that had been specifically proscribed by West German law and court practice, such as anti-Semitism or the advocacy of hatred or hostilities toward other nations. The third wave, however, the Republikaner party of the 1980s, is too far removed from the active life span of most pre-1945 Nazis to share this description. Although it is still apologetic of the Third Reich and would prefer to draw a bottom line under its crimes and offenses, its radical populism really appears to be fueled mostly by new and contemporary issues such as the presence of foreign workers and asylum-seekers. What appears left of the old Nazi legacy has taken the "bourgeois" turn of the historical revisionism of the New Right and the maintenance of Nazi culture among aging nationalists and not very militant youth groups.[6]

Yet there is a new and rather virulent strain of violent radical right activities that resembles neither the pre-1933 SA storm troopers nor the ideological National Socialist proselytizers of old. As Zimmermann and Saalfeld show, they include Neo-Nazi action groups such as the People's Socialists, the outlawed Military Sport Group Hoffmann, or the Action Front of National Socialists of Michael Kühnen, who died in 1991 at the age of thirty-five, presumably of AIDS. In tiny Mackenrode, near Göttingen, the Lower Saxon leader of the Free Workers party has turned his farmhouse into a fortress with barbed wire, dark netting, dogs, and a platoon of very young skinheads with bomber jackets and boots, and armed with axes, machetes, and guns. All of these organizations as well as the old NPD and Republikaner party have now discovered the former German Democratic Republic as a fertile recruiting area for the Radical Right. It seems debatable whether all of these groups are truly political, in any conventional sense of the word, even though they bandy Nazi slogans and symbols about and are capable of an extraordinary degree of violence. Increasingly in recent years, local skinhead groups and soccer rowdies have launched their own brand of "spontaneous violence" upon visible foreigners—Turks, Poles, Africans, Vietnamese—and members of the left-wing, anarchist, or "alternative," scene. Their actions show less evidence of partisan coordination beyond the local boundaries and sometimes seem as unpolitical as violent juvenile gang

wars over turf or girl-friends. Typical news items of just a few weeks in eastern Germany tell of characteristic patterns of violent incidents:

Potsdam, April 29, 1991; "Riots of Skins and Hooligans": About thirty
skinheads blocked a highway with their cars south of Berlin on Sunday, and
accosted other motorists. Some of them later extorted several bottles of alcoholic beverages from a store in Trebbin. In nearby Jüterbog, skinheads
later assaulted a group of foreigners with knives, clubs, and brass knuckles.
One of the victims had to be treated in a hospital.

Friday night fifteen to twenty [soccer] hooligans broke up furniture in a
roadside inn. Two guests from Kiel suffered head injuries from clubs and
kicks. One hundred and fifty hooligans from Berlin invaded Frankfurt on
the Oder to attend the game between FC Victoria (Berlin) and FC Leipzig. A
very large police presence curbed incidents in the city, but in Müllrose the
hooligans stopped a bus returning with Leipzig fans, inflicted damage on
the vehicle, and attacked the fans. The police reported further offenses of
the hooligans on their own return to Berlin, such as thefts, property damage, and physical injuries ... in [three towns].

Frankfurt/Oder, April 9, 1991; "Screams of *Sieg Heil* and Police Barriers":
On the day the Polish-German border was opened to Polish tourists without
visas, the bus with the orchestra Gorzowska Orkiestne Rozrykowa stopped at
the crossing before the Frankfurt bridge when the first rock came flying. A
hundred ski-masked youths stormed the vehicle, shouting "Sieg Heil" and
throwing more rocks and beer bottles. They broke the windshield and surrounded the bus. The driver honked his horn and accelerated his vehicle,
whereupon the attackers had to jump aside, and then the police arrived and
went after them with their truncheons. Two of the frightened musicians
were cut by flying glass. [There were unconfirmed rumors that both ANS
leader Kühnen and Republikaner chief Schönhuber had come to Frankfurt
to put in an appearance on the day thousands of Polish transit passengers
were expected to cross the border.] A local advertising flyer, *Oder-Anzeiger*,
carried an ad about "Führer Kühnen" under the headline "The Neo-Nazis
Are Coming to the Oder." Undeterred by the police presence, the masked
horde of assailants later mugged in front of the television cameras, shouting
"Only a dead Pole is a good pig" and "Germany for the Germans. Out with
the foreigners." The nervous police continued, among cries of "Stasi pigs,"
to cruise up and down Karl Marx and Rosa Luxemburg streets, using their
truncheons against groups of skinheads and sometimes on passersby as well
and, with considerable use of force, arresting juveniles and carrying them
off in trucks.

Mahlsdorf, May 28, 1991; "Attack on Fête of Homosexuals": About sev-
enty skinheads and their friends invaded a large gathering of homosexual
men and women, beating some of them so severely with wooden clubs and
iron bars that two women had to be hospitalized. They also damaged parked

cars and set several fires. The gay gathering had received a last-minute warning about the impending attack and a few guests left at this point. The rest were assaulted with, among other weapons, plastic bags of paint and gas pistols.

Zittau, May 15, 1991, "Attack on Russian Children": Ten right-wing radicals led by the local Republikaner chief marched on Friday night in front of a Zittau resort that had taken in forty Russian children from Chernobyl, the site of the 1986 nuclear disaster. An employee in charge of protecting the children was injured when he attempted to stop the radicals.

This was not the first attack on Russians whose soldiers in East German bases have drawn political protests, provocations, and physical attacks, including fatal stabbings, from skinheads and the like. The violence meted out to a variety of victims is a part of a rising tide of physical aggression and psychological displacement in the former German Democratic Republic.[7]

WHY IN FORMERLY COMMUNIST GERMANY?

There are a number of reasons why this phenomenon is particularly acute in the former East Germany and at this moment, not long after the collapse of the Communist dictatorship and unification with West Germany. First and foremost are the elements of the legacy of the Communist dictatorship, such as the enforced isolation of the population from travel and contact with other peoples. Despite official talk of antifascism and "friendship among peoples," the crudest prejudices were tolerated against Poles, Czechs, Russians, Jews, and especially the small number of visibly foreign trainees and workers from such places as Mozambique and Vietnam. The GDR population knew all along that the "proletarian internationalism" of the Communist regime was a sham and that even police misconduct toward foreigners was not unusual.[8]

A second set of reasons stems from the atmosphere of the transition, which opened the floodgates of racist discrimination and violence against Poles and other foreigners as about 160,000 foreign workers were brought in under Erich Honecker, including 60,000 Vietnamese, 14,000 Mozambicans, and 10,000 Cubans, many of whom were not in a position to leave the inhospitable land in 1990. There were frequent incidents of people being refused service in stores or being robbed in the street of what they had already purchased. In particular young East Germans were reported to be disoriented by the great change of authority structures and the "collapse of [Communist] values" in their families and schools.[9] As many as 80 percent of the youngsters were said to be possessed by a generalized sense of angst, a fear of their future, and a negative self-image of being "second-class citizens" of the new united Germany, which seemed to trigger in them a virulent search for their German identity and for scapegoats, and a violent hatred of foreigners. The resulting climate of aggressiveness and violence among young East Germans has spread a fear of rape among young women and of brawls and melees among young men attending the few youth clubs that remained open. Some 15 percent to 20 percent of young people in the former GDR are considered open to right-wing radicalization of a violent sort, and of course organizers of right-wing radical groups (both pre and post-1989) have been hard at work to channel the mobilized youths into their various organizations—third set of reasons for the growth of right-wing aggression there. One expert on the situation, Norbert Madlock, has pointed out that in East Germany the relations between skinhead groups and such parties as the NPD, the Republikaner, and the DVU are much closer than in West Germany. The rightists there also are far more militant and frequently mix their violence with robbery, looting, and extortion. Unlike the western part of the country, the "Wild East" of Germany also has yet to close its doors to U.S. Nazi Gary Lauck, historian David Irving, or to the public advocacy of nazism.

According to the head of the State Protection Service of the Common Criminal Police Office of the five new *Länder*, Bernd Wagner, the pre-1989 core of the Radical Right in the GDR already numbered about 1,500 active Neo-Nazis—a phenomenon hushed up by the Communist regime. They had been active throughout the 1980s and in 1987–1988 organized elite cadre parties with the names National Alternative, Free Workers party, German Alternative, and Nationalist Front that now lead assaults on left-wing and anarchist groups, including "alternatives" (and squatters in the abandoned houses typical of the rundown old towns of East German cities), foreigners, gays, and sometimes even the police. One step removed from this Neo-Nazi hard core are the Fascho groups, who have absorbed much of the Neo-Nazi ideology but are not yet organizationally integrated, and the skinheads, whose antisocial, anarchistic demeanor is often at variance with their unevenly distributed Neo-Nazi views: Not all skinheads are of right-wing persuasion or likely to remain with its causes. The soccer hooligans, finally, lack a unifying ideology other than their delight in physical confrontation, although they frequently sport Neo-nazi symbols and seem ready for recruitment.[10] Wagner also mentioned the appearance of new, hitherto unknown small groups of assailants of foreigners and left-wing or anarchist groups at the margins of this social movement of the East German Radical Right. He described their mushrooming membership as mostly fifteen- to seventeen-year-olds, and more often in small towns between 20,000 to 50,000 inhabitants than in larger places.[11]

Wolfgang Brück of the Central Institute for Youth Research of the GDR Council of Ministers reported on a pre-1989 study of a sample of 3,000 youths between fourteen and twenty-five years of whom 30 percent expressed some understanding for the skinheads, 4 percent "sympathized,"

and 1 percent "believed" in them. From 1987 to 1989 the GDR police examined fifty cases of criminal prosecutions of right-wingers, of whom over half
were skilled workers and another fourth apprentices to a craft. Some 82 percent were between eighteen and twenty-five years old, and three-fourths
came from families of skilled workers (47 percent) and the university-
educated intelligentsia (in other words, the Communist social elite) even
before the fall of the Wall. Although some of the pre-1989 skinheads later
went to West Germany, many came back with new Neo-Nazi affiliations, politicized and ready to recruit old friends for the FAP, NF, or NPD.

FROM PUNK TO NEO-NAZI

In the 1980s the new phenomenon typically occurred in the larger cities and
their environs, where alienated teenagers turned away from "official socialism" to the apolitical autonomy of the punk scene and, eventually, were confronted with official anti-Fascist propaganda and police repression. This
trend was especially evident from about 1987 on, after a major Stasi-
manipulated confrontation at St. Zion's Church in Berlin, when the Communist regime began to lash out at those "seduced by the West." Up until
this misguided campaign, according to some of the young people themselves, their rebellion had been unfocused and unpolitical, although obviously in contempt of the straitjacket dogma of the SED and its youth organization, the Free German Youth (FDJ). The autonomous youth culture,
moreover, experienced a great deal of differentiation: In addition to the styl-
ish and musical punks, there were the irrational Grufties, the first skinheads
and soccer hooligans, all of them a living provocation to Communist con-
formity that was unable to dominate the small groups of high school, apprenticeship, or juvenile-home buddies out of which these groups grew.

The harsh Communist clampdown, along with the official bagatellization
of their group membership, politicized the youngsters. To quote one of
them, "Since they put me in jail I developed such an extraordinary hatred
for this whole system here, a hatred for everything 'red' or left-wing. This hatred really has eaten into me; it is an extremist attitude." Stigmatized by all-
too-well-meaning Communist educators and law enforcement personnel,
he evidently decided in his despair to emulate the historical Nazis whom his
punitive tormentors probably paraded before him as horrifying examples
from the German past.[12] Parents of troubled teenagers and social workers
often understand this counter-productive mechanism whereby the rebel-
lious youngster may pick up precisely the role model that his or her parents
most warn against. With vengeance worthy of a better cause, the autonomous information networks of the various small groups seized upon all the
taboo subjects of the Communist regime: foreigners, the history of the war
and the Third Reich, the division of Germany, and the economic misman-

agement and political manipulation of the Communist regime. Self-taught, they turned toward crude displacement of their agonies upon scapegoats. After being punished for having taunted the Communists with what were in fact apolitical calls for tearing down the Berlin Wall or for German reunification in 1987–1988, moreover, the actual occurrence of these events in 1989–1990 must have left them in existential limbo. Instead of glorying in the demise of their Communist enemies—or physically attacking them—however, the skinheads, Faschos, and Neo-Nazis of today seem to concentrate their angry violence on defenseless Jewish cemeteries, "colored" foreigners, gays, and alternative groups.[13] There is a curious contradiction between the high levels of criminality among the young Right Radicals and their desperate assertion of moral and cultural superiority to the allegedly dirty and criminal foreigners who are said to be "not fit to live among Germans."

There is a fourth set of reasons why the radical right scene in East Germany has tended to go out of control, to confuse law enforcement agencies. The old People's Police (Vopo), not to mention the State Security Service (Stasi), was so deeply involved in the political and human repression of the Communist dictatorship that the collapse of the latter left most police and court personnel quite insecure and disoriented—feeling despised and blamed for their role in the repressive atmosphere of the dictatorship and in the confrontations with the popular demonstrations for democracy, in which the Radical Right often participated. For a while after the fall of the old regime, consequently, police were so disturbed they could not even be depended upon to intervene in street violence or investigate simple thefts and robberies. East Germans fell into an interlude of anarchy of varying local duration that could still be felt in 1991 by such potential victims of right-wing violence as foreigners or gays or Jewish cemeteries. To make matters worse, entire administrative structures were being reorganized, regiments of East German administrators were phased out, or ominously asked to reapply for their own jobs, and a trickle of West German civil servants were coming in to take over in the face of East German resentments. This transitional chaos after a startling paucity of Communist administrative efforts to cope with either the foreigner's need for advice or the need to supervise the young Right Radicals meant further anarchy, a situation made for skinheads, hooligans, and West German right-wing recruitment among them. The remaining Communist loyalists, moreover, were delighted to witness the discomfiture of the new regime and to see their self-fulfilling prophecy come true: that fascism would return the moment the Communist dictatorship collapsed.[14] Some Vopo policemen and former National People's Army soldiers, by the way, have joined the Republikaner.

The point of this discussion of Neo-Nazi mobilization in the former GDR is to establish a counterpoint to the usual description of Neo-Nazi politics predominantly in terms of the legacy of the Nazi past. The present Radical Right in East Germany, of course, cannot be understood without reference to the role models of the past, but the motivation is clearly from contemporary confrontations and predicaments.[15] The prejudice against foreigners emerging in public opinion polls, for example, does not stem from the xenophobia of the Nazis of another generation: 13 percent of East Germans "have reservations" about the foreign workers there—23 percent of East Berliners and, for that matter, 28 percent of West Berliners would not visit foreigners nor invite them to their houses—and 41 percent are against their working anywhere in united Germany, most of them for fear of a loss of jobs (83.4 percent) or because "we have nothing to give away" (15 percent), or because of objections to their way of life (10.1 percent—multiple mentions).[16] Because of their age composition or for more complex reasons, the voting strength of the East German Radical Right has so far remained well below expectations, with less than 1 percent in the state elections of October 1990 or under 2 percent in the federal elections the following December.[17]

HOW MUCH CONTINUITY WITH THE PAST?

A quick look through the contributions to this book exemplifies the strands of continuity of radical right groups with the past and the relative weight of such continuities as compared to contemporary dynamics and issues. The most important distinctions relate to what kind of continuity we are looking for, and sometimes it is not clear to which "past" period, if this can be determined at all, a radical right group could refer. One kind of continuity, that of personnel, has little chance of surviving thirty, forty, or fifty years, at least among the young activists who are mostly under thirty or even under twenty-five years of age. The German skinheads, hooligans and young NPD members of today generally underwent the formative years of their political socialization in the 1980s and have neither firsthand experience of the Third Reich of which they flaunt symbols and shout slogans nor secondhand experience through old Nazi parents. Even the Republicans and the older NPD members, say in their thirties and forties, went through their formative years fighting left-wing activists in the late 1960s and early 1970s and have never glimpsed the brown paradise itself, although they may have absorbed enough of it as the children of Nazi families that created a nostalgic Nazi subculture for the decades after the death of Hitler. We encounter their equivalents among the Italian *missini* and members of Pino Rauti's Ordine Nuovo who cut their teeth fighting the Italian student rebels and left-wing radicals of that same generation.

Among older groups of Neo-Nazis, there are probably very few of the immediate postwar generation who grew up amidst the overwhelming signs of the catastrophic Nazi defeat and destruction—unlike in Italy, where a large

amnesty let the old Fascists off the hook and thus spared them the embarrassment before their children. This group is are between about fifty-one
and sixty-three years old today. After them in age, there are the original Nazis (and the Italian Republicans of Salo), now sixty-four and older, who may
vividly remember the war years and the Third Reich. Such a one is Franz
Schönhuber, the Republikaner chief and a former SS officer in France.[18]
Obviously, this old war-horse and skillful television communicator would
not only appeal to other veterans of the war and the movement over sixty-
four but also represents a personal link to younger cohorts—though only up
to a point. There is a limit to the appeal of old veterans to young activists,
and even the number of voters over sixty-four—not to mention real
activists—is fortunately not very large and contains as well anti-Fascists and
Nazi victims.

Table C.1 makes an attempt to tabulate the dimensions of continuity of
the various radical right movements. It is not meant to be exhaustive, of
course, but only to help order the evidence. In the first column, "personal
experience" refers mostly to major factors of mobilization for the bulk of
the young Radical Rightists, such as Communist repression and internationalism in the cases of East German Neo-Nazis, the Russian Pamiat, and Vatra
Romanesca. In the 1980s, the reaction to immigrants and foreigners provided the impetus to right-wing mobilization, as in the case of the French
Front National, the British National Front, and German Neo-Nazis, West
and East.[19] The pitched battles of the Radical Right against the left-wing mobilization of the late 1960s and the 1970s also explain the Italian, French,
German, and even the American right-wing mobilization of an earlier set of
Right Radicals. Theirs was already a movement that was relatively less related
to historical antecedents except for the continuities that tied their left-wing
adversaries to the past.

These personal experiences play a different role from the socializing
background of family and right-wing subcultures of the second column.
Here we can contrast Radical Right activists from not particularly right-wing
family or cultural backgrounds—the "brown sons of red fathers," East German skinheads and Neo-Nazis, are a striking example—with those of strong
socializing backgrounds, such as the families of old Italian Fascists or German Nazis of the 1950s and 1960s that often passed on their convictions to
their offspring.[20] A more complex but obviously potent source of such family socialization may be religious or nationalist rather than partisan. The religious fanaticism that drives members of the American Christian Right or the
Israeli Gush Emunim and similar groups is largely family-taught and reinforced in small groups from an early age. It is more difficult to link a traditionalist cultural setting of, say, *la France profunde,* xenophobic Russian, Romanian provincialism or, for that matter, the imposed cultural isolation of
communist regimes to aggressive nationalism and racism.

TABLE C.1 Dimensions of Radical Right Continuity with the Past

Countries and Movements	Personal Experience	Radical Right Family Socialization	Reaction to Decline of Empire	A Distant Golden Age	National Orthodox Ideology
FRANCE					
Front National	Immigrants	–	–	Before 1968	Diffuse
Pieds Noirs, OAS	Algerian War	Family	Anticolonial emancipation	French empire	Imperialism, civilizing mission
Poujadists	Tax revolt	Small-business family	–	Middle Ages	Diffuse
GERMANY					
Republikaner	Immigrants	–	–	Third Reich	Diffuse
East German Neo-Nazis	Communist repression	–	–	Third Reich	Diffuse
NPD of 1960s	Conflict with the Left	Family	Memory of Eastern empire, Third Reich	Third Reich	National Socialist ideology
SRP, etc. of 1950s	Third Reich	Family		1871–1945	National Socialist ideology
GREAT BRITAIN					
National Front	Immigrants, race riots	Memory of empire	Pre-1918 or pre-1914 Britain	Nation and empire	Superior British race
ISRAEL					
Gush Emunim	Settlements in occupied areas	Religious family and school	Reconquest of Judea, Samaria	Biblical Palestine	Judaism
ITALY					
MSI of 1980s	–	Fascist subculture	–	1922–1943	Diffuse
Ordine Nuovo, etc.	Conflict with the left	Fascist subculture	–	1922–1943	Fascist renaissance
MSI of 1950s	Mussolini's Italy	Fascist culture	Fascist empire	1922–1943	Fascism

Movement	Reaction to modernism	Military-authoritarian subculture	Wartime empire	Pre-1945 Japan	Military-authoritarian beliefs
JAPAN Seikijuku	Reaction to modernism	Military-authoritarian subculture	Wartime empire	Pre-1945 Japan	Military-authoritarian beliefs
PORTUGAL MDLP/PDC	Conflict with Communist Left	Conservative family	–	Salazar's Portugal	Catholic integralism
ROMANIA Vatra Romanesca	Communist repression	Traditional family, religion	Defense of empire over Hungarians	Mythical age of organic nation	Ultranationalist agrarian populism
SOUTH AFRICA Weerstandsbeweging	End of apartheid	Boer family and small group	Defense of racial empire	Era of the great trek	White supremacy
SOVIET UNION Pamiat/Soyuz	Communist repression	Traditional religious family	Disintegration of Soviet power, Russian supremacy	Mythical age of Old Russia	Ultranationalist religious populism
SPAIN Fuerza Nueva	Fall of Franco regime	Falangist subculture	Decline of Spanish supremacy	Franco Spain	Catholic integralism
UNITED STATES KKK, New Christian Right, etc.	Disintegration, women's emancipation	Traditional family	Fear of declining U.S. empire	Mythical age of white supremacy	White supremacy, patriarchy

This brings us to the two symbolic levels of specifically historical orientation that characterize many movements of the Radical Right. Such movements have long been associated with a profound cultural pessimism, a belief that the nation or national culture is in a state of decline that, of course, can easily lead to a search for scapegoats or enemies responsible for the deterioration. The first symbolic level is usually linked to the loss of empire and in its milder manifestations enjoys the broadest popularity. In his study of the British National Front, Stan Taylor cogently relates its ideological antecedents to the persistent concern with the erosion of the economic and military predominance of the empire, and the disintegration of the empire itself, throughout the twentieth century. Conservative die-hard empire loyalists could easily focus their frustration on the "internationalism, liberalism, and socialism" that allegedly caused the decline and turn their fury on immigrants from Pakistan, India, East Africa, and the Caribbean isles. There were similar reactions to the loss of empire on the French Radical Right at the time of the Algerian War and its aftermath. The sense of loss was no less acute among the Right in the United States, where, in the Reagan and Bush era, it culminated in a widely popular revival of gunboat diplomacy and patriotic festivals to "overcome the Vietnam syndrome." From the sputnik era to the current demise of the "evil empire," conservative Americans have been motivated by the alleged decline of the country from greatness, and it was easy for radical right agitators to link this mood of pessimism to liberalism, to race issues, or simply to the presence of "Communists" throughout the system. Shades of the reaction to the loss of empire could very likely be found also among Japanese, Russian, Yugoslav-Serbian, Italian, and German hard-liners.

The second symbolic dimension, the fourth column, is usually represented by a distant golden age, a utopia, or a period when the Radical Right was actually in control of the country in question, as were the Italian Fascists under Mussolini. The compelling myth of a golden age, of course, omits most negative aspects of an actual historical period and is highly selective about what it does single out. In many cases, the golden age is mythical indeed, a utopia that never existed, a time of harmony and organic unity between rulers and the ruled and between God and the simple people. History has always had to endure quixotic projections by tormented minds, and the distance between these images and present life is probably no larger than that between some of the violent deeds of radical right movements and their rationalizations about them.[21] Suffice it to say that all of these movements, and many others, seem to have a great psychological need to believe in a historical myth.

The last column of the table seeks to record the presence and cohesiveness of an ideology, in particular a national orthodoxy, as radical right movements almost by definition tend toward the imposition of a single, unifying faith—everything else gets stigmatized as "un-American," "un-German," or "cosmopolitan," as Eastern European Communists liked to say during their frequent proto-Fascist lapses. As Table C.1 shows, however, some of the contemporary movements tend to be uncharacteristically diffuse in their ideology, either because they care little about it or because they are heterogeneous and composed of different groups, some of which, like the soccer hooligans and skinheads, are still on the periphery of serious political involvement. We might take this as another sign that there is a rather different and new Radical Right evolving that owes less to its antecedents and more to present crises. But the rest of the radical right ideologies also are far from uniform. Some involve more religion than the old Fascists or Nazis ever mustered; others are simply racist.

INDIVIDUAL CRAZIES OR SOCIAL MOVEMENTS?

Unlike, say, during the 1920s in Weimar Germany, the phenomenon of radical right violence in the 1980s and 1990s tends to appear as incidents involving disturbed individuals or small, disorderly groups. Even when larger numbers and perhaps even planning are involved, the violent actions look more like voluntary, spontaneous mayhem than the quasi-military operations of the uniformed ranks of storm troopers or Mussolini's Blackshirts of another generation.[22] The universal use of quasi-military garb and organization in those days suggests the close linkage of the Radical Right of the 1920s and 1930s to the intensely mobilizing experience of World War I that seemed to pattern them all, even if they had been too young to serve: the Blackshirts and Brownshirts, the Hungarian Arrow Cross, the Romanian Iron Guard, the several French and Belgian Fascist organizations, and the English biff boys of Oswald Mosley. By way of contrast, the contemporary Neo-Nazis, Fascho groups, skinheads, and their equivalents in other countries seem anything but disciplined and quasi-military, except perhaps in the sense that they like bomber jackets and combat boots. Only insiders can tell them from unpolitical motorcycle toughs. Even their occasional displays of Neo-Nazi symbols and insignia is playful and enough to make old drill sergeants wince. To intensify this impression, they usually appear quite inebriated and frequently become violent after only loud altercations with their victims. To be sure, there are also massed appearances and attacks, as seen in the examples at the beginning of this chapter. The question appears justified, nevertheless, to what extent the Radical Right of various movements acts individually or in spontaneous small groups and to what extent in larger, well-coordinated organizations.

American law enforcement policy, with the statistics it collects on so-called hate crimes, obviously assumes a preponderance of individual right-wing crazies and small groups. After the outbreak of the Gulf War, for example, the American-Arab Anti-Discrimination Committee reported a quintupling of acts of violence, harassment, or intimidation against Arab-Americans throughout the United States, from ten incidents in the first two weeks of January 1991 to forty-eight for the rest of the month.[23] At the same time, the number of anti-Semitic incidents reported for the year 1990 by the Jewish Anti-Defamation League was a record 1,685, including 927 acts of vandalism (arson, bombings, cemetery desecrations, swastikas daubed on buildings and other objects) and 758 incidents of harassment, assaults, and threats— and even a public assassination, that of Meir Kahane. The incidents included graffiti on three synagogues and a high school in Ventura County, California, that referred to the phrase the "synagogue of Satan" (Revelations 2:9), within a week after pop singer Madonna's song "Justify My Love," in which the phrase occurs, was first aired.[24] To curb the rising tide of hate crimes against blacks, Hispanics, gays, and other minorities, a bill setting new penalty levels was introduced in the California senate, and the state lieutenant governor warned against "a wave of hate crimes greater than we have seen since the heyday of the Ku Klux Klan."[25]

The preponderant evidence of Radical Right activities in the United States confirms the impression of considerable numbers of small hate groups with grandiloquent names but often consisting mostly of a newsletter published by a Mom-and-Pop team that makes a living from the contributions it solicits for "saving the world" from sundry conspiracies. In spite of the documented decline of prejudice in the public at large, moreover, there are thousands of individuals committing prejudicial acts somewhat in the vein of what students of German left-wing terrorism have dubbed "weekend terrorists": individuals or small groups of friends previously unknown to the police who suddenly commit solitary acts of violence, probably after bouts of drinking and other revelry have removed their normal inhibitions. Even the few larger organizations, such as the Klan or the Christian Right groups, are far from centralized, disciplined organizations; they resemble more a relatively unorganized social movement of like-minded individuals and small local groups than, say, the Nazi storm troopers of yesterday.

On the West German postwar radical right, too, in contrast to the several tightly organized but small cores of parties such as the NPD, the Republikaner, and small militant groups, there has always been a large fringe of loners and spontaneous small circles that committed acts of vandalism and violence against the usual targets. The police has kept a tally but has had a difficult time tracking down one-time offenders, vandals smearing swastikas, or even assailants in physical attacks with hardly a witness other than the victim and some ambiguity about the likely motive. What is different about East German Neo-Nazis and skinheads is their social cohesion, a youth subculture of mostly unemployed, ganglike social groups that meet in youth clubs and taverns for prolonged "coma drinking" and roam the streets at night armed with brass knuckles, iron bars, nunchakus, baseball bats, and other lethal weapons for "Fiji bashing." Except for occasional, organized mass attacks, their violence appears random and a (nonpolitical) purpose in itself.

They, too, more closely resemble a social than a political movement, and this impression is reinforced by their lively social subculture. Their social groups and clubs attract younger recruits and women who may not share their political attitudes to begin with. The hard-core Neo-nazis, of course, try to draw the young toughs into a more disciplined organization as fast as they can, but the desire of the youngsters for freedom from regimentation gets in the way. The same postmodern dynamics that drove East German youth of the 1980s to flee official regimentation in search of free living space with the punk scene—and, after repressive government measures, on to the skinhead and Fascho persuasions—makes them reluctant to submit to the discipline of a Neo-Nazi party. Even when they seem to cooperate with Neo-Nazi plans of coordinated, violent attacks, in other words, their subjective, individual engagement in violence may be expressive of their suggestibility rather than politically instrumental in the Neo-Nazi sense. Perhaps this is also the reason why their ideology seems so diffuse in comparison to that of party-trained cadres for whom ideology is a lever to enforce discipline in the organization.[26]

Even in France, where the Radical Right appears most prominently in the form of the literary Nouvelle Droite and Le Pen's National Front, there is a large fringe of individuals and small groups that commit acts of vandalism and mayhem spontaneously: The French Ministry of the Interior counted 722 racist incidents in 1990, far more than occurred in the previous eleven years.[27] In May 1990, after a nighttime raid in the Jewish cemetery of Carpentras left thirty-four gravestones broken and a freshly buried body horribly desecrated, more than 10,000 silent demonstrators at the Place de la République in Paris, in Marseilles, Bordeaux, Rouen, Strasbourg, and Grenoble expressed their dismay. Nevertheless, there were additional daubings of swastikas in a Paris cemetery, and Le Pen held a television conference at the time of the largest demonstration, at which he praised Marshall Pétain, the head of the collaborationist and anti-Semitic Vichy regime, and attacked the "Jewish lobby" in France. Behind these antics there is obviously a large constituency that agrees and likes to hear them, and among them are many individuals who are quite likely on occasion to take matters into their own hands. This is what I mean by a "large fringe" of loners and groups that may act without specific instructions or coordination by a radical right organization.

These relationships between fringe and organizational core are present also where the core may be an eastern Communist regime of a Ceausescu or

Iliescu or another potentate who condones or actively manipulates ethnic hatred and prejudicial action to his advantage. In such an environment, the differences between ethnochauvinism, agrarian fascism, integral nationalism, and alleged communism under a *conducator* disappear behind the white flames of Romanian hatred for Hungarians, Jews, and Gypsies, and the Vatra Romanesca can engage in massive street violence in Cluj or Tirgu Mures, safe in the knowledge that the dictator would approve of their actions. The Romanian Flame, with many former Securitate and Communist party members, is supposed to be only a "cultural association," but its xenophobia and anti-Semitism burns its victims with the same ardor with which Ceausescu tried to brutalize all the non-Romanians and their villages in his country into Romanization.[28]

Another example that the virulent fringe of ethnochauvinism can often count on police and other official connivance is the existence of the Russian Pamiat and similar organizations, with names such as Fatherland, Union (Soyuz), Committees for National Salvation, Russian Monarchist party, and Russian Communist party. They include organizations of Russians in Lithuania and Latvia and other former union republics anxious to assert their separate nationalities, and they have worked hand in glove with the KGB and the Soviet military there to squelch their rebellions violently. Pamiat's National Patriotic Front (headed by Vasil'ev) claims chapters in thirty cities and has 400 members in Moscow alone. In Moscow and St. Petersburg, Pamiat has generated such fear with threats of pogroms that large numbers of Russian Jews have been emigrating. Its several souls (see Chapter 5 by Vladislav Krasnov) include the familiar nationalist images of pious old women in churches of the Slavophile tradition as well as neo-Stalinists bent on rolling back the dissolution of the Soviet empire of nationalities by any means necessary. But they all share a virulent anti-Semitism that threatens to break out into massive pogroms at any time. The nativist subculture is very large and the fringe elements ready and willing to act spontaneously. Colonels Nikolai Petrushenko and Victor Alknis, two prominent members of the Soyuz delegation in the Congress of People's Deputies, wielded power in the street as well as in the congress. In the meantime, the Moscow prosecutor's office and a few other authorities have undertaken to dilute Pamiat threats and go after some individuals but to little avail. Early in May 1991, 3,000 St. Petersburg citizens marched through the inner city, calling on the "Soviet army to save us from the Jewish-Bolshevik slaughterers" and accusing the Russian president, Boris Yeltsin, of being an "errand boy of Jewish-international capital." Pamiat cosponsored the parade and supplied posters, warning against renewed diplomatic recognition of "Fascist, racist Israel." Half a year later, in an independent Russian republic, Yeltsin's nationalist rival, Zhirinovsky, proposed that Russia's Muslim population be "packed off to their native lands" and a great wall be built to keep them out until a resurgent Russian empire could once more subdue all the other republics.

PARTIES AND POLITICAL PURPOSES

At the other end of the scale from the social-movement component of the Radical Right are centralized organizations of a partisan, paramilitary, or religious nature. The picture is often complicated by the presence of several, probably competing, organizations that if carried to an extreme, may again resemble the many small social groups of a social movement. Nevertheless, it is safe to say that the predominant feature of the French Radical Right in the 1980s and 1990s is the centralized party organization of the Front National and its considerable electoral success. We can say the same for the nonelectoral, anti-Gaullist *Algérie Française* opposition of the early 1960s or the Poujadist party of the late 1950s, the Italian MSI, or (at the peaks of electoral performance) the West German Republikaner, the NPD of the 1960s, and the Lower Saxon SRP of the early 1950s.

In between the peaks, the social movement character may come out more strongly for lack of a unifying will to power. Unity and centralized command (see Table C.2) may also have religious or nationalist roots, as with the Gush Emunim and the Kach party, Vatra Romanesca, Pamiat and perhaps the Soyuz patriotic coalition, the Weerstandsbeweging and the South African Conservative party, or Fuerza Nueva and, at least in the first post-Franco years, the Alianza Popular of Spain. It will be noted that most of these organizations come in pairs with a division of labor, usually between zealots or paramilitaries on the one hand and an ultra-conservative political party on the other that, though sharing most of the views of the radical right activists, participates in the hated system by competing for votes.

As Table C.2 shows, most Radical Right movements have been backed up by a strong, centralized party, even though at times the control lapsed and there were several competitors on the far right. The degree of street violence (column four) seems to be related to the presence of a strong party, but not the terrorism produced by some of the radical right fringe or subcultures. Perhaps, centralized direction encourages systematic street violence, especially if it can promise protection against prosecution. Terrorism, though, is more often the product of individual frustration and desperation, the weapon of the impotent. The tally of electoral successes, finally, suggests no immediate danger of a government takeover by any of these movements, and probably none in the immediate future. This is hardly a reason for complacency, however, as long as substantial radical right movements are, by their mere presence, subverting the climate of public opinion in their direction. There is a subtle interplay, as we shall see, between the public mood—

TABLE C.2 Social Movement or Radical Right Party: Violence or Elections?

Countries and Movements	Lower Activities	Subculture or Small Groups	Partisan Organization	Degree of Street Violence	Electoral Success (%)
FRANCE					
Front National	Large fringe	Large subculture	Strong	Medium	11–13
Pieds Noirs, OAS	Considerable (including terrorism)	Large subculture	–	High	–
Poujadists	–	Large subculture	Strong	None	11
GERMANY					
Republikaner	Large fringe	Small groups	Declining	Low	7.1
East German Neo-Nazis	Large fringe	Young subculture	Disjointed	High	0.2
NPD of 1960s	Large fringe	–	Strong	Medium	4.3
SRP, etc. of 1950s	Small fringe	Small groups	Disjointed	Low	11 (Lower Saxony)
GREAT BRITAIN					
National Front	Large fringe	Small groups	Weak	Medium	15 in cities (1976)
ISRAEL					
Gush Emunim	Large fringe (including terrorism)	Intense subculture	Declining	High	–
ITALY					
MSI of 1980s	Considerable (including terrorism)	Large subculture	Strong	Medium	6.8
Ordine Nuovo, etc.	Considerable (including terrorism)	Disjointed subculture	Strong	High	8.7
MSI of 1950s	Considerable	Large subculture	Strong	Medium	5.8

JAPAN Seikijuku	Assassinations	Subculture Small groups	–	Sporadic	–
PORTUGAL MDLP/PDC	Large fringe	Large subculture	Disjointed	Sporadic (ELP)	1.1
ROMANIA Vatra Romanesca	Large fringe (including terrorism)	Large subculture	–	High	–
SOUTH AFRICA Weerstandsbeweging	Large fringe	Large subculture	Strong (Conservatives)	Medium	25
SOVIET UNION Pamiat/Soyuz	Large fringe	Large subculture	Weak (Soyuz)	Rising	21
SPAIN Fuerza Nueva	Small fringe (including terrorism)	Small groups	Medium	Medium	–
UNITED STATES KKK, New Christian Right, etc.	Considerable (including terrorism)	Small groups	–	–	–

for example, in the face of ever-increasing masses of immigrants—and the right-wing demagoguery of prominent politicians.

FLIRTING WITH THE RADICAL RIGHT

We could even stretch these concepts a little and suggest that, in France, Radical Right loners and small bands of violent militants are acting in collusion with the efforts of Jean-Marie Le Pen's National Front to win parliamentary seats and political influence. In Britain, the race rioters and toughs of the National Front defer to what used to be the Powell wing of the Conservative party. In the United States, at least in the 1980s, the crazies the Klan and of the New Christian Right were not all that far from the conservative political direction of the religious Right and the various other conservative camps—the economic, racial, and foreign policy conservatives—united by President Reagan, the "great communicator" who, it was said, made us at ease with our prejudices.

But then again, it is very important to maintain fine lines of distinction and at least consider the possibility that the largely cosmetic Reagan revolution may actually have stolen the thunder of the Right for the benefit of preserving the status quo, give or take some minor adjustments. Consider, for comparison, the situation in France, where recent polls of Insee Institute revealed that two-thirds of the families now fear a further rise in unemployment (twice the level of mid-1990) and nearly that many say that they have seen their living standards decline "visibly."[29] In mid-June 1991 the unemployment levels and other discontents touched off widespread incidents of rioting and clashes with the police among the Islamic and North African immigrants, especially young Maghrebis in the outskirts of Paris.[30] With regional elections in the offing, there was widespread expectation that Le Pen and his Front National would take advantage of the emotions aroused by the immigrant violence. But instead of the Radical Right, former premier and presidential candidate Jacques Chirac, the present Paris mayor and chair of the Gaullist party (RPR) jumped into the fray with a speech in Orléans that was pitched at the basest racial prejudices. He spoke of a French worker who sees "a family with a father, three or four wives, and about twenty kids who, without working, pull down 50,000 francs [about $10,000] in social benefits." For good measure, Chirac also threw in some words about the "odor" and "noise" of immigrant families, for his equivalent of Reagan's "welfare mother picking up her benefits in a Cadillac" or of the Bush campaign's Willie Horton, the black rapist on a prison furlough.[31] Later on television, the Gaullist leader added that he was only trying to embolden public authorities that were unwilling to "do something" about the crisis. There were the expected expressions of shock about Chirac's "xenophobic hysteria" from government figures and groups such as SOS Racisme. A surprised and upstaged Le Pen could only say that "more and more the people were coming around to the point of view of the Front National" and that they should not keep "picturing him as a devil."[32] Not to be outdone, a few months later, former president Giscard d'Estaing (UDF) wrote in a magazine article about the "immigrant invasion" facing France.

The point of describing the role of Chirac vis-à-vis Le Pen is to demonstrate the importance of focusing on the whole political context in which the Radical Right may function and not only on the Radical Right itself. In its electoral campaigns and in the political impact derived therefrom, the Front National is a product of the whole political system and reflects the reactions, prejudices, and choices made by all French citizens among changing everyday challenges. There is a constant battle to keep the extremist party and its doctrines marginalized—"picturing them as a devil" in Le Pen's words—to save the liberal, humane values of French civilization from the baser proclivities of the French themselves in a multicultural environment. The battle is addressed to all the French and not just Le Pen's followers, somewhat in the manner that all children are told to wash their hands in a dirty environment.

But there is also a political struggle to deny extremist politicians the facile victory of capitalizing on people's prejudices in a charged situation, and it is not an easy battle, short of undemocratic tricks and manipulations to keep the extremist party at bay.[33] Chirac's sally, then, amounted to telling the child that dirt is fine and in accord with French mainstream values, which from such an exalted public bully pulpit may have the effect of miseducating the nation. The same may be true of other conservative helpmates of the Radical Right in Great Britain, Germany, Italy, or Israel except that, like the "great communicator," Ronald Reagan, many of them never claimed to protect the liberal and humane values of the nation from its baser instincts.[34] If a major statesman's resort to racist appeals is bad, the eventual return to emphasizing mainstream values—for instance, after the hotly contested elections are over and the challenge of the Radical Right has been defeated at the polls—is no consolation, unless the "respectable" spokesperson is removed from office in disgrace. Otherwise, the child will not only remember that dirt is an acceptable mainstream value but also that it is alright for people in authority to speak out of both corners of their mouths whenever the situation demands it.

NOTES

INTRODUCTION

1. Karl Popper, *The Poverty of Historicism* (New York: Harper Torchbooks, 1964) p. 115.

2. John Maginnis, "The Hazards of Duke," *New Republic* (November 25, 1991) pp. 25–29.

3. Michalina Vaughan, "The Extreme Right in France: 'Lepenisme' or The Politics of Fear," in Liciano Cheles, Ronnie Ferguson, and Michalina Vaughan (eds.), *Neo-Fascism in Europe* (London: Longman, 1991) pp. 211–233.

4. Ian S. Lustick, *For the Land and the Lord* (New York: Council on Foreign Relations, 1988) pp. 153–176.

5. For the classic statements, see Daniel Bell (ed.), *The Radical Right* (Garden City, NY: Doubleday, 1963).

6. For a discussion, see Klaus von Beyme, "Right-Wing Extremism in Post-War," *West European Politics* 11:2 (1988) pp. 1–18.

7. Anti-Defamation League, *Extremism on the Right* (New York: Anti-Defamation League, 1983); Franco Ferraresi (ed.), *La destra radicale* (Milan: Feltrinelli, 1984).

8. Overviews of the debate may be found in Renzo De Felice, *Interpretations of Fascism* (Cambridge Harvard University Press, 1977); A. James Gregor, *Interpretations of Fascism* (Morristown, NJ: General Learning Press, 1974); and Stanley Payne, *Fascism* (Madison: University of Wisconsin Press, 1980). But even these summary discussions represent only a few books among a large number of overviews. See also Stein Larsen et al., *Who Were the Fascists? Social Roots of European Fascism* (Oslo: Norwegian University Press, 1980).

9. For a discussion along these lines, see Seymour Martin Lipset and Earl Raab, *The Politics of Unreason* (New York: Harper & Row, 1970) pp. 3–31.

10. See, for example, Seymour Martin Lipset, *The First New Nation* (New York: Basic Books, 1963) pp. 61–98.

11. See, for example, Russell Dalton, *Citizen Politics in Western Democracies* (Chatham, NJ: Chatham House, 1988) pp. 118–121.

12. Roger Eatwell, "The Nature of the Right, 2: The Right as a Variety of 'Styles of Thought'," in Roger Eatwell and Noel O'Sullivan (eds.), *The Nature of the Right* (Boston: Twayne Publishers, 1989) pp. 62–76.

13. Michael Billig, "The Extreme Right: Continuities in Anti-Semitic Conspiracy Theory in Post-War Europe," in Eatwell and O'Sullivan, op. cit., pp. 146–166.

14. Gill Seidel, *The Holocaust Denial: Antisemitism, Racism and the New Right* (Leeds: Beyond the Pale Collective, 1986) pp. 38–128.)

15. See, for example, Zvi Gitelman, "Glasnost, Perestroika and Anti-Semitism," *Foreign Affairs* 70:2 (1991) pp. 141–159.

16. For a summary of activities in Western Europe from the end of World War II through the 1970s, see Christopher Husbands, Contemporary Right-Wing Extremism in Western European Democracies: A Review Article," *European Journal of Political Research* 9 (1981) pp. 75–99.

17. For an account, see Anti-Defamation League, *Neo Nazi Skinheads: A 1990 Status Report* (New York: Anti-Defamation League, 1990).

18. Lawrence Powell, "The Makeover of David Duke," *New Republic* (October 15, 1990) pp. 18–22.

CHAPTER 1

1. UDCA is the Union pour la Défense des Commerants et des Artisans.

2. In addition to the Poujadists, these included the Ordre Nouveau (New Order), established in 1970 and banned in 1973; Occident, a virulently anti-Semitic group; (Groupe de Recherche et d'Étude sur la Civilisation Européenne (GRECE), an elitist and racist association; and the Parti des Forces Nouvelles, founded by Jean-Louis Tixier-Vignancour in 1974.

3. RPR is the Rassemblement pour la République (Rally for the Republic), the successor of older Gaullist parties; UDF is the Union pour la Démocratie Française, a federation of the Republican, Radical-Socialist, and (Catholic) centrist parties created in 1978 for the purpose of promoting the reelection of President Giscard d'Estaing.

4. Such as the Ordre Nouveau, the Parti des Forces Nouvelles, the Groupes Nationalistes Révolutionnaires (National Revolutionary Groups), and the Féderation d'Action Nationale et Europeénne (FANE).

5. Jean Chatain, *Les Affaires de M. Le Pen* (Paris: Editions Messidor, 1987) pp. 106–107.

6. Philippe Vilgier, ed., *La Droite en Mouvement: nationaux et nationalistes, 1962–81,* (Paris: Vastra, 1981) p. 91.

7. See Jean-Marie Le Pen, *Les Français d'abord* (Paris: Carrere-Michel Lafon, 1984); François de la Rocque, *Service public* (Paris: Grasset, 1934) p. 8 et passim; and Ariane Chebel, "La Culture politique du front national: présentation de l'évaluation d'une tradition politique française" (Paris: Institut d'Etudes Politiques, 1986, mimeograph) p. 118.

8. Louis Pawels, *Ce que je crois* (Paris: Grasset, 1974) pp. 50–51. The author, who is the editor of *Figaro* magazine, is a supporter of Le Pen.

9. See J. S. McClelland, *The French Right from De Maistre to Maurras* (London: Jonathan Cape, 1970) pp. 26–31.

10. PS stands for Parti Socialiste; PCF for Parti Communist Français.

11. This court was set up in 1963 to try subversives and was abolished by the Socialist government in 1981.

12. Pascal Perrineau, "Le Front national: un électorat de la crainte," in *CFDT aujourd'hui*, 88 (February 1988) p. 26.

13. Jérome Jaffré, *Le Monde*, February 14, 1984.

14. Pascal Perrineau, "Les Ressorts du vote Le Pen," in Philippe Habert and Colette Ysmal, eds., *L'Election Présidentielle de 1988*, (Paris: Figaro, 1988) p. 19.

15. Le Monde, Dossiers et Documents, *L'Election présidentielle de 1988* (Paris: Le Monde, 1988) p. 42.

16. CNI(P) is the Centre National des Independents (et Paysans); *Enarques* are graduates of the prestigious Ecole Nationale d'Administration; Michel Labro, "Le Pen et les Siens à l'Assemblée," in *L'Express*, January 24–30, 1986, pp. 56–57.

17. Note that only 61 percent of the "hard-core" Le Pen electorate who voted for him in April 1988 and only 28 percent of new voters (i.e., who had previously voted for someone else or had never voted before) who supported him for the presidency were prepared to vote for the FN in the ensuing parliamentary elections. Perrineau, "Les Ressorts," p. 30.

18. Catherine Pégard, "Faut-il avoir peur de Le Pen?" in *Le Point*, February 13, 1984, p. 38.

19. Alain Rollat, *Les Hommes de l'extrême droite* (Paris: Calmann-Lévy, 1985) pp. 16, 24.

20. Alain Rollat, "M. Le Pen et l'héritage Lambert," *Le Monde*, October 25, 1983.

21. Désiré Calderon, *La Droite française: formation et projet* (Paris: Messidor–Editions Sociales, 1985) p. 201.

22. Chatain, op. cit., p. 27.

23. Jean Raspail, "Serons-nous encore français dans 30 ans?" in *Figaro*, October 26, 1985, and the refutation in *Le Monde*, October 30, 1985.

24. Pierre-André Taguieff, "La Métaphysique de Jean-Marie Le Pen," in Nonna Mayer and Pascal Perrineau, eds., *Le Front national à découvert* (Paris: Presses de la Fondation Nationale des Sciences Politiques, 1989) pp. 201–203.

25. Paul-Jean Francescini, "M. Le Pen, un surdoué du Simplisme," in *Le Monde*, October 19, 1985, and "Immigrés: des chiffres erronés," in *Le Monde*, October 18, 1985.

26. Pégard, op. cit.

27. Ibid.

28. Rollat, *Les Hommes*, op. cit., pp. 98, 198.

29. Pierre-André Taguieff, "La Rhétorique du national-populisme" in *MOTS*, 8, March 1985.

30. Le Pen, op. cit., p. 135.

31. *Droite et démocratie économique: doctrine économique et sociale du front national*, preface by Jean-Marie Le Pen, supplement to *National Hebdo* (October 1984).

32. See Jean-Claude Eslin, "L'Effet Le Pen," in *La Revue nouvelle*, special issue, "La Perturbation Le Pen" (May-June 1984), pp. 73–74.

33. Philippe Baucher, "Le Pen," in *Le Monde*, October 16, 1985. See also Stéphane Rials, "La Droite ou l'horreur de la volonté," in *Le Débat*, 33 (January 1985), pp. 34–48, which distinguishes between the irrationalist and rationalist Right.

34. See Julien Brunn, *La Nouvelle droite* (Paris: Nouvelles Editions Oswald, 1979) pp. 9–11.

35. Alain Rollat, "M. Le Pen tel qu'en lui-même," in *Le Monde,* October 22, 1985.

36. Vilgier, op. cit.

37. Le Pen, op. cit., pp. 172, 215. One defender of Le Pen, Roger Holeindre (a member of the FN executive committee and himself elected to the National Assembly in 1986), argues that the presence of a Muslim (Mourad Kaouah) and a Jew (Robert Hemmerdinger) on the FN list of candidates for the 1986 legislative elections proves that the party is not racist. See his *Aux armes, citoyens!* (Paris: Robert Laffont, 1987) p. 17. These activists are found in the Association de Français Juifs, an FN front organization led by Hemmerdinger, a decorated veteran of World War II and an FN regional councillor of Ile-de-France.

38. Rollat, *Les Hommes,* op. cit., p. 98.

39. For example, politicians Simone Veil, Robert Badinter, Jack Lang, and Laurent Fabius; presidential adviser Jacques Attali; trade union leader Henri Krasucki; and media personalities Jean-Pierre Elkabbach, Michel Polac, and Anne Sinclair, all of whom have been the object of vehement attacks by Le Pen.

40. *La Vrai opposition: le front national,* point 2 (c) (Paris, no date).

41. Chebel, op. cit. p. 89.

42. Roland Gaucher, "Le Monde de silence," in *National Hebdo,* 80 (January 30-February 5, 1986) p. 4. For the commentary in question, see Maurice Duverger, "La Situation des fonctionnaires," in *Revue du droit public,* 57:3 (June 1941), pp. 277–332.

43. "Les Français et le racisme," in *Le Point,* April 29, 1985, pp. 46–47. According to a more recent poll, only 1 percent of the French expressed hostility toward Jews in 1988 (compared to 4 percent in 1978 and 10 percent in 1966). Gérard Mermet, *Francoscopie: les français—qui sont-ils? ou vont-ils?* (Paris: Larousse, 1988) p. 203.

44. In a representative sampling of opinion in Grenoble in 1985 on the question about minority communities in France considered too large, 90 percent of FN supporters (and 55 percent of the general electorate) mentioned North Africans; 50 percent, Black Africans (20 percent); 20 percent, Jews (7 percent); 27 percent Asians (11 percent); 37 percent Spaniards and Portuguese (15 percent); and 33 percent Italians (14 percent). Mayer and Perrineau, *Le Front National,* p. 244.

45. Jean-Marie Le Pen, *Pour la France: programme de front national* (Paris: Editions Albatross, 1985) p. 14.

46. See Robert Solé, "La Campagne de M. Le Pen sera axée sur l'immigration," in *Le Monde,* September 24, 1985.

47. On Le Pen's allegedly insincere use of slogans, see Jacques Fremontier, *Les Cadets de la droite* (Paris: Seuil, 1984) pp. 244–250.

48. See Daniel Singer, "The Resistible Rise of Jean-Marie Le Pen," in *Nation,* September 7, 1985. He has referred to Le Pen as "a French Spiro Agnew."

49. CDS is the Centre des Démocrates Sociaux (Center of Social Democrats), the Christian Democratic component of the UDF.

50. Jean-Marie Colombani, "Du bon usage du diable," in *Le Monde,* February 17–18, 1985.

51. Jean Vincour, "Far Right Seeking French Foothold," in the *New York Times,* March 3, 1985, Alain Rollat, "Le Consensus éxtrémiste," in *Le Monde,* October 31, 1984.

52. Chatain, op. cit., pp. 16–17.

53. Le Pen, *Les Français d'abord,* op. cit., pp. 167–168. See also Chebel, op. cit., pp. 36, 145, and J. P. Honoré in *Temps modernes,* April 1985, pp. 1850–1851.

54. *Le Monde,* February 23, 1985.

55. Discourse d'Egletons (Corréze), October 3, 1976.

56. Quoted in Calderon, op. cit., p. 139.

57. *Le Monde,* January 17, 1986.

58. *Le Monde,* September 14, 1985.

59. *Le Pointe,* February 13, 1984, p. 42.

60. See "CNIP: Le Pen Club," in *L'Express,* February 1, 1985, p. 19.

61. Ibid.

62. Rollat, *Les Hommes,* op. cit., pp. 157–160. See also Club de l'Horloge, *L'Identité de la France* (Paris: Albin Michel, 1985); and Jean-Yves LeGallou and the Club de l'Horloge, *La Préférence national* (Paris: Albin Michel, 1985).

63. *Le Monde,* March 13, 1985.

64. Jean-Yves Lhomeau, in *Le Monde,* March 13, 1985; *National Hebdo,* July 26, 1985, p. 3.

65. Cf. Colette Ysmal, "La Droite de 1990," in *Perspectives,* 19 (May 1984), pp. 39–44.

66. *Playboy* (French edition), July 1987, and *Cánard enchainé,* (Chained duck, a satirical and cartoon weekly for intellectual tastes), June 17, 1987.

67. The popularity of the FN fluctuated between 12 percent and 18 percent between 1984 and 1987. It fell from about 11 percent in mid-1987 to 8 percent in September of that year but by the spring of 1988 had risen again to over 12 percent. See SOFRES, *L'Etat de l'opinion 1988* (Paris: Seuil, 1988) p. 95.

68. *National Hebdo,* July 26, 1985, p. 3.

69. Le Monde, *L'Election présidentielle de 1988,* p. 61.

70. In the Assembly elections of 1988, the FN produced a single deputy, Yann Piat, from a Bouches-du-Rhône constituency. But she was expelled from the party soon thereafter for having criticized Le Pen's remarks about the gas chambers. The following year, however, Marie-France Stirbois, the widow of Le Pen's comrade-in-arms, was elected as an FN deputy from Dreux.

71. *Le Monde,* September 10, 1988. This decision was caused in large part by the evolution of attitudes of party sympathizers. A poll taken immediately after the second ballot of the presidential elections of 1988 showed that 52 percent of RPR sympathizers and 63 percent of UDF sympathizers opposed any alliance with the FN. SOFRES, *L'Etat de l'opinion 1989* (Paris: Seuil, 1989), p. 119.

72. For example, Jacques Chaban-Delmas, the mayor of Bordeaux, refused to make public facilities in his city available to the FN to hold its convention in 1990. Earlier, Jacques Médecin, the mayor of Nice, a member of the CNI who was close to Le Pen, had permitted the FN to meet there; but soon thereafter Médecin was indicted for embezzlement and forced to flee the country.

73. Jean Noli, "Front national," in *Le Point,* January 9, 1989, p. 35.

74. *Le Monde,* September 7, 1988, p. 9. "Mme. Piat affirme que M. Le Pen s'emploie à tirer son parti vers le bas," in *Le Monde,* October 12, 1983, p. 9.

75. *Le Point,* October 23, 1989, p. 61.

76. See David Beriss, "Scarves, Schools and Segregation: The *Foulard* Affair," in *French Politics and Society,* 8:1 (Winter 1990) pp. 1–13.

77. Edwy Plenel, "Les Militants soldats du front national," in *Le Monde,* March 20, 1990.

78. In a public opinion poll (reported in *Le Monde,* October 6, 1990, p. 10), 34 percent of the respondents attributed Le Pen's position to a desire to differentiate himself from other politicians, 24 percent to anti-Semitism, and only 11 percent to a desire to defend the interests of France. See also Michel Soudais, "Pourquoi Le Pen a choisi l'Irak," in *Politis,* 113, (November 8–14, 1990), pp. 12–17.

79. See Denis Jeambar, "Le Pen: le front serein," in *Le Point,* September 24, 1990, p. 44.

80. Perrineau, "Les Ressorts," op. cit., p. 21.

81. René Rémond, "Front national: un extrémisme modéré?" in *Le Point,* February 13, 1984, p. 41.

82. Olivier Biffaud, "Le Pen seul candidat à la succession," in *Le Monde,* March 31, 1990.

83. Yvon Blot, quoted in Pierre Milza, *Le Fascisme français: passé et présent* (Paris: Flammarion, 1987) p. 427.

84. René Rémond, *The Right Wing in France from 1815 to de Gaulle,* 2nd edition (Philadelphia: University of Pennsylvania Press, 1969). Translation of *La Droite en France.*

85. Rials, op. cit.

86. See Zeev Sternhell, *Ni droite ni gauche: L'idéologie fasciste en France* (Paris: Seuil, 1983).

87. Perrineau, "Les Ressorts," op. cit., pp. 19–21.

88. Milza, op. cit., pp. 417–419. See also Mayer and Perrineau, *Le Front* op. cit., passim.

89. SOFRES, *L'opinion publique 1985* (Paris: Gallimard, 1985) pp. 179–180.

90. Ibid., p. 88.

91. See Martin A Schain, "The National Front in France and the Construction of Political Legitimacy," in *West European Politics,* 10:2 (April 1987), pp. 229–252.

92. Milza, op. cit., p. 410.

93. SOFRES, *L'Etat de l'opinion 1988,* p. 84; and Milza, op. cit., p. 433.

94. SOFRES, *L'Etat de l'opinion 1988,* p. 132.

95. SOFRES, *L'Etat de l'opinion 1989,* pp. 156–157.

96. Ibid., p. 121.

97. *Le Monde,* May 7, 1990.

98. Roberts Solé, "L'immigration et les mots," in *Le Monde,* June 22, 1991.

99. *Le Monde,* June 22, 1991, p. 10.

100. Jean-Louis Bourlanges, "Le Rendez-vous manqué de la rénovation," in Olivier Duhamel and Jérome Jaffré, eds., SOFRES, *L'Etat de l'opinion 1990* (Paris: Seuil, 1990) pp. 37–40.

101. According to Mermet, 43 percent, *Francoscopie,* p. 203; and 48 percent according to an IPSOS poll of April 1988, *Le Monde,* April 15, 1988. Even in 1984—the year the FN made impressive gains in the elections to the European Parliament—less than two-thirds of FN voters wanted the number of immigrants to be reduced (SOFRES, *L'Opinion publique 1985,* p. 181). Between 1984 and 1988 the proportion of French citizens opposed to granting alien residents the right to vote in municipal

elections declined from 74 percent to 60 percent (SOFRES, *L'Etat de l'opinion 1989,* op. cit., p. 132). In 1988 the problem of immigrants was no longer the priority item: It was considered most important by only 33 percent of respondents, compared with the problem of employment by 87 percent, poverty by 46 percent, and education by 46 percent (ibid., p. 127).

102. See Seymour Martin Lipset, *Political Man* (Garden City, N.Y.: Doubleday, 1960) pp. 105, 134–149.

103. Chebel, op. cit., p. 140.

104. Le Monde, *L'Election présidentielle de 1988,* p. 13.

105. Olivier Biffaud, "Un entretien avec M. Bruno Megret," in *Le Monde,* March 31, 1990.

CHAPTER 2

1. Harald Neubauer, "Wo bleibt die deutsche Rechte?" in *Deutsche Annalen. Jahrbuch des Nationalgeschehns* (vol. 21, no. 4, 1990) p. 135, our translation.

2. Oskar Niedermayer, "Sozialstruktur, politische Orientierungen und die Unterstützung extrem rechter Parteien in Westeuropa," in *Zeitschrift für Parlamentsfragen* (vol. 21, no. 4, 1990) pp. 570–571, with cross-national data from the *Eurobarometer.*

3. Richard Stöss, *Die Extreme Rechte in der Bundesrepublik: Entwicklung—Ursachen—Gegenmassnahmen* (Opladen; Westdeutscher Verlag, 1989).

4. The criterion of 5 percent was chosen because according to German electoral law, a party will secure parliamentary representation either if it has gained at least 5 percent of the national vote or if at least three of its candidates are able to win a relative majority in their constituencies.

5. The German names are Sozialistische Reichspartei (SRP), Deutsche Reichspartei (DRP), Deutsche Gemeinschaft (DG), Nationaldemokratische Partei Deutschlands (NDP), and the Republikaner (REP).

6. Stephen Fisher, The *Minor Parties of the Federal Republic of Germany: Toward a Comparative Theory of Minor Parties* (The Hague: Martinus Nijhoff, 1974) pp. 129–130.

7. Horst W. Schmollinger, "Die Sozialistische Reichspartei," in Richard Stöss, ed., *Parteienhandbuch: Die Parteien der Bundesrepublik Deutschland 1945–1980,* vol. 4, (Opladen: Westdeutscher Verlag, 1986); and Fisher, op. cit., p.129

8. The percentage figures were taken from Fisher, op. cit., p. 132. It remains unclear to which extent former National Socialist party and SRP members overlap.

9. That is, in elections where the DRP was not part of the broader right-wing electoral coalition, such as in Bavaria (1954) and Bremen (1963), where it formed a common ticket with the All-German Bloc (Gesamtdeutscher Block/BHE) and the German party, respectively, but could not secure any parliamentary seats for its own representatives.

10. Horst W. Schmollinger, "Die Deutsche Reichspartei," in Stöss, 1986, op. cit., Vol. 4, p. 1181; and Fisher, op. cit., pp. 131–132.

11. Fisher, op. cit., p. 132

12. Schmollinger, "Die Deutsche Reichspartei."

13. Fisher, op. cit., p. 136.

14. Ibid.

15. Ibid.

16. In 1966, 35 percent of all NPD members, 46 percent of its officials on the local and county level, 67 percent of its functionaries on the federal state level, and 73 percent of its functionaries on the national level had previously been members of the Nazi party or of some postwar right radical movement, according to Fisher, ibid.

17. Fisher, op. cit., pp. 145–154.

18. Gerhard Paul, "Der Schatten Verblasst: Die Normalisierung des Reichsextremismus in den Achtziger Jahren," in Paul, ed., *Hitlers Schatten Verblasst: Die Normalisierung des Reichsextremismus* (Bonn: J.H.W. Dietz, 1989) pp. 18–19.

19. Stöss, 1989, op. cit.

20. Horst W. Schmollinger, "Die Nationaldemokratische Partei Deutschlands," in Stöss, 1986, Vol. 4, op. cit.; Giselher Schmidt, "Ideologie und Propaganda der NDP," in *Aus Politik und Zeitgeschichte* (no. 7, 1968); Federal Ministry of the Interior, *Verfassungsschutzbericht*, 1990.

21. Strauss had arranged a major bank loan of DM 1 billion for East Germany that was rejected by conservative CSU activists as an inappropriate stabilization of the Communist East German regime.

22. Uwe Backes, "Extremismus und Populismus von Rechts: Ein Vergleich auf europäischer Ebene," in *Aus Politik und Zeitgeschichte,* (B46–47, 1990) p. 11; Paul, op. cit., pp. 41–42; as to the DVU, see the section on "Voting, Membership, Violence" in this chapter.

23. Backes, op. cit., pp. 13–14.

24. Norbert Lepszy, "Die Republikaner: Ideologie—Programm Organisation," in *Aus Politik und Zeitgeschichte* (B41–42, 1989) pp. 6–7.

25. Ibid, pp. 8–9.

26. Backes, op. cit., pp. 9–12; Deutscher Bundestag in *Woche im Bundestag* (vol. 20, no. 20, 1990) p. 6.

27. Hans-Gerd Jaschke, "Verschlungene Traditionen: Zur Geschichte des Rechtsextremismus in der Bundesrepublik," in *Gewerkschaftliche Monatshefte* (vol. 40, no. 9, 1989) pp. 515–516; Stöss, 1989, op. cit., pp. 129–133.

28. Jaschke, op. cit., p. 517.

29. The German name of the group is Deutsche Volksunion.

30. 1989: 25,000; Federal Ministry of the Interior, 1990, op. cit.

31. Stöss, 1989, op. cit., pp. 184–191.

32. Paul, op. cit., p. 18.

33. Ibid., pp. 19–20.

34. Frey's publications include *Deutsche Wochenzeitung, Gesamtdeutscher Anzeiger,* and *Deutsche Nationalzeitung.*

35. Jaschke, op. cit., p. 519.

36. The German names are Volkssozialisten, Aktionsfront Nationaler Sozialisten, and Wehrsportgruppe Hoffmann.

37. The German name is Freie Arbeiter Partei. See Jaschke, op. cit., p. 519; and Stöss, 1989, op. cit., pp. 157–158.

38. Jaschke, op. cit., pp. 519–520; Margit Feit, *Die "Neue Rechte" in der Bundesrepublik* (Frankfurt: Campus, 1987).

39. We have entered all parties that—on the basis of their programs—were classified as antidemocratic right-wing parties by Stöss, 1989, op. cit.

40. The common ticket of both parties gained twenty-six seats, of which the BHE received twenty and the DG six. Subsequently, the BHE turned into more of an interest group for refugees than a right-wing party and was absorbed by the major parties of the FRG. See Stöss, 1989, op. cit., p. 120.

41. Schmollinger, op. cit., Vol. 4, "Die Sozialistische Reichsparten" in Stöss, 1986, p. 2309.

42. Stöss, 1989, op. cit. p. 97.

43. Schmollinger, "Die Nationaldemokratische Partei Deutschlands," in Stöss, 1986, op. cit., Vol. 4, pp. 1923–1926.

44. In 1966 Bavaria (7.4 percent of the vote and fifteen parliamentary seats), Hesse (7.9 percent, eight seats), Schleswig-Holstein (5.8 percent, four seats), Rhineland-Palatinate (6.9 percent, four seats), Lower Saxony (7 percent, ten seats), Bremen (8.8 percent, eight seats); in 1968 Baden-Württemberg (9.8 percent, twelve seats).

45. Stöss, 1989, op. cit., p. 217.

46. Federal Ministry of the Interior, Verfassungsschutzbericht 1969/1970.

47. Paul, op. cit., p. 15.

48. Ibid., p. 16.

49. Federal Ministry of the Interior, 1969/1970, op. cit., pp. 142–143.

50. Stöss, 1989, op. cit., p. 98.

51. Figures vary depending on the conceptualization of extremist right-wing attitudes in opinion surveys. Fisher and Sinus (see n. 86) assume a potential of 8 percent to 15 percent. Falter and Schumann (see n. 72) use a more restrictive initiation, namely, a person's ideological position in a left-right continuum from one to ten as applied in the Eurobarometer surveys. They characterize 3.7 percent of the electorate (ie., those who see themselves as occupying position ten on this continuum) as right-wing extremists.

52. Fisher, op. cit., p. 146.

53. Seymour Martin Lipset, Political Man: The Social Bases of Politics (Garden City, New York: Doubleday, 1960) pp. 131–134.

54. Ibid., pp. 134–152.

55. Heinrich August Winkler, Demokratie und Nationalsozialismus: Die Politische Entwicklung von Handwerk und Kleinhandel in der Weimarer Republik (Cologne: Kiepenheuer und Witsch, 1972); and Jürgen W. Falter and Reinhard Zintl, "Weltwirtschaftskrise und NSDAP-Wahlerfolge: Ein Erklärungsversuch mit Hilfe eines 'Rationalistischen' Ansatzes und Ökologischer Regressionsanalysen," in Falter and Klaus G. Troitzsch, eds., Wahlen und Politische Einstellungen in der Bundesrepublik Deutschland (Frankfurt am Main: Lang, 1989) p. 165.

56. Schmollinger, 1986, "Die Deutsche Reichspartei," pp. 1173–1174; Stöss, 1986, op. cit., pp. 895–896.

57. Schmollinger, "Die Nationaldemokratische Partei Deutschlands," pp. 1955–1956.

58. Klaus Liepelt, "Anhänger der Neuen Rechtspartei: Ein Beitrag zur Diskussion über das Wählerreservoir der NDP," in Politische Vierteljahresschrift (vol. 8, 1967) pp. 241–247.

59. This assessment refers to those respondents who *intended to vote* for the Republikaner. However, Bauer and Niedermayer also found that among those who consider themselves extremely right-wing in terms of *ideology and beliefs*, the old middle classes are grossly overrepresented (see n. 94). This would confirm Lipset's thesis.

60. For example, Stöss, 1989, op. cit., pp. 235–236.

61. Niedermayer, op. cit., p. 573.

62. The German Conservative party–German Right party (DReP, Deutsche Konservative Partei–Deutsche Rechtspartei) was a nationalist conservative party in the tradition of the Weimar German Nationalist People's party (DNVP, Deutschnationale Volkspartei) and existed from 1946 to 1950. See Horst W. Schmollinger, "Die Deutsche Konservative Partei–Deutsche Rechtspartei" in Stöss, 1986, op. cit., Vol. 4.

63. Werner Kaltefleiter, *Wirtschaft und Politik in Deutschland: Konjunktur als Bestimmungsfaktor des Parteiensystems*, 2nd edition (Cologne and Opladen: Westdeutscher Verlag, 1968) pp. 134–136.

64. A party's propaganda should, of course, not be equated with its voters' motives. However, in the absence of data on the DG's voters, we have to take these bits of information as a substitute, bearing in mind the risk of fallacy. See Fisher, op. cit., p. 136.

65. Ibid., p. 135.

66. Liepelt, op. cit., pp. 255–256.

67. Ibid. pp. 255–256.

68. Infratest Sozialforschung, "Sonderauswertung Republikaner: Kumulierte Ergebnisse von vier Repräsentativuntersuchungen," in *Sozialstruktur und Einstellungen von Wählern rechtsextremer Parteien* (Bonn: Vorwärts Verlag, 1989) p. 27, and Niedermayer, op. cit., p. 574.

69. Dieter Roth, "Sind die Republikaner die Fünfte Partei? Sozial und Meinungsstrukturen der Wähler der Republikaner" (unpublished paper presented to the International Colloquium on "Rechtsextremismus im Westeuropäischen Kontext," Antwerp, 1990) pp. 7–8.

70. Niedermayer, op. cit., pp. 572–574.

71. Erwin K. Scheuch and Hans D. Klingemann, "Theorie des Rechtsradikalismus in westlichen Industriegesellschaften," in *Hamburger Jahrbuch für Wirtschafts- und Gesellschaftspolitik* (vol. 12, 1967) p. 29.

72. Jürgen W. Falter and Siegfried Schumann, "Affinity Towards Right-Wing Extremism in Western Europe," in *West European Politics* (vol. 11, 1988) pp. 107–108.

73. Hans Dieter Klingemann and Franz Urban Pappi, *Politischer Radikalismus: Theoretische und Methodische Problems der Radikalismusforschung. Dargestellt am Beispiel einer Studie Anlässlich der Landtagswahl 1970 in Hessen* (Munich: Oldenbourg, 1972) p. 51.

74. Ibid., pp. 50–51.

75. Dieter Roth, "Sind die Republikaner die Fünfte Partei? Sozial und Meinungsstruktur der Wähler der Republikaner," in *Aus Politik und Zeitgeschichte* (no. 4, 1989) pp. 12–13.

76. William Kornhauser, *The Politics of Mass Society* (London: Routledge and Kegan Paul, 1960) p. 237.

77. Jürgen W. Falter, "Radikalisierung des Mittelstandes oder Mobilisierung der Unpolitischen? Die Theorien von Seymour Martin Lipset und Reinhard Bendix über die Wählerschaft der NSDAP im Lichte neuerer Forschungsergebnisse," in Peter Steinbach, ed., *Probleme Politischer Partizipation im Modernisierungsprozess* (Stuttgart: Klett-Cotta, 1982) pp. 457–458.

78. Schmollinger, "Die Deutsche Reichspartei," pp. 1173–1174; Schmollinger, "Die Sozialistische Reichspartei Deutschlands," p. 2330; Kaltefleiter, op. cit., p. 136.

79. Schmollinger, "Die Nationaldemokratische Partei Deutschlands," pp. 1955–1956.

80. Liepelt, op. cit., p. 245.

81. Roth, 1990, op. cit., p. 5; Roth, 1989, op. cit., p. 14; Niedermayer, op. cit., p. 579.

82. Liepelt, op. cit., p. 241; Roth, 1990, op. cit., pp. 3–6.

83. Roth, 1989, op. cit., pp. 11–12; Niedermayer, op. cit., pp. 577–578.

84. Roth, 1990, op. cit., pp. 5–6.

85. Liepelt, op. cit., pp. 262–263; Niedermayer, op. cit., pp. 580–581.

86. Fisher, op. cit., p. 146; Sinus Gesellschaft für Sozialforschung und Marktforschung, *5 Million Deutsche: Wir Sollten Wieder einen Führer Haben* (Sinus-Studie über Rechtsextremistische Einstellungen bei den Deutschen, Reinbek: Rowohlt, 1981).

87. Ekkart Zimmermann and Thomas Saalfeld, "Right Wing Extremism in West Germany from 1949 to the Present: Towards a Supply-Side Model" (submitted for publication 1991).

88. Stöss, 1986, op. cit.; Stöss, 1989, op. cit.

89. Liepelt, op. cit.; Roth, 1989, op. cit., p. 16.

90. Infratest, op. cit.

91. Roth, 1989, op. cit., p. 19.

92. Liepelt, op. cit., pp. 268–269.

93. Sinus, op. cit.; *Der Spiegel*, February 27, 1989, p. 49; Wilhelm Heitmeyer, *Rechtsextremistische Orientierungen bei Jugendlichen: Empirische Ergebnisse und Erklärungmuster einer Untersuchung zur Politischen Sozialisation*, 2nd edition (Weinheim: Juventa, 1988).

94. Petra Bauer and Oskar Niedermayer, "Extrem rechtes Potential in den Ländern der Europäischen Gemeinschaft," in *Aus Politik un Zeitgeschichte* (no. 46–47, 1990) p. 21.

95. Falter and Schumann, op. cit., p. 99.

96. Elisabeth Noelle-Neumann originally intended this concept to address the reluctance to express sympathy in public for the conservative parties during the 1970s. In her view, in many instances the opinion climate as influenced by the mass media was hostile to openly expressed support for the conservatives.

97. "Ausländerhass in den neuen Ländern," in *Frankfurter Allgemeine Zeitung* February 22, 1991.

98. Erwin K. Scheuch, "Die Suche nach der Besonderheit der heutigen Deutschen," in *Kölner Zeitschrift für Soziologie und Sozialpsychologie* (vol. 24, 1990) p. 739.

99. The prediction of Roth (1989, op. cit., p. 19) that the Republikaner party provided no suitable answer to the economic and political issues they raised, largely re-

lied on protest votes, and possessed no firm roots in the social structure, that their votes showed a low allegiance to the Republikaner party, and that they had grown too fast to sustain their organizations—all these factors have so far indeed become true.

CHAPTER 3

1. The Nouvelle Droite has nothing in common with the so-called New Right. The first is a cultural movement developed in France in the 1970s that aims at refounding the ideology of the Right (P. A. Taguieff, "La strategie culturelle de la Nouvelle Droite en France [1968–1983]" in Union des Ecrivains, ed., *Vous Avez Dit Fascimse,* Paris: Arthud/Montalba, 1985). The Nouvelle Droite has no partisan politician alignment; its leading figure, Alain de Benoist, has repeatedly manifested his disdain for the French National Front. The New Right, in contrast, acts inside the conservative movement and was originated by the reaction to the welfare state and permissiveness (A. King, *The New Right: Politics, Market, Citizenship,* London: Macmillan Education, 1987).

2. The MSI flanking organizations are Fronte della Gioventù (Youth Front, FDG), Fronte Universitario di Azione Nazionale (University Front, or FUAN), Fare Fronte (Work Front, a new student and youth organization loosely linked to the party), Confederazione Nazionale Italiana Sindicati Lavoratori (Italian National Confederation of Union Workers, or CISNAL), Federazione Nazionale Combattenti Republicani (National Federation of Republic Veterans, or FNCR), *Fiamma* (Flame, sport and leisure groups), the emigrant group Comitato Tricolore Italiani nel Mondo (Tricolor Committee of Italians in the World, or CTIM), and a cultural foundation, the Instituto di Studi Corporativi (Institute of Corporatist Studies).

3. On the radical side, we see R. Catanzaro (ed.), *Ideologia, movimenti, terrorismi* (Bologna: Il Mulino, 1990); R. Catanzaro (ed.), *La politica della violenza* (Bologna: Il Mulino, 1990), F. Ferraresi, "La destra eversiva," in F. Ferraresi (ed.), *La destra radicale* (Milan: Feltrinelli, 1984), F. Ferraresi, "La destra eversiva,"in D. della Porta (ed.) *Terrorismi in Italia* (Bologna: Il Molino, 1984); F. Ferraresi, "The Radical Right in Postwar Italy," *Politics and Society,* 16, no. 1 (1988), 71–120; and Leonard Weinberg and William Eubank, *The Rise and Fall of Italian Terrorism* (Boulder, Colorado: Westview Press, 1987).

4. On the Italian Nouvelle Droite, see D. Confrancesco, "Fascismo: destra a sinistra?" in K. Brachen and L. Valiari, eds., *Fascismo e nazionalsocialismo* (Bologna: Il Mulino, 1986); G. Tassani, *Vista da sinistra. Ricognizioni sulla nuova destra* (Firenze: Arthaud, 1986); and M. Zucchinali, *A destra in Italia oggi* (Milan: Sugarco, 1986).

5. This distinction has been developed by P. Ignazi, "La cultura politica del movimento sociale italiano," in *Rivista italiana di scienza politica* 3:19 (1989): 431–405.

6. On Julius Evola's thoughts, see Ferraresi, 1988, op. cit.

7. An ideological profile of the Italian *nouvelle droite* from the inside is provided by *Le Forme del politico. Idee della nuova destra* (Firenze: La Roccia de Erec, 1984), and E. Raisi, *Storia de idee della nuova destra italiana* (Rome: Settimo Sigillo, 1990).

8. An overview of the MSI is found in M. Caciagli, "The Movimento Sociale Italiano–Destra Nazionale and Neo-Fascism in Italy," in *West European Politics* 11, no.

2 (1988): 19–33, G. Galli, *La destra in Italia* (Milan Gammalibri, 1983); and P. Ignazi, *Il polo escluso. Profilo del movimento sociale italiano* (Bologna: Il Mulino, 1989).

9. The phases of the MSI's history have been treated in more depth by Ignazi, *Il Polo Escluso.*

10. On this very wide topic, refer to E. Gentile, *Le origini dell'ideologia fascista* (Bari: Laterz,: 1974); G. Mosse, *The Nationalization of the Masses* (New York: Howard Ferting, 1974); S. G. Payne, "The Concept of Fascism," in S. U. Larsen, B. Hagtvet , and J. P. Myklebust, eds., *Who Were the Fascists* (Oslo: Universitetsforlaget, 1980); Z. Sternhell, "Fascist Ideology," in W. Laqueur, ed., *Fascism: A Reader's Guide* (Berkeley and Los Angeles: University of California Press, 1976); Z. Sternhell, *Ni droite ni gauche: l'idéologie fasciste en France* (Paris: Edition Complexe, 1987); and Z. Sternhell, *Naissance de l'idéologie fasciste* (Paris: Fayard, 1989); and P.G. Zunino, *L'Ideologia del fascismo* (Bologna: Il Molino, 1985).

11. See R. De Felice, *Intervista sul fascismo* (Bari: Laterza, 1975).

12. In 1972 the MSI added to its identifying title and symbol the term *Destra Nazionale.*

13. A portion of the Ordine Nuovo did not support Rauti's return and established a new movement, the Movimento Politico Ordine Nuovo (Political Movement of the New Order), which organized terrorist activities.

14. In the 1979 parliamentary elections, DN received 0.6 percent of the votes and no deputy. It disappeared following this defeat.

15. Both the left and right wings expressed this sentiment, the Left in the once extremist newspaper *Lotta continua* (The Struggle Goes On) and the Right in journals such as *La voce della fogna* (Voice from the Sewer) and *Elementi* (Elements). A new look at those years, from the right viewpoint, is presented by Cabona and Solinas, eds., *C'eravamo tanto a(r)mati,* Vibo Valentia: Sette Colori, 1984.

16. MSI developments in recent years are highlighted by G. Tassani, "The Italian Social Movement: From Almirante to Fini" in R. Y. Nannettia and R. Catanzaro, eds., *Politics in Italy 1988* (London: Pinter, 1990).

17. On this subject see Ignazi, 1989, op. cit.; and P. Ignazi and C. Ysmal, "New and Old Extreme Right Parties: French Front National and the Italian Movemento Sociale," in *European Journal of Political Research* 22, no. 4, July 1992, pp. 101–122.

18. A definition of middle-level elites is provided by R. Cayrol, "L'Univers politique des militants socialistes: une enquête sur les orientations, courant et tendances," in *Revue française de science politique,* 25, no. 4 (Feb. 1975), pp. 23–52; and H. van Schuur, *Structure in Political Beliefs* (Amsterdam: CT Press, 1984).

19. See van Schuur, op. cit., p. 31.

20. This figure includes those who did not respond (26.5 percent) and those who explicitly declined to give their position (5.6 percent). These missing values must be included because of their extremely high level—ten *times higher* than the missing values in preceding and subsequent questions.

21. S. H. Barnes, and M. Kaase et al., eds., *Political Action: Mass Participation in Five Democracies* (Beverly Hills: Sage, 1979).

22. See C. Ysmal, "The Browning of Europe: Right Wing Extremism in European Elections," paper presented at the American Political Science Association meeting, San Francisco, September 1990.

23. See the insightful comments in R. Chiarini, "'Sacro egoismo' e 'missione civilizzatrice': la politica estera del MSI dalla fondazione alla metà degli anni cinquata," in *Storia contemporanea* 21 (1990): 541–560.

24. In this case, slightly different wording could have favored a more "liberal" choice: In fact, in the 1987 survey the item referred to illegal immigrants *without jobs*, whereas the 1990 survey referred only to illegal immigrants.

25. See P. Ignazi, "The Silent Counter-revolutionn: Hypothesis on the Emergence of Extreme Right-wing Parties in Europe," *European Journal of Political Research* (1991): 1–41, and Ignazi and Ysmal, 1991, op. cit.

CHAPTER 4

1. For example, A. James Gregor, *The Ideology of Fascism* (New York: Free Press, 1969); A. James Gregor, *The Fascist Persuasion in Radical Politics* (Princeton, N.J.: Princeton University Press, 1974); and John A. Armstrong, *Nations Before Nationalism* (Chapel Hill: University of North Carolina Press, 1982), especially chapter 7, pp. 201–241.

2. Ibid.

3. E.g., Peter F. Sugar (ed.), *Native Fascism in the Successor States, 1918–1945* (Santa Barbara: ABC-Clio, 1971), especially Lyman H. Legter's Introduction (pp. 1–13) and Sugar's conclusion (pp. 145–156).

4. A great deal of literature has been summarized here. An example of literature that deals with this material is Andrei Otetea (ed.), *Istoria poprului roman* (Bucharest: Editura Stiintifica, 1970), especially pp. 349–378.

5. A classic is still Robert Lee Wolff, *The Balkans in Our Time* (Cambridge: Harvard University Press, 1979), especially chapter 5 (pp. 69–101) and chapter 6 (pp. 101–159).

6. One of the standard works remains Peter F. Sugar and Ivo J. Lederer (eds.), *Nationalism in Eastern Europe* (Seattle: University of Washington Press, 1969).

7. Coupled with this sense of collective destiny was the abhorrence of foreign rulers; see, for example, André Guillou, *La Civilisation byzantine* (Paris: Arthaud, 1974), and Nicolae Iorga, *Geschichte des osmanischean Reiches* (Gotha: Friederich Andreas Pertes Aktiengesellschaft, 1908).

8. See, for example, R. W. Seton-Watson, *A History of the Roumanians* (Cambridge: Cambridge University Press, 1934), especially chapters 1 and 2 (pp. 1–50).

9. See, for example, Mihai Fatu and Ion Spalatelu, *Garda de fier—organizatie terorista de tip fascist* (Bucharest: Editura Politica, 1980), especially chapters 1, 2, and 3 (pp. 11–51).

10. The volume by Fatu and Spalatelu is superb on interwar fascism in Romania. On the issue of the royal dictatorship, see chapter 13 (pp. 184–200).

11. Ibid., pp. 52–53.

12. Ibid., pp. 68–88.

13. E.g., Otetea, op. cit., pp. 389–402.

14. Ghita Ionescu, *Communism in Roumania, 1944–1962* (London: Oxford University Press, 1964), especially chapter 5 (pp. 107–126) and chapter 9 (pp. 197–218).

15. The most extreme example of this personality cult was always the occasion of the general secretary's birthday in January. See, for example, *Munca,* January 21, 1988.

16. One of the best volumes on Ceausescu's personal power is Mary Ellen Fischer, *Nicolae Ceausescu: A Political Biography* (Boulder, Colo.: Lynne Rienner Publishers, 1988).

17. See, for example, *Nationalism and Communism in Romania: The Rise and Fall of Ceausescu's Personal Dictatorship* (Boulder, Colo.: Westview Press, 1990), especially chapter 5 (pp. 83–111).

18. A revealing "dictionary" of the personality cult, including many religious and mystical terms used to celebrate the Ceausescus, was compiled by Dan Ionescu in "An A to Z of the Personality Cult in Romania," *Radio Free Europe Research,* February 2, 1989.

19. A good example of Nicolae Ceausescu's political philosophy was his speech to the plenum of the Romanian Communist party's Central Committee in April 1989; see *Scinteia,* April 15, 1989.

20. E.g., Ionescu, op. cit.

21. The execution of the Ceausescus was announced on television and in the press. See, for example, *Adevarul* (Bucharest), December 26, 1989.

22. A good analysis of the National Salvation Front elite is found in Dan Ionescu's "The National Salvation Front and Social Democracy," *Radio Free Europe Research,* January 25, 1991.

23. The official reaction of the Romanian leadership to the clashes between Romanians and Hungarians in Tirgu Mures is symptomatic of such chauvinism. See, for example, *Rompres,* March 21, 1990.

24. Iliescu's statement to the nation on this issue was close to Ceausescu's usual chauvinism; see, for example, *Rompres,* March 25, 1990.

25. Iliescu personally called upon miners to deal with the "rebellion" of "reactionary students" in Bucharest. See *Rompres,* June 13, 1990.

26. Particularly disturbing is the role of the ultranationalist organization Vatra Romanesca. Even Prime Minister Petre Roman, who professes to be a modern intellectual, appeals to this organization; see, for example, his article in *Cuvintul Liber* (Bucharest), July 17, 1990.

27. Ionescu, 1989, op. cit.

28. Roman, op. cit.

29. This attitude is fostered by various organizations such as Vatra Romanesca. See statements by the leader of this organization, Radu Ceontea, in *Vatra* (Tirgu Mures), April 1990.

30. Recent statements by some of the leaders of the National Salvation Front are Neo-Communist and have elements of the Ceausescu era's rhetoric. See, for example, Claudiu Iordache, first deputy chairman of the front, in *Rompres,* January 7, 1991.

CHAPTER 5

1. See, e.g., Walter Laqueur, "Glasnost's Ghosts," an article distributed by U.S. Information Agency (USIA) on August 10, 1987; Howard Spier, "Soviet Anti-Semitism

Unchained: The Rise of Pamiat" and "Russian Chauvinists and the Thesis of a Jewish World Conspiracy: Three Case Studies," Institute of Jewish Affairs Research Reports numbers 3 and 6 (July and August 1987); Vladimir Tolz, "Zhido-Masonskii mif Sovetskoi propagandy i pravda istorii," a program script, broadcast in Russian by Radio Liberty (RL) on June 1, 1987; Julia Wishnevsky, "The Emergence of Pamiat and Otechestvo," RL 342/87, August 26, 1987; Julia Wishnevsky, "A Second Pamiat Emerges," RL 463/87, November 16, 1987; Julia Wishnevsky, "Reactionaries Tighten Their Hold on the Writers' Union," RL 148/88, March 28, 1988; Julia Wishnevsky, "Ligachev, Pamiat, and the Conservative Writers," RL 113/89, February 28, 1989; Adrian Karatnycky, "The Secret of Pamiat's Success," *Wall Street Journal,* April 3, 1989; "Mother Russia on a New Course," *National Geographic,* vol. 179, no. 2, February, 1991. There was also an exchange about Pamiat's place in the spectrum of Russian nationalism. Aron Katsenelinboigen, in his article "Will Glasnost Bring Reactionaries to Power?" argued that Pamiat was virtually indistinguishable from other manifestations of the Russian national and religious revival. But George Gibian, in a letter to the editor, urged a more discriminating approach (*Orbis,* spring-summer 1988).

2. See Julia Wishnevsky's article on Pamiat and Ligachev (note 1 above). She portrays Pamiat as "neo-Stalinist" and in league with such "conservative" Communists as Egor Ligachev and Nina Andreeva.

3. According to the latest count (Garem Razh, "Metastazy," in *Sobesednik,* no. 49, December 1990), in Moscow alone there are at least seven groups vying for the right to be a "true" Pamiat. In addition to Vasil'ev's group, (1) Natsional Nopatrioticheskii Front Pamiat (National Patriotic Front Memory), there is (2) N. Filimonov's and I. Kvartalov's group with exactly the same full name. The remaining four are (3) Pravoslavny Natsional'nyi Patrioticheskii Front Pamiat (Orthodox Christian National Front Memory), a splinter from the former led by A. Kulakov and S. Vorotyntsev, who allegedly seek to combine monarchism with Stalinism; (4) Russkii Narodno–Demokraticheskii Front Dvizhenie Pamiat (Russian People's Democratic Front–Movement Memory) led by Igor' Sychev, who in 1987 challenged Vasil'ev's "extremism" by proclaiming his loyalty to Marxism-Leninism (this group later evolved toward an "Orthodox Christian monarchist" ideology); (5) Spoiz za Natsional'noproportsional'noe Predstavitel'stvo Pamiat (Association for a Proportional National Representation), a splinter group from Sychev's led by K. Smirnov-Ostashvili; (6) Vsemirnyi Antisionistskii and Antimasonskii Front Pamiat (World Anti-Zionist and Anti-Masonic Front Memory) led by Valerii Emel'ianov (in his book *Desionizatsiia* [De-Zionization], published in Paris in 1979, allegedly with the help of the PLO, Emel'ianov claimed that Christianity is a "variety" of Zionism); (7) Koordinatsionnyi Sovet Patrioticheskogo Dvizheniia Pamiat (Coordinational Council of the Patriotic Movement Memory) led by the brothers Viacheslav and Evgenii Popov (this group was expelled from Vasil'ev's group in 1986 for exhibiting "nationalist Communist views"). There are also a number of Pamiat'-like groups in other cities.

I focus on Vasil'ev's group because it seems to be the largest. Its hard-core membership in Moscow is about 400 people, and there are some 20,000 sympathizers. The membership of the others is usually in the dozens. In spite of the ideological differences, all these groups exploit the theme of memory and blame, in various degrees, the Zionists, Jews, and Masons for the abuse of the Russian past by the Soviet regime.

4. I use *Judophobia* in lieu of *anti-Semitism* because the latter seems especially unsuitable in the discussion of Pamiat, whose leaders profess sympathy for the Arabs—who are, after all, no less Semitic than the Jews.

5. There exist different versions of Pamiat's history. According to *Ogonek,* November 21, 1987, it originated in the early 1980s under the wing of the Ministry of Civil Aviation. However, in Pamiat's own proclamation (see note 8), issued in December 1987, the group expresses pride in its three-year span of activities. In any case, Pamiat predates perestroika. In English, see Wishnevsky's Radio Liberty research articles (note 2).

6. Whether this hypothesis is true or not, there is no doubt that the official Soviet anti-Zionist policy during the pre-glasnost period offered an umbrella of legality without which Pamiat could not have started. Recently, my hypothesis was corroborated by two independent Soviet sources. One is the anonymous author of the "Chronicle of 1979–1988." Subtitled "Ot preddveriia kommunizma do Tysiacheletiia Kreshcheniia Rusi," it appeared during 1990 in the Russian right-wing nationalist magazine *Veche* (headquartered in Germany). In a segment of this "Chronicle" that was reprinted in *Russkaia Zhizn'* (February 6, 1991), the author claims that "in the beginning, the movement was tacitly supported by [Moscow] authorities" and that the KGB tried to recruit itself as one of its conduits. "Later, the movement overran the barriers [set by the KGB]," and the government began a campaign of discrediting it as an "anti-Semitic" movement, says the "chronicler." Another source is Oleg Kalugin, a former KGB general whom Gorbachev deprived of his rank for his critique of the KGB, only to see him elected a deputy of the Soviet parliament. In an interview with the independent news magazine *Novii Peterburg* (December 1990), Kalugin claimed that the KGB still tries to infiltrate "Pamiat and other patriotic organizations." He said he was sure that "among leaders of Pamiat there are (some) KGB agents."

7. Elena Losoto, "Vbespamiatstve: Kuda vedut rukovoditeli tak nayvaemogo obsch estva Pamiat," in *Komsomolskaia pravda,* May 22, 1987.

8. Andrei Cherkizov, "O podli'lnykh tsennostiakh i mnimykh vragakh," in *Sovetskaia kul'tura,* June 18, 1987.

9. Elena Losoto, "Slishkom pokhoshe!" in *Komsomolskaia pravda,* December 19, 1987.

10. Some tried to accentuate a distinction between Pamiat's "hysterical" leaders and well-meaning "patriotic" members, who have done some "good deeds." *Ogone's* Anatolii Golovkov and Aleksei Pavlov (November 21, 1987), for instance, said that they "could have written a whole article devoted to Pamiat's good deeds" (but they did not). Pavel Gutiontov (*Sovetskaia Rossiia,* July 17, 1987) mentioned that he could not ignore "the bitter facts" of the destruction of Russian culture, but he failed to describe a single such fact. Anatolii Ezhelev (*Izvestiia,* August 1, 1987) defended a Leningrad cultural preservation group, Spasenie (Salvation), from Cherkizov's insinuation that it was just as anti-Communist as Pamiat.

11. One notable exception was Franz Kossler's report on Austrian television, which included an interview with Vasil'ev. In his own interview with *Moscow News* (November 7, 1988), Kossler pointed out that "the atmosphere of being semi-legal and

'harassed' is an asset for Pamiat, because it gives some mythical aura and creates a legend around its martyrdom. ... The criticism should be business-like, specific and well-reasoned. All too often a caricature is drawn, which is then criminalized." It was prudent advice to Soviet journalists. But it has been hardly followed by Kossler's Western colleagues. One report in *Spiegel*, a Hamburg weekly, for August 3, 1987, was illustrated by a photograph of Pamiat demonstrators carrying placards proclaiming Pamiat's demands to "stop construction (harmful to historical monuments)" and to recognize it as one of the "informal groups." But the caption under the photograph read "Nieder mit den Juden" (Down with the Jews). Two weeks later the same weekly carried a report under a title-slogan "Rettet Russland! Schlagt die Juden" (Save Russia! Beat the Jews). The two slogans were indeed typical of prerevolutionary Russian anti-Semites. They may have even surfaced during demonstrations, but they are not part of (Vasil'ev's) Pamiat ideology. Esther Fein's report in the *New York Times* (February 27, 1989) has no such overt inaccuracies, but it falls short of objective reporting because it is based on interviews with whoever wanted to pass as a Pamiat member and says nothing about Pamiat's programmatic documents.

Remarkably, Soviet samizdat publications have shown more objectivity in their reporting on Pamiat than either the Western or Soviet press. Aleksandr Podrabinek's *Ekspress-Khronika* ran an interview with Vasil'ev (reprinted in *Russkaia mysl'* on June 17, 1988), and Sergei Grigoriant's information bulletin, *Glasnost' Russian People?* offered one of the most objective assessments of Pamiat (see English edition, *Glasnost'*, issues 13–15, October 1988, pp. 55–61). The Russian émigrée newspaper *Novoye Russkoye Slovo* (New York) has given short shrift to Pamiat, but in January 1988 it carried a series of articles by Vladimir Kozlovskii that could qualify as objective and responsible reporting.

12. The four-page, double-spaced, typewritten appeal was issued by Pamiat's governing body on May 21, 1986. Its full title is "Obrashchenie patrioticheskogo istoriko-literntumogo ob 'edineniia Pamiat' k russkomu narodu, ko vsem narodam nashei velikoi derzhavy, zhelaiushchim sokhranit' otechestvo svoe ot poshara" (Appeal of patriotic literary-historical association Pamiat to Russian people and to all peoples of our great country who wish to protect their fatherland from conflagration). It is available in the Radio Liberty archival collection, *Arkhiv Samizdata*, no. 6079, October 9, 1987. The seventeen-page proclamation was issued on December 8, 1987 (*Arkhiv Samizdata*, no. 6138, February 1, 1988). Its full title is "Vozzvanie patrioticheskogo ob 'edineniia Pamiat' k russkomo narodu, k patriotam vsekh stran i natsii" (Proclamation of patriotic association Pamiat to Russian people and to patriots of all countries and nations).

13. Appeal, p. 1.

14. Proclamation, p. 16.

15. Appeal, p. 1.

16. Proclamation, p. 2.

17. Il'ia Suslov, in his article "Nepoliticheskii manifest" (*Novoye Russkoye Slovo*, October 9, 1989), quotes a number of statements from a "manifesto of the National Patriotic Front Pamiat." Because he fails to identify it by its exact title and date, however, this "manifesto" cannot be considered here.

18. Proclamation, p. 2.

19. Ibid., p. 9.

20. Ibid., p. 2.

21. Ibid., p. 12.

22. Ibid., p. 3.

23. Ibid., p. 13.

24. Ibid., p. 12.

25. Ibid., p. 7.

26. Ibid., p. 2.

27. Ibid., p. 14.

28. Ibid., p. 2.

29. Vladimir Petrov, in a *Pravda* article entitled "Pamiat and Others" (February 1, 1988), linked Pamiat with Sergei Grigoriant's *Glasnost'*. According to Petrov, both Pamiat and *Glasnost'* discredit the informal movement by undermining our "patriotic, internationalist upbringing and socialist ideals."

30. "Pamiat kak ona est'," in *Soglasie,* no. 4, March 14, 1989.

31. Vadim Kozhinov, "My meniaemsia?" in *Nash sovremennik,* no. 10, October 1987, pp. 160–174. It is hard to judge Kozhinov's sincerity when he appeals to Lenin's authority because by 1987 such appeals were regarded as effective both as a polemical tool and as a means of assuring the publication of one's article.

32. Valentin Rasputin, "Zhertvovat' soboiu dlia pravdy: Protiv bespamiatstva" (speech delivered at the fifth congress of VOOPIK (All-Union Association for the Preservation of the Monuments of History and Culture), July 1987), in *Nash sovremennik,* November 1, 1988, p. 171.

33. G. Kh. Popov and Nikita Adzhubei, "Pamiat' i 'Pamiat'," an interview about "problems of historical memory and contemporary nationalities relations" in *Znamia,* no. 1, January 1988, pp. 188–203, especially p. 196.

34. Ibid., p. 193.

35. Nina Andreeva, "Ne mogu postupat'sia printsipami," in *Sovetskaia Rossiia,* March 13, 1988.

36. Alla Latynina, "Kolokol'nyi zvon-ne molitiva," in *Novyi mir,* no. 8, August 1988.

37. Alla Glebova, "Kak stat' mirom?" in *Vek XX i mir,* November 1, 1989 (includes the interview with Zelinskaia).

38. See I. Bespalpva's article in *Sovetskii zhurnalist,* December 12, 1989.

39. See Norinskii's interview "Interv'iu s antigeroem," in *Ogonek,* no. 9, February 25-March 4, 1989.

40. See M. Salop's letter in *Ogonek,* November 14, 1989.

41. The court decision on the Romanenko case was published in *Sovetskaia kul'tura,* April 27, 1989.

42. S. Zhdanov, "Kogo i kak my poteriali," in *Molodaia gvardiia,* November 6, 1990. *Znamia iunosti* (Banner of Youth) (July 19, 1990) marked the anniversary of Begun's death by criticizing a laudatory article in his honor in *Politicheskii sobesednik* (The Political Debater) (November 7, 1990).

43. For a report of Evseev's death, see *Moskovskaia pravda,* February 17, 1990, p. 4; about Evseev's "committee", see *Russkaia mysl',* December 12, 1988.

44. Interview with Valerii Emel'ianov, "Ia otsidel sem' let za ideiu 'Pamiat'," in *Baltiiskoe vremia,* no. 44, November 13, 1990.

45. See Wishnevsky, "Second Pamiat' " (note 1).

46. *Argumenty i fakty* (no. 23) reported that on May 28, 1988, Dmitrii Vasil'ev was warned by the KGB to cease and desist from "antisocial activities that might provoke national discord." (See his interview with the *Ekspress-Khronika* reprinted in *Russkaia mysl'*, June 17, 1988). In October 1988 the *Washington Times* reported that Vasil'ev sued the KGB for "defaming" Pamiat (Novoye Russkoye Slovo [a New York Russian daily news report]), November 2, 1988).

47. *Ekspress-Khronika,* no. 39, September 25, 1988.

48. "Printsipy perestoiki: revoliutsionnost' myshleniia i deistvii," in *Pravda,* April 5, 1988.

49. Aleksandr Shtil'mark, "Pamiat': my—za dukhovnoe vozrozhdenie Otechestva," in *Sobesednik,* no. 23, June 1989.

50. According to Shtil'mark, Pamiat has been giving free labor for the restoration of monuments, churches, and monasteries; the re-creation of traditional Russian handicrafts; the burial of Soviet soldiers' remains left unburied from World War II; and the advocacy of ecological protection. These activities will be left out of consideration in this chapter for lack of space.

51. Gorbachev did, indeed, cite those figures during a press conference in France in 1986. Gorbachev's statistics are probably correct or at least not too far off the mark. In June 1987 three prominent Soviet women, Vera Briusova, Galina Litvinova, and Tamara Ponomareva, complained in their letter to the plenary session of the Central Committee of the Communist party that "according to published data," Jews constituted as many as 45 percent of all Soviet Ph.D.'s (see Vladimir Kozlovskii's article in *Novoye Russkoye Slovo,* January 6, 1988). Moreover, Soviet statistics show that in spite of massive Jewish emigration, in January 1989 over 215,000 Communist party members were Jewish. Although they formed only 1.1 percent of the total membership, Jews were the eighth largest ethnic group in the party. These figures make Soviet Jews one of the most "Communist" nations in the union, which corresponds to their prominence in the Soviet establishment (KPSS v tsifrakh in *Izvestiia Ts.K. KPSS,* November 2, 1989). Yet as one of the respondents to Shtil'mark's article pointed out, in 1986 Soviet Jews had only one Jewish newspaper and one magazine with a total circulation of 17,000 (*Sobesednik,* no. 23. August 1989). It seems that none of the Soviet nationalities has been so deprived of its cultural institutions as have Soviet Jews.

52. See, for instance, the report "Hatred's Just Reward" in *Time,* October 22, 1990.

53. Aleksandr Podrabinek, "Dva goda dlia Ostashvili—mnogo ili malo?" in *Russkaia mysl',* October 26, 1990.

54. There were some joint demonstrations of Pamiat with the Democratic Union, an informal organization unsuspected of anti-Semitism, against "persecution for political convictions." The Democratic Union protested the arrest of one of its leaders, Valeriia Novodvorskaia, charged with comparing Gorbachev to Hitler (*Kommersant,* no. 38, September 24-October 1, 1990).

55. John B. Dunlop's "A Conversation with Dmitrii Vasil'ev, the Leader of Pamiat'" (RL 554/89,, December 12, 1989). This is perhaps the only article in which a serious attempt at an objective analysis of Pamiat's program is made. See also the less revealing interview with Vasil'ev in *Soviet Nationality Survey* (vol. 6, no. 6–7, June-July 1989).

56. Vasil'ev's interview in "Chto v imidzhe tvoem?" in *Volzhskie novosti*, April, 1990, p. 8.

57. See also Vasil'ev's interview in "Za dukhovnoe vozrozhdenie Rossii," in *Znamia kommunizma* (Noginsk), September 9–10, 1989; and Aleksandr Segen', "V logove 'chernosotentsev'" (an interview with several Pamiat' activists, including Vasil'ev), in *Sovetskaia literatura*, November 4, 1990. In a letter published in the nationalist *Literaturnaia Rossiia* on March 16, 1990, Vasil'ev protested against the disparaging remark about Pamiat as "a few masquerading buffoons" contained in "The letter of Russian writers" published by the newspaper. He accused the newspaper of yielding to the "Russophobia" Soviet mass media.

58. The lowest estimate (by the Marxist historian Roy Medvedev) is 40 million; the highest goes to up 80 million. This imprecision itself is macabre, for it shows how cheap life was during most of Soviet history. The Soviet holocaust experience suggests yet another similarity (as well as dissimilarity) between Kach and Pamiat—the passion of those who have survived.

59. Aleksandr Solzhenitsyn, "Misconceptions About Russia Are a Threat to America," in *Foreign Affairs*, April 1980, pp. 797–834. See also Solzhenitsyn et al., *From Under the Rubble* (Boston: Little, Brown, 1975) pp. 138–140.

60. For more, see Vladislav Krasnov, *Russia Beyond Communism: A Chronicle of National Rebirth* (Boulder, Colo.: Westview Press, forthcoming).

61. John B. Dunlop, *The Faces of Contemporary Russian Nationalism* (Princeton, N.J.: Princeton University Press, 1983) p. 290.

62. In another article, "The Contemporary Russian Nationalist Spectrum" (Radio Liberty Research Bulletin, special issue of December 19, 1988), Dunlop identified the moderates with the "liberal nationalists," such as academician Dmitrii Likhachev, the philosopher Sergei Averintsev, a number of the "villagers," and the group of intellectuals around Sergei Zalygin's magazine, *Novyi mir*. Close to them, in his opinion, stands an even larger group of the "centrists" represented by many authors of the magazine *Nash sovremennik* (Valentin Rasputin, Vadim Kozhinov, and others) and the painter Il'ia Glazunov.

CHAPTER 6

1. See author's *The Ascendance of Israel's Radical Right* (New York: Oxford University Press, 1991). On Gush Emunim, see Gideon Aran, "From Religious Zionism to Zionist Religion: The Roots of Gush Emunim," in Peter Medding (ed.), *Studies in Contemporary Jewry*, vol. 2 (New York: Oxford University Press, 1986); David Newman (ed.), *The Impact of Gush Emunim* (London: Croom Helm, 1985); Zvi Raanan, *Gush Emunim* (in Hebrew) (Tel Aviv: Sifriyat Poalim, 1980); Danny Rubinstein, *On the Lord's Side: Gush Emunim* (in Hebrew) (Tel Aviv: Hakibbutz Hamaeuchad, 1982); Ehud Sprinzak, "Gush Emunim: The Iceberg Model of Political Extremism" (Hebrew), in *Medina Mimshal Vevehasim Beinleumiim*, no. 17 (Fall 1981); Ehud Sprinzak, "Gush Emunim: The Politics of Zionist Fundamentalism in Israel" (New York: American Jewish Committee, 1986); Eliezer Don-Yehiya, "Jewish Messianism, Religious Zionism and Israeli Politics: The Impact and Origins of Gush Emunim," in *Middle Eastern Studies*, vol. 23, no. 2 (April 1987).

2. Cf. Yair Kotler, *Heil Kahane* (New York: Adam Books, 1986) chapter 16; Ehud Sprinzak, "Kach and Kahane: The Emergence of Jewish Quasi-Fascism," in Asher Arian and Michael Shamir (eds.) *The Elections in Israel 1984* (Tel Aviv: Ramot, 1986) p. 182. Also essays by Aviezer Ravitzki, Ruth Gabizon, Jerald Krumer, and Ehud Sprinzak in *The Ideology of Meir Kahane and His Supporters* (in Hebrew) (Jerusalem: Van Leer Institute Publications, 1986).

3. The Jerusalem Van Leer Foundation conducted three surveys of the political attitudes of Israel's high school generation (those fifteen to eighteen years old). The September 1984 study found that 60 percent of the respondents thought Arabs did not deserve full equality and 42 percent were in favor of restricting rights for non-Jews. A subsequent survey, taken in May 1985, showed that 40 percent agreed with Kahane's opinions and 11 percent were ready to vote for him. A further breakdown of the results indicated exceptionally strong support for Kahane's ideas among religious youth (59 percent) and among young people of North African and Far Eastern origin (50 percent). The April 1986 survey, which was conducted after an intense anti-Kahane campaign throughout most of the political system, showed a small decline in support for the rabbi's positions. Only one-third of the respondents thought Kahane's opinions were right and 7.5 percent said they would vote for him. However, 50 percent were still favorable to the idea of restricting the rights of Arabs and 56 percent opposed equal rights for non-Jews. For a further description of the growth of Israeli ultranationalism, see Charles S. Liebman, "Jewish Ultra-Nationalism in Israel: Converging Strands," in William Frankel (ed.) *Survey of Jewish Affairs* (London: Associated Universities Press, 1985).

4. Cf. Yaacov Shavit, *Jabotinsky and the Revisionist Movement* (London: Frank Cass, 1988) chapters 3 and 4.

5. Ibid., pp. 149–150.

6. Cf. Joseph Heller, *Lehi: Ideology and Politics* 1940–1949 (Jerusalem: Keter, 1989) pp. 19–35.

7. Ibid., pp. 24–31.

8. Ibid.

9. For a different version, see Joseph Schechtman, *The Life and Times of Vladimir Jabotinsky: Fighter and Prophet* (Silver Springs, Md.: Eshel Books, 1986) pp. 434–441.

10. Cf. Shlomo Avineri, *Varieties of Zionist Thought* (in Hebrew) (Tel Aviv: Am Oved, 1980) pp. 195–202.

11. For an impressive although somewhat ahistorical attempt to portray Jabotinsky as a classical Western liberal, see Raphaella Bilski Ben-Hur, *Every Individual Is a King: The Social and Political Thought of Zeev (Vladimir) Jabotinsky (in Hebrew)* (Tel Aviv: Dvir, 1988) chapter 2.

12. See Yonathan Shapira, *The Road of Herut to Power: A Socio-Political Explanation* (in Hebrew) (Tel Aviv: Am Oved, forthcoming) pp. 30–36.

13. Cf. Charles S. Liebman and Eliezer Don Yehiya, *Civil Religion in Israel* (Berkeley: University of California Press, 1983), pp. 74–76.

14. Shapira, op. cit., pp. 42–52.

15. Cf. Avineri, op. cit., pp. 210–215.

16. Sasson Sofer, *Begin: An Anatomy of Leadership* (New York: Basil Blackwell, 1988) pp. 19–24; Shapira, op. cit., pp. 76–81.

17. On Stern and Lehi, see Heller, op. cit., chapter 4.

18. See, for example, Yonathan Shapira, *Democracy in Israel* (Ramat Gan: Massad, 1977); Dan Horowitz and Moshe Lissak, *The Origins of the Israeli Polity* (Tel Aviv: Am Oved, 1977 [Hebrew]); Peter Medding, *Mapai in Israel: Political Organization and Government in a New Society* (Cambridge: Cambridge University Press, 1972); Myron Aronoff, *Power and Ritual in the Israeli Labor Party* (Assen: Van Gorcum, 1977).

19. Cf. Shavit, op. cit., pp. 350–357; Ehud Sprinzak, "Atalena, Thirty Years After; Some Political Thoughts" (in Hebrew) in *Medina mimshal vevehasim bein leumiim*, no. 14 (Spring 1979).

20. Cf. Horowitz and Lissak, op. cit., pp. 114–117.

21. Cf. Michael J. Cohen, *Palestine and the Great Powers, 1945–1948* (Princeton: Princeton University Press, 1982) chapter 10.

22. Cf. Horowitz and Lissak, op. cit., pp. 137–146; Itzhak Galnur, *Steering the Polity: Communications and Politics in Israel* (in Hebrew) (Tel Aviv: Am Oved, 1985) pp. 103–112.

23. Cf. Heller, op. cit., pp. 113–135.

24. Cf. Shapira, op. cit., p. 92; Amos Perlmutter, *The Life and Times of Menachim Begin* (New York: Doubleday, 1987) and Sofer, op. cit., chapter 5.

25. On Herut's maximalist program and radical myths, see Shapira, op. cit., pp. 138–151.

26. Cf. Heller, op. cit., chapter 12.

27. Cf. *Sulam*, vol. 3, no. 3 (June 1951) p. 32. For a general background on the group, see Israel Eldad, *The First Tenth* (Tel Aviv: Hadar, 1975) pp. 385–400, and Isser Havel, *The Truth about the Kastner Murder* (in Hebrew) (Jerusalem: Edanim, 1985), pp. 47–48.

28. Cf. Isser Harel, *Security and Democracy* (in Hebrew) (Tel Aviv: Edanim, 1989) chapter 10.

29. Personal interview with Israel Eldad, February 28, 1985.

30. Cf. Baruch Kimmerling, *Zionism and Territory: The Socio-Territorial Dimension of Zionist Politics* (Berkeley: Institute of International Studies, University of California, 1983) pp. 170–171.

31. Cf. Rael Jean Isaac, *Israel Divided : Ideological Politics in the Jewish State* (Baltimore: Johns Hopkins University Press, 1976) chapter 3.

32. On the distinction between Gush Emunim fundamentalism and messianism, see Ehud Sprinzak, "Fundamentalism, Terrorists, and Democracy: The Case of Gush Emunim Underground" Occasional Paper (Washington, D.C.: Woodrow Wilson International Center for Scholars, 1987) p. 9.

33. Cf. Sprinzak, "Gush Emunim: The Iceberg Model," op. cit., p. 23.

34. Personal interview with Meir Kahane, April 18, 1973.

35. Cf. Kotler, op. cit., p. 21.

36. Personal interview with Kahane.

37. Meir Kahane, "The Activist Column: Reflections on the Elections" in *The Jewish Press* (June 3, 1977) p. 20.

38. Danny Rubinstein, op. cit., pp. 147–152; Sprinzak, "the Iceberg Model," op. cit., p. 27.

39. Personal interview with Geula Cohen, August 23, 1985.

40. Personal interview with Gershon Solomon, February 14, 1985.

41. Cf. Rubinstein, op. cit., pp. 152–156; personal interviews with Geula Cohen and Gershon Solomon.

42. Meir Kahane, "The Second Revolution," in *Jewish Press* (October 20, 1978).

43. Meir Kahane, *Thorns in Your Eyes* (in Hebrew) (New York: Druker, 1981) chapter 4.

44. Sprinzak, "Kahane and Kach," op. cit., pp. 175–176.

45. Cf. Haggai Segal, *Dear Brothers* (in Hebrew) (Jerusalem: Keter, 1987) pp. 47–57; Sprinzak, "Fundamentalism, Terrorism," op. cit., pp. 5–6.

46. Cf. David Rapoport, "Messianic Sanctions for Terror," in *Comparative Politics*, vol. 20, no. 2 (January 1988) pp. 204–205.

47. Segal, op. cit., p. 55; Ehud Sprinzak, "From Messianic Pioneering to Vigilante Terrorism: The Case of Gush Emunim Underground," in *Journal of Strategic Studies*, vol. 10, no. 4 (December 1987) p. 200.

48. In May 1980 Menachem Livni, the "leader" of the underground, told Rabbi Levinger, his religious mentor, "for these purposes we have to choose pure people, highly observant and sinless, people with no shred of violence in them and who are disciplined to reckless action." M. Livni, interrogation (court documents, May 18, 1984).

49. Cf. Gideon Aran, *Eretz Israel: Between Politics and Religion* (Jerusalem: Institute for the Study of Israel, 1985, Hebrew publication) pp. 36–43.

50. On Herut's New Zionism as an ideology, culture, civic religion, and symbolic system, see Ofira Seliktar, *New Zionism and the Foreign Policy System of Israel* (London: Croom Helm, 1986) chapters 3 and 4; Liebman and Don-Yehiya, op. cit., p. 234; Myron J. Aronoff, "Establishing Authority: The Memorialization of Jabotinsky and the Burial of the Bar-Kocha Bones in Israel Under the Likud" in Myron J. Aronoff (ed.), *The Frailty of Authority*, vol. 5 of *Political Anthropology* (New Brunswick: Transaction Books, 1986).

51. Moshe Levinger, "Old Flags Should Not Be Thrown Away" (in Hebrew), in *Nekuda*, no. 97 (March 25, 1986) p. 8.

52. Personal interviews with Geula Cohen and Gershon Solomon.

53. *We Struggle for the Integrity of the Land* (in Hebrew), undated early pamphlet of Gush Emunim.

54. For an excellent discussion of the fundamentalism of ultraorthodoxy in Israel in relation to the new Zionist fundamentalism of the Radical Right, see Aviezer Ravitsky, "Messianism, Zionism, and the Future of Israel in the Divided Religious Schools in Israel," (in Hebrew) in Alouph Haraven, ed., *Towards the 21st Century* (Jerusalem: Van Leer, 1984); Menachem Friedman, "Radical Religious Groups in Israel: Conservatism and Innovation," in Emanuel Sivan and Menachem Friedman, (eds.), *Religious Radicalism and Politics in the Middle East* (Albany, N.Y.: State University of New York Press, 1990).

55. Benny Katzover, "The Gravitation Point," in *Nekuda*, no. 27 (April 17, 1981) p. 11.

56. The main representative of this approach was the late Eliezar Livneh in *Israel and the Crisis of Western Civilization* (Tel Aviv: Schoken, 1972). For years the same approach dominated *Zot haretz*, the magazine of the Land of Israel Movement that was later channeled into *Nekuda*.

57. Cf. Ehud Sprinzak, "Extreme Politics in Israel," in *Jerusalem Quarterly*, no. 15 (Fall 1977), and Sprinzak, "Gush Emunim: The Iceberg Model," op. cit.

58. Many members of Gush Emunim never trusted Begin and his declarative, but impractical, commitment to settling Judea and Samaria. Personal interview with Rabbi Yoel Ben Nun, June 20, 1985.

59. Judith Carp, "Investigation of Suspicions Against Israelis in Judea and Samaria: A Report of the Follow Up Committee" (in Hebrew), May 23, 1982. See also Dedi Zuker, "A Study of Human Rights in the Territories Administered by the IDF, 1979–1983: Interim Report" (International Institute for Peace in the Middle East, 1983).

60. David Weisburd with Yered Vinitzky, "Vigilantism as Rational Social Control: The Case of the Gush Emunim Settlers," in Myron J. Aronoff (ed.), *Cross Currents in Israeli Culture and Politics, vol. 4 of Political Anthropology* (New Brunswick: Transaction Books, 1984) p. 74.

61. Cf. *Nekuda*, no. 93 (November 22, 1985).

62. Cf. Avinoam Bar Yosef and Yehoshua Bitzur, "A Prime Minister That Surrenders Parts of Eretz Israel Will Be Considered a Traitor," in *Yediot Achronot* (November 8, 1986).

63. Meir Kahane, "The Second Revolution," in *Jewish Press* (October 20, 1978).

64. Cf. *Nekuda* editorial and Yehoshua Zohar, "The Retreat from Lebanon: Spiritual Weakness," in *Nekuda*, no. 83 (February 1, 1985) pp. 5–7; also, the Tzfia report on the establishment of a *gariin* (a settlement nucleus) for a future settlement in Lebanon in *Tzfia*, no. 2 (Spring 1985) pp. 95–96.

65. Elyakim Haetzni, "A State with No Protection Against Internal Erosion," in *Nekuda*, no. 84 (March 1, 1985) p. 22.

66. Elyakim Haetzni, "The 'Focus' That Was Not Focused," in *Nekuda*, no. 97 (March 3, 1986) p. 14.

67. Cf. Myron Aronoff, "The Internationalization and Cooptation of a Charismatic, Messianic, Religious-Political Revitalization Movement," in Newman, op. cit.

68. Cf. Meron Benvenisti, *The West Bank Data Project* (Washington, D.C.: American Enterprise Institute, 1984) pp. 52–63; and Sprinzak, "Gush Emunim," op. cit., pp. 18–22.

69. Cf. Meron Benvenisti, *1986 Report: Demographic, Economic, Legal, Social and Political Developments in the West Bank* (Jerusalem: Jerusalem Post, 1986) pp. 57–62.

70. Otniel Schneller, the secretary general of Moetzet Yesha, told me in an interview (August 5, 1985) that the government's most secretive deliberations about Judea, Samaria, and Gaza are confided to him by friendly cabinet members within half an hour of the discussion. See also Yael Yishai, *Land or Peace: Whither Israel?* (Stanford: Hoover Institution Press, 1987) pp. 124–126.

71. "We have become such an influential body that no minister can afford not to see me, not even Itzhak Rabin. Rabin knows that if he wants Judea and Samaria quiet and the settlers out of the roads, he has to talk to me." Personal interview with Otniel Schneller, August 5, 1985.

72. See Tehiya original manifesto, *Kol korah*, 1979. In the 1992 elections, Tehiya failed to return to the Knesset. Tzomet and Moledet, however, increased their share to 11 seats (9.5 percent).

73. The approach is mostly stressed by the influential *chug* (circle) Ein Vered, which is composed of Mapai and Hakibbutz Hameuchad Veterans. Personal interview with Ephraim Ben Haim, May 5, 1985.

74. Cf. *Moledet: The Movement of the Eretz Yisrael Loyalists*, no. 1 (platform explanations, 1988).

75. Cf. Sprinzak, "Kahane and Kach," op. cit., pp. 185–187.

76. Cf. Daniel Bell, "The Dispossessed," in Bell, ed., *The Radical Right* (Garden City, N.Y.: Doubleday, 1963), pp. 1–45; M. Billig, *Fascists: A Social Psychological View of the National Front* (London: Harcourt, Brace, Jovanovich, 1978); E. Bonachich, "The Past, Present and Future of Split Market Theory," in *Research in Race and Ethnic Relations*, no. 1 (1979); S. Cummings, "White Ethnics, Racial Prejudices and Labor Market Segmentation," in *American Journal of Sociology*, no. 85, 4, (1980); G. P. Freeman, *Immigrant Labor and Racial Conflict in Industrial Societies: The French and the British Experience, 1945–1975* (Princeton: Princeton University Press, 1979); C. T. Husbands, "Contemporary Right-Wing Extremism in Western European Democracies: A Review Article," in *European Journal of Political Research* no. 9 (1981); and S. M. Lipset, "The Sources of the Radical Right," in D. Bell, op. cit.

77. Cf. Gershon Shafir and Yoav Peled, "Thorns in Your Eyes: The Socioeconomic Basis of the Kahane Vote," in Arian and Shamir, op. cit.

78. Cf. Sprinzak, "Kahane and Kach," op. cit., pp. 181–185; Ehud Sprinzak, "The Kahane Movement in Comparative Perspective," in *The Ideology of Meir Kahane and His Supporters* (in Hebrew) (Jerusalem: Van Leer Publications, 1986).

79. This judgment is based on interviews with Yoel Lerner (December 12, 1984), Rabbi Israel Ariel (January 31, 1985), Ephraim Caspi (July 16, 1984), and Rabbi Dov Lior (January 19, 1985).

80. Cf. Yehuda Etzion, *Temple Mount* (in Hebrew) (Jerusalem: E. Caspi, 1985).

81. Personal interview with Ariel. See also Ariel's essay, "Is It Really a Rebellion Against the Kingdom?" in *Nekuda*, no. 73 (May 25, 1984); Ariel, "Things as They Are" in *Tzfia*, no. 1 (Summer 1984); and Ariel, "When Will the Temple Be Built?" in *Tzfia* no. 2 (Spring 1985).

82. My estimation is conservative and is based on regular opinion polls that indicate an 8 percent to 12 percent support for Tehiya, Tzomet, and Kahane; a 10 percent to 12 percent support for the Sharon camp and other radicals in the Likud and an additional 3 percent to 5 percent support for the Radical Right within such parties as NRP, Shas, and the right-wing fringes of Labor.

CHAPTER 7

I am grateful to my collegue Dr. Zig Layton-Henry, who read an early draft of this chapter and made valuable suggestions for its improvement.

1. S. M. Lipset and E. Raab, *The Politics of Unreason* (London: Heinemann, 1971) pp. 7–17.

2. A. Gregor, *The Fascist Persuasion in Radical Politics* (Princeton: Princeton University Press, 1974) pp. 139–188.

3. R. Thurlow, *Fascism in Britain: A History, 1918–85* (Oxford: Blackwell, 1987) p. 277.

4. R. Sidelsky, *Oswald Mosley* (London: Macmillan, 1975) p. 302.

5. G. Lebzelter, *Political Anti-Semitism in England* (London: Macmillan, 1978) pp. 47–67.

6. Z. Layton-Henry, *The Politics of Race* (London: George, Allen and Unwin, 1984) pp. 16–29.

7. A. Richmond, *The Color Problem* (London: Pelican, 1955) pp. 254–268.

8. G. Thayer, *The British Political Fringe* (London: Blond, 1965) pp. 53–65.

9. M. Walker, *The National Front* (London: Fontana, 1977) pp. 57–65.

10. S. Taylor, *The National Front in English Politics* (London: Macmillan, 1989) pp. 64–81.

11. Ibid., pp. 78–81.

12. M. Hanna, "The National Front and Other Right-Wing Organizations," in *New Community*, (no. 111 (1974) pp. 49–55; D. Scott, "The National Front in Local Politics: Some Interpretations," in I. Crewe (ed.), *British Political Sociology Yearbook* (London: Croom-Helm, 1975) pp. 214–238; and S. Taylor, "The National Front: Backlash or Boot Boys?," in *New Society*, August 18, 1977, pp. 283–284.

13. Taylor, 1989, op. cit.

14. Ibid., p. 103.

15. N. Fielding, *The National Front* (London: Routledge and Kegan Paul, 1981) pp. 137–156; Scott, op. cit., pp. 214–238; Taylor, 1989, op. cit., pp. 96–107.

16. Quoted in *Searchlight* (a news service reporting on the "fascist" Radical Right), 1977, p. 22.

17. R. Clutterbuck, *Britain in Agony* (London: Faber and Faber, 1978) pp. 162–163.

18. B. Smithies and P. Fiddick, *Enoch Powell and Immigration* (London: Sphere, 1979) pp. 19–22.

19. D. Schoen, *Enoch Powell and Powellites* (London: Macmillan, 1977) pp. 33–34.

20. Taylor, 1989, op. cit., pp. 21–22.

21. R. Johnson and D. Schoen, "The Powell Effect: Or How One Man Can Win," in *New Society*, July 22, 1976, pp. 168–172.

22. Taylor, 1989, op. cit., pp. 25–27.

23. C. Husbands, *Racial Exclusionism and the City: The Urban Support for the National Forest* (London: George, Allen and Unwin, 1983) pp. 403–405.

24. P. Whitely, "The National Front's Vote in the 1977 GLC Elections: An Aggregate Data Analysis," in *British Journal of Political Science*, no. 9 (1979) pp. 370–381.

25. M. Steed, "The National Front Vote," in *Parliamentary Affairs*, 31 (1978) pp. 282–293; and Taylor, 1989, op. cit., pp. 121–131.

26. "World in Action," ITV, January 31, 1978.

27. M. Steed, "The National Front's Vote in the May 1979 Election," paper presented to the Conference on Right Wing Politics in Western Europe, sponsored by the Social Science Research Council, London School of Economics, June 1979; C. Husbands and J. England, "The Hidden Support for Racism," in *New Statesman*, May 11, 1979, pp. 674–676; and Taylor, 1989, op. cit., pp. 166–167.

28. M. Harrow and G. Zimmerman, "Anatomy of the National Front," in *Patterns of Prejudice*, 11 (1977) pp. 12–13; M. Harrow, J. England, and C. Husbands, "The Bases of National Front Support," in *Political Studies*, 28 (1980) pp. 271–283.

29. S. Weir, "Youngsters in the Front Line," in *New Society,* April 27, 1978, pp. 190–192; S. Taylor, "Racism and Youth," in *New Society,* August 3, 1978, pp. 249–250.

30. Husbands, 1983, op. cit., p. 101.

31. Whitely, op. cit., pp. 370–381; pp. 250–255; S. Taylor, "The National Front: Anatomy of a Political Movement," in R. Miles and A. Phizacklea (eds.), *Racism and Political Action in Britain* (London: Routledge and Kegan Paul,1979) pp. 139–141.

32. Taylor, pp. 141–144; C. Husbands, "The 'Threat' Hypothesis and Racist Voting in England and the United States," in Miles and Phizacklea, op. cit. pp. 147–181.

33. Husbands, 1983, op. cit., pp. 52–55.

34. J. Williams, E. Dunning, and P. Murphy, *Hooligans Abroad* (London: Routledge and Kegan, Paul, 1984) pp. 149–179.

35. But see D. Baker, "A. K. Chesterton, the Strasser Brothers and the Politics of the National Front," in *Patterns of Prejudice,* (no. 19, 1985) pp. 23–33.

36. R. Cochrane and M. Billig, "I'm Not National Front Myself, But ...," in *New Society,* May 17, 1984, pp. 255–258.

CHAPTER 8

1. Anti-Defamation League, *Hate Groups in America,* rev. ed. (New York: Anti-Defamation League, 1988) pp. 4, 24.

2. Sidney Blumenthal, *The Rise of the Counter-Establishment* (New York: Times Books, 1986); and Robert Liebman and Robert Wurthrow, eds., *The New Christian Right* (Hawthorne, N.Y.: Aldine, 1983).

3. For an excellent accounting, see David Bennett, *The Parts of Fear* (Chapel Hill: University of North Carolina Press, 1988).

4. Don DeLillo, "Silhouette City: Hitler, Manson and the Millennium," in *Dimensions,* 4:3 (1989) pp. 29–34.

5. James Aho, "Reification and Sacrifice: The Goldmark Case," in *California Sociologist* (Winter 1987) pp. 79–95.

6. For an account, see Stephen Singular, *Talked to Death* (New York: William Morrow, 1987).

7. *Washington Post* (January 9, 1987) p. 1.

8. Tamara Jones, "Violence by Skinheads Spreads Across Nation," in *Los Angeles Times* (December 19, 1988) p. 22.

9. *Hate Groups in America,* op. cit., pp. 89–90.

10. David Wyman, *The Abandonment of the Jews* (New York: Pantheon Books, 1984) p. 9; and Arnold Forster, *A Measure of Freedom* (New York: Doubleday, 1950) pp. 222–227.

11. Anti-Defamation League, *Extremism on the Right* (New York: Anti-Defamation League, 1983) pp. 1–50.

12. See, for example, Seymour Lipset, "Blacks and Jews: How Much Bias?" in *Public Opinion,* 10:2 (1987) pp. 4–5, 57–58.

13. Dennis King and Patricia Lynch, "The Empire of Lyndon LaRouche" in *Wall Street Journal* (May 27, 1986) p. 26; and Anti-Defamation League, *The LaRouche Political Cult* (New York: Anti- Defamation League, 1986).

14. Gill Seidel, *The Holocaust Denial* (Leeds, England: Beyond the Pale Collective, 1986) pp. 66–92.

15. Anti-Defamation League, *The Populist Party: The Politics of Right Wing Extremism* (New York: Anti-Defamation League, 1985); and Anti-Defamation League, *The American Farmer and the Extremists* (New York: Anti-Defamation League, 1986) pp. 2–3.

16. Jeff Coplon, "Skinhead Nation," in *Rolling Stone* (December 1988) p. 62.

17. Anti-Defamation League, *Shaved for Battle: Skinheads Target America's Youth* (New York: Anti-Defamation League, 1987) pp. 1–6.

18. *Hate Groups in America*, op. cit., pp. 4, 24.

19. Coplon, op. cit., p. 58.

20. John Judis, "The Making of a Madman," in *New Republic* (May 29, 1989) pp. 35–39.

21. *Extremism on the Right*, op. cit., pp. 65–178.

22. Ibid., p. 167.

23. Author interview with Reno police detective David Jenkins, January 18, 1989.

24. Raphael Ezekiel, "Racism, Isolation and Terror: Encounters with Neo-Nazi Youth" (paper delivered at the annual scientific meeting of the International Society of Political Psychology, New York, July 1988).

25. *San Francisco Chronicle* (December 17, 1986).

26. Leonard Weinberg, "Fantasy and Vengeance: Observations on the Origins of Right-Wing Violence in Italy and the United States," in *Bulletin Research Committee on Political Education, International Political Science Association* (April 1989) pp. 16–17.

27. Simon Winchester, "Hayden Lake," in *Present Tense* (May-June, 1987) pp. 6–13.

28. James Aho, *The Politics of Righteousness* (Seattle: University of Washington Press, 1990) p. 66.

29. Anti-Defamation League, *Extremism Targets the Prisons* (New York: Anti-Defamation League, 1986) pp. 1–10.

30. Aho, 1990, op. cit., pp. 135–163.

31. Ibid.

32. *Extremism on the Right*, op. cit., pp. 58–59.

33. James Coates, *Armed and Dangerous* (New York: Hill and Wang, 1987) pp. 123–156.

34. Michael Barkun, "Millenarian Aspects of White Supremacist Movements" (paper delivered at the 1988 annual meeting of the American Political Science Association, Washington, D.C., September 1–4, 1988).

35. Ibid., p. 18.

36. See, for example, David Bennett, *The Party of Fear* (Chapel Hill: University of North Carolina Press, 1988).

37. *Hate Groups in America*, op. cit., pp. 91–92.

38. Ibid., pp. 27–28.

39. Anti-Defamation League, *Computerized Networks of Hate* (New York: Anti-Defamation League, 1985).

40. S. Robert Lichter, Stanley Rothman, and Linda Lichter, *The Media Elite* (Bethesda, Md.: Adler and Adler, 1986) pp. 20–53.

41. James Guth, "The New Christian Right," in Liebman and Wurthrow, op. cit., pp. 31–45.

42. *Extremism on the Right,* op. cit., p. 64.

43. Bennett, op. cit., pp. 353–354.

44. Bruce Marr, "Talk Radio Programming," in Susan Eastman, Sidney Head, and Lewis Klein, eds., *Broadcast/Cable Programming,* 2nd ed. (Belmont, Calif.: Wadsworth, 1985) pp. 383–400.

45. See, for example, Murray Levin, *Talk Radio and the American Dream* (Lexington, Mass.: D. C. Heath, 1987) pp. 13–26.

46. "The News and News/Talk Report," in *Bond Report* (1981) pp. 2–6.

47. Jane Bick, *Changing Audiences for Two-Way Talk Radio* (Washington, D.C.: National Association of Broadcasters, 1981) pp. 3–4.

48. Levin, op. cit., pp. 27–72; and Bob Secter and Tracy Shryer, "Talk Radio Adds Its Voice to Chicago's Racial Split," in *Los Angeles Times* (April 2, 1989) pp. 12–13.

49. *The American Farmer and the Extremists,* op. cit.; and Anti- Defamation League, *The Politics of Right-Wing Extremism* (New York: Anti- Defamation League, 1985).

50. Dennis King, *Lyndon LaRouche and the New American Fascism* (New York: Doubleday, 1989) pp. 85–86.

51. Ibid., pp. 105–108.

52. Anti-Defamation League, *The 1986 LaRouche Primary Campaign: An Analysis* (New York: Anti-Defamation League, 1986) p. 1.

53. Seidel, op. cit., pp. 42–43.

54. *ADL Latin American Report* 7:1 (1989) p. 6.; and King, op. cit., pp. 166–167.

55. John Leo, "A Chilling Wave of Racism," in *Time* (January 25, 1988) p. 57.

56. Anti-Defamation League, *1986 Audit of Anti-Semitic Incidents* (New York: Anti-Defamation League, 1987) p. 2.

57. Coates, op. cit., pp. 168–171.

58. Bruce Hoffman, *Recent Trends and Future Prospects of Terrorism in the United States* (Santa Monica, Calif.: Rand Corporation, 1988) pp. 6–7.

59. Jeffrey Ross and Ted Gurr, "Why Terrorism Subsides: A Comparative Study of Trends and Groups in Canada and the United States" (paper delivered at the annual meeting of the American Political Science Association, Chicago, September 1987) p. 11.

60. Thomas Martinez (with John Gunther), *Brotherhood of Murder* (New York: McGraw-Hill, 1988) pp. 83–84.

61. See, for example, Bill Miller, "Supremacists Plead Guilty," in *Idaho Statesman* (September 9, 1988) pp. 1–3.

62. Seymour Lipset and Earle Raab, *The Politics of Unreason* (New York: Harper and Row, 1970).

63. Robert Reich, "As the World Turns," in *New Republic* (May 1, 1989) p. 23.

64. David Rapoport, "Messianic Sanctions for Terror" in *Comparative Politics* (January 1988) pp. 195–201.

CONCLUSION

1. Always much closer to the Catholic conservatism of the People's party than to the Nazis, Waldheim seems to have committed two chief offenses—his shameless

wartime careerism under the Third Reich and his nimble cover-up of this wartime re-
cord since—rather than specific and demonstrable crimes. See also Hans-Georg
Heinrich and Slawomir Wiatr, *Political Culture in Vienna and Warsaw* (Boulder, Colo.:
Westview Press, 1991) pp. 66–71.

2. Blas Piñar had once been a member of Youth for Catholic Action and, from the
Falangist *Fuerza Nueva*, soon spun off a student group called the Guerrilla Fighters
for Christ the King. There were other groups as well, with names like Youth Front
and Adolph Hitler Sixth Commando of the New Order. See José Mana Bernaldez,
Ruptura o Reforma? (Barcelona: Plaza & Janes, 1984). The FN sported blue shirts and
red berets, like the old Falange.

3. See especially Sheelagh Ellwood, "The Extreme Right in Spain: A Dying Species," in Luciano Cheles et al., eds., *Neofascism in Europe* (London and New York:
Longman, 1991) pp. 147–166, for the gaggle of groups and activities associated with
it. The Falange Española de las Juntas de Ofensiva Nacional Sindicalista (Committees for National Syndicalist Attack) received about 24,000 votes each time.

4. See also Antonio Costa Pinto, "The Radical Right in Contemporary Portugal,"
in Cheles, op. cit., pp. 167–190. On Belgium, see also Christopher T. Husbands's essay in Paul Hainsworth, ed., *The Extreme Right in Europe and America Since 1945* (London: Pinter, 1991); and newspaper reports on the November 1991 elections in which
the Vlaams Blok won a plurality of the vote in Antwerp.

5. See also the Neo-Nazi history in Peter H. Merkl, "Rollerball or Neo-Nazi Violence in West Germany," in Merkl, ed., *Political Violence and Terror: Motifs and Motivation* (Berkeley and Los Angeles: University of California Press, 1986) pp. 233–248.

6. The Republikaner tend to belong to the generation born between about 1945
and 1965, whereas skinheads and soccer hooligans are usually younger and the real
ex-Nazis considerably older. See also Markus Wallenbern in *Neues Deutschland*, March
4, 1991, on the foundation of Republikaner organizations in East Berlin. West Berlin
had been a location of their early electoral triumphs in West Germany, and they began recruitment among the receptive East Germans as soon as the Wall came down.

7. A dramatic increase of unconventional political participation, including violence, was observed during the 1980s in West Berlin and West Germany as well, but it
was neither as abrupt nor of quite the magnitude of the East German right-wing violence. The worst incident to date was a massive skinhead attack on residences for foreign refugees in the coal-mining town of Hoyerswerda in fall 1991, which led to the
evacuation of hundreds of asylum seekers. One result of the Hoyerswerda incident
and similar occurrences were massive anti-Nazi demonstrations on Crystal Night
(November 9) all over Germany. Another upshot was a government plan to house
the vast numbers of refugees in more easily guarded camps. *Der Spiegel* magazine often reports details and analyses under titles such as "Geil auf Gewalt?" (Turned on
by violence?). Holiday weekends at giant resorts of big cities frequently feature massive brawls involving large groups of skinheads and large police units.

8. To quote the head of the Foreign Residents Office, Almuth Berger, "in GDR
schools they thought and spoke far too little about racism, anti-Semitism and about
hostility toward other nations." There was no education in tolerance. See the interview in *Der Spiegel* 44, no. 14, April 2, 1990, pp. 106–110. Frequently observed prejudicial incidents included the treatment of foreign students from "fraternal socialist
countries" such as Hungary or Czechoslovakia on trains. Identified from their pass-

ports, they often found themselves ordered to alight from transit trains and thereupon were arrested and prosecuted by local authorities for being in a place without a residence permit. The segregated workers of color sometimes fared worse. See also *Der Spiegel* 44, no. 14, April 2, 1990, pp. 98–119. The racist GDR jargon for them was and still is "Fijis."

9. Particularly in families where the parents were officials and active members of the state Communist party (SED) or its mass organizations—often currently demoted or unemployed—the teenage children have tended to be soccer hooligans or politically radicalized in the direction of the radical right, the "brown sons of red fathers," as observers have put it in a reversal of the 1960s left-wing radical syndrome in ex-Nazi families of the sixty-eighters, the "red sons and daughters of brown fathers." See also Walter Friedrich and Peter Förster, "Ostdeutsche Jugend 1990," in *Deutschland Archiv*, no. 4, April 1991, pp. 348–360, especially pp. 352–355.

10. See my description of the soccer hooligan scene in Merkl, op. cit., pp. 229–233. Wagner believes that with the "majority of incidents of attacks on foreigners and other such targets, there is evidence of careful preparation and planning attributable to the organized core groups, including the rallying of large hordes of assailants."

11. See "Gefahr von rechts wächst," in *Berliner Zeitung*, April 23, 1991. Also Walter Friedrich, "Mentalitätswandlungen der Jugend in der DDR," in *Das Parlament*, no. 17 (1990), supplement B16; and Loni Niederlander, "Zu den Ursachen rechtsradikaler Tendenzen in der DDR," in *Neue Justiz*, no. 1 (1990). Psychologists have described the disorientation and angst the collapse of communism caused mostly among twelve- to fifteen-year old students in the public schools, but there is probably a time lag and age-group lag between the mental agonies of beginning puberty and the violent acting out by the dropouts of the next teenage stage.

12. "Rechtsextremistische Orientierungen in der DDR-Jugend: Wie sind sie entstanden?" in Magistratsverwaltung für Jugend, Familie und Sport, Jugendförderung, *Jugend und Rechtsextremismus in Berlin-Ost* (Berlin, no date [1990]), pp. 9–18, which relates the twenty- to twenty-five-year-old activists of 1990 to the alienated punks and hooligans of much younger age in the 1980s.

13. See especially Peter Ködderitzsch and Leo A. Müller, *Rechtsextremismus in der DDR* (Göttingen: Lamuv Verlag, 1990) pp. 11–28, where the generational basis is said to be among the birth cohorts between 1965 and 1975 (p. 13) and the clash between skinheads and young people, presumably punks attending a rock concert at St. Zion's church, is described in some detail, as well as its judicial aftermath (pp. 15–17). To the extent that today's attacks are indeed planned and directed by the Neo-Nazi cadre, they appear to be intended for recruitment and reinforcing small-group solidarity in the movement of the new members rather than for combatting a real enemy.

14. One consequence of this kind of anarchy has been the incompleteness of information about the radical right organizations. There have been widely varying estimates of membership, for example, that range from partial figures of 3,000 to 4,000 political hard-core members and perhaps 10,000 skinheads, Faschos, and hooligans—550 skinheads in Brandenburg alone and 500 right radicals in Dresden, a hot bed—to wild exaggerations such as the 30,000 Neo-Nazis claimed by an anti-Fascist group to be present in the greater Leipzig area. There are far lower estimates: Bernd Wagner believes the political hard-core members not to have grown much be-

yond the original 1,500. Some groups are known to have lost half of their members since 1989. See also *Sachsenspiegel*, April 19, 1991.

15. See also Rudi Pahnke, "Unbehagen, Protest, Provokationen, Gewaltaktivität von Jugendlichen in neofaschistischer Gestalt," in *Jugend und Rechtsextremismus in Berlin-Ost*, pp. 19–32 who denies that these fourteen- to twenty-year-olds are "fascists in the sense of the period 1933–1945" (p. 19) and describes typical subgroups and their attitudes, including authoritarianism, a Führer cult, and physical culture.

16. Polls, however, differ about this situation. A Trend poll of late fall 1990, for instance, revealed that two-thirds of East Berliners had no leisure-time contact whatsoever with foreigners. Emnid reported in mid-1990 that this same majority was ready for broader social contacts, but not on a private basis. The Leipzig Institute for Youth Research found that young East Germans, especially males, had a more negative attitude toward foreigners than did their elders. One out of five apprentices and one of ten students is a Republikaner, one of twenty each sympathizes with "skins," Faschos, and hooligans. See *Der Tagesspiegel*, April 6, 1991, p. 12, and the account of attacks against foreigners in East Berlin–where only 1.4 percent (as compared to 14 percent in West Berlin) of the population are foreigners—by Anetta Kahane, "Ausländerfeindlichkeit in Berlin," in *Jugend und Rechtsextremismus* in Berlin-Ost, pp. 76–85.

17. In December 1990, the *Republikaner* polled 1.4 percent, or 117,000 voters, the NPD another .4 percent or 34,000 of the second ballots (and sometimes of first ballots) in addition. Other groups, such as the Federation of German Democrats (DDD), Patriots for Germany, and National Alternative, together received less than 1,000 votes. Regional strong points were Saxony (1.6 percent), Brandenburg (2 percent) and Mecklenburg-Vorpommern (2.1 percent).

18. See also Claus Leggewie, *Die Republikaner, Phantombild der Neuen Rechten* (Berlin: Rotbuch, 1989); and Kurt Hirsch and Hans Sarkowitz, *Rechts von der Union: Ausflüge in den Denkfabriken der Wende* (Berlin: Rotbuch, 1989).

19. With 4.5 million foreigners in West Germany as compared to only 100,000 in East Germany, explaining the great virulence of xenophobia in the latter area remains a challenge for social scientists and public authorities.

20. The media have even reported cases of former Communist youth (FDJ) organizers and Stasi informers who became Neo-Nazi leaders. See *Der Spiegel* 45, no. 22, May 27, 1991, pp. 78–85.

21. To stay with the examples from East German Neo-Nazis, it is as difficult to reconcile their robberies, arson, and mayhem against blacks and Vietnamese with their emphatic promise to bring law and order to society as it is to reconcile their image of the Third Reich with what that regime really entailed. Movements and clienteles on the extreme left, moreover, have shown the same proclivity for inventing myths of the past or future and to rationalize their present crimes and oppression.

22. See also the description and comparison in Peter H. Merkl, *The Making of a Stormtrooper* (Princeton: Princeton University Press, 1980), reprinted as an Encore edition, without ornamental swastikas, by Westview Press in 1988. See especially the final chapter.

23. This compares to only one incident in January 1990. The incidents of January 1991 consisted of reported threats (70 percent), physical assaults (14 percent) and

vandalism (16 percent). In the five months after the Iraqi invasion, there were another thirty-seven incidents, according to the *Los Angeles Times*, February 7, 1991. There are about 2 million Americans of Arab descent, one-sixth of them in California.

24. Ibid. California, with 129 incidents, had a high share, one-half in the greater Los Angeles area. Two San Francisco synagogues suffered firebomb attacks.

25. The bill proposed to double the sentence for misdemeanor hate crimes to a year of incarceration, provide for one to four years of prison for hate-crime felonies, increase civil penalty limits to $25,000, and remove the limit on punitive damages (*Los Angeles Times*, February 9, 1991).

26. "The citizens of ex-GDR shy away from [political] commitments, even the ultras do: they reject the 'party'—for forty years they were stuck with communists (SED)," wrote B. Grill in his report on the Radical Right in East Germany. *Die Zeit*, no., 25, June 14, 1991.

27. The ministry recorded 650 threats of violence and seventy-two racial attacks, including fifty-two against *Maghrebis*, leaving one dead, thirty-six injured. There were incidents of vandalism also in the cemeteries of Quimper, Weissenburg (Alsace), and Clichy-sous-bois (Paris). Immediately prior to the outrage at Carpentras, the site of the oldest synagogue in France (1367), and one of the earliest Jewish settlements, there had been commemorations of the end of the Third Reich forty-five years earlier and television documentary on the Holocaust.

28. During the disturbances in Romania, leaflets of the Iron Guard of the 1930s and 1940s—a virulent nemesis of the eastern Hungarian minority that the 1919 Treaty of Trianon handed over to Romania—appeared and called upon Romanian volunteer fighters against them.

29. Reported in *Le Figaro,* June 21, 1991.

30. There are about 3.7 to 4 million immigrants in France and perhaps as many as another 1 million illegal residents. They are blamed for 40 percent of crimes committed in the Paris region. Their average family size of seven should be compared to the average size of three for each French family.

31. Chirac's statement drew an immediate correction from the state secretary for family affairs, Laurent Cathala, who pointed out that such a family would only receive 25,800 francs (about $5,000) of which 18,700 francs would be child and dependents' support and about 5,300 francs a housing subsidy. The secretary challenged Chirac to produce this family of twenty-five and pointed out that if the facts were true, benefits would not exceed about 1,000 francs ($185) per person per year.

32. *Le Figaro,* June 20–21, 1991. President François Mitterrand also commented on the crisis, promising greater watchfulness with regard to illegal immigration and criticizing "racist statements aimed at electoral gains."

33. Typically, the political struggle against radical right groups is fought by denying them meeting halls to speak and permits to stage public parades. In the days of Poujadist UDCA, which had over fifty deputies elected to the National Assembly, their parliamentary colleagues even denied them the use of the cafeteria and jostled them on the stairs of the parliament building.

34. There are revealing differences between, say, Enoch Powell's unrestrained racial polemics and the contradictions of Margaret Thatcher, whose opportunism on questions of race immigration could not but clash with some of her liberal convictions.

ABOUT THE BOOK AND EDITORS

The cold war may be over, but there is no shortage of enemies in a world beset by resurgent nationalism, ethnic conflict, and economic rivalry. Right-wing extremists from David Duke to Jean-Marie Le Pen know how to exploit the pressure points of race, religion, and culture in a bid to keep the national and international conflict industry cooking.

Encounters with the Contemporary Radical Right introduces us to the personalities as well as the systems of rightist repression. It shows, in clearly written and carefully documented essays, how radical right groups have made electoral headway in France, Germany, and Israel while increasingly making headlines in the United States, Great Britain, and other points East and West. The phenomenon is by no means limited to all skinheads and jackboots; many official governments shelter radical rightism or even sponsor it outright.

Reflecting a broad geographical distribution that includes Eastern Europe and the former Soviet Union, the essays in this book lend themselves to comparative analysis on three important dimensions: the historical and intellectual backgrounds of various rightist groups, the way each group fits within the context of social movements theory, and the assessment of relative electoral participation and success. The book goes on to outline both the patterns and peculiarities of radical right action in the settings represented and concludes that it is no accident that the radical right is on the rise internationally, admonishing us of the movement's power without overstating its potential.

Peter H. Merkl is professor of political science at the University of California at Santa Barbara. **Leonard Weinberg** is professor of political science at the University of Nevada at Reno.

ABOUT THE CONTRIBUTORS

Trond Gilberg was formerly professor of political science at the Pennsylvania State University and is currently an independent analyst.

Piero Ignazi is research fellow in Political Science at the University of Bologna.

Vladislav Krasnov is professor and director of Russian Studies at the Monterey Institute of International Studies.

Thomas Saalfeld is a political scientist at the University of the Bundeswehr in Munich.

William Safran is professor of Political Science at the University of Colorado at Boulder.

Ehud Sprinzak is professor of political science at the Hebrew University of Jerusalem.

Stan Taylor is lecturer in politics at the University of Warwick.

Ekkart Zimmermann is professor of sociology at the University of the Bundeswehr in Munich.

INDEX

Barbie, Klaus, 39
Barnes, S. H., 87
Barre, Raymond, 29, 45
BDP. *See* British Democratic party
Beam, Louis Ray, 190
Begin, Menachem, 134, 140–141, 145, 148, 253(n58). *See also* Camp David accords
Begun, Vladimir, 114, 123
Belgium, 2, 206–207
Bell, Daniel, 192
Ben Gurion, David, 138, 154
Ben-Shoshan, Yeshua, 143
Berg, Alan, 186, 191
Bernadotte, Count Folke, 137–138
Betar (Israel), 135–136, 141
Bevin, Ernest, 141
BHE. *See* Federation of the Homeless and Dispossessed
Black Hundreds (Russia), 111, 116, 120, 128, 129
Blackmail potential, 14–15
Black Order. *See* Ordine Nero
Blance, Eugene Terre, 206
Block of the Faithful. *See* Gush Emunim
BNP. *See* British National party
Board of Deputies of British Jews, 179
Boer War, 166
Brasillach, Robert, 31
Brecht, Bertolt, 72
Brezhnev, Leonid, 127
Briand, Yvon, 28
Brissaud, Jean-Marc, 207
Britain. *See* British radical right; National Front (Great Britain)
Brith Habirionim (Palestine mandate), 134, 135, 136
Brith Hakanaim (Israel), 138
British antiimmigrant sentiment, 7, 168, 169, 173–174, 218
and electoral support, 14, 176, 177, 178, 179–180, 181
British Council of Churches, 179
British Democratic party (BDP), 181, 182
British-Israelism. *See* Christian Identity
British National party (BNP), 169, 175, 181
British radical right, 10, 13–15, 181–182, 226. *See also* British antiimmigrant sentiment; National Front (Great Britain)
British Union of Fascists (BUF), 167–168, 172, 181, 182
Britons Society (Great Britain), 169
Briusova, Vera, 248(n51)
Brück, Wolfgang, 211–212
BUF. *See* British Union of Fascists
Bukharin, Nikoly, 113, 127
Bulldog (Great Britain), 182
Burger, Norbert, 206
Bush, George, 38, 197, 226
Butler, Richard Girnt, 193–194

Camp David accords, 139, 141, 142–144, 148, 156
Carignon, Alain, 46
Carter, Jimmy, 142. *See also* Camp David accords
Carto, Willis A., 189
Caspi, Ephraim, 157
Cathala, Laurent, 262(n31)

CDS. *See* Centre des Démocrates Sociaux
CDU. *See* Christian Democratic Union
Ceausescu, Elena, 103, 105
Ceausescu, Nicolae, 102–105
Ceausescu, Nicu, 105
Center for Democratic Renewal (United States), 190
Center of Social Democrats. *See* Centre des Démocrates Sociaux
Centre des Démocrates Sociaux (CDS) (France), 36
Centre National des Independents (et Paysans) (CNI[P]) (France), 28, 38, 231(n16)
Chaban-Delmas, Jacques, 233(n72)
Chamberlain, Neville, 142
Cherkizov, Adrei, 114, 121, 123, 126, 245(n10)
Chernobyl, 210
Chesterton, A. K., 168, 169, 182
China, 2
Chirac, Jacques, 15, 37, 40, 45, 46, 47, 226–227, 262(n31)
Christian Constitutionalists (United States), 192
Christian Democratic Union (CDU) (Germany), 55, 60, 65, 68, 69, 71, 73
Christian Democrats (DC) (Italy), 79, 80, 82, 84
Christian Identity (United States), 14, 188, 189–190, 192, 193–194, 200, 201, 202
Christian Patriots Defense League (United States), 190
Christian Social Union (CSU) (Germany), 55, 60, 65, 68, 69, 71, 73, 236(n21)
Chug Sulam (Israel), 138
Church of the Living Word (United States), 193
CISNAL. *See* Confederazione Nazionale Italiana Sindicati Lavaratori
Citizens Emergency Defense System (United States), 193
Club de l'Horloge (France), 38, 43
Clutterbuck, R., 175
CNI(P). *See* Centre National des Independents (et Paysans)
CNPF. *See* Employers' Association
Codreanu, Corneliu Zelinski, 100, 103
Cohen, Geula, 139, 153
Comitato Tricolore Italiani nel Mondo (CTIM), 240(n2)
Commando Unit 191, 138–139
Committees for National Syndicalist Attack. *See* Falange Española de las Juntas de Ofensiva Nacional Sindicalista
Communism, 6, 119
collapse of, 1–2, 4, 10–11
See also Anti-Communism; Marxism-Leninism; Pamiat; Soviet Union; *specific parties*
Communist party of Romania. *See* Partidul Comunist Roman
Communist party of South Africa, 206
Confederazione Nazionale Italiana Sindicati Lavaratori (CISNAL) (Italy), 240(n2)
Conservative fascism (Great Britain), 167, 168
Conservative party (Great Britain), 14, 168, 169, 176, 177, 179–180, 182, 226
Conservative party (South Africa), 206
Conspiracy theories, 8, 12, 165, 167–168, 171. *See also* Anti-Semitism; Anti-Zionism

Heterick Memorial Library
Ohio Northern University

	DUE	RETURNED	DUE	RETURNED
1.			13.	
2.			14.	
3.			15.	
4.			16.	
5.			17.	
6.			18.	
7.			19.	
8.			20.	
9.			21.	
10.			22.	
11.			23.	
12.			24.